REVEALING ANTIQUITY

17

G. W. BOWERSOCK, GENERAL EDITOR

HISTOIRES GRECQUES

SNAPSHOTS FROM ANTIQUITY

Maurice Sartre

Translated by Catherine Porter

THE BELKNAP PRESS OF

HARVARD UNIVERSITY PRESS

Cambridge, Massachusetts

London, England

2009

This book was originally published as *Histoires Grecques,* copyright
© 2006 by Editions du Seuil, Paris.

Publication of this book has been aided by a grant from the
French Ministry of Culture.

Library of Congress Cataloging-in-Publication Data
Sartre, Maurice.
[Histoires grecques. English]
Histoires grecques : snapshots from antiquity / Maurice Sartre ;
translated by Catherine Porter.
p.   cm. — (Revealing antiquity ; 17)
Includes bibliographical references and index.
ISBN-13: 978-0-674-03212-5 (alk. paper)
1. Greece—History.   2. History, Ancient.   I. Title.
DF214.S3413 2009
938—dc22   2008027034

Contents

Maps

MANY OF THE place names cited in the text appear on at least one of the three maps presented here. The maps themselves are followed by a list of the cities that are marked with numerals; to ensure readability, only the most important cities are indicated by name on the maps.

Each chapter of the book has been situated geographically on one of the maps by means of a white numeral inside a black circle.

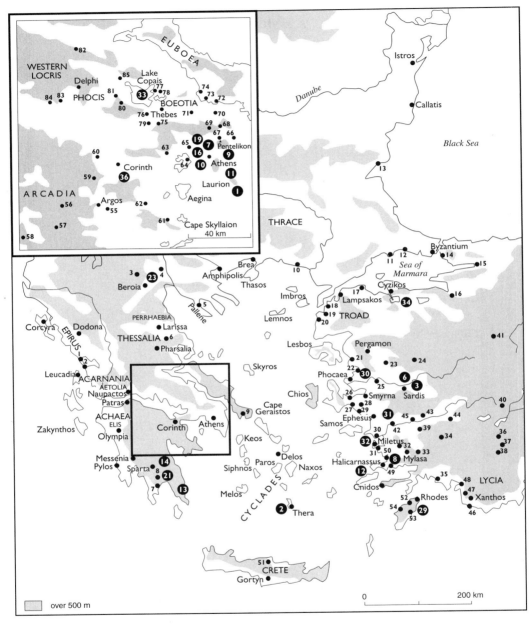

Map I. The Aegean World

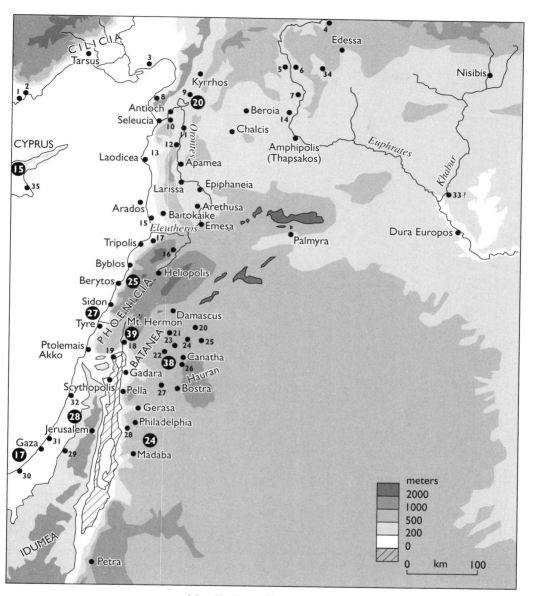

Map II. Greco-Roman Syria

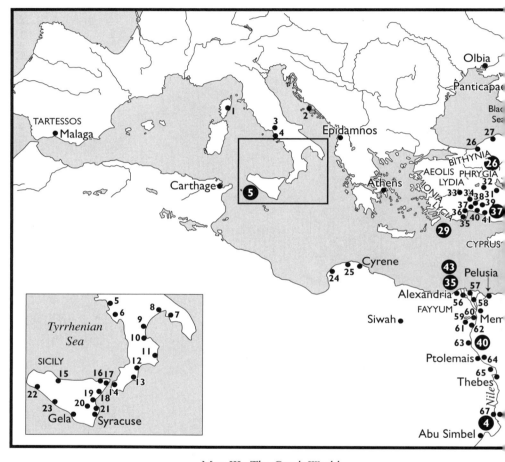

Map III. The Greek World

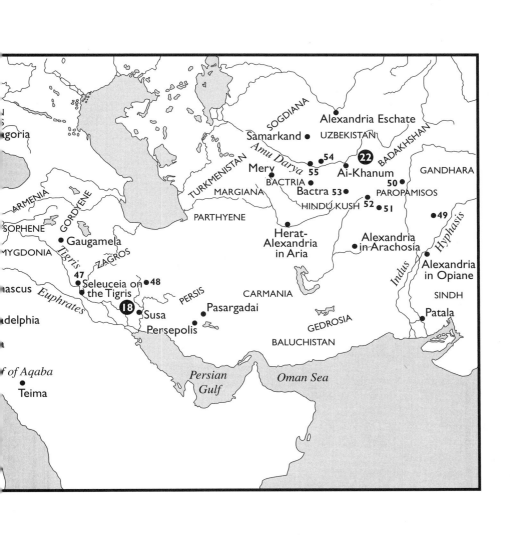

SOGDIANA

Alexandria Eschate

Samarkand • UZBEKISTAN

Amu Darya 55 54

Mery • BADAKHSHAN

BACTRIA Ai-Khanum 22

Bactra 53• GANDHARA

TURKMENISTAN PAROPAMISOS 50

MARGIANA 52 •51

PARTHYENE HINDU KUSH

goria

ARMENIA

SOPHENE

MYGDONIA • Gaugamela

GORDYENE

Tigris ZAGROS

47 •48

ascus • Seleuceia on

Euphrates the Tigris

delphia 18 •Susa

PERSIS

Herat-
Alexandria
in Aria

Alexandria
in Arachosia

Indus Alexandria
in Opiane

Hyphasis •49

SINDH

CARMANIA

Pasargadai

• Persepolis

GEDROSIA

Patala

BALUCHISTAN

f of Aqaba

• Teima

*Persian
Gulf*

Oman Sea

Place Names Corresponding to Numerals

The Roman numeral indicates the map on which the site appears; the Arabic numeral situates the site on the map.

Abai, I, 85
Abonuteichos, III, 27
Abydos (Dardanelles), I, 18
Abydos (Egypt), III, 65
Acraephia (Boeotia), I, 77
Actium, I, 2
Adada, III, 34
Adraha, II, 27
Aegae, II, 3
Agrigentum, III, 23
Alalia, III, 1
Alexandria Bucephala, III, 49
Alexandria of the Caucasus, III, 52
Amisos, III, 29
Amrit, II, 15
Amyclae, I, 8
Aornos, III, 50
Apamea on the Euphrates, II, 6
Aphrodisias, I, 39
Aphytis, I, 5
Arsinoeia, II, 1
Arsinoite (nome), III, 61
Ascalon, II, 31
Aspendos, III, 39
Astacos, I, 15
Atarneus, I, 21
Attaleia, III, 36

Balbura, I, 36
Barca, III, 25
Batanea, II
Bathyra, II, 21
Berenike Aqaba: see Aila, III

Caesarea Cappadocia, III, 43
Caesarea Maritima, II, 32
Caesarea Panias, II, 18
Caesarea-Arca of Lebanon, II, 17
Caryanda, I, 50
Carystos, I, 9
Catania, III, 19
Caulonia, III, 12
Caunos, I, 35
Celaenae, I, 40
Chaeronea, I, 81
Chalcedonia, I, 14
Chalcis of Euboea, I, 74
Chaleion, I, 83
Charakipolis, I, 24
Cholargos, I, 67
Cibyra, I, 36
Citium: see Cyprus, III
Claros, I, 29
Clazomenae, I, 26
Colophon, I, 28

Preface

THIS BOOK IS neither a history of the Greek world nor a history of Greek civilization. If the chapters that follow appear to cover more than a thousand years, they nevertheless represent, all things considered, only a fairly brief moment in a history that begins much earlier (it can certainly be called Greek history as early as the era of the Mycenean kingdoms) and that is still going forward today. But then, is it really a history? Stories, rather: as though, having reached the age when one should finally be able to produce some great synthesis by drawing on the learning of a lifetime, I pulled back before the obstacle and chose to settle for fragmentary narratives. Really, who today would dare to write, independently, a complete history of the Greeks, when the shortest textbook requires the collaboration of half a dozen specialists? But it was not fear that held me back, and it was a desire for something else that pushed me onto the side roads where I should like to take the reader. When Michael Winock was kind enough to ask me for this book, I immediately had the idea of starting from documents, sometimes anecdotal ones, and trying to show their significance. In other words, I wanted to put the historian's work and methods before the reader's eyes; I wanted to show how a document can prove to be rich in teachings if one knows how to interrogate it, place it in a series, look at it in relation to others that can shed light on it. Without question, there is a pedagogical thrust here—we do not reinvent ourselves!—aimed at younger readers, but older ones may find pleasure both in coming across documents they know well and in encountering others that have been discovered recently, some of which remain essentially unpublished.

But friendship does not explain everything, and there had to have been a nagging desire to transmit some idea that was dear to me. Having spent most of my time as a researcher exploring the Syrian margins of the Greek world, I confess that I have remained more fascinated by the periphery of that world than by its center. Is this because, right after I earned my *agrégation,* thanks to Jean Pouilloux's good offices I was able to go on a dig with Paul Bernard at Ai-Khanum in Afghanistan? Or might it have been my taste for exoticism that made me volunteer instinctively for this mission, just as I agreed at once, when I came back, to take charge of the corpus of Greek and Latin inscriptions found in Arabia? However this may be, the pressing needs of teaching have constantly brought me back from the margins toward the center, and this has had the advantage of constantly reminding me of the unity of a civilization behind the diversity of its manifestations. Whether the gymnasium is made of marble or crude bricks, what is important is the competition that takes place there! Throughout the forty-three chapters—I might just as well call them "sequences," as in a film—which I have arranged in approximate chronological order, I have sought to demonstrate the diversity of Greek experiences, trying to show, as it were, what gives these their profound originality, through time and space. Along the way, a sort of Greek history may begin to take shape, but the gaping holes I have left rule out such a description. Readers need to understand, then, that they will encounter only selected episodes, chosen in a completely subjective way, I confess, but chosen because they struck me as particularly significant. And it should be obvious that I took pleasure in exploring, explaining, dissecting—a pleasure I hope my readers will share.

HISTOIRES GRECQUES

CHAPTER ONE

Theseus Unites Attica's Inhabitants,
or the Origins of the City-State

After the death of Aegeus, Theseus conceived a wonderful de-
sign, and settled all the residents of Attica in one city, thus making one people of one city out of those who up to that time had
been scattered about and were not easily called together for the
common interests of all, nay, they sometimes actually quarreled
and fought with each other. He visited them, then, and tried to
win them over to his project township by township and clan by
clan. The common folk and the poor quickly answered to his
summons; to the powerful he promised government without a
king and a democracy, in which he should only be commander
in war and guardian of the laws, while in all else everyone
should be on an equal footing. Some he readily persuaded to
this course, and others, fearing his power, which was already
great, and his boldness, chose to be persuaded rather than
forced to agree to it. Accordingly, after doing away with the
town-halls and council-chambers and magistracies in the several communities, and after building a common town-hall and
council-chamber for all on the ground where the upper town of
the present day stands, he named the city Athens, and instituted
a Panathenaic festival.

Plutarch, *Theseus*, in *Plutarch's Lives*, trans. Bernadotte Perrin
(Loeb Classical Library, 1914), vol. 1, pp. 51–53 (XXIV, 1–3)

ATHENS, AROUND 1250 B.C.E., perhaps even around 1450; in any
case, before the Trojan War, according to the ancient authors.
Of the merits they readily attributed to themselves, the Greeks
counted as among the most remarkable the fact that they lived in organized city-states, that is, in communities of limited size covering relatively
small territories and remaining entirely independent of one another. And
in numerous pseudohistorical narratives of the sort we have just read, they

1

came close to crediting themselves with inventing the civic institution itself. The success of this self-proclamation cannot be denied; after all, it is widely believed that what best characterized the Greeks of antiquity was indeed life in city-states, and few people doubt that the Greeks were its inventors. We can acknowledge that the first point remains true to a large extent (although there were Greek communities organized according to other models); the same cannot be said of the second.

In fact, this type of organization in small, isolated communities independent of one another within a common culture was found elsewhere long before the Greeks adopted it. We need only consider the Sumerians of the third millennium or, closer to the Greeks in time and space, the Phoenicians on the east coast of the Mediterranean. Among the Phoenicians, the division into city-states was achieved before the end of the second millennium, that is, three or four centuries before the Greeks adopted that formula in turn.

Might the Greeks simply have copied the Phoenicians? There would be nothing astonishing about this, for it was around the time the first Greek city-states were founded that the Greeks borrowed writing from their neighbors in the Levant. But it is not necessary to look so far afield for models for the Greek city-state. In fact, in the Aegean and Balkan world of the second millennium, there was a long tradition of political splintering, of small communities jealous of their own autonomy existing side by side. Without neglecting the Cretan kingdoms dating from the period of the earliest palaces, we need only note that in the second millennium the Mycenean kingdoms already shared a relatively small space, and that none of them succeeded in unifying the Greek world politically. For we have to recall that the Myceneans themselves were Greek.

At the time when the first city-states *(poleis)* of the archaic age were being established, the Greek world had thus been practicing life in scattered communities for a long time, thereby situating itself at the opposite pole, ideologically, from the great centralized empires that dominated the Nile Valley or the valleys of the Tigris and the Euphrates. The innovation, around the ninth and eighth centuries, thus lay not so much in the infinite splintering of these communities as in the new way they were structured. And this is where the myth developed by Plutarch takes on its full relief.

Plutarch, a Greek writer from Chaeronea in Boeotia, lived during the period of the Roman Empire, roughly between 50 and 125 C.E. He was a public figure, and, more important for our purposes, he was an immensely cultivated man. Although historians have long made good use of his countless works, Plutarch did not claim to be a historian. Even in his *Parallel Lives,* where he placed biographies of famous Greeks and Romans side by side, as mirror images, his primary aim was moral edification. This does not prevent us from recognizing the general quality of his historical information, which was often drawn from older authors whose works have since disappeared.

In the present case, a modern historian is adopting a paradoxical attitude, using the biography of a legendary hero for historical purposes. For although the Greek historiographical tradition puts Theseus's life before the Trojan War, which is to say, according to the same tradition, around 1250, the fact remains that, like Romulus, his Roman alter ego in Plutarch's account, Theseus was a legendary figure. Plutarch's narrative thus tells us nothing at all about the way Athens was established, but it does shed light on the way the Athenians conceived of the event. And this is no less interesting.

Theseus belonged to the most illustrious of Athenian families, that of the earliest kings. Through his father, Aegeus, the fourth king of Athens, he was descended from the city's founder, Erichthonius/Erechtheus, a king born of sperm deposited by Hephaestus on Attic soil and thus born of the very soil of the country. Theseus covered himself with glory by delivering his city-state from having to pay the Minotaur of Crete, after an unhappy war, a hateful tribute: seven adolescent boys and seven girls from noble families. Forgetting to signal his triumphant arrival from afar—he had arranged with his father that he would unfurl a white sail in case of victory—he involuntarily caused his father's death, for the latter, despairing, threw himself into the sea that has borne his name ever since. Becoming king in his turn, Theseus undertook to unite what had remained divided.

According to the Athenian tradition (for it is certain that Plutarch is retelling a canonical Athenian legend), Theseus is thus not the founder of Athens in the sense that Romulus was the founder of Rome, but the author of a gathering of communities, a *synoikismos,* giving rise to a new political entity: the city-state of Athens. According to the legend, Attica was divided at the time among a host of small, independent communities, each with its own institutions, its own magistrates, and its own deliberative council. No doubt aware that they all have links with one another,

Plutarch does not call them city-states, but demes; he notes that it was hard to get them to act in concert, giving the impression that they nevertheless had common interests. Theseus undertook to visit all the demes and families (the latter must not be understood as nuclear families in the modern sense, but as all the family lineages, noble and otherwise). Ordinary people accepted his proposal right away, especially the poor, who presumably saw it as a way to escape from the economic and political control of the handful of wealthy families that dominated their village. The influential people (the Greek term is *dynatoi,* "powerful") were more divided, but in the end they all gave in, out of conviction or fear. What is most surprising, finally, is what Theseus said he would do for them: he promised to abolish royalty and to establish democracy. The first proposition is easy enough to understand, for it would have been hard to get the local leaders to submit to a single king governing the entire country; the second, however, is surprising, for it appears totally anachronistic at such an early period. Now, Plutarch knew his Athenian history, and he knew that democracy had been established only much later, in stages, during the time of Solon (around 596–594), Cleisthenes (510–507), and Pericles (around 460–430). The word *democracy* probably stands for a way of designating a certain equality of rights. Not equality for all, however: Theseus did not make this offer to all the residents of the new city-state, but only to the "powerful," those who had political rights, as it were. By renouncing royalty, he opened up the possibility that these local leaders could express themselves politically. By giving them equality of rights, he allowed them to constitute a recognized group destined to govern the city-state. For, in a passage located a little farther on, Plutarch recalls that although Theseus turned the Athenians into a single people, "he did not suffer his democracy to become disordered or confused from an indiscriminate multitude streaming into it"; consequently, he distinguished the nobles *(eupatridai)* from the peasants and the artisans, and charged the former with "the care of religious rites, the supply of magistrates, and the interpretation of the will of heaven."[1] The governing role that he reserved for the influential families of Attica thus appears to have been the condition sine qua non for obtaining their support for his project.

Plutarch's narrative accounts in its way for the situation that prevailed on the eve of the crisis Athens underwent in Solon's era, at the beginning of the sixth century: a landed aristocracy held all the power—religious, political, legal, and economic. But it is especially interesting in that the creation of the city-state is imagined as a voluntary measure, accomplished in a short time. Theseus is represented as playing the same role in the foundation of the city-state that Cleisthenes played in the institution of democracy at the end of the sixth century. What is more, Plutarch imagines the foundation of the *polis* as very similar to the new creations undertaken by Hellenistic kings and later by Roman emperors, from the fourth century B.C.E. on: the promotion of sometimes dispersed communities to a superior status. We shall come back to this point.

But the parallel with the establishment of democracy and the mention of this specific regime in Plutarch's account are not innocent. Theseus, an Athenian hero, did not take on real importance until quite late. In reality, at the outset he was probably just a local hero from the Marathon region in northeastern Attica. He does not figure among the ten heroes whose names were given to the new tribes created by Cleisthenes (Chapter 7). It was only after the Greco-Persian Wars that he appeared in the foreground and acquired a "national" (by which I mean Pan-Attic) character. Around 475, Cimon, a political figure who had become prominent after Themistocles—the hero of the Greco-Persian Wars, all-powerful until the end of the 460s—was eliminated, "discovered" Theseus's bones on the island of Skyros in the Aegean Sea, and brought them back to Athens with solemn honors. This choice had a political resonance that was not neutral. In the face of those who claimed to be Cleisthenes' heirs in order to push through further reforms in favor of the people, the celebration of Theseus, an incontestable hero, must have recalled the terms of the initial contract on which the city-state was founded, with power going to the *eupatridai* and the others having to settle for "a balance of privilege, the noblemen being thought to excel in dignity, the husbandmen in usefulness, and the handicraftsmen in numbers."[2] The promotion of Theseus to the rank of national hero marked a halt in the appropriation of power by the lower classes and announced a clearly conservative program.

While we can now clearly see the legend's political usefulness in classical Athens, this does not shed much light on the real conditions and processes that led the inhabitants of Attica to group together at the heart of a political community that was uniquely progressive in the ninth and eighth centuries B.C.E. Each city-state must have its own history, but for Athens, as for Sparta, a specific development has to be recognized, for these were giant city-states in relation to the usual norm of the insular and Balkan Greek world. After all, more than three-quarters of the city-states possessed territories measuring less than a hundred square kilometers: small islands such as Keos (modern Kea) were divided among four city-states (Poiessa, Iulis, Koresia, Karthaia). Boeotia, about the same size as Attica, harbored eleven at the end of the classical period, but smaller city-states had already been absorbed by larger ones during the fifth century. With its four thousand square kilometers, Spartan Laconia looked like a veritable monster, but even Attica, with twenty-five hundred square kilometers, covered a disproportionately large area in relation to the other city-states. Both Sparta and Athens succeeded in imposing themselves very early, by persuasion or by force, over vast expanses, absorbing previously autonomous communities. We find traces of these later, in the maintenance of particular statuses, local cults, or specific organizations—for example, in Amyclae (Amykles), on Sparta's territory, or in Marathon and Eleusis in Attica.

So when and how was this model propagated, this polis that was so characteristic of the Greek world? All the accounts of the foundation of colonies outside insular and Balkan Greece (Chapter 2) indicate that the colonists left constituted city-states and went elsewhere to reproduce the model they were leaving behind. This is probably why historians thought for a long time that the civic structures in Greece proper were fully established before the mid-eighth century, perhaps around 800. But it is quite possible that the migratory process and the demands of establishing a colony in a foreign and sometimes hostile environment may have contributed to finding new solutions, and that, in a way, colonization may have favored the development of unprecedented community structures. During the same period, the resumption of closer relations with the Near East during the ninth century put the Greeks in contact with a model of political organization structured around a king, magistrates, and a council. The importance of the Phoenician model must not be overlooked: at around the same time, the Greeks borrowed the Phoenician writing system and readily introduced Phoenicians into their myths. Cadmos, a Sidonian, was represented as the founder of Thebes, and beautiful Europa, seduced by Zeus, was of the same origin.

The difficulties begin with the definition of the polis, the city, or, as it is often called to avoid confusion with the ordinary sense of the word in

Western languages, the city-state. Generally speaking, to the extent that historians (and not only historians) see the Greek city-state as the primitive model for the modern nation-state, the political structures of the city-state have been stressed: the codification of laws, the designation of magistrates, the creation of councils and assemblies, the definition of citizens' rights (and thus of causes for exclusion), the promulgation of laws. In short, the city-state has been represented as a model of participatory political structure (whatever limits may have been imposed on the participants), at the opposite pole from the monarchic regimes in force in the great empires of the Near East. But such a definition seems too restrictive, and on this account we would have to move the establishment of the poleis fairly far forward in time, perhaps not before the late seventh or even the sixth century. And while the importance of the institutional aspects of the city-state cannot be denied, the city-state cannot be reduced to these alone.

Thus it is preferable to start with a broad definition and to view as a polis any community that—for reasons to be spelled out later on—established relations of solidarity at its core that imposed a minimum number of common rules and obligations upon all its members. The polis is in some sense the recognition of common interests by a limited group that is established on a limited territory and that sees itself as different from its neighbors.

A definition as broad as this one has the advantage of taking the entire group into account, whatever limitations on the rights of certain of its members may have been imposed for political reasons. For example, such a definition of the city-state fully integrates women, whereas a definition that privileges the political and institutional aspects naturally sets them apart, because they were deprived of participatory rights. Now, the polis was not a community of males, and still less a community of citizens; it was actually a community of families, where men, women, and children, free and not free, citizens and rural dependents, all had their places and their roles to play in the economic, social, and religious realms. It was only later, when the political dimension in the narrow sense seemed to be the very essence of the city-state, that those who did not enjoy political rights were viewed as excluded.

The question is how these groups became conscious of their community of interests, how and when they constituted themselves, that is, how the boundaries between them were finally established. Economic, military, political, religious, and cultural factors have all been invoked, sometimes one or another of these exclusively, and this has tended to mask the complexity of the phenomenon.

Let us note to begin with that the creation of poleis appears to have affected at first only the eastern and southern regions of the Balkan Peninsula, along with the Aegean Islands. Thus at the outset this phenomenon did not involve the Greek world as a whole, although it quickly spread both into the colonial world and into Asia Minor (if it did not in fact appear there at the same time as in Greece proper). Whole regions in the north and the west (Thessalia, Aetolia, Acarnania, Epiros) remained apart from the movement. We may note that this area included the one in which Mycenean palatial civilization developed, also divided up in small territorial units; this obliges us at least to wonder about a possible continuity between the Mycenean and archaic Greek worlds.

Secondly, we must not lose sight of the fact that, of the very high number of Greek city-states (more than five hundred in the classical era, perhaps as many as fifteen hundred in all in antiquity), it is not certain that the same causes were equally important everywhere in the process of establishing poleis. Moreover, among the factors behind the appearance of poleis, we probably have to eliminate from the outset what were in reality only secondary aspects, or even consequences. For example, the development of a monumental center with public buildings *(prytanea)* and ramparts was probably the result rather than the cause of a given community's self-awareness. Moreover, the monumental center was by no means obligatory or generalized, and scholars have long emphasized that the monumentalization of Athens was exceptional. Thucydides had already noted that no one could have imagined Sparta's power if that city-state had suddenly disappeared: "As Sparta is not compactly built as a city and has not provided itself with costly temples and other edifices, but is inhabited village-fashion in the old Hellenic style, its power would appear less than it is."[3] In the same way, the modifications in battle technology that came about during the seventh century—the hoplite revolution that gave a preponderant place to heavily armed foot soldiers at the expense of the cavalry, and that, more importantly still, privileged collective fighting to the exclusion of individual combat—account for evolutions at the heart of the political system that was then in place, but they cannot explain the actual birth of the polis.

Some have attributed this development to an economic factor. In this account, there would have been a transition around the ninth and eighth centuries from an extensive pastoral economy to more-intensive agricultural practices under the pressure of strong demographic growth. No one doubts today that there was indeed a population increase, but the break was not significant enough to provoke a shift from a pastoral to an agricultural society. At most, there may have been an awareness of the need to manage the available lands better in order to ensure the subsistence of a larger community. This may have imposed new constraints, such as common defenses against the incursions of neighbors. But this cannot have been the sole or even the main cause; it has to be viewed as one element among others—and perhaps not everywhere—that may have helped define a community.

More often, thanks in particular to the work of François de Polignac and Claude Bérard, scholars have stressed the cultic aspects that affected the Greek communities in the ninth and eighth centuries. During this period, we can observe a multiplication of votive repositories in places that seem specialized enough to have been called "sanctuaries" from then on. In other words, we see the beginnings of a fairly strict differentiation between secular and religious spaces; this was not the case in the Aegean world during the second millennium, nor did it appear in the Homeric epics. Moreover, a number of these sacred repositories are situated on the periphery of a community's territory (for example, Hera's temple in Argos), as if they were marking the territorial limits of the collectivity. This may well indicate a taking of control, as it were, a delimitation of the collective territory; it surely translates an awareness of previously unknown convergences of interests. There were doubtless already some common elements among the lineages grouped together this way (for example, dialects: the inhabitants of Attica spoke a dialect that distinguished them from their neighbors in Boeotia or from the Megarians), but here we find for the first time an attempt at geographical delimitation on the part of a group, a way of saying just how far it extends and what is excluded from it. This fundamental role of the cultic element in the definition of a group would explain in particular the intimate fusion that never ceased to prevail in the Greek city-states between the religious and political dimensions, that is, between religious phenomena and everything that stemmed from the group's collective manifestations. The mention of the gods and the common cults has pride of place in every classical definition of the city-state; to integrate a foreigner into the polis was thus not only to grant him political rights but above all to have him participate in the common cults, to give him the same gods one had oneself.

A grasp of the solidarity that was based on sharing common cults constitutes, today, the most solid and most fruitful element of reflection and explanation regarding the birth of the polis. We must note that its defenders have emphasized that this phenomenon was produced in a particular context, the "heroizing frenzy" that clearly affected the eighth and seventh centuries. Indeed, it has been observed that a number of votive repositories were set up on the funerary remains (or vestiges perceived as such) of earlier periods, Mycenean in particular, remains interpreted as traces of mythic ancestors common to the entire community. Perhaps the phenomenon should not be seen as limited to this period alone, for as early as the tenth century we have evidence that certain men were given a hero's burial. At Lefkandi in Euboea, in front of a building that has been seen as the earliest example of a Greek temple, the charred remains of a man have been discovered in a bronze amphora alongside the remains of a woman who had simply been buried and those of three or four sacrificial horses. These funeral rites of the heroic or even Homeric type meant that the beneficiary had to have been viewed as a hero by his own community, which associated his tomb with a sacred space. In any case, it is essentially incontestable that this pronounced taste for the world of heroes reached its peak toward the end of the eighth century and the beginning of the seventh, in the era in which the Homeric poems were first written down, the era in which writing was again used for purposes that were more poetic than practical.

By the same token, the establishment of the city-states would be at best contemporary with the colonial movement, and not anterior to it. The Greeks did not export a preexisting model, but the colonists presumably helped refine this new conception of communities, given that the cohesion of a community was all the more necessary when it was being established in a foreign and sometimes hostile environment.

Under these conditions, it seems probable that communities rapidly created political instruments for themselves—political in the strict sense—enabling them to ensure that everyone would respect rules applying to all. They must have moved fairly quickly from becoming aware of common interests and of the need for solidarity to consolidating the group through the recuperation of a shared past, real or mythical, and then establishing collective institutional structures. Did the same thing happen everywhere, and at the same pace? We still know too little to make such a claim, but the overall schema appears credible, and must have functioned, with local variations, in every region where, in the seventh century, the existence of this new political form, the polis, is attested.

CHAPTER TWO

The Theraeans Embark for Cyrene, or How to Found a Colony: A National Legend

It pleased the assembly. Given that Apollo himself has ordered Battos and the Theraeans to colonize Cyrene, may it please the Theraeans to decide this: that they send Battos to Libya as *archegetes* [founder] and king; that the Theraeans will set off to accompany him; that they will embark on equal and similar conditions for each household, sending one son per family; that the list of all men of an age to leave will be drawn up for the entire country and that, among the Theraeans, every free man, if he wishes, may go along; if the colonists succeed in becoming masters of the colony, that any of their compatriots who later land there will enjoy full citizenship and receive a lot from among the vacant lands; if the colonists do not succeed in becoming masters of the colony, if the Theraeans cannot bring them aid and if after five years they have not surmounted the difficulties that they must face, that they may return without fear from this country to their own properties in Thera and resume the right of residence. Anyone who does not wish to embark whereas the city-state has designated him to do so, that he be subject to the death penalty and that his property be confiscated. Anyone who shall receive him or shelter him, should this be a father and son or brother and brother, that he be subject to the same penalties as the one who does not wish to embark. Those who remain here and those who leave to found the colony have sworn an oath in these terms and they have formulated imprecations against those who transgress these oaths and fail to keep them, whether it be among those who live in Libya or among those who remain here. Having made figurines of wax, they burned them while pronouncing imprecations, men, women, boys, and girls: "He who does not remain faithful to these oaths but transgresses them, may he melt and be liquefied

13

like these figurines, he and his lineage and his property. To those who remain faithful to these oaths, whether they be among those who embark for Libya or among those who remain in Thera, may much good befall them and their descendants."

Supplementum Epigraphicum Graecum (Alphen aan den Rijn: Sijthoff and Noordhoff, 1923–), vol. 9, 3

YRENE (IN LIBYA), fourth century B.C.E. The city-state had a peculiar document engraved on a stone stele. It was a decree, an ordinary sort of document in the classical and Hellenistic Greek world, announcing a decision made by the entire body of citizens meeting in an assembly of the people. But this particular decree is intriguing for at least three reasons. First, even though it was erected on the agora at Cyrene, it was not a decree from Cyrene but from Thera, that is, from the city-state that occupied the island of Santorini in the Cyclades during antiquity. Next, the engraving of the decree, which can be dated fairly precisely toward the end of the fourth century by virtue of the writing style, does not correspond at all to the era when the decree was approved by the Theraeans, toward the middle of the seventh century. Finally, and this is a consequence of the preceding affirmation, it is astonishing to find a decree drafted in this form as early as the mid-seventh century. What is this all about?

The city of Cyrene, in today's Libya, is thought—quite rightly, let us be clear at the outset—to have been founded by the Greeks around the middle of the seventh century B.C.E. Certain ancient sources even specify 644 B.C.E. Nothing in the archaeological discoveries contradicts this assertion, and thus historians have by and large accepted this date, not as absolutely certain, but as a reasonable approximation. The founders were not Greeks from just anywhere, adventurers setting off at random, but Greeks from the island of Thera, on a very official mission. By good fortune, in addition to the narrative preserved on the stele in Cyrene, we have a long account by Herodotus about the foundation and history of Cyrene. In reality, there are two parallel accounts, for Herodotus recorded variants. Despite minor difficulties, it is worth summarizing Herodotus's narrative, for in it we find a number of elements common to most Greek colonial foundations, a movement that dispersed Greeks from Spain to the Crimea.

An embassy of Theraeans, led by their king, received the order from the god at Delphi to go found a city in Libya (this is what the Greeks called Africa west of Egypt), whereas the goal of their embassy had seemed to be unrelated to such a project (in one of the accounts, the embassy was led by Battos, who had come to consult the god about his voice, for he was a stutterer). Confused, the Theraeans did nothing after they returned home, for they had no idea even where Libya was. Whereupon a drought settled upon their island for seven years, killing even the trees. The Theraeans then sent a new embassy to Delphi, whereupon the god reminded them of his earlier injunction. This time the Theraeans acted accordingly, first seeking out someone who could guide them, as they still did not know how to get to Libya. In Crete they found a murex fisherman who by chance had once been carried away to Libya by the winds, onto an island called Plataea. A small group of Theraeans set off with him to Plataea, reconnoitered the space, left a certain Corobios behind with food supplies, and returned to Thera to report to the authorities. The Theraeans were absent much longer than expected, and poor Corobios would have died of hunger if a boat from Samos, thrown off course by the winds, had not stopped by chance at Plataea and left him some food.

Back in Thera, the first envoys reported that they had found Libya and had created a colony there. It was thus decided that each family would send one of every two brothers, designated by lot, with a leader, Battos, who would be the king of the new city-state. We can see that Herodotus's text differs somewhat from the Cyrene document, in which just one son per family was designated. In concrete terms, the two versions may have amounted to more or less the same thing. In any case, the group was not small: two fifty-oar boats had to be outfitted to accommodate everyone. Several hundred people thus went off.

In one of the versions reported by Herodotus, this group was unable to settle in Libya and returned in haste to Thera. There, the returnees were greeted by people throwing stones, and they were forced to turn around and go back to Libya. It was at this point that the colony of Plataea was founded.

But the conditions were harsh, and after two years the colonists sent an embassy to Delphi to ask the god why he had sent them to such a poor place. The god's response was unambiguous: "If you know Libya, rich in herds, better than I, You who have never seen it, when I myself have gone there, I truly admire your knowledge!"

The god was clearly letting them know that he had ordered them to go

15

to Libya itself, not to an island at some distance from the coast. The colonists thus left Plataea to settle on the coast across from the island, in Aziris, a place "framed with beautiful wooded glens, beside a river." After six years, local people led them to a better site, toward the west. They were made to travel at night—so they would not see that they were traversing the prosperous indigenous villages and lands—toward the interior, onto a well-irrigated plateau overlooking the sea: as Herodotus reports, the natives told them that "there, the sky has holes." This, finally, was the site of Cyrene. From then on, the colony prospered, even though the number of colonists did not increase. Thus, under the third king, Battos the Fortunate, an oracle of Pythia convoked all the Greeks to come settle in Cyrene, promising to distribute lands. Greeks came from all over, and the natives began to worry, because, naturally, they found themselves dispossessed by the new arrivals.

This text can be read in many ways, and some have rightly emphasized that it was above all a matter of developing a national legend whose historical character in the strict sense remains of little importance. This is true enough, but the narratives of colonial foundations present so many common features that it is difficult not to use them as sources of information about the general conditions of Greek colonization during the archaic period. For one undeniable fact remains: between 770 and 550, roughly speaking (although the pattern continued until around 500), thus for more than two centuries, Greeks from all over the Aegean basin left to settle in Sicily, in southern Italy, on the Adriatic coast, in southern Gaul, in Spain, in Libya, in Thrace, around the Black Sea, on the southern coast of Anatolia, and possibly on the Syrian coast. They were sometimes so numerous that the new territories looked like a new Greece. This was the case in southern Italy, which earned the name Great Greece, and in eastern Sicily. Even where they were more isolated, their numbers were not negligible, and they usually succeeded in founding city-states that prospered and survived. This is a significant phenomenon, then, that needs to be understood and explained.

The Greeks probably crossed the Mediterranean as early as the second millennium, but despite efforts to prove that there had already been Mycenean colonization, we have to acknowledge that, while we have evidence that merchandise traveled, nothing proves that there were permanent settlements populated by Greeks before the eighth century. The fact that the

Theraeans did not even know where Libya was shows that the sea had not been entirely explored, and even the Cretans, although they were closest to Libya, had rarely gone there except by chance. The Greeks probably knew southern Italy and Sicily better; Greek products arrived there as early as the end of the second millennium. Still, we cannot assert that they were brought by Greeks; the Phoenician merchants who were crisscrossing the Mediterranean in those years may have served as transporters. In contrast, there is no doubt that as early as the thirteenth and twelfth centuries, Greeks from the European continent and the islands (the Cyclades) colonized the Asiatic bank of the Aegean and the islands close by, founding cities such as Ephesus, Miletus, Smyrna, Phocaea (modern Foça in Turkey), Samos, Chios, Lesbos, Rhodes (in fact three different cities, Ialysos, Lindos, and Kamiros), Cnidos, and so on. At the time when what is called colonization in the archaic period was beginning, these city-states were already well established and a number of them participated in that adventure.

In any case, according to a tradition that archaeology does not contradict, a first Greek colony is said to have been installed in Pithecussae (Ischia), a small island at the entrance to the Bay of Naples, around 770, and then about twenty years later on the continent, at Cumae. Let us note at once that these dates must not be taken as clear-cut reference points. They are the result of *a posteriori* speculations on the part of learned men of antiquity who did not rely on documentation that would have preserved absolute dates, but who made calculations according to the number of generations. We do not always know what interval they set between two generations (it varied from thirty to forty years, often thirty-three or thirty-five), and this gave their calculations a more or less mechanical character in any case. But, except for instances in which archaeology formally contradicts these calculations, we shall retain them here, because they give an at least approximate idea of the era during which these new Greek cities were founded.

When Greeks were landing in Campania, around 750, colonies had been founded in eastern Sicily, Naxos (on Capo Schiso) in 734, Syracuse in 733, Catania and Leontinoi (on the southern Catania plain) the same year (729), Megara Hyblaea in 728, Zancle (Messina) on the east coast, and then Gela on the south coast (688). In the same period, colonies had been founded around the gulf of Tarentum and in Calabria: Rhegium (Reggio)

17

between 750 and 720, Sybaris around 720, Croton in 709, Tarentum around 706, Epizephyrian Locri around 680. These colonies were sometimes so successful that they founded secondary settlements in turn: thus Zancle founded Mylae and then Himera further to the west, Sybaris created Metapontum, and Croton populated Caulonia.

But Sicily and Italy were not the only destinations of this first wave of colonizers. Greeks left for the north and the northeast: Chalcedonia on the Asiatic bank of the Bosporus, shortly before 700, Parium around the same time in the Dardanelles, Thasos around 680, Cyzicos around 676 on the southern coast of the Sea of Marmara, Byzantium around 660.

A second wave of colonization, starting in the mid-seventh century, touched almost all the banks of the Mediterranean and the Black Sea. Thus Lampsakos and Perinthus on the Sea of Marmara were founded in the second half of the seventh century, then around the Black Sea, Heraclea Pontica, Sinope, Amisos (now Samsun in Turkey) on the south bank, Messembria, Istros, Callatis, and Olbia on the west bank, Panticapaeon (now Kerch) and Phanagoria in Crimea. We have seen that the Theraeans founded Cyrene around 644, while tradition holds that Marseille was founded in 600. Other colonial expeditions led to the creation of new Greek outposts in Thrace (Maronea). It was during this second wave that the colonists who had moved in during the first wave founded new settlements in southern Italy and Sicily: the Sybarites moved into Posidonia-Paestum around 650, Acragas (Agrigentum) was founded by the city-state of Gela around 580, Selinus by the residents of Megara Hyblaea in 628. This also happened in Libya, where the Cyrenians populated Barca around 560–550 and Euhesperides (now Benghazi) around 520. But many other regions also witnessed the arrival of Greek colonists: the Adriatic (Corcyra, Epidamnos), Cilicia (Nagidos, Soloi), Pamphylia (Side), Lycia (Phaselis).

Some regions were not very much affected by the movement, generally because they were under the domination of a strong power that kept the Greeks from entering as they pleased (this was the case in Egypt and Phoenicia), but also sometimes because the Phoenicians had colonized them at the same time as the Greeks or a little earlier. This was the case in North Africa (Carthage was founded in 814, according to the ancient sources, although archaeology has found nothing there before the end of the eighth century), the Spanish coasts (although the Greeks did have a few small settlements there, such as Mainake-Malaga—of which no vestiges have yet been found—and Emporion-Ampurias), Sardinia, and western Sicily (Selinus notwithstanding). Generally speaking, the Greeks had to choose sectors in which control of the territory by the indigenous populations was incomplete and thus allowed newcomers to seize the lands they needed.

Why this vast movement of emigration, over such a long period of time? We need to note first of all that the causes were not necessarily the same for all the colonies or throughout the entire period. For a long time, historians privileged a single cause: the lack of land. The Greeks were thus thought to have set out to conquer new lands, following a large population increase. No one denies that Aegean Greece underwent perceptible demographic growth as early as the end of the ninth century, and an improvement in living conditions might have made the populations eager to consume more. It is thus not impossible that certain civic territories may have been too cramped, especially on the islands, which were often arid and offered little in the way of agricultural land. But there could also have been local or structural causes. Local, as in Chalcis of Euboea (famine), or in Thera, if the national legend is to be believed: a persistent drought ruined the island's agriculture. This is possible, but the designation of one brother for every two, or one son per family, may also indicate structural causes (in Chalcis, one resident in ten was designated). Demographic growth made it necessary to divide up inheritances, thus splintering property to the point where no one's lands sufficed for sustenance. We also have to take the structures of land ownership into account. Hesiod's long poem *Works and Days* (from the eighth century B.C.E.) describes a deeply inegalitarian society in which the powerful monopolized the land. Indebtedness obliged small landowners to give up their holdings (whatever form these may have taken), perhaps ending up as farmworkers on what had been their own property. In Athens, early in the sixth century, Solon declared that "Earth was in bondage," both because very large numbers of owners of small and medium-size landholdings were obliged to mortgage their lands, and because certain categories of agricultural workers were subject to frightful conditions, close to slavery, owing considerable debts to large landowners or to creditors who profited from mortgages.[1] To solve these problems, leaders may well have decided to expel segments of the population, urging them to go elsewhere to look for lands to cultivate.

These internal tensions in the city-states appear in several other foundation narratives. Thus Tarentum is said to have been founded by Spartan bastards driven from the city-state after the return of husbands who had been kept away too long by war (there are in fact several versions that end up with more or less the same results). In Corinth, a certain Archias, a member of the reigning Bacchiad dynasty, was condemned for the murder of a young boy and had to flee: he went off with companions to found Corcyra (Corfu) and then Syracuse; behind that private matter with an anecdotal flavor may in fact have lain a rivalry between the city-state's prominent families.

The accounts we have do not allow us to put all the colonial foundations in the same mold. Thus the Samians, who had helped Corobios when he was abandoned on the islet of Plataea, were there to trade, and whereas they wanted to go to Egypt, it is said, the winds pushed them to Hercules' columns—that is, to the Strait of Gibraltar, where they engaged in the tin trade with residents of Tartessos.

Moreover, whether we are observing the colonies' origins or their later development, the agricultural dimension is sometimes lacking. To be sure, some accounts clearly highlight the distribution of land. This was the case twice over at Cyrene, since the appeal for reinforcements was translated by new distributions, to the detriment of the natives. It was also the case at Syracuse, where lots had already been drawn on shipboard (one of the colonists lost his at dice even before disembarking), and the wealthy Syracusans later bore the name *geomoroi,* "those who have divided up the land" or "those who have received a share of land."

But this was not always the case. Thus for a long time Marseille had only a minuscule territory around the city proper, along the edge of the Old Port. And that did not seem to keep it from prospering, as if its primary function was to be an intermediary between the Greeks and the natives, and as if its initial subsistence depended on this mercantile role. Similarly, the settlement on Pithecussae can hardly be explained by agriculture, because the territory is so small. Yet the colonists themselves came from Euboea, a rich region known for the fertility of its soil. It is hard to see why they would have chosen this small island if they had lacked land at home. In contrast, Pithecussae was an easily defended site for people who sought to participate in the traffic of all sorts that was developing along the western coasts of Italy, especially trading in metals. The quest for metals seems to have been an obsession, moreover, for it explains the foundation of Thasos, across from the mines of Mount Pangaeus, or Maronea, right on the Thracian coast. But trading in other goods may have been involved, and the cities on the north coast of the Black Sea sent the Aegean world wood, furs, wheat, and dried fruit produced by the indigenous peoples of the region.

Thus we cannot reduce the causes of archaic Greek colonization to a single explanation. Moreover, the very nature of the settlements changed over time, and for each one we would need to find dominant features rather than a single, defining trait. Even the trading posts most oriented toward commerce needed to ensure a minimum of subsistence, as they could not count exclusively on imports from outside to meet the needs of daily life. Conversely, colonies obviously founded for demographic reasons, such as Cyrene and also most of those in southern Italy and Sicily, were able to profit from the resources of their territory and engage in commerce. Cyrene thus based part of its wealth on collecting and exporting silphium, a highly sought-after medicinal plant that is no longer extant and that we cannot identify with precision.

The geography of the city-states the colonists left behind can also shed some light on the conditions underlying this vast movement. The small city-states of Euboea, Chalcis, and Eretria were the ones that started the movement: they were small, but no doubt more advanced in terms of material culture than many others, in particular because they maintained active relations with the Near East. It is astonishing that a city-state such as Chalcis could have founded in turn Pithecussae, Cumae, Naxos, Catania, Leontinoi, and Rhegium (with the help of the Messenians). Corinth, already an important center of ceramic production, founded Corcyra and Syracuse. But even some tiny city-states, in Locris and Achaea, for example, were founders (of Epizephyrian Locri and of Sybaris, respectively); we find Cretans and Rhodians in Gela, Theraeans in Cyrene. One of the European Greek city-states is prominent for its absence: Athens, which did not participate in the movement. This may be explained both by the extent of its territory (it had enough usable land to accommodate population growth) and by its leaders' ability to resolve its political and social crises without having to expel part of its population. Draco, by establishing written laws, and Solon, by forbidding enslavement for debtors and by reducing or eliminating debts, had improved conditions enough so that the poorest Athenians did not seek self-imposed exile. It was only later, and in a very different context, that of Athenian imperialism at the time of the Delian League, that Athens in turn embarked on two singular colonial enterprises, at Brea in Thrace and at Thurioi in southern Italy.

In the second period, major city-states in Asia Minor sent colonists far and wide: in particular, colonists were sent from Miletus (to Parium, Cyzikos, Abydos, Sinope, Amisos, Istros, Olbia, Panticapaeon), but also from Phocaea (to Lampsakos, Marseille, Alalia in Corsica, Emporion, Elea), Samos (Perinthus), Teos (Phanagoria), Cnidos (to the Lipari Islands), while at least one European city-state, Megara, was active in colonization (Astacos, Chalcedonia, Selymbria, Byzantium). It is striking that, with rare exceptions (such as Thera), the poorest or the most isolated city-states were not the ones that sent off colonists. To be sure, the landlocked city-states hardly had that possibility, because they did not have boats, but poverty alone does not explain why the wealthy city-states of Asia Minor, which also had vast agricultural territories, went off to look for land in the Crimea, even though there were possibilities for expansion close at hand. The evidence militates in favor of commercial objectives that seem obvious. Does this mean that the city-states engaged in a policy of territorial expansion to serve mercantile ends? Caution is called for, but some indications, still too few, nevertheless show that Greek products reached certain zones a short time before the phase of colonization properly so-called set in, for example in Francavilla Marittima, in Calabria. Here and there, colonization may well have come after an exploratory phase that revealed the interest of the site.

In all these foundations, one man played a preponderant role, the one the later texts called the *oikistes* or *archegetes,* the founder. We have seen that the Greeks did not leave in a haphazard fashion; the city-states took the initiative, with very rare exceptions in which the colonial enterprise seems to have been quasi-private: a certain Dorieus, a Spartan, thus managed to found a colony in North Africa, while the Athenians Miltiades the Elder and Hippias in turn established outposts near the Dardanelles (Hellespont), the first in Chersonese of Thrace, the second in Sigea in the Troad region. But as a general rule, the city-states dictated the rules of designation to the colonists, assigned them their goals, and decided on their destination, at least approximately, after consulting the gods, especially Apollo of Delphi. There has been much commentary on the role of Delphi, promoted to the rank of information center regarding the colonial movements in the Mediterranean; the city-states are said to have gone there for information so as to avoid sending colonists to a zone already occupied by others, or to an area that was too dangerous. It may be that people hoped to gather information at Delphi from Greeks who had traveled far and wide, for the great sanctuary at Phocis received visitors from the entire *oikoumene* ("the inhabited part of the earth"). But I believe that it was mainly the trust placed in the god at Delphi that justified sending embassies: one could not embark on such an adventure without having the god's agreement, without having gotten him or her to approve the project.

Once the colonists had been designated, the head of the expedition was named; he was responsible for carrying out operations and also for fulfilling the sacred rites of foundation. After his death, he received quasi-divine honors and his tomb was installed on the agora of the new city-state. For there was indeed a new city-state, and the "colonies" did not find themselves in the relation of dependence in which the colonies of the European powers were placed starting in the sixteenth century. The Theraeans provide a good example. Battos was designated to be oikistes and king of the new city-state, Cyrene. He actually founded a dynasty, the Battiads, which remained in power in Cyrene until the middle of the fifth century. Cyrene was a fully autonomous city-state that made its own laws and its own decisions about its future. When a serious political and social crisis arose around 560–550, it called upon a legislator, Demonax of Mantinea, to find a solution acceptable to all parties in the conflict.

Nevertheless, we can guess that ties with the metropolis, the "mother city," persisted. First of all, as the stele of the founders of Cyrene shows, Thera retained the prerogative of sending new colonists who would automatically have the right of citizenship in Cyrene and would receive lands. This is both proof that Cyrene was a fully autonomous city-state (it had its own citizenship) and that the Theraeans enjoyed privileges there, because the granting of citizenship was one of the prerogatives the city-states protected most jealously.

Moreover, it is probable that a number of the political institutions and laws of the new city-states were borrowed from the metropolis, and many parallels have been observed over time. Thera was governed by a king (like Sparta, from which Thera's inhabitants came originally), and it established Battos as king in Cyrene. This did not preclude innovations, and the colonists had to confront new situations that obliged them to make new

23

laws. It is doubtless no accident that several of the great, more or less mythical lawmakers of the archaic period came from the colonies (Zaleucos of Locri, Charondas of Catania, Diocles of Syracuse) or worked in them (Demonax of Mantinea in Cyrene). In addition, the colonists took their gods with them when they left, and this constituted a patrimony held in common with the mother country, even if the colony's pantheon was enriched by new gods owing to contact with the natives.

For another aspect we must take into consideration is that the Greeks did not go to deserted lands. Indigenous populations, more or less numerous, existed everywhere. Several narratives mention very harmonious relations at the time a colony was founded, as if the natives helped the newcomers settle in. This was the case in Thera, where the Libyans ended up taking pity on the Greeks, unsatisfactorily settled in Aziris, and showed them a better site, at Cyrene. It was also the case at Marseille, where the Greeks landed just as a local leader was preparing to marry off his daughter. And the leader of the Greeks was the one chosen to be her spouse! Only rarely did the foundation itself take place after violent battles against the locals. In contrast, the situation often worsened afterward, and the colonists had to confront peoples dispossessed of their lands or of their access to the sea. This was the case in Sicily, where the colonists were pitted against the Sikeles, and in southern Italy, where the colonists had to face the Messapians, the Lucanians, and the Bruttians. We have seen that the Libyans ended up mobilizing against the influx of new colonists. They appealed to the pharaoh, Apries, who tried to come to their aid but was crushed by the Greek troops around 580. For long periods, the colonies sought to reinforce themselves in the face of pressure from the natives. The events that took place in the Aegean world led on several occasions to massive departures. Thus when the Lydian king Gyges seized Greek city-states in Asia Minor around 560, there were large-scale emigrations from some sites, including that of the Phocaeans, some of whom naturally went to join their compatriots who had settled in Marseille. But the colonies also willingly received individuals who were outside the law, badly integrated into the collective structures of their original city-states, or lacking the means to subsist. The colonies allowed people to start over.

But the relations between Greeks and natives were not limited to indifference or conflict. Very few colonial expeditions included women, and thus the colonists had to find women where they were. This is the lesson to be drawn from the pious Marseille legend according to which the city was founded when Gyptis, a lovely and sought-after young native princess, turned down her other suitors in favor of Protis, a handsome young explorer from Phocis, a region of central Greece. Such intercommunity marriages undoubtedly led to cultural exchanges, even if their nature is hard for us to grasp. Nevertheless, digs in indigenous settlements in proximity to Greek colonies show the presence, very early, of Greek artisanal products (ceramics, bronzes, small objects), and these objects undoubtedly denote a certain form of acculturation or hybridization, in that their use is tied to typically Greek behaviors: the consumption of olive oil and wine, the introduction of ceramics painted with Greek mythological motifs, and so on. Without speaking of a Hellenization whose effects were felt only in the long term, it is not going too far to say that the colonists got the natives used to certain forms of Greek life, certain customs involving food, clothing, and art. It is probable that the Hellenized natives ended up being accepted into the new cities and ultimately reinforced the Greek city-states. From this standpoint, archaic colonization, despite all the uncertainties that surround it, appears to be one stage among others in the long process that led the Greeks to emigrate farther and farther away and to accept at the heart of their own communities people who adopted Greek culture in the broadest sense. The process went into dormancy after the Greco-Persian Wars, but it took on new impetus after Alexander's conquest.

CHAPTER THREE

Lydian Coins,
or the Origins of Money

Lydian electrum stater, with striations, coll. Cabinet des Médailles.
Athenian drachma in silver, second half of the fifth century B.C.E.

ASIA MINOR, around 600, perhaps a little earlier. For the first time, we find fragments of hammered metal that can be identified by specialists as coins—although at first glance they are merely bits of metal that look pretty much like all the others. The one chosen here (above left) from among many similar specimens is a small metal disc resembling a slightly thickened wafer, or perhaps a droplet; it has been marked by striations on one side only. We are far removed from the lovely Athenian coinage that came later, featuring an owl (above right). So why do we call the first piece of metal a coin? Indeed, what is a coin? What distinguishes it from a piece of metal of the same weight and thus, a priori, of the same value?

Money figures among the inventions that are attributed to the Greeks. Or, rather, the Greeks themselves and the historians who came later agree that coinage appeared first in the kingdom of Lydia, that is, in the west of what is Turkey today, in the rich and prosperous state that had as kings two men who are known for different reasons: Gyges because, it is said, he had a ring that allowed him to appear and disappear at will, Croesus because his wealth surpassed anything that had ever been seen before. But while the Lydians were credited with inventing money, everyone agreed that the Greeks were the ones who propagated this innovation, if only because the Lydian kingdom disappeared as early as 546, carried off by the Persian whirlwind (Chapter 6).

Accustomed as we are to the use of money, even though ours differs greatly from the ancient metallic coinage, we have a hard time imagining a world without it. The Greeks themselves told stories on the subject that were intended to explain how one could carry out exchanges without falling back on that convenient mediation. For everyone knew perfectly well that exchanges had been unending, both within Greek communities and between the Greeks and the surrounding peoples. Yet the invention of money could be dated, at least approximately, to a not very distant period.

Naturally, the simplest way to proceed was to barter: in exchange for a given item of merchandise, one supplied a certain quantity of other merchandise, the two parties reaching agreement to establish the equivalence. But it is clear that this very cumbersome and complicated system was hardly suited for everyday exchanges. In reality, as far back as we have written documents to consult, that is, as early as the third millennium in Mesopotamia, we observe that the ruling powers sought to establish equivalences acceptable to all, or even imposed them. Thus, around 2600, in Mesopotamia, a basket of barley could be an officially defined measure of weight, which implied that every item of trade could be evaluated in numbers of baskets of barley (or fractions of baskets). In the nineteenth century B.C.E., King Sin-Kasid of Uruk (1865–1804) counted among the great achievements of his reign the fact that he had established equivalences to help with exchanges. "One shekel of silver [a measure of weight] according to the local standard had the same value as three measures of barley, twelve minae of wool, ten minae of copper, or three measures of sesame oil."[1]

To facilitate taxation, the state rapidly established a system of weights and measures and imposed it on everyone. Thus a first step had been taken toward a system of equivalence. In the Annals of Sin-Kasid, it is symptomatic that the weight of reference was not a basket of barley but a shekel of silver, that is, a certain quantity of precious metal. In fact, the preponderant role that fell to precious metals, gold and silver in particular, appears at the same period in the accounts of the Assyrian merchants who had settled in Cappadocia. But the system remained inconvenient in that the metals used as means of exchange could take any form at all: jewelry, ingots, bars, even axes ànd sickles in Mesopotamia, cauldrons, spindles, skewers, or any other metallic object among the Greeks. This meant that the metal had to be weighed and trimmed until the exact weight was obtained. Treasures discovered both in Mesopotamia and in Egypt have provided numerous examples of metal objects cut up for this purpose; in Greece itself we know of such objects up to around 600 B.C.E., and in the Persian Empire much later, after the invention of money, and after the point when the Great King himself, the king of Persia, had acquired the habit of striking coins for his own use.

A system of weights on the one hand, an emphasis on precious metals on the other: the first elements that led to the invention of money were now in place. Certain scholars are not unwilling to speak, in specific cases, of protocoinage, insofar as states or temples began to stamp ingots. Doing this was not only a way of marking the metal so as to designate its owner, or even to indicate the weight for accounting purposes (so it would be easy to add up what was in the state's treasury, or the god's), but also a way to give a sort of legal value to the ingots thus stamped. The stamping authority guaranteed the accuracy of the weight but also, most importantly, the purity of the metal or alloy.

These practices show that, by trial and error and quite unsystematically, the various authorities that intervened in commercial dealings tried to find a way to facilitate exchange by guaranteeing the honesty of the transactions. Still, it was probably not until the end of the seventh century that the threshold was really crossed. For until that period, everywhere in the eastern Mediterranean and in Mesopotamia, people continued to trim metal and adjust weights until the required sums were obtained.

It is not before the middle of the seventh century, in fact, that we find what can be truly viewed as money: the little droplets stamped on one side. What differentiates these from stamped ingots or one of the other metallic objects in use at the time? It seems to me that several fundamental elements can be taken into account. We cannot speak of money unless there is regularity in the weight and in the alloy used in a given continuous series. Thus the first issues were produced in electrum, a natural blend (although not as natural as might be supposed, as we shall see later on) of gold and silver, which is found in its natural state in Asia Minor. Issues included series of coins of equal weight (but there could be several series of different weights to satisfy different needs) and struck of the same metal. This regularity was accompanied, in the second place, by a guarantee from the state or some other recognized public authority. All the small wafers in a given series marked by the kings of Lydia were reputed to have the same weight and the same value: the royal stamp served as a guarantee. From then on, in principle, no one needed to weigh a coin and adjust his payment if the coin had lost weight owing to wear. The authority of the state imposed a legal tender, at least within the zones where that authority was in force. Consequently, and this is a third piece of evidence to take into consideration, no one could refuse to accept that instrument, guaranteed by the state, in settlement of a debt. To be sure, money did not replace barter from one day to the next; barter continues to reign widely even today, even in the developed countries. But money has universal value as legal tender. It has become the absolute reference in terms of evaluating worth, and, for those who have some, it constitutes a reserve of values that can be used at any time.

The revolution was thus considerable. We shall see later on that it did not succeed as rapidly, and certainly not as universally, as might have been expected. But before briefly examining the way the invention spread, we need to take another look at the reasons that led the Lydian kings to create such an instrument. As a matter of fact, the experts are still debating whether the Lydian kings were really the first, or whether money was invented at the same time by the Lydians and by the Greek city-states of Asia Minor, neighbors and subjects of the Lydian kings. The date, too, poses a problem. The only certain fixed point has been established by the discovery of small metal discs of several types in the digs at the temple of Artemis in Ephesus (one of the seven wonders of the world) in an archaeological context that antedates 560–550 B.C.E., when the sanctuary was rebuilt by Croesus. As these discs were probably among offerings to the goddess deposited there over a period of a hundred years or so, the oldest may date from the mid-seventh century, or perhaps only from the end of that century. The archaeological evidence does not allow us to be any more precise.

Whatever the exact date may have been, the invention did not come about all at once, for there does seem to have been an evolution in the way these metal discs were produced. Initially, they were practically smooth, without marks; they nevertheless constituted series in terms of weight and size. Then we begin to see striations, and especially, on one side, at the point when the discs start to thicken, a hollowed-out mark that is difficult to identify. Next, as the discs began to take the form of wafers, true monetary symbols appeared, evoking the Lydian kings (the forequarters of lions or wild boars facing each other) or, soon, the Greek coastal city-states (a seal in Phocaea, a lion in Miletus, but every city-state used several symbolic images). There was a period of trial and error, then, before money really caught on and took over in a large part of the Greek world.

But we have to go back to the causes of this innovation, for there is no novelty without necessity. Scholars have debated these ad infinitum without reaching any real agreement. The first argument that comes to mind is that money was intended to facilitate exchange. This is certainly a possibility, but does it not confuse causes with results? For a long time, the innovation remained confined to Asia Minor alone; thus it was of limited economic interest. And the Lydian kingdom did not stand out, in terms of its commercial activity, in relation to its neighbors. When we also note that a number of city-states that were very active traders in the region were slow to adopt money—even very slow, in the case of the Phoenician city-states—we find that this "economic" vision of the origins of money has to be largely abandoned, or at least deemed quite secondary. Scholars have also invoked the needs of the state. This path appears more promising; it was the Lydian state, after all, that took the initiative in minting coins. Would this not have been a convenient way for a state to settle its debts: paying wages to soldiers and mercenaries, purchasing materials for daily life at the palace, paying for major construction projects, and so on? The king (or rather his stewards and accountants) would have found it convenient to pay everyone in the same way, with metal weighed and stamped in advance that could simply be given to creditors when the need arose. As the Lydian king acquired metal at little cost (the Pactolus River, which flowed in the vicinity of his capital, produced flakes of gold mixed with silver that could be harvested by panning), he could easily have it processed and stockpiled. This explanation cannot be completely dismissed, for it entails an undeniable simplification of the management of the royal treasury, and, once again, the crucial role of the state in the creation of money prevents us from rejecting the hypothesis out of hand.

But an observation made by numismatists leads us to complete this explanation with another. As harvested in the Pactolus, the natural blend of gold and silver—the substance known as electrum—consisted of a large amount of gold and a smaller proportion of silver, generally about 20 percent. This is the proportion found in the coins of Croesus, moreover, around the mid-sixth century. But the oldest coins, those attributed to the reign of Croesus's predecessor Alyattes, had quite different proportions: 52 to 55 percent gold, versus 43 to 46 percent silver, the balance made up of copper or other metals. This is quite different from the natural alloy, and thus the royal artisans must have melted down what they found to make a new alloy with less gold, because from time immemorial (already in Mesopotamia in the second millennium) silver had been worth at least ten times less than gold. Hence the conclusion of the great numismatist Georges Le Rider that money was manipulated by the state from the start: the king imposed a legal value on every disc of electrum produced according to its weight, but without regard for the composition of the alloy in question. Earlier, when an individual had to pay a debt of 14.3 grams of electrum, he had to give his creditor 14.3 grams of natural electrum, weighed with precision, no matter what form the metal came in (jewelry, ingots, and so on). Henceforth, the king gave his guarantee that every coin bearing his mark was to be understood to weigh 14.3 grams (this was the weight of the heaviest Lydian unit, the stater). Before putting the metal into circulation, however, he replaced part of the gold with silver, thus giving a coin made of a less costly alloy the same value as legal tender that the coin of natural electrum had had before. By this manipulation, the king pocketed the difference between the real value of the metal and that of the coinage. But at the same time, unwittingly and unintentionally, Alyattes created a fiduciary coinage whose intrinsic value was inferior to its value as legal tender. And this notion is the basis for the very idea of money: coins may wear out, the alloy may vary (a little or a lot), but coins of a given type are all deemed equivalent, with no need to weigh or calibrate them.

The return to a better alloy under Croesus had little impact, for the actual transition essentially involved shifting from minting electrum to minting gold and silver separately. This was henceforth the case in most of the city-states that adopted coinage: a little gold (or, sometimes, none at all), silver, and bronze—that is, various alloys of silver and lead or zinc. Only kings like those of Lydia, Persia, and, later, the Macedonians or the Greco-Bactrian and Greco-Indian sovereigns minted large quantities of gold. Silver was the coinage of reference, the one that was used for important transactions, while bronze had more localized uses.

The considerable innovation represented by the invention of money did not succeed the way we might imagine retrospectively. The city-states of Asia Minor quickly took it up, but it appeared in Greece proper only much later. While scholars have sometimes been tempted to push the earliest continental or insular mintings back to the first half of the sixth century, specialists now agree that there is no justification for situating the earliest series before 530–520. These series seem to have appeared more or less at the same time in Aegina (not much before 525–500), Athens (perhaps a few years earlier, but the adoption of the famous owl symbol came about at the very end of the sixth century), Euboea (Chalcis, Eretria, Carystos), and Corinth, at the same time as in Thrace and Macedonia. Very soon afterward, the innovation took hold in Sicily (Selinus, Himera, Agrigentum, and Syracuse) and in southern Italy. Thus a significant number of city-states, and not the least important ones, were minting coins around the year 500. At first glance, this seems to support the idea of a commercial use of money, but the link may not have been as strong as some have thought. In fact, the primary condition for minting coins was the possession of metal, and the city-states that engaged in long-distance trade, like the ones just cited, were better placed than others to acquire it. Unless they themselves had mines, like the small city-states of Thrace, Ainos, Maronea, and Abdera: these were in fact among the earliest to mint coins, which allowed them to export a local product (metal) at a high price.

It is striking to see that great trading city-states were slow to adopt coinage: the Phoenician city-states began to issue coins only in the second half of the fifth century, more than a century and a half after the appearance of the earliest coinages—evidence that they were not particularly struck by the commercial usefulness of the invention. Similarly, the treasure troves of Greek coins found in Egypt that had been buried in the first half of the fifth century show that the coinage was not accepted there for its nominal value but only for its weight as metal: every collection contained many coins that had been trimmed or chipped and many fragments of silver that had not been struck. In Greece itself, few city-states minted coins regularly. This was the case for Athens, which had silver mines (actually lead mines from which silver could be extracted) on its own soil, southwest of the city (the Laurion mines). But certain city-states undertook to mint coins only sporadically, content to use the coins of other city-states as such, or else they minted bronze coins to meet local needs. When Athens decided, shortly after the middle of the fifth century, to impose the use of its coins on all of its allies in the Delian League (Chapter 12), most of the latter had not in fact issued any coins for a long time. And a handful of city-states did no minting at all before the Hellenistic period. Sparta rejected this innovation—on moral grounds, it claimed later, for money created inequalities between citizens. Thus until the beginning of the third century the Spartans used *obeloi,* inconvenient iron spindles. But we also know that huge fortunes existed in Sparta as early as the fifth century, some of which must not have been lacking in silver and gold coins—Athenian, Corinthian, and, starting with the Peloponnesian War, Persian.

Money cannot be confined to utilitarian uses. For city-states, it emblematized their freedom, their independence, and they knew how to make it an effective ideological support. By their choice of monetary symbols, they popularized their gods and their founding myths; they displayed their prosperity and their power. The simple fact of minting coins manifested to everyone's eyes that the city-state was fully free and independent, that it was subject to no one. The kings, especially from Alexander on, succeeded in adapting this practice to display their own titles, victories, and ambitions. The Roman emperors were no different, when they disseminated their portraits and the images that best manifested their power. Whatever the practical utility of coinage may have been, the political dimension of its production must never be overlooked, for it is first and foremost a symbol of power on the part of whoever is issuing it. And who can say that our modern states do not remain broadly indebted to this legacy?

CHAPTER FOUR

Graffiti on Ramses II's Leg, or Greek Mercenaries and Merchants in Pharaonic Egypt

When King Psammetichos came to Elephantine, those who were sailing with Psammetichos son of Theocles wrote this: they came upstream from Kerkis as far as the river allowed; and Potasimto commanded those who spoke a foreign language, and Amasis [commanded] the Egyptians; [this has been] engraved by Archon son of Amoibichos and Pelekos, son of Eudamos.

André Bernand and Olivier Masson, "Les inscriptions grecques d'Abou-Simbel," *Revue des études grecques* 70 (1957): 3–10, no. 1

ABU SIMBEL (EGYPT), 591 B.C.E. The tourists who hurry along by the hundreds or thousands along the shores of Lake Nasser contemplate from the appropriate distance the gigantic statues that decorate the façade of the temple built by Ramses II before they enter the magnificent painted rooms that justify their trip. Those who take the time to approach the statues and look closely at the details will not be surprised to find, as on all historical monuments, a host of graffiti left there by visitors over several centuries. But here the tradition is ancient. Anyone looking closely at the first colossus to the left of the entrance will see several archaic Greek inscriptions engraved in the soft stone, on the left leg of Ramses II. What do they say?

The graffito retained for consideration here takes up five lines, and has to do with an episode in Egyptian history that is well known from other sources. King Psammetichos II, pharaoh of the twenty-sixth dynasty (known as the Saite dynasty because it originated in the city of Sais in the Delta), reigned from 594 to 588 B.C.E. Herodotus, the Greek historian most interested in Egyptian history, knew him as Psammis, and reports that he led an expedition to Ethiopia (*Histories* II, 161)—referring to what we know as Sudan today rather than to Ethiopia proper. Egyptian sources mention this expedition, which might have reached the Fourth or even the Fifth Cataract (a little below Khartoum) by 591 B.C.E.: the site of Kerkis, mentioned here, marks the extreme limit of the expedition, but it is not formally identified. The king himself stopped at Elephantine, at the level of the First Cataract, at Aswan. The troops continued along the Nile Valley and, before reaching the Second Cataract, stopped at the rocky temple that Ramses II had had built at Abu Simbel at the beginning of the thirteenth century, nearly seven centuries earlier.

The troop sailed up the river as far as possible, up to Kerkis. Their leader was a certain Psammetichos, homonym of the pharaoh, but he must have been a second-generation Greek, for his patronymic, Theocles, vouches for his foreign origin. He must have been the descendant of a family long in the service of the Saite dynasty and was presumably the namesake of one of the two Saite pharaohs called Psammetichos. In any case, he knew the river and its dangers well, for he was undoubtedly the pilot of the fleet. The little troop included two very different elements: Egyptians, led by the Egyptian Amasis, and mercenaries of foreign origin, especially Greek, led by another Egyptian, Potasimto. Two Greek members of the expedition, Archon and Pelekos, decided to engrave this text, signing their names at the end. But they were not the only ones tempted by the soft stone of Ramses' leg. Other, shorter graffiti can be read on the same leg and another on the knee of the second colossus, at the far left of the façade. They clearly belong to the same period and the same group: one bears the name of Python, son of Amoibichos, unquestionably Archon's brother. They supply precious information, for several include an *ethnikos*.

36

Thus Telephos of Ialysos (one of the three cities of Rhodes) left his name, along with Helesibios of Teos, Pabis of Colophon, and Anaxagoras of Ialysos. They all clearly came from Asia Minor. Some did not indicate their origin: Archon and Python, but also Pelekos and a certain Krithis. Was this because they had been settled in Egypt for several generations and had lost all ties to their city-state of origin? This is one possible hypothesis. In any case, the desire to leave a trace of one's passage on "historic" monuments was not unique to the soldiers serving under Psammetichos II. Other Greeks similarly engraved their names on the Memnonion of Abydos, in Upper Egypt; these were clearly Greeks living in Egypt, because one of them said he was from Daphne, the other from Memphis, both Egyptian cities.

These Greeks in the service of the Egyptian pharaohs at the beginning of the sixth century were in the company of other mercenaries of diverse origins: Carians, Syrians, and also Jews—a Jewish garrison has been found at Syene (Aswan). According to Herodotus (II, 154), Psammetichos I (663–609) had already given lands to his Carian and Ionian mercenaries to thank them for their help, in the Delta, on the Pelusiakos—the easternmost—branch of the Nile. These are the first Greeks we can identify in the Nile Valley, where many others were to follow. According to Herodotus, the pharaoh Apries, successor to Psammetichos II, employed thirty thousand Greek mercenaries in his army when he was beaten by the usurper Amasis in 569. Did Egypt hold a particular fascination for them, or was it simply chance that made them mercenaries? We shall probably never know, but it must be noted that colonization was not the only outlet for landless men; one could also seek one's fortune as a mercenary in the service of some king, in Lydia, in Egypt, and before long in Persia. For, in the fourth century, a number of Greeks voluntarily put themselves in the service of the Great King, helping him in particular in his attempts to reconquer Egypt.

The social aspect is not what I want to consider here, however; instead, I want to examine the relations between the Greeks and Egypt before Alexander's conquest. But we need not go back to the dawn of time, that is, to the second millennium, when the Egyptians established the first contacts with Greeks from Cyprus or Crete; I propose to consider the relations that prevailed in the archaic period and during the classical era. To begin with, let us recall the proximity between the Aegean world and

Egypt. All indications converge: it took only five days to go from Crete to Egypt, barely four from Rhodes to the entrance of the Delta, in good weather.

Egypt occupies a not inconsequential place in Greek mythology. For example, one of the most popular Greek legends, the story of Io, daughter of the first king of Argos, takes place partly in Egypt. Seduced by Zeus, who had used a golden veil to try to hide his unfaithfulness from Hera, Io was abruptly turned into a heifer by her lover when Hera passed through the intriguing veil. It did not take Hera long to grasp what was hidden behind what appeared to be a lovely heifer; she thus sent a furious horsefly that endlessly pursued poor Io, on a frenzied course leading to Egypt. There, from her union with Zeus, was born Epaphos, who himself engendered Libya; she gave birth to Belos, father of two sons, Danaos and Aegyptus; the first fathered fifty daughters (the Danaids), the second fathered fifty sons (the Egyptiads), and the latter wed the former. But we know that the wives killed their husbands on their wedding night, with one exception. These Danaids were thus condemned to fill a bottomless barrel for all eternity. Other episodes also took place in the Nile Valley. Is this sufficient to indicate that all Greek civilization was borrowed from Egypt (and beyond that, from black Africa), as Martin Bernal argued in the late 1980s?[1] Clearly not, and the correspondences that can be established among various Egyptian and Greek divinities stem more from theological reflection than from historical affiliation. Neith of Sais may well have had features in common with Athena of Athens, but this does not make Athena a Greek double of Neith, nor does it require us to believe that the Greeks went to find their goddess in Egypt.

But without adopting Bernal's fanciful musings, we have to recognize that Egypt did exercise a sort of fascination over the Greeks of antiquity. Herodotus, who devoted all of Book II and the beginning of Book III of his *Histories* to the history and description of Egypt, contributed powerfully to this infatuation, but he himself may already have been simply reflecting an Egyptophilia, if not an Egyptomania, that can be discerned in Greece. The Greeks acknowledged a number of borrowings from the Egyptians, and Herodotus tells some surprising stories. He asserts, for instance, that the Eleans—organizers of the Olympic games—sent an embassy to Egypt during the reign of Psammetichos II to present the rules applied during the competitions, on the assumption that "even the Egyptians, albeit the wisest of men, could not better" the invention; however, the wisest of the Egyptians, summoned by the king, pointed out that the right granted the Eleans to participate in competitions organized on their home ground broke the rules of equity, for the organizers would necessarily tend to favor their fellow citizens.[2]

There were contacts between the Greeks and Egypt very early. I chose as the point of departure for this chapter the presence of Greek mercenaries in the armies of the Saite pharaohs, and I pointed out that Psammetichos I had them settle in the Delta, not far from the sea, in a place the Greeks called Stratopeda, "the Camps": they were charged with training young Egyptians and teaching them Greek. Herodotus even specified that this was the origin of the interpreters who were still at work during his time in Egypt. Another pharaoh, Amasis (569–525), the last in the Saite dynasty, made the mercenaries leave these "camps" and move to his capital, Memphis, where he made them his bodyguards, which attests to the high regard in which he held them. But during the same period, other Greeks had come to trade in Egypt. Ceramics have been found that attest to their presence in the Delta starting in the late seventh century. For the most part, these were Greeks from Asia Minor, and Herodotus points out that many of those who came to do business without settling down obtained from Amasis the right to build sanctuaries. Among these, he identifies a common sanctuary, Hellenion, that served nine city-states from Ionia (Chios, Teos, Phocaea, and Clazomenae), Doris (Rhodes, Cnidos, Halicarnassos, and Phaselis), and Aeolis (Mytilene), but there were also private sanctuaries for the Samians and the Milesians. Among the Greeks from Greece proper, only the Aeginetans are mentioned. All benefited from official institutions managed by magistrates appointed collectively by the city-states.

In addition, according to Herodotus, Amasis granted Greeks living in Egypt—whom he clearly distinguished from Greeks passing through—the city of Naucratis for their residence. This city located on the westernmost branch of the Nile (the Canopic branch) unquestionably harbored Greeks well before Amasis's time, as archaeological discoveries show, but the Greeks who lived there blended in with the indigenous population and had no special rights. Amasis granted them full ownership of part of the city (probably the northern part, according to archaeological evidence), and the Greek community could organize as it chose; but contrary to what had long been supposed, Naucratis did not then constitute a Greek city-state, a *polis,* in the full sense of the word, because the king could intervene, especially in the realm of taxation. The city did not obtain the status of polis until some time during the fourth century, perhaps shortly before Alexander's conquest. Moreover, at the same time Naucratis became the only authorized port of entry to Egypt: ships that were caught by surprise elsewhere had to prove that they had been driven by opposing winds and had thus been obliged to make long detours to reach Naucratis. Digs have revealed great quantities of Greek ceramics at Naucratis, coming in particular from workshops in Asia Minor, and chiefly from Rhodes, but we know that the city was frequented by Greeks from farther away, such as Syracusans. This concentration of Greco-Egyptian trade in the single port of Naucratis obviously made the city very important; it facilitated trade for the Greeks, while at the same time it must have allowed the pharaoh better control of the tax revenues he expected it to produce. This rule was abolished after 525, when the Persians took over Egypt, and the Greeks could then trade freely throughout the country. But Naucratis did not lose its importance, for the Greek community there remained strong, up to Alexander's conquest and beyond; Alexander in fact named one of these Greek traders, Cleomenes of Naucratis, to serve as governor of Egypt. After the foundation of Alexandria and Ptolemais, Naucratis was one of the three Greek city-states in Egypt.

While the Greeks undoubtedly found the pharaoh's protection to their advantage, the pharaoh himself benefited from it just as much, for supplying Egyptian products to Greeks of the Aegean region and elsewhere was not the only goal of the Egyptian Greek traders; the pharaoh and other wealthy Egyptians consumed the Greek products that the Naucratites procured. Consecrations made by several pharaohs in major Greek sanctuaries show that they valued their friendship and alliances with the Greeks: Nechao II (611–595) consecrated the tunic that he had worn when he defeated the Syrians in Gaza to the Apollo of Didymae, on the territory of Miletus (Herodotus, II, 159); Amasis contributed a thousand talents of alum—a double sulfate widely used to make dyes—toward the reconstruction of the temple of Apollo at Delphi after the fire of 548, and he made sumptuous gifts to the Athena of Cyrene, to the Athena of Lindos in Rhodes, and to the Hera of Samos.

After the conquest of Egypt by the Achaemenid Persian king Cambyses in 525, the Greek presence did not falter, and the Greeks who had been established there for several generations remained in the country without being subjected to the limitations that Amasis had imposed on their trade. After Cyrus's conquest of Asia Minor in 546, the city-states that administered the Hellenion in Naucratis were themselves under Achaemenid domination. But political ties were restored between certain Greek city-states not subject to the Persians and those who, in Egypt, were trying to drive the Persians out.

In fact, starting in 486, a revolt—about which we know nothing—broke out in Egypt just as Darius was preparing to launch an expedition against the Greeks to avenge the Persian defeat at Marathon. Death overtook him at that point, and Xerxes, his successor, seems to have taken measures of revenge against Egyptian temples, evidence of troubles whose full extent we do not know. In contrast, the revolt of Inaros—an Egyptian—in 464 was a serious threat to the Persian presence, at least in the Delta. Inaros turned at once to Athens, which responded enthusiastically to his requests. An Athenian fleet that had been operating in Cyprus headed immediately toward Egypt. A combined sea and land campaign took place in 460–459 (a list of the Athenians who died in the war that year, notably in Phoenicia, has been preserved); it went on for six years, until the Persians counterattacked and the Athenians suffered a military disaster at the entrance to the Mendesian mouth of the Nile. But the matter did not stop there, despite Inaros's execution by the Persians, for on the one hand another Egyptian rebel whom the Greeks called Amyrtaeus, known as Prince of the Swamps, held the north of the Delta, around Lake Burulus, and in 445–444 a certain Psammetichos, who must have held part of the Delta, sent a large cargo of wheat to Athens. Similar shipments took place again in 412, and also to Athens, which proves that autonomous powers remained active in Egypt and that there were close links between these rebels and Athens. It is true that they had a common enemy, the Persians. Even if these indigenous dynasties represented an older tradition of local autonomy in the Delta rather than a "nationalist" tendency that had never existed, it is interesting to see Atheno-Egyptian solidarity hold up in the face of Persian power during a good part of the fifth century.

When the Egyptian revolt extended into the fourth century—the pharaoh Amyrtaeus was recognized in Elephantine in 400 at the latest; Nepherites founded the twenty-ninth dynasty in 398, and when he died, in 393, Hakoris succeeded him (393–380)—the Greeks were again present, not only Athenians but also Spartans and Greeks from Cyprus. The details are not important here, but we should note that at the time of Alexander's conquest the Greeks and the Egyptians already had a long-standing habit of collaborating against the Persians. It had been less than ten years since the energetic Persian reconquest, led by Artaxerses III in 343–334, when Alexander showed up on the threshold of the country.

Many Greeks thus had direct knowledge of Egypt. And yet few described it before the Hellenistic or Roman eras. A number of details turn up here and there, but between Herodotus around 425 and Strabo around 25–20 B.C.E. no one provided a detailed description to match the accounts of those firsthand observers. Let us set Strabo aside and look more closely at Herodotus, who witnessed the crises that shook Egypt in the second half of the fifth century, and who gathered a good deal of information personally in Egypt. Despite some errors and nontrivial oversights, he gave the first sustained history of Egypt after the end of the third millennium, with abundant details on the Saite period (664–525) and the Persian conquest. Not that he is always reliable, for he got his information from Egyptian priests, some of whom spoke Greek, and the latter were sometimes extremely biased regarding the Persian occupier. Thus Herodotus reports that Cambyses wounded the sacred steer, Apis, and had his priests executed upon his return from Memphis after a disastrous expedition into Libya. But the archaeological documents do not confirm this information in any respect; on the contrary, when an Apis died during his stay in Egypt, Cambyses had him embalmed according to all the rules, and he assumed the role that had fallen to the pharaoh in these ceremonies, as the inscriptions from the Memphis Serapeum attest.

Thus we must be cautious, and not take Herodotus to be a totally trustworthy informant. Still, what counts here is not what he actually tells us about Egypt but the picture he paints of the country, one that prevailed for centuries among the Greeks and the Romans. This picture is made up of contradictory features. On the one hand, Herodotus, like many others after him, is full of admiration for the wisdom of the Egyptian priests, especially those of Heliopolis, who seem to have given him a lot of information, true or false. Similarly, he lauds the Egyptian climate and the fertility of the soil; he has understood the primordial role of the flooding of the

Nile, whose fertilizing silt deposits increase the extent of the land itself each year; this leads him to assert that Egypt is land "given . . . by the river."[3] Finally, he praises the country's administration, being familiar with the broad outlines of the governance system.

But at the same time he is astonished at the Egyptians' behavior: compared to other peoples, as he sees it, they do everything backward. Is this not already the case with the Nile itself? Herodotus has tried to understand the phenomenon of flooding and proposes a highly original explanation. He is astonished that the river swells during the summer (the flood reaches its height at Aswan in June and in the Delta in September), precisely at the moment when the water level in all the other rivers is going down, if they are not completely dry. Because the farther south one goes the hotter it gets, Herodotus thinks, this flooding cannot result from rains or melting snow. He then imagines an ingenious system: the flooding must result from the summer winds that blow from the north during the season of fine weather, and these must create a barrier to the natural flow of the river! Ingenious, but absurd, for Herodotus ought to have noticed that the flooding began not in the Delta but rather in Upper Egypt.

But it was not just the river that behaved strangely. "[The Egyptians have] made all their customs and laws of a kind contrary for the most part to those of all other men."[4] And he lists several that he finds shocking: the women urinate standing up, the men crouched down; people relieve themselves in their houses and eat in the streets; men practice circumcision. Other things are also astonishing: women can never be priestesses, not even of a goddess; men are priests of feminine divinities! People show mourning by letting their hair grow, whereas everywhere else people shave their heads. The list goes on: weaving is done from top to bottom and not from bottom to top; women go to the marketplace and do business while the men take care of the house and do the weaving; finally, writing is done from right to left and not left to right.

Religion fascinates Herodotus, and he views the Egyptians as the most religious of people. He describes in minute detail the purification rites of the priests, the sacrifices, the feasts, the sacred animals (cat, crocodile, hippopotamus, phoenix, snake, ibis), knows the local differences among the cults, and tries to establish equivalences between the Greek and Egyptian gods. But he ends up concluding that "wellnigh all the names of the gods came to Hellas from Egypt," and by "names" he really means the divine personalities.[5] Even the most famous of the Greek oracles owe something to Egypt, in his view: thus the oracle of Zeus at Dodona in Epiros is a twin of the oracle of Ammon in the Siwa oasis in Libya, both created by two consecrated women kidnapped from Thebes in Egypt. Herodotus completes his anthropological tableau with a study of mores, banquets, and funerary rites.

Herodotus's influence was considerable, and for a long time his description constituted the sum of Greek knowledge about Egypt. Even after Greeks had settled in Egypt, Herodotus's opinion prevailed on most points, especially where Egyptian history and religion were concerned. We cannot say that there was an "Egyptomania" like the one that ran through Europe after Bonaparte's expedition, and we find hardly any Egyptian or Egyptian-like objects in the houses or tombs of the Greek world. But Herodotus imposed the idea of Egypt's strangeness, which spurred the curiosity of many (a number of Roman emperors made the trip). That had its negative side: the supposed weirdness of Egypt nourished a whole tradition of hostility that could almost be described as "racist" if the term were not an anachronism. This anti-Egyptian sentiment is very clearly expressed by certain Roman authors, such as Juvenal, but it is present as well in the Greek authors, who consider the Egyptians particularly barbarous because they behave in the opposite way not only from the Greeks but from most other peoples as well. The environmentalist theory that emerged from the Hippocratic treatise *On Airs, Waters, and Places*—a theory so named by the moderns because it attached specific traits to people as a function of their geographical localization, or more precisely their climate—was particularly justified in Egypt's case, it seemed, because the Egyptians lived at one of the ends of the earth, far from the ideal center constituted by the Greek Aegean basin. Their peripheral position and their extreme climate sufficed to explain why they did everything backward compared to the Greeks and virtually everyone else. Just as the Nile's behavior, as it were, was the opposite of that of other rivers, geography explained why Egyptian mores were at the opposite pole from those of civilized people.

CHAPTER FIVE

Phalaris's Bull, or One Aspect
of the Crisis: Tyranny

But universal execration overwhelms Phalaris, that man of piti-
less spirit who burned men in his bronze bull.

> Pindar, *Pythian Odes*, in *Pindar*, trans. William H. Race (Loeb
> Classical Library, 1997), vol. 1, p. 225 (I, 95–96)

Peoples, in general, without trying to find out what sort of man
the head of state is, whether just or unjust, simply hate the very
name of tyranny, and even if the tyrant is an Aeacus, a Minos,
or a Rhadamanthus, they make every effort to put him out of
the way just the same, for they fix their eyes on the bad tyrants
and include the good ones in equal hatred by reason of the common title. Yet I hear that among you Greeks there have been
many wise tyrants who, under a name of ill repute have shown
a good and kindly character.

> Lucian, "Phalaris I," in *Lucian*, vol. 1, trans. A. M. Harmon
> (Loeb Classical Library, 1927), pp. 11–13 (I, 7)

AGRIGENTUM (SICILY), sixth century B.C.E. The city-state, founded
around 600 as a colony by its neighbor Gela, experienced the tyranny of a certain Phalaris. According to Aristotle (*Politics*,
1310b), Phalaris headed an important magistracy in his city-state before
he confiscated power to his own benefit. This indication is indirectly confirmed by the speech that Lucian of Samosata (second century C.E.) attributes to the tyrant: in this purely rhetorical address to the inhabitants
of Delphi, who have criticized his offering of a bronze bull to their god

45

Apollo as in bad taste, Phalaris declares that he was not born in modest circumstances, but comes from a prominent family in Agrigentum. In reality, we know almost nothing about him beyond the episode that serves as a pretext for Lucian's fictional discourse: Phalaris was said to have put his enemies inside a hollow bronze bull with a fire blazing underneath. The anecdote may have been embellished over time, but there is a long tradition behind it; Pindar had already mentioned it in the first half of the fifth century, and Pindar himself had spent some time in Agrigentum, at the invitation of the tyrant Thero, who seems to have ruled there around 488–472. In any case, Phalaris's bull, real or not, rapidly became the very symbol of the arbitrariness and cruelty of tyranny, a regime that Aristotle deemed the most harmful of all, for it combined the worst defects of the most extreme forms of oligarchy and democracy.

Phalaris's horrifying behavior was not an isolated instance. Opponents were murdered, their wives and daughters forced to marry slaves or mercenaries, their goods confiscated—Greek tyrants often directed violence of this sort against potential adversaries. Still, other images come to mind: Peisistratus, tyrant of Athens, reorganized the Great Pan-Athenian contests, the greatest festivals in honor of Athena, and had the text of Homer set down in writing; Gelo of Gela and his brother Hiero attracted artists and poets (Pindar, among others) to their court, as Dio of Syracuse later attracted Plato; Clearchos of Heraclea Pontica created the first library. The ancients knew all there was to know about the horrors perpetrated by certain tyrants, but they were also aware of other tyrannies with more positive aspects, and a saying in vogue in Athens accurately conveyed a popular sentiment: according to Aristotle, people said in effect that "the tyranny of Peisistratus was the Golden Age of Cronos," a way of referring to "the good old days."[1] The fact that the tyrants Pittacos of Mytilene and Periander of Corinth were included among the Seven Sages of Greece points in the same direction.

It is true that tyranny took on a negative image early, especially in Athens. After the Athenian tyrants were overthrown in 510 (Chapter 7), all members of the council were made to swear an oath that they would never help reestablish tyranny. A little later, the first ostracism decisions (Chapter 9) targeted men suspected, rightly or wrongly, of favoring tyrants. But the image created after the fact does not help us understand the deep reasons for a phenomenon that affected the entire Greek world over a long period of time. For there were tyrants in the Greek city-states as early as the seventh century, and there were still tyrannies in the late first century C.E. when the Pax Romana was instituted. But we should doubtless not confuse epochs, and we should not attempt to apply the same analysis to the archaic tyrannies of Cypselos of Corinth, Polycrates of Samos, or Phalaris of Agrigentum as to the tyrannies of Nabis of Sparta early in the second century B.C.E. (Chapter 21), or Nicias of Cos and Boethos of Tarsus in the era of Mark Antony and Augustus. We shall focus only on the first form here, in that it appears to have been a widespread phenomenon that could touch virtually any *polis* and that undoubtedly betrayed moments of profound crisis in the city-states.

The phenomenon was indeed a general one, and very few regions of the Greek world escaped it. An overall inventory would be tedious, but we can consider a few names and regions that were particularly affected. The city-states of Asia Minor were the first, with tyrants such as Thrasybulos of Miletus, Pittacos of Mytilene, Polycrates of Samos, and Lygdamis of Naxos, before the flowering of the tyrannies set up by the Persians in the late sixth century. Greece proper also saw tyranny flourish, especially in the Peloponnesus and the Isthmus of Corinth, with men such as Phido of Argos, Cypselos and Periander of Corinth, Theagenes of Megara, the dynasty of the Orthagorids of Sicyon (one of whom, Cleisthenes, was the grandfather of Cleisthenes of Athens; Chapter 7), and, of course, Peisistratus and his sons in Athens. A third great geographic pole where tyranny developed lay in Sicily and Magna Graecia, with men such as Panaetius of Leontinoi, Phalaris and Thero of Agrigentum, Gelo and Hiero in Gela and Syracuse, later Dionysius of Syracuse, whereas Aristodemos reigned as tyrant over Cumae in Campania, Anaxilas over Rhegium, and others over Sybaris. Although the phenomenon was especially pronounced in the archaic period, it persisted throughout the entire classical era, for the Sicilian tyrants prospered in the fifth and fourth centuries, and tyranny reappeared in the fourth century in Asia Minor (Hermias of Atarneus, Clearchos of Heraclea Pontica) and in Greece proper (Euphron of Sicyon, Jason of Pherae).

Despite significant variations in the circumstances in which they appeared, tyrannies had several common features that struck the ancient authors: the way tyrants took power, their attitude toward aristocratic families, their adoption of policies favorable to ordinary people, and their personal behavior—features that created something like an ideal image of a tyrant.

First, taking power: this was done everywhere more by ruse than by violence. Tyrants tended to profit from a moment when the citizen-soldiers were unarmed (during a religious festival, for example) to impose themselves. But there were variations: Peisistratus claimed to have been the victim of an attack by his political adversaries while he was heading peacefully toward his fields, in order to get the people to award him personal bodyguards, his "cudgel-bearers." In a number of cases, the tyrant (or aspiring tyrant) held power either legally (like Peisistratus) or because he put together his own mercenary force (Periander's "lance bearers" in Corinth or Thrasybulos's mercenaries in Syracuse).

Tyrants needed armed forces in order to fend off those who seem to have been their designated adversaries: the aristocrats in power. Virtually everywhere, tyrants appear to have been staunch opponents of the men in power, even if they themselves had been part of this governing milieu (as Peisistratus had). They often took concrete measures to eliminate these opponents: they had the aristocrats murdered or exiled, compelled the aristocrats' wives and daughters to marry slaves or the tyrants' own mercenaries (who might be former slaves themselves), and confiscated their goods. Sometimes they took steps to humiliate their former masters. Herodotus recounts in detail, for example, the measures taken by Cleisthenes of Sicyon. In particular, Cleisthenes is said to have changed the names of the four traditional civic tribes so as to give them degrading labels: "[To the members of his own tribe] he gave a name signifying his own lordship, and calling its folk People-rulers; the rest were Swinites and Assites and Porkites."[2] Herodotus saw this as part of a systematic anti-Argive policy, but its meaning is not very clear, except that it was intended to humiliate the tribes to which Cleisthenes' political adversaries—members of major aristocratic families—belonged. But this attitude was not widespread, and it is not certain that the practice of humiliation was as systematic as the ancient sources seem to indicate. In Athens, about which we have a little more information than for other city-states, we see clearly that Peisistratus was at the head of one of three aristocratic factions competing for power. Although he initially won out over the other two factions, after he had been driven out of power the first time he returned by making an alliance with one of the other factions, the one led by Megacles the Alcmaeonid.

And in fact, despite later propaganda proclaiming that Alcmaeonid resistance to tyrants was unbroken, we have proof that Megacles' son Cleisthenes served as archon under Peisistratus, which could not have come about without political collusion between the two groups.

The very nature of tyrannical power lies in the fact that, without abolishing the laws, the tyrant places himself above them. This is easy to see in Athens, where magistrates continued to be elected according to the rules, but the only powers at their disposal were the ones Peisistratus granted them. The ancient authors agreed that Peisistratus governed wisely and showed a great respect for the laws, at least during his first tyranny. He probably managed to gain power owing to the great military prestige he enjoyed after a war against Megara that Athens had won brilliantly. He was driven from power after six years, but, Herodotus's testimony notwithstanding, it is not certain that he really went into exile; he may have simply withdrawn to his own lands. This seems to prove that he was not deemed dangerous for the city-state. His return eleven years later ended in a new failure after six more years. The tyrannical regime was thus tempered in this case by the possibility of driving out the tyrant: the struggles among factions remained sufficiently intense to provide a counterweight to the tyrant's power. It was only after his second exile that Peisistratus undertook to disarm the population and ensured his power by force.

In almost all the reasonably well-documented examples, we observe that the tyrant was actually popular, at least early on. Aristotle even established a list of the tyrants who held their power from "demagogy," that is, from the people. Even when such a tyrant came from the local aristocracy, he appeared as the defender of the powerless against those who exploited them, and he advocated a certain degree of equality. Thus Lygdamis of Naxos established his power by struggling against the oligarchy (the "fat ones"); after being driven out by them, perhaps following an attempted coup d'état, he returned and was made tyrant. Panaetius of Leontinoi, in Sicily, is said to have persuaded the people to rise up against the aristocrats. Pittacos of Mytilene, rewarded by his fellow citizens by being granted a piece of land, is said to have distributed it in equal parts to all, on the grounds that "the equal is better than the more." Cypselos of Corinth, before becoming a tyrant, had won the gratitude of ordinary people by acting humanely during his service as *polemarch* (commander). That function gave him control over the city-state's prison, but he had refused to lock up anyone who was a citizen, had refused to accept his share of the proceeds from fines, and had not hesitated to pay the poorest people's fees himself.

Did this favorable attitude toward ordinary people lead to sharing land with dispossessed peasants? There is no evidence that all tyrants of the archaic period proceeded in that way; when Cypselos seized the property of his adversaries, members of the aristocratic Bacchiad family, he donated it to the city-state, but we do not know whether the land was redistributed. In another domain, Peisistratus tried to make the life of ordinary people easier by appointing village judges; his adversaries represented this as a measure intended to keep citizens from coming to the city, but the action may well have been received favorably by the beneficiaries. However, the *demos* did not always support tyrants. Thus Gelo, tyrant of Gela, seized the tyranny in Syracuse in the 480s, responding to the appeal of the oligarchs against the demos. When he took control of Megara Hyblaea a little later, he made the wealthy people citizens of Syracuse, while he sold the poor as slaves.

The idea of a "popular" tyrant no doubt belonged largely to the antidemocratic ideology of the fourth century more than to the realities of the archaic period. For no tyrant was ever seen carrying out political reforms that led to increased participation by the people in the affairs of the city-state. On the contrary, tyrants took care to distance the people from participation (this may have been the purpose behind Peisistratus's creation of judges in the demes), and the various anecdotes relating to the struggle against idleness betray the tyrants' interest in keeping the people fully occupied with their own personal affairs, to the exclusion of those of the city-state.

A whole tradition credits certain tyrants with cultural and religious preoccupations that must have had considerable political impact. Thus when Cleisthenes of Sicyon eliminated the hero Adrastes from the city-state (Adrastes was an Argive hero judged intolerable because of his presumed links with Sicyon's landed aristocracy), he replaced him with a Theban hero, Melanippos (Adrastes' worst enemy, in Greek mythology), and more importantly with Dionysus, the god of wine and vineyards whose festivals were extremely popular in modest milieus. This exaltation of Dionysus showed that the tyrant was aligning himself with ordinary people against the local aristocracy. Dionysus was celebrated in the same way in Athens by Peisistratus, who created several festivals in his honor. In addition, Peisistratus and his sons implemented far-reaching policies in the religious realm in particular: the first is credited not only with having Homer's texts written down in fixed form and with reorganizing the Pan-Athenian contests, adding lavish touches, but also with refurbishing the monumental entry to the Acropolis through which the procession arrived for the contests; his sons are credited with embellishing the great temple of Athena on the Acropolis (or one of the temples, for we do not know whether there were one or two) by replacing the pediments made of local limestone with others made of marble. This was also the period during which painted ceramics reached their apogee in Attica, first black figures, around 520, then red ones. These ceramics gradually displaced almost all others in Mediterranean markets (we have evidence of this in Marseille as well as in Etruria). Athens under the tyrants thus stands out as an intellectual and artistic haven of the first order. The same thing is true of Hiero's court in Syracuse, where Pindar, Aeschylus, and Simonides all spent some time. The tradition continued in the fourth century, with Plato's voyage to Dio's court in Syracuse. The presence of highly reputed artists alongside a tyrant is evidence that the latter was concerned with his image even beyond his own city-state: the arts contributed to a ruler's prestige and thus to his power. Little by little, we see a quasi-royal behavior emerge, announcing certain aspects of the Hellenistic monarchies. Thus the tyrant Clearchos of Heraclea Pontica is credited with being the first to create a library, an institution that could be found half a century later in all kingdoms of any importance: in Alexandria, but also in Antioch and Pergamon.

The appearance of tyrannies in the course of the seventh century and their development throughout the sixth century undoubtedly reflect a political crisis within the city-states. But what exactly was in crisis, and for what underlying reasons? Moreover, must we seek a common explanation for such diverse phenomena spread over more than a century?

As we have seen, the tyrannies appeared most often in city-states that included an urban core of a certain importance, such as Miletus, Samos, Corinth, Megara, Argos, Athens, Syracuse, city-states that were generally centers for an above-average amount of artisanal and commercial activity. The pastoral and agricultural regions located away from the major exchange routes (Arcadia, Phocis, Doris, Elis, Crete) did not experience tyranny in the archaic period, or if they did it was only episodically (there is a reference to an Elean tyrant who did not last very long). Establishing a link between tyranny and socioeconomic upheavals from here is a step that has often been taken. Thus Cypselos of Corinth has been called the representative of the new classes: nouveau-riche families unhappy with the decline of trade in Corinth under the Bacchiad dynasty. But this is probably putting the problem in anachronistic terms; the case of every city-state was unique. It is no doubt true that Miletus, Samos, Corinth, Athens, and Syracuse underwent important transformations on the social level owing to accelerated economic development, but the situation in Naxos, Megara, and Sicyon is less clear. The texts we have offer glimpses of open hostility between aristocratic clans, and perhaps between families enriched more recently whose fortunes did not rest primarily in land. But we must be skeptical of the ancient sources: they all date from much later than the tyrannies they describe, and they are often hostile. The information they provide is contradictory on some essential points. For example, the Orthagorids of Sicyon are generally presented as people of modest origins (their ancestor Andreas was said to be a cook or a sacrificer), but the texts do not hesitate to show us the highest-placed aristocrats of the Greek world seeking the hand of Agariste, the daughter of Andreas's descendant Cleisthenes! Even if the family had become wealthy and acquired a degree of honorability over time (Cleisthenes was Andreas's great-grandson), the throng of aristocratic pretenders for Agariste's hand contradicts the accusations that Cleisthenes was politically hostile to the Sicyonian aristocracy.

The city-states unquestionably underwent transformations and rapid evolutions in the sixth century, and it was probably no accident that the ones that fell prey to tyranny were among those that adopted coinage, participated or had participated in colonization (except for Athens), and carried out political activity that went beyond local or regional horizons. But on this last point it is difficult to sort out how much stemmed from the tyrant's politics of prestige and how much corresponded to the expectations of his popular supporters. Polycrates of Samos maintained a powerful fleet that allowed him to intervene against the Persians (who ended up killing him by trickery); Cleisthenes of Sicyon made himself the standard-bearer of an anti-Argive policy that must have satisfied a certain number of the Sicyonians; Cypselos and Periander founded Corinthian colonies on the Ionian coast all the way to the entrance to the Adriatic, while Hippias of Athens founded a settlement at Sigae in Troad.

It is certain that, for a time, tyranny weakened the landed aristocracy, by dispossessing it sometimes of its wealth and invariably of its political and religious power. And even after getting rid of its tyrants, a city-state could not simply return to the previous state of affairs. Tyrants destroyed the prevailing structures but did little to build new ones, because they were content to confiscate power. Nevertheless, the overall situation evolved: city-states grew wealthier and stronger, and the social equilibrium was modified. This is easy to see in Athens, where the resumption of the struggle among the aristocratic factions took place on entirely new bases. The tyranny had helped firm up civic identity by restoring the cults and giving them more prominence (as in Athens) or by driving out cults reputed to be foreign (as in Sicyon). But once these objectives had been attained, many people in the city-states must have thought that the tyrant had fulfilled his task. Yet very few followed the model of Pittacos of Mytilene (who did not bear the title of tyrant, moreover) and withdrew of their own accord. Quite to the contrary, authentic tyrannical dynasties were created almost everywhere; the longest-lasting ones were found most notably in Sicyon, Corinth, Syracuse, and Agrigentum. Yet across the board, following a founder who came across as rather gentle and benevolent, the regime hardened. We see this in Athens (with the assassination of Hipparchos), but also in Syracuse (it was only the third tyrant, Thrasybulos, who surrounded himself with mercenary bodyguards). What solution remained, then, other than assassination or a coup d'état (Chapter 7)?

CHAPTER SIX

"You Will Destroy a Great Empire!" or Oracles and Soothsayers

When the Lydians came to the places whither they were sent, they made present of the offerings, and inquired of the oracles, in these words: "Croesus, king of Lydia and other nations, seeing that he deems that here are the only true places of divination among men, endows you with such gifts as your wisdom merits. And now he would ask you, if he shall send an army against the Persians, and if he shall take to himself any allied host."[1] Such was their inquiry; and the judgement given to Croesus by each of the two was the same, to wit, that if he should send an army against the Persians he would destroy a great empire. And they counseled him to discover the mightiest of the Greeks and make them his friends.

Herodotus, trans. A. D. Godley (Loeb Classical Library, 1920), vol. 1, p. 61 (I, 53)

S ARDIS, IN LYDIA, mid-sixth century. To the west of Asia Minor, a powerful Lydian kingdom had been in place for a long time, with Sardis as its capital. Sardis exercised political and economic control over the Greek city-states in the coastal region; its oversight was not heavy-handed, but it was real. To the east, the powerful Assyrian empire fell between 612 and 609 under the assault of a new Babylonian empire. Still farther east, the Medes controlled the Iranian plateau. In the late 550s, the Medean Empire fell under the sway of a new power, the Persians. Cyrus the Great, perhaps a son of the Persian Cambyses and the Mede Mandana, daughter of King Astyages, took control of the latter's empire following a successful revolt against his grandfather, and he placed Persians at the highest levels of the administration, establishing his capitals in Pasargadae, Persepolis, and Susa. Even if we cannot follow the Greek authors' accounts of this conflict between Medes and Persians without serious reservations, all the authors insist on the continuity between the two powers and the relative ease with which Cyrus triumphed. In any case, this is not what matters in relation to our text.

Did the period of troubles and uncertainties that was beginning in the east—at least that is how Croesus saw things—strike the ruler as propitious for an expansion in an eastward direction? His closest neighbor, the Babylonian Nabonides, did not seem preoccupied by the Persians' growing power, given that he went off in 553 to settle in Arabia, in the Teima oasis. Croesus was ambitious, and rich, thanks to the gold that was panned in the Pactolus, the river that came down from the mountains near Sardis (Chapter 3). But he was also pious and prudent. He had just given evidence of his prudence: before questioning the gods about a decision that would affect the future of the kingdom, he undertook an investigation. He sent embassies to all the oracles, famous or not, and instructed them to ask each one the same question on the same day, the one hundredth after their departure from Sardis (and they all left the same day), in effect, "What is the king doing at this very moment?" Croesus had invented an unimaginable occupation: having a chopped-up tortoise and a lamb cooked together in a bronze cauldron with a lid of the same metal. When the embassies returned, it became clear that only Apollo, the god at Delphi, had been able to inspire his priestess to give the correct answer, formulated in hexameters as was the local custom:

> What is it now that I smell? 'Tis a tortoise mightily armoured,
> Sodden in vessel of bronze, with a lamb's flesh mingled together;
> Bronze thereunder is laid and a mantle of bronze is upon it.[2]

The response of the oracle of Amphiaraos at Oropos in Boeotia has not survived, but Croesus found it valid to some extent as well. Thus when he had a question to ask that concerned the future of his kingdom, he was satisfied to consult these two oracles; they both agreed and gave the same response, the one reported by Herodotus in our epigraph.

Not all the faithful turned out to be so mistrustful, but few had such serious questions to ask. In reality, each person chose an oracle according to its proximity and in relation to the trust he or she placed in the god.

Hundreds of oracular sanctuaries existed in the Greek world. Those of Apollo are the most famous: these have been found at Delphi, in the Ptoion and in Thebes (Boeotia), in Abai (Phocis), in Claros (Asia Minor) and at the sanctuary of Didymae in the territory of Miletus, in Patara (Lycia), and in Telmessos (Caria). But Apollo had no monopoly in this area, and people also consulted Zeus in Dodona (Epiros), the heroes Amphiaraos in Oropos and Trophonios in Lebadea, two city-states in Boeotia, not to mention sanctuaries that lay outside the Greek world, such as the famous oracle of Ammon in the Siwah oasis in Egypt, which the Greeks knew of long before Alexander ensured its glory. After Alexander's conquest, the possibilities multiplied, because new oracles became available for consultation by the faithful. The oracle of Bel in Apamea (Syria) received illustrious visitors such as Trajan and Septimus Severus, while that of the serpent Glykon, in Abonuteichos (Pontus), installed by a certain Alexander (not to be confused with Alexander the Great), became a popular favorite and aroused the ire of Lucian of Samosata.[3]

Not all the Greeks' uneasiness was alleviated through consulting the gods, a long and costly procedure; there were always soothsayers in the city-states as well. Peisistratus sought the advice of Amphilytos; the help of soothsayers was especially indispensable in times of battle. Every army marched behind a soothsayer, whom the commander in chief consulted before every confrontation. Herodotus never fails to point these out, and we witness veritable jousting matches between soothsayers. The predictions of Hegesistratos, an Elean accompanying the Persians on the eve of the battle of Plataea (479), were paralleled by those of his colleague in the service of the Greeks, Tisamenos, another Elean who had agreed to enter Sparta's service on condition that he would receive Spartan citizenship, something that had never been seen before and was never seen again; as for the Greeks who were allied with the Persians during this same battle, they had their own soothsayer, Hippomachos of Leucadia. Curiously, the predictions were in agreement. We know that Tisamenos emerged victorious from this war of soothsayers. But he himself had not known how to interpret the oracle at Delphi, whom he had consulted before for personal reasons (to find out if he would have children one day); the oracle had responded that Tisamenos would be victorious in five great battles. He had thought that meant he was to win at the pentathlon in Olympia, and he had trained zealously. However, he failed in one of the trials. Told about the oracle, the Spartans had insisted on procuring his services, even at the exorbitant price he had set, Spartan citizenship for himself and his brother. But they had no cause for regrets, because thanks to Tisamenos they defeated their adversaries five times in a row; Plataea was the first in the series of victories.

Every city-state thus had one or several official soothsayers who declared on a daily basis whether or not the signs were favorable for embarking on a particular project or taking a specific action. They were often foreigners in the city-states they served, and some had itinerant careers. One of Hegesistratos's family members, Tellias, advised the Phocidians. Hegesistratos himself, at first a soothsayer in Elis, was taken prisoner by the Spartans; he escaped and joined the Persian forces, then those of Zakynthos. Another Elean, Callias, entered the service of the Crotoniates around 510, after fleeing Sybaris, where he had not managed to obtain favorable omens for a war against Croton. A certain Cleander of Phigalia (Arcadia) worked in Tiryns (Argolis). It is clear that people preferred foreign soothsayers, who may have been less responsive to the divergent interests of the groups that made up the city-state.

But let us come back to the oracles. If the soothsayers acted on behalf of the city-state, individuals could turn either to interpreters of divine signs—who were more or less credible, more or less charlatanic—or else to sanctuaries of gods recognized for the quality of their oracles. In the classical period, Delphi, Dodona, and Oropos were among the most famous. People went there to consult either in a public capacity, through official embassies like those sent by Croesus, or as private individuals. The questions asked were of all sorts, varying with the origin of the consultant. Delphi received many visits from Greeks preparing to set out to found new city-states on the shores of the Mediterranean or the Black Sea. But people also consulted, as Croesus did, to find out what was just and advantageous for the city-state. The Athenians had the Pythia of Delphi select from a list of one hundred names the ten that would be given to the new tribes created by Cleisthenes. But private individuals raised more down-to-earth issues: should they marry, would they have children, was it right to conclude a particular transaction? The sanctuary of Zeus in Dodona has given us a large number of small strips of metal each bearing an engraved question, thus letting us see people's everyday preoccupations. For one did not question the god by speaking aloud; questions were asked through the intermediary of a priest, who brought back the answer. The god responded in a variety of ways: through the sound made by the leaves of an oak tree, through the prophecies of a woman (the Pythia of Delphi), through the intermediary of a priest who examined the entrails of an animal, the flight of birds, or the ripples made by the fish in a sacred basin, and sometimes directly by inspiring a dream in the faithful follower. The procedures for consultation were infinitely varied, and it would be pointless to list them all here.

In all cases, people tried to ask their questions in a manner that would leave the god no way out. For the reproach addressed most often to the gods was that their responses were unclear. When the Athenians went to consult Apollo at Delphi to find out what attitude they should adopt toward the Persian invasion in 481, there were bitter debates in Athens about the meaning of the response: the god had announced to the Athenians that their salvation would come from a wooden wall. Was this the sign that the Acropolis—which had once been surrounded by a palisade—would stand firm? Or, on the contrary, must the Athenians abandon the city and take refuge on the boats that Themistocles had had built starting in 483 in view of a war against Aegina? We have to admit that the meaning remained obscure. And the obscurity may have been intentional. The sanctuary at Delphi was frequented by Greeks from all over; as it happened, a minority of city-states chose to resist the Persians while the majority let the Persians have their way. In anticipation of the victories to come, was it not wise to give responses that left a good deal of room for interpretation—a clever way to preserve credibility for the future? But this precaution did not prevent the conquerors—Sparta, Athens, and their allies—from accusing the Pythia of having "spoken scandalously," that is, of having sided with the "Medes," who were in reality Persians.

Thus people frequently tried to trap the god by imposing a yes or no answer, or at least by presenting a clear alternative—"Will it be preferable or better to do such-and-such?"—as if to leave the god no escape route, no margin for interpretation. Curiously, however, we know very little about the ceremonial aspects of the consultation, even in a sanctuary like Delphi, for which more than six hundred consultations have been preserved in literary texts or inscriptions. This is because the procedure was so well known to the Greeks that no one bothered to leave a precise description. Everywhere, the consultants first had to introduce themselves to the priests who managed the sanctuary, so an order of passage could be established. A few privileged persons benefited from the privilege of *promanteia*—the right to go ahead of the others without waiting in line (unless they were behind other privileged persons like themselves). Depending on the sanctuary, the faithful saw or did not see the person prophesying; the ceremony might take place in dim light (Claros) or in broad daylight (Delphi). The faithful inscribed their questions on a tablet or a strip of lead (Dodona), or transmitted them orally to a priest (Delphi). For official consultations on behalf of city-states, the questions were probably always asked in writing and the answer given in the same form, so it would be clear that the ambassadors had not betrayed the popular will or made some clumsy mistake.

But the divination procedures varied from one sanctuary to another, and sometimes even within a single sanctuary. In Dodona the sound of oak leaves and the flight of doves were interpreted; in Delphi the god could express himself directly through the voice of the Pythia as well as through a drawing of lots using beans, dice, or knucklebones. Thus when the Athenians sent an embassy in 352 to find out what should be done after a sacrilege committed at Eleusis (fallow lands dedicated to the local goddesses had accidentally been put into cultivation), they did not take the risk of receiving a vague or incomprehensible answer: they had two possible responses written down (praise for cultivation or on the contrary for fallow lands) on two strictly identical strips of lead, so that the Pythia would simply have to draw one or the other! Moreover, when Apollo expressed himself through the Pythia's voice, he did so clearly, although the lovely oracular texts preserved by the literary tradition were probably subject to rewriting by the priests of the sanctuary. For it is hardly likely that the Pythia herself, a young woman chosen at random from among the women of Delphi, always had literary talent. There must have been professional versifiers capable of polishing the god's response. Thus a ceramic fragment found at Salamis on Cyprus has preserved the response to a question that a faithful follower had put to an oracle of Zeus Epikoinios. The questioner asked whether or not a stream near the sanctuary should be filled in. In prose, the god had responded quite briefly: "Decision of the god: I absolutely forbid the filling of the stream." But this must have seemed a little too harsh or unpoetic on the god's part, so the consulting party had the same oracle rewritten in verse: "I appreciate and approve your zeal, but I strike my enemy with lightning. By the stream bed, I receive fresh water for the herds, and in the spring plants grow there. If someone is in doubt and implores my aid, I shall answer his prayer." The god suddenly seemed closer and more benevolent, even if, at bottom, the answer remained the same.

The gods expressed themselves through the intermediary of soothsayers. Thus the Pythia of Delphi was inspired by the god as soon as she was seated on the tripod and ceased to be inspired as soon as she left it. Much has been said about the divine breath *(pneuma)*, the mastication of bay leaves, and other purification rites. The frightening tableau drawn up by the poet Lucan in the first century, making it a sort of delirious frenzy going on all day, like the picture provided, understandably enough, by the Church Fathers, finds no support in the documentation. The divine inspiration of which the texts speak does not signify delirium, and no one indicated that the pneuma emanated from the ground, from a crack in the earth under the tripod, in the form of gas or vapors that could have provoked a disordered verbal outburst that would have had to be interpreted. The pneuma was only the breath with which the god surrounded his interpreter, something no more astonishing than the Christian idea of the Holy Spirit.

The oracular procedures, which surprise us by the trust the Greeks placed in them, were in reality just an ordinary form of behavior common to all citizens through which people sought to know the future so as to control it as best they could. Croesus did not act any differently from his contemporaries. But let us look once more at Croesus, and recall what an abundance of precautions he took to determine the most trustworthy god to consult. His impressive offerings at Delphi were supposed to protect him against a deceitful oracle. Croesus thus entered into a war against Cyrus the Great, and the war ended in the collapse of a great empire: his own. The god had not lied, but Croesus had failed to understand the message.

CHAPTER SEVEN

"And Cleisthenes Had the People Join His Hetaireia," or the Bases of Athenian Democracy

Athens, which had before been great, grew now yet greater when rid of her tyrants; and those that were of chief power among them were two, Cleisthenes an Alcmaeonid (it is he who is reputed to have over-persuaded the Pythian priestess), and Isagoras son of Teisandrus, a man of a notable house, but of what lineage I cannot tell; his kinsfolk sacrifice to Zeus of Caria. These men with their factions fell to contending for power, wherein Cleisthenes being worsted took the people into his hetaireia. Presently he divided the Athenians into ten tribes, instead of four as formerly; he called none any more after the names of the sons of Ion, Geleon, Aegicoreus, Argades, and Hoples, but invented for them names taken from other heroes, all native to the country save only Aias; him he added, albeit a stranger, because he was a neighbor and an ally.

> *Herodotus,* trans. A. D. Godley, rev. (Loeb Classical Library, 1920), vol. 3, p. 73 (V, 66)

ATHENS, 510–508 B.C.E. Thus ended, for Herodotus as for Aristotle, a crisis of several years' duration, probably dating from the death of Peisistratus in 528–527. By an unexpected and unprecedented move, an Athenian aristocrat, one of the most prominent, from a family whose reputation had spread far beyond its own city-state, had invited the people—the mass of ordinary citizens, those who had few rights—to belong to his group of companions. For that is indeed the meaning of *hetaireia:* companions in combat, belonging to the same social milieu, sometimes linked by family and matrimonial alliances. They got together to drink and party, to work out in the gymnasium and relax in the baths, but they did not hesitate, during their gatherings, to discuss the affairs of the city-state and to work out political strategies from the vantage point of men who had come by power naturally. For, despite Solon's reforms early in the sixth century, ordinary people remained largely excluded from decision making and even from political discussions.

Yet Solon had introduced essential innovations, by ruling out the withdrawal of civic rights from debtors, and by ruling out any consideration of the degree of nobility of one's birth in the definition of the rights of citizenship. In actual fact, this latter provision, essential though it was on the legal level, probably had no effect whatsoever in practical terms: until the mid-fifth century, aristocratic families dominated Athenian political life, holding monopolies on wealth, prestige, talent for governance, and the art of persuasion. But as it happened, the semifailure—in the short run—of Solon's reforms was temporarily canceled out by a much more significant factor: the installation of tyranny in Athens.

The matter was not settled without difficulty—for the tyrant, that is. For Peisistratus, the head of an aristocratic clan that was said to be particularly well implanted "beyond the hills" (in the region of Marathon and the eastern plains of Attica), had to make three attempts, and had to invent more or less incredible ruses in order to assume power. Initially, probably in 561–560, during a simulated attack by his political adversaries, he ran to the agora and got the people to grant him a bodyguard of three hundred men armed with clubs. This did not keep him from being removed from power six years later (555–554). Eleven years after that (in 544–543), he came back by making allies of his former adversaries, the Alcmaeonids, and he impressed the public with a spectacularly staged event: a young peasant woman of imposing stature was disguised as Athena and charged with accompanying Peisistratus to Athens. The people's credulity, noted by Herodotus, did not prevent the tyrant from being driven from power once again at the end of six years (539–538); he came back four years later (535–534) and remained in power until his death in 528–527.

For the aristocrats accustomed to leading the city-state, the establishment of a tyranny was in principle a hard blow, because the tyrant confiscated all powers for his own benefit by relying on a personal armed guard (Chapter 5). The aristocrats thus generally took a dim view of the establishment of a tyranny, if only because it deprived them of all decision-making power at the heart of the city-state.

However, Peisistratus's tyranny seemed to escape this model. First, because there was never a question of persecutions against the wealthiest citizens. Moreover, Peisistratus seems to have succeeded in imposing himself thanks to an alliance with other important families, including the Alcmaeonids, headed at the time by Megacles (father of our Cleisthenes), at least when he came back to power in 544; Peisistratus is said to have married Megacles' daughter. And this situation persisted, later Alcmaeonid propaganda notwithstanding: in 525–524, Cleisthenes son of Megacles figured among the archontes elected in Athens. Some scholars will object that, under the tyrant's reign, the regular magistrates no longer played much of a political role; this is probably true, but it is no less certain that the tyrant would not have allowed a member of a family with which he was openly at war to be elected as a magistrate. Thus when the Alcmaeonids present themselves as the most constant adversaries of tyrants, we have to challenge the assertion and seek the political reasons behind this after-the-fact rewriting of history.

It was probably not until Peisistratus's death in 528–527 that the situation deteriorated. His successor, his youngest son Hippias (for, contrary to Aristotle's claim, the eldest, Hipparchos, played only a secondary role), seems to have stiffened the tyranny, although we do not know exactly in what ways. Certain families may have gone into exile, including the Alcmaeonids, whose numerous ties outside of Attica no doubt made exile bearable. Furthermore, they had taken responsibility for the reconstruction of the temple of Apollo in Delphi, which had been destroyed by fire in 548, and they had made it more beautiful than expected, using marble from Paros rather than the local limestone for the façade and generously offering to cover the additional expense. This earned them great prestige throughout the Greek world and unequivocal support from the Delphic priests. But in 524 they were once again in Athens—if indeed they had ever left.

In 514, following an episode of rivalry in love with a homosexual connotation (the tyrants' youngest brother Thessalos, smitten with Harmodios, had been rejected by the latter), Hipparchos, the brother of the reigning tyrant, was assassinated by two young aristocrats, Harmodios and Aristogiton; their gesture was interpreted, after the tyrants' fall, as the first step on the path to the city-state's liberation. Statues and drinking songs galore later celebrated their heroic act. But at the time, a terrible repression was visited upon the opponents, and it was undoubtedly at this point that many families were obliged to go into exile. On the strength of the support they could gather outside Athens, and also thanks to the support of the god of Delphi, whose priests sang of the generosity of the Alcmaeonids, they attempted an assault on the fortress of Leipsydrion, on Attica's northern border, but they failed miserably. It ultimately took an armed invasion by the Spartans—persuaded by the Pythia of Delphi, who was in the Alcmaeonids' pay—to drive out Hippias along with his entire family. Hippias took refuge in his properties in Asia Minor (Troad), that is, in the Persian Empire.

The political interplay of which the aristocrats had been so long deprived could finally be resumed. The *hetaireiai* had unquestionably never ceased to function, and the political divisions persisted, even though it is impossible for us to know what underlying divergences opposed one group to another. Was it just a question of immediate interests, tied to the exercise of power? Probably not, for it is hard to imagine that Cleisthenes had proposed such fundamental reforms merely for circumstantial reasons— merely to look good in the eyes of the people and triumph over his adversaries.

For in fact, despite the determining role played by the Alcmaeonids in evicting the tyrants, Cleisthenes did not succeed in imposing himself as the city-state's leader; he was shunted aside in favor of a coalition of his adversaries. And it was then that he had the totally revolutionary idea of associating the entire population with a political struggle from which it had been excluded up to that point: he "made friends with the popular party" by bringing the people into his hetaireia, thus giving his own faction a numerical and political weight against which no other faction was big enough to fight—except by starting a civil war whose outcome no one could predict but that had every chance, given the balance of powers, of ending up with the installation of a new popular tyranny with Cleisthenes himself at its head.

To convince the people to support him, Cleisthenes must have had something to offer. For how could people have been interested in participating in the struggle for power if they were going to keep on being excluded from its exercise on a daily basis? Cleisthenes' objectives and his sources of inspiration have given rise to endless speculation, but there is no doubt that Cleisthenes was the spiritual heir of the sixth-century Ionian philosophers who had developed the earliest reflections we have on the nature of politics.[1] To be sure, we know the Ionians' political philosophy only through fragments, but they had been able to develop solutions for establishing a certain degree of equilibrium at the heart of city-states that were deeply divided among groups with divergent interests. The idea later developed by Cleisthenes that power must be situated "at the center" of the city-state emanated from the Ionians' reflections.

Cleisthenes seems to have had the goal of ensuring that all citizens, whatever their level of fortune and birth, would participate in one way or another in what the Greeks called the *politeia,* that is, in political life, the working of institutions, the constitution, the exercise of citizenship. There was no question of advocating political equality; no city-state ever achieved that, not even Athens at the height of its democratic life. It was rather a question of making it possible for each citizen to intervene in the political debate, in decision making, if only by voting in the assembly.

To achieve this aim, Cleisthenes proposed a series of measures so revolutionary in appearance that Athens's neighbors and also Sparta, which had helped drive out the tyrants, after all, took fright and banded together to drive out the Alcmaeonids in turn, along with—we are told—seven hundred families against whom an old charge of sacrilege was resurrected. In fact, after a victory in the Olympic games in 640 or 636, a certain Cylon had tried to seize power in Athens. After the failure of his coup d'état, he took refuge as a suppliant next to the statue of Athena, which protected him from a brutal counterattack. But after promising that he would not be condemned to death if he left his refuge, the magistrates massacred him along with his accomplices. As Herodotus concludes laconically (V, 71), "the slaying of them was laid to the door of the Alcmaeonidae,"[2] probably because one of their number held an essential magistracy. The accusation was serious and the risk extreme: Cleisthenes fled from the city in secret, along with his supporters. But the coalition of city-states was insufficiently coordinated to intervene in a concerted fashion, which allowed the Athenians to defeat them one by one, and the king of Sparta let himself be bribed! Cleisthenes was soon back in power and the people were prepared to follow him.

What, then, were these reforms for which the Athenian population had proved ready to fight? No single one of them can be considered as the unmistakable sign of a democratic regime (the word *democracy* did not yet exist), but, taken together, Cleisthenes' reforms appeared sufficiently innovative to be understood as keystones of the democracy to come.

The system was based on a new organization of the civic body designed not so much to weaken existing solidarities as to create new ones among groups that had not been in relation before. For Attica, as we have seen (Chapter 1), was something rare in the Greek world: it was a giant city-state possessing a vast territory (twenty-five hundred square kilometers), which meant that it was impossible for everyone to know everyone else. It cannot be claimed, even for the period in question, that this was a "face-to-face" society into which no foreigner could blend. Attica doubtless remained for the most part a juxtaposition of regional groups that were more or less dominated by great aristocratic families implanted locally. This is what Herodotus and Aristotle confirmed, moreover, when they explained that, on the eve of Peisistratus's takeover, three families were struggling for power: the Pedians, led by a certain Lycurgus, were people of the plains; the Paralians, headed by Megacles the Alcmaeonid, drew their numbers rather from coastal groups; finally, the Diacrians (Aristotle) or the Hyperacrians (Herodotus) who supported Peisistratus came from the mountains, or rather from "beyond the hills," that is, they were farthest away from the civic center. We may be astonished by the rather mechanical character of the distribution, but it is not impossible that the major political factions indeed benefited from a geographical anchoring related to their leaders' bases on the land. In order to move beyond these regional divisions and create a civic body concerned with the interests of the city-state as a whole, it was necessary to create structures that went beyond the local framework.

Cleisthenes thus began by making the basic unit the deme (we know of at least 150 of these in the fourth century). Each deme was made up of one or two villages, or a village and the surrounding hamlets, or a quarter of the city of Athens: these were small units in which everyone actually did know everyone else. The demes maintained the civic registers, enrolled as new citizens males who had reached the age of majority, after a vote by the *demotai* (members of the deme). From then on, Cleisthenes decided, everyone would have to be designated not by a patronymic—a practice that made it possible to identify citizens of foreign origin, or to highlight a brilliant family genealogy—but only by the name of a deme: for example, Pericles, of the deme of Cholargos. The measure was actually applied, but only in part: the rule was indeed always to give the name of one's deme, but the habit of adding the patronymic was retained, perhaps as a way of distinguishing among homonyms. Nevertheless, the rules were followed in a number of official documents, such as in the headings of decrees.

Once citizens were divided up into demes, their descendants would automatically belong to the same deme. Although the initial distribution was geographic (everyone was inscribed in his or her place of residence), there was no question, afterward, of deviating from the geographical rule: a family remained forever enrolled on the registers of the same deme and participated in the resulting distributions. This rule was fundamental, for reasons that will soon become clear.

As the demes had been established in a very uneven fashion (some were highly populated, others much less so), Cleisthenes undertook to distribute all citizens, deme by deme, among ten tribes. We must not imagine these tribes as some vestige of an ancient period in which the Athenians might really have lived in tribes. Athenians were already distributed among four tribes (known as "Ionian"): Cleisthenes left this institution in place, Herodotus's claim notwithstanding (and Herodotus is contradicted on this point by Aristotle and the Attic inscriptions), but he added an additional distribution of the population into ten new ("Cleisthenian") tribes completely unrelated to the previous ones. These new tribes were given names of Athenian heroes selected by the Pythia of Delphi from a list of one hundred that had been submitted to her. To constitute each tribe, Cleisthenes adopted a geographical principle that was fairly complex but that made it possible to blend the population together. He first divided the entire territory *(chora)* into three large zones: the city *(astu)*, the coast *(paralia)*, and the interior *(mesogeia)*. Then each of these zones was divided in turn into ten smaller units, or *trittyes,* making a total of thirty units. Once the country had been divided in this way, each tribe was made up of three trittyes: one from the city, one from the coast, and one from the interior. Thus within a given tribe there were citizens from three very different sectors of the chora.

The general principle is beyond question: the point was indeed to mix the Attic population together. But a detailed study of the geography of each tribe has led some historians to more political conclusions. It has thus been noticed that the trittyes of a single tribe were never contiguous, except in a few cases where communications from one to the other proved to be particularly difficult. In addition, small village communities that were highly unified, organized, for example, around a common cult, like the tetrapolis of Marathon, found themselves split among two or three different tribes. Similarly, great aristocratic families saw their members dispersed among several tribes, which prevented them from dominating a

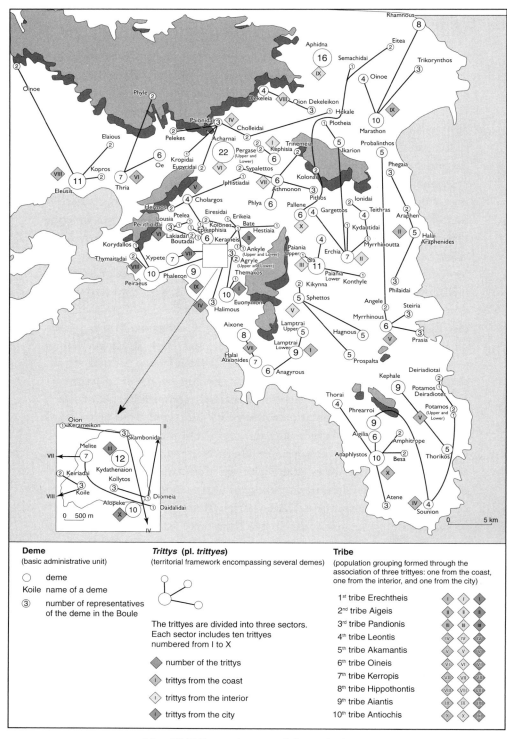

Deme
(basic administrative unit)

○ deme

Koile name of a deme

③ number of representatives of the deme in the Boule

Trittys (pl. trittyes)
(territorial framework encompassing several demes)

The trittyes are divided into three sectors. Each sector includes ten trittyes numbered from I to X

◆ number of the trittys

◇ trittys from the coast

◇ trittys from the interior

◆ trittys from the city

Tribe
(population grouping formed through the association of three trittyes: one from the coast, one from the interior, and one from the city)

1st tribe Erechtheis
2nd tribe Aigeis
3rd tribe Pandionis
4th tribe Leontis
5th tribe Akamantis
6th tribe Oineis
7th tribe Kerropis
8th tribe Hippothontis
9th tribe Aiantis
10th tribe Antiochis

Map IV. Tribes, *trittyes*, and demes in Attica

single one. In short, Cleisthenes may have sought not only to intermingle the population, but also to break down the old solidarities and to weaken his adversaries.

I find these conclusions very dubious; Cleisthenes must not be confused with a politician engaged in gerrymandering. The absence of contiguity among the trittyes of a given tribe seemed to be the condition sine qua non for a real mixing of citizens, but it was not systematic, and there were exceptions (see the map on the preceding page); I am thus not sure that a systematic rule was applied. As for weakening the great families, Cleisthenes would have weakened his own first of all, for the Alcmaeonids found themselves in three different tribes. It is obvious that Cleisthenes wanted to combat his political adversaries. But one cannot conclude that he weakened his adversaries by placing them in two or three different tribes and that he reinforced his own family by putting it in a position to control three tribes: the same causes produced the same effects in each case. Similarly, it is not clear what advantage Cleisthenes would have achieved from splintering the regional groupings: moreover, how did the fact that the four villages of the tetrapolis of Marathon were in different tribes destroy their traditional religious solidarity?

I think, then, that these analyses lead us along a false trail, and that Cleisthenes never manifested such Machiavellianism. First, Aristotle and Herodotus agree on one point: Cleisthenes did not eliminate any of the old structures. This was the guarantee that he was not attempting to break the existing bonds at the heart of the communities. In addition, if Cleisthenes had proposed a distribution that was disadvantageous both to the great aristocratic families and to the regional communities, he would have run the risk of seeing his reform rejected and losing the support of the people. Yet his distribution was never called into question, even when his adversaries returned to power. Thus this new distribution must have appeared satisfying to most of the population.

The "anomalies" noted above can be explained in reality simply by the need to establish equilibrium among all the tribes. The tribe became in effect the key to the distribution of most functions and responsibilities. Each tribe would supply fifty *bouleutai,* one thousand hoplites, one hundred horsemen, one archon, and so forth. Not only did the population of all the tribes thus have to be roughly equivalent, but the distribution of wealthy families also had to be balanced, because only they would furnish horsemen and most of the magistrates. This, rather than a desire to harm political adversaries, accounts for the distribution of the aristocrats among the tribes. This concern for tribal equilibrium in both quantitative and qualitative terms explains why Cleisthenes proceeded to this geographic division of the civic body while deciding that in the future everyone would remain enrolled in the ancestral tribe and deme, no matter what changes of residence occurred later on. One could in effect recognize that, over all, the population of each tribe would evolve in the same way.

An attentive reading of Herodotus and Aristotle indicates that the reform of the tribal structure is the only reform explicitly attributed to Cleisthenes, at least the only one of any real importance. The Council of the Five Hundred seems to have been created a few years later, like the College of the Ten Strategoi; it is not clear that Cleisthenes was their creator. He has also been credited with creating ostracism (Chapter 9), but this penalty was first applied only in 488, well after Cleisthenes had disappeared from Athenian political life. Nevertheless, the creation of the ten tribes suffices to make Cleisthenes appear to be the true founder of Athenian democracy. To be sure, Herodotus does not use this word—which appears in a composite form only in Aeschylus's *Suppliants* in 472—but rather the word *isegoria* or *isonomia*. These terms are difficult to translate, but they have to be understood as equal access to speech *(isegoria)* or a certain equality before the law *(isonomia)*. This by no means signified equality pure and simple, in the sense in which we understand it today, but rather a right of participation according to the census category to which one belonged. For Cleisthenes did not tamper with the Solonian organization of the Athenian civic body: the four census classes that Solon had established at the beginning of the sixth century remained in place, and only the first two classes had access, for example, to the archontate and to the cavalry. The innovation, in the Cleisthenian system, was that political power was placed "at the center" of the community, and that all adult males had access to it in one way or another—some through election to the most prestigious magistracies, some by lottery in the Council of the Five Hundred, all through participation in the popular assembly. All could speak out and try to convince others; all could express themselves by their votes. This was certainly not yet Periclean democracy, but the structures that made the latter possible were henceforth in place.

One enigma remains: what became of Cleisthenes? Partisans and adversaries alike recognize him as the father of Athenian democracy. At the time of his reforms, he was probably no longer a very young man, nor was he very old. The point is of no particular importance in any case, but he disappeared from the documentation as soon as the tribes had been created, and no one took the trouble to tell us what happened to him. Was he dead? The texts we have say nothing whatsoever about this, whereas his death might well have made an impression on people if it had come soon after such upheavals. Nor is there any legendary tradition at hand to fill in this gap in history, whereas Solon is made to travel throughout the world. For Cleisthenes, there is nothing—no narrative, no legend, as if he had disappeared from Athenian memory. Plutarch wrote numerous lives of illustrious men, legendary founders of city-states (Theseus, Lycurgus) and audacious reformers (Numa, Solon, Agis and Cleomenes, and so on), but Cleisthenes did not inspire him. This was doubtless not a personal choice on Plutarch's part, but the reflection of a total absence of a historiographical tradition regarding the father of democratic Athens. The mystery remains intact.

CHAPTER EIGHT

Histiaeus of Miletus and the Tattooed Slave, or Greeks and Persians in Asia Minor ca. 550–ca. 490

For Histiaeus desired to signify to Aristagoras that he should revolt; and, having no other safe way of so doing (for the roads were guarded), he shaved and pricked marks on the head of his trustiest slave, and waited till the hair grew again; as soon as it was grown, he sent the man to Miletus with no other message save that when he came to Miletus he must bid Aristagoras shave his hair and examine his head. The writing pricked thereon signified revolt, as I have already said. This Histiaeus did, because he surely misliked his enforced sojourn at Susa; now he had a good hope that if there were a revolt he would be sent away to the sea-coast; but if Miletus remained at peace, he reckoned that he would return thither no more.

Herodotus, trans. A. D. Godley (Loeb Classical Library, 1920), vol. 3, p. 39 (V, 35)

SUSA (IRAN), 499 B.C.E. A secret messenger crossed Asia. From Susa, the administrative capital of the Great King, almost on the banks of the Persian Gulf, to Miletus, the most powerful and richest of the Greek city-states on the coast of Asia Minor. This region, too, had been situated within the Persian Empire, ever since the fall of Croesus and the conquest of his kingdom by Cyrus the Great, in 546 (Chapter 6), more than half a century earlier. In 499 the Greeks of Asia, or at least some of them, were restive. The Great King was suspicious: the roads were under surveillance. Now, we can justifiably be astonished at this abrupt change in the attitude of the Greeks living under Persian rule. For the conquest of

546 had not marked a break in the history of the region. The Greeks of Asia were used to living under the authority of a foreign monarch. The Achaemenid tutelage does not seem to have been more onerous than that of the Mermnads, the royal dynasty of Lydia. The archaeological evidence does not reveal any decline in prosperity, and the embellishment of the city-states continued apace. In many respects, the Greece of Asia looked like a leader among the Greeks. Its philosophers—the term encompasses all facets of knowledge and wisdom—were unquestionably at the forefront of the movement of ideas. Thales of Miletus for mathematics and astronomy, his compatriot Hecataeus of Ephesus somewhat later, and also of course Pythagoras of Samos, whose school emigrated to the west, in Croton, profoundly renewed Greek knowledge and thought. The Persian presence does not seem to have harmed the development of intellectual life, despite Pythagoras's exile.

Nevertheless, after Darius's advent—in reality, his usurpation—in 522, the situation deteriorated. Darius clearly had ambitions of conquest in Europe. In 512 he led a major expedition that crossed the Straits, seized Thrace, crossed the Danube, and launched an endless pursuit of the Scythian peoples south of the Ukraine, until he realized that winter was coming on and he could go no farther. In this short-lived and inconsequential adventure (Darius retained only the Thracian bridgehead), he received valuable help from the Greeks of Asia, in the form of manpower, ships, and competent technicians. Mandrocles of Samos was the one who built the bridge of ships on the Bosporus that allowed the royal army to cross into Europe. The Ionians built a similar bridge at the head of the Danube delta and protected it while the Great King was crossing the lands of the Scythians. To be sure, because they did not see the king return within the promised sixty days, some of the Ionians were tempted to break up the bridge and leave the king to his fate. But Histiaeus of Miletus argued strongly against that proposal; then, standing up to the Scythians who had caught Darius's army unawares and were pressing it to destroy the bridge, he used a ruse to get rid of them and save the expedition. Darius rewarded him by taking him to Susa as an advisor. It was in that remote capital that Histiaeus plotted against the king in 499.

But if the Greeks of Asia were grumbling about the Great King at the end of the sixth century, it was not out of solidarity with Histiaeus. In fact, since taking power, Darius had installed men of confidence as tyrants in the city-states. The Asian Greeks found it hard to tolerate being subjected to a political regime that had been very widespread in the seventh and sixth centuries (Chapter 5) but that was on the verge of disappearing more or less everywhere throughout the Greek world. On the finest figures in Greek political thought, Darius imposed the most archaic regime there was. One sign of the importance of the Asian Greeks' protest seems to me to be the fact that the first measure taken by the tyrants who initiated the revolt was to renounce their tyranny.

Were there other causes? Probably, but Herodotus says nothing about them, except to accuse the tyrant Aristagoras of Miletus and his predecessor Histiaeus of defending their own interests. It is certain that Aristagoras played a personal game and practiced a sort of headlong rush forward. In fact, following a civil war in Naxos, some Naxian exiles had taken refuge in Miletus, hoping to get Histiaeus's help in order to regain power on their island. As Histiaeus had been replaced as tyrant of Miletus by his son-in-law and cousin Aristagoras, the latter succeeded in convincing the Persian governor of Sardis to mount an expedition against Naxos, which might thus fall into the power of the Persians. But in the wake of a trivial disagreement between Aristagoras and the Persian general in charge of operations, the expedition failed. Considerable sums had been spent to no avail: the Persian satrap of Sardis demanded reimbursement from Aristagoras. Unable to pay, the latter mobilized the other Asian Greeks by brandishing the flag of freedom, and headed to the western Aegean region—to Athens and Sparta in particular—to seek help.

Aristagoras's misadventure may have served to trigger the revolt, but the deeper causes probably lay elsewhere. Herodotus notes a climate of civil war in several city-states, and in many places there must have been bitter debates over the best attitude to adopt toward the Persians. But Herodotus, our principal source regarding this conflict, was probably biased (he himself was originally from Halicarnassos in Caria). He clearly knew that the revolt had ultimately failed and that this was a disaster for the region. Violently hostile to the tyrants (his family had been among their victims), he defended the thesis according to which the movement was bound to fail from the outset. He laid maximum blame on the tyrants who had led the Greeks into the adventure for personal ends of their own. He thus took care to stress the differences of opinion, the lack of preparation on the part of the civic armies, even the selfishness of certain city-states, which withdrew their contingents immediately after an initial victory. In reality, all this may betray profound differences in the rebels' objectives. Whereas the tyrants had no way out but the end of Achaemenid domination (any Persian victory would actually have brought them harsh punishment at the hands of the ruler from whom they held their authority), many Greeks might well have been satisfied with the abolition of the tyranny. As it happened, the tyrants abandoned their posts at the very start of the rebellion, and this seemed a sufficient victory for many. This may explain the varying attitudes on the part of the city-states and, within a given city-state, the diversity of attitudes among political groups.

Herodotus notwithstanding, the fact remains that the revolt began in an atmosphere of unanimity (only the historian Hecataeus of Miletus argues otherwise). Aware of their weakness, the Ionians sent Aristagoras as an ambassador to seek help from the free Greeks. That mission met with limited success, because only Athens and Eretria ended up promising and sending aid, twenty ships and four ships respectively. But Sparta, far and away the leading Greek military power, refused to go along, after an exchange in which Aristagoras revealed a total ignorance of Sparta's sociopolitical system. Boasting of the empire's fabulous wealth, shoring up his claims with a map made in Asia Minor (which must have left the Spartans more confused than admiring), he thought he could convince King Cleomenes to throw himself into an effort to conquer the Persian Empire. He was clearly unaware that Sparta officially professed contempt for wealth and tried to maintain at least a superficial social egalitarianism, which would have been shattered by an influx of booty. When after this series of blunders Aristagoras revealed that it took three months to get to Susa from the Aegean Sea, he was invited to leave as quickly as possible.

With virtually no outside support, the Ionians nevertheless threw themselves into the battle and met with some initial success. With the Athenian and Eretrian contingents, they took the city of Sardis, the Persian capital of Asia Minor, and set it on fire (498). The victory was short-lived, for the conquerors could not take the acropolis; they quickly fled but were massacred on the way out. That false victory convinced the Athenians and the Eretrians to return home, but it triggered an extension of the revolt in Asia Minor, from the Straits all the way to Cyprus. The matter was becoming serious for the Persians, who reacted vigorously. Cyprus was reconquered in just under a year; then the cities of the Straits fell one after another.

However, the central sector, in Ionia and Caria, resisted, despite the disappearance of Aristagoras. Histiaeus, who had gone back to Miletus with the king's approval after hinting to the king that he could conquer Sardinia, did not succeed in preventing the coalition from unraveling. On the eve of the decisive naval battle, near the small island of Lade, the Samians defected with their 60 ships (of the 353 on the rebels' side); the Persians had bought them off. A crushing naval defeat of the Ionians and their allies was the last straw, dispersing the few city-states that had remained united. The Persians then laid siege to Miletus and took the city thanks to major undermining efforts and to their war machines (493). The revolt had lasted five years. As for the Milesians, the men were massacred, the women and children sold into slavery; the prestigious oracular sanctuary of Apollo at Didyma was sacked and burned. According to Herodotus, a few surviving prisoners were deported to a place called Ampe, on the mouth of the Tigris in the Persian Gulf.

One might suppose that this episode in the history of the Asian Greeks was of only marginal importance with respect to the Greek world as a whole, but this is not the case. First, because the conquest of Miletus and its destruction had considerable repercussions: the richest and most powerful of the Asian city-states, the fatherland of Thales and Hecataeus, the place where Hellenism had been the most brilliantly developed in the sixth century, was totally lost. Emotions ran so high in Athens that after Phrynichos's tragedy *The Fall of Miletus* was performed, the author was sentenced to pay a fine of one thousand drachmas for having made the entire population burst into tears at the evocation of a national drama, and no more performances of the play were allowed.

Next, because the failure of the revolt had as a corollary the perceptible decline of the region. Generally speaking, the city-states of Asia Minor remained impoverished during most of the fifth century, even after their liberation from the Persian yoke in 478, following the Greek victories in the second Greco-Persian War. The losses must have been significant, and it took the city-states a long time to recover. Athens's supremacy over the Aegean basin was made all the easier. Above all, the center of Greek intellectual life left Asia for a long time, and it was not until the Hellenistic and imperial era that the great cities of Asia once again had roles to play in that arena.

Finally, and perhaps not least importantly, Athenian propaganda, skillfully relayed by Herodotus, made this upheaval the basis for a half-century-long confrontation between the Greeks and the Persians. Very early on, the Athenians established a causal link between the attack on Sardis and the Persians' two successive expeditions against Greece, in 490 and in 481–479. The first in particular, according to them, was dictated solely by Darius's desire for revenge. The proof of this, in their eyes, lay in the fact that the naval expedition commanded by the Persians Datis and Artaphernes focused particularly on Eretria (handed over owing to Gongylos's betrayal), and then on Athens (the Marathon landing). These two facts certainly cannot be denied, and conquest of the two city-states was indeed one of the Persian objectives. But along the way the Persians defeated many other insular city-states that had not participated in the Ionian revolt, proof that their war aims went well beyond mere punishment for the attack on Sardis. In other words, punishing Athens may have been one goal of the first Greco-Persian War, but not necessarily the most important one. We can measure what this change of perspective introduces into the history of the war: the Persian defeat at Marathon unquestionably saved Athens from Persian domination, but this was only a minor episode in a wider war. Although the Persians, after this failure, preferred to go back home (the season of bad weather was beginning), the balance sheet for the expedition remained quite positive: the islands had come under the control of the Great King, a stage that could be seen as a sign of a more complete domination of both banks of the Aegean in the future. By proclaiming their city-state the quasi-unique "war goal" of the Persians, the Athenians made the expedition by Datis and Artaphernes look like a failure. Marathon then took on considerable relief, because it symbolized the victory of a single small Greek city-state over the Achaemenid tyranny. This propaganda image worked extremely well: the victory at Marathon has been understood right up to our day, even by otherwise scrupulous historians, as a victory of freedom over Oriental despotism! In reality, the Athenians had not saved Greece at Marathon; they had saved only themselves, and their success was just one small episode in a war in which the Persians had in fact piled up victories. The only freedom they had managed to protect was their own. And for how long?

CHAPTER NINE

An Ostracizing Potsherd,
or the Progress of Democracy
after the Greco-Persian Wars

Ostracism shards bearing the name of
Themistocles, son of Neocles, and of
Hippocrates, son of Anaxilas

[The popular assembly met in Athens to decide on an ostracism.]

As the voters were inscribing their *ostraka*, it is said that an unlettered and utterly boorish fellow handed his *ostrakon* to Aristides, whom he took to be one of the ordinary crowd, and asked him to write *Aristides* on it. He, astonished, asked the man what possible wrong Aristides had done him. "None whatever," was the answer, "I don't even know the fellow, but I am tired of hearing him everywhere called 'The Just.'" On hearing this, Aristides made no answer, but wrote his name on the *ostrakon* and handed it back. Finally, as he was departing the city, he lifted up his hands to heaven and prayed—a prayer the opposite, as it seems, of that which Achilles made—that no crisis might overtake the Athenians which should compel the people to remember Aristides.

Plutarch, *Aristides*, in *Plutarch's Lives*, trans. Bernadotte Perrin
(Loeb Classical Library, 1914), vol. 2, pp. 233–235 (VII, 7–8)

ATHENS, 484 B.C.E. The involuntary hero: Aristides, an Athenian politician known for his perfect integrity, a political adversary of Themistocles, who seems to have had fewer scruples in this area. Aristides defended a fairly traditional policy, basing the safety of the city-state on its hoplites, whereas Themistocles wanted to develop the navy, as a means toward a bolder approach.

This brief anecdote illustrates perfectly one of the most curious institutions of Athenian democracy: ostracism. Today, the term has taken on pejorative value, not so much for the one who is its victim as for those who practice it. But at the same time the term has lost some of its force; ostracism now signifies only "sending to the sidelines," exclusion from a group, with no particular political connotations. To the contrary, in Athens, it designated a powerful measure whose political significance must not be underestimated. It is worth explaining in some detail what was involved.

The procedure was described by Aristotle in *The Athenian Constitution* and by Plutarch in the chapter cited above of his *Aristides;* the archaeological finds from the Athens agora have added very useful complementary information.

Once a year, during the principal assembly of the sixth *prytaneia,* the question of ostracism was put before the assembled population. Every citizen received a potsherd *(ostracon)* on which he wrote the name of the person he wanted to ostracize. For the vote to be counted, there had to be at least six thousand potsherds deposited on the agora, in a round enclosure built for the purpose, and thus at least six thousand people had to be present at the assembly—in other words, depending on the period, between a quarter and an eighth of the civic body. This ruled out any decision made stealthily by a tiny minority of the citizenry. The very fact that the question was raised on just one date, always the same, allowed everyone to prepare, for or against. Once the voting was closed, the archontes counted the number of potsherds; if there were fewer than six thousand, the matter was dropped, and no one was driven from the city. If, on the contrary, the required number was reached, the person whose name was cited most often was declared banished for ten years.

The procedure was complex enough that the crowd could not act hastily or under the influence of a sudden angry impulse; the date was established in a stable way and no one could change it. This did not exclude manipulations, as we shall see, but in principle there could be no surprise ostracisms. Let us note, however, that one could be ostracized by the accumulation of a small number of potsherds, if votes were spread among a large number of "candidates." In fact, among the thousands of potsherds (more than ten thousand) recovered on the slopes of the acropolis and on the agora, many well-known names appear: Themistocles remained on top of the list for a long time, but a discovery has placed at the head of the Athenians' list the most ill-regarded of their fellow citizens, Megacles the Alcmaeonid, Cleisthenes' nephew, ostracized in 487–486. However, many potsherds bear the names of people entirely unknown to us.

Three questions require our attention: When? Why? Who? But first, a word about the practical consequences of ostracism for its victims.

The ostracized person had to leave Athens, and his period of exile lasted ten years. Starting in 480, it was established even that he had to go beyond Cape Geraistos and Cape Skyllaion, the first marking the southernmost point of Euboea, the second marking the easternmost point of the Argolid, under penalty of definitive *atimia,* for there was concern that an influential man might manage to continue to weigh in on Athenian public life if he remained too near the civic territory. But this exile was not accompanied by any public degradation or deprivation of property. This last was managed from a distance by the exiled person himself or by members of his family who remained behind in Athens. For ostracism was never a legal measure, but a strictly political position.

Aristotle indicates that the first ostracism took place in 488, and he explicitly links this event to the success of the Athenian hoplites at Marathon in 490. Encouraged by their victory, aware of having saved the city-state (and, beyond that, the Greeks in general), the citizen-hoplites, and probably the entire set of citizens, who had very little access to the magistracies despite Cleisthenes' reforms, used their right of ostracism. The exact meaning of Aristotle's statement has been much discussed. The simplest approach, it seems to me, is to take it literally. Ostracism indeed appears as one of Cleisthenes' democratic innovations, and its origin must go back to the final years of the sixth century, but it was applied for the first time only in the wake of the first Greco-Persian War, in 488. Were there earlier attempts at ostracism that failed for want of a "qualified" majority, as defined above? This is quite plausible, for it is hard to see why or how the sitting magistrates could have failed to pose the question at the principal assembly of every sixth prytaneia. But for reasons that escape us and about which we might speculate indefinitely, no ostracism was pronounced. The key date thus remains that of 488, and it is not insignificant that Aristotle closely associates this first ostracism with a greater "assurance" on the part of the *demos*. Saving the fatherland gives rights, and the people were determined to mark this.

This precision on Aristotle's part leads to an emphasis on the strictly political character of ostracism. Nowhere is it a question of exiling anyone at all for reasons that would have to do with justice. Aristotle indicates clearly that ostracism aims to protect the democracy against those who would threaten it. Plutarch, in his moralizing language, says nothing else: "Now the sentence of ostracism was not a chastisement of base practices, nay, it was speciously called a humbling and docking of oppressive prestige and power; but it was really a merciful exorcism of the spirit of jealous hate, which thus vented its malignant desire to injure, not in some irreparable evil, but in a mere change of residence for ten years."[1] Which Aristotle translates as the concern for maintaining a regime of strict equality at the heart of the city-state (*Politics*, III, 15).

But this concern for distancing any overly influential individual seems rather secondary, and ostracism actually appears to have been an instrument in the struggle between political clans. Even Aristides' ostracism, in 484, which seems to have been situated, in the light of the anecdote cited above, within the very spirit of the institution as Plutarch defines it, must not have escaped the most classic political combat: in his confrontation with Themistocles, partisan of a more ambitious politics for Athens, he temporarily lost out.

Does the clearly political aim of ostracism account for the difficulty of making the procedure work over a long period of time? Citizens were not supposed to vote lightly, and the anecdote about Aristides probably gives an inaccurate picture of their real behavior. In fact, in a city-state that had perhaps twenty thousand citizens at most, it must not always have been easy to bring together six thousand men; moreover, the city-state was so ill prepared that, for this exceptional vote, the assembly met on the agora and not on the Pnyx, which could not accommodate so large a crowd before it was renovated in the late fifth century. In addition, in the struggle among Athenian factions, the risks of failing must have been palpable: if the adversaries of two or three rival factions were mobilized, the six thousand voters could be brought out, but one had to be sure that one's own champion was not going to be at the top of the list. The procedure could be manipulated, more or less, by a few malcontents acting in concert, and it could unexpectedly punish the head of one rival faction or another.

For there is no doubt about the fact that the factions, or, as the Greeks called them, the *hetaireiai*, mobilized their troops for this vote, whether to vote or to abstain. Contrary to what Plutarch implies, not every citizen filled out his own potsherd or had it filled out by a cooperative neighbor if he were illiterate: the discoveries on the agora show that a number of potsherds were written by the same hand. A collection of 190 potsherds bearing the name of Themistocles found on the slopes of the Acropolis contains writing by no more than fourteen different hands! Prominent political figures must have had potsherds inscribed in order to distribute them to their supporters, and perhaps also to undecided participants. The ostracism session was thus carefully prepared in advance, and it gave rise to complex manipulations. In cases where there was a risk of exclusion, it was presumably in the interest of a prominent man to round up his supporters and keep them from participating in the vote, so that the quorum of six thousand would not be reached—or, worse, to reach an agreement with his adversary so that ostracism would fall on a third man. This is the way Alcibiades and Nicias are said to have agreed, in 418 or 417, to have all their supporters write the name of a third person, Hyperbolos, on the potsherds, for it was clear that the angry populace would put one of their names at the head of the list; by mobilizing against a third party, these two diverted the procedure from its goal.

We have no specific information about the votes, but we note that apart from the period 488–481, when an ostracism seemed to take place every year, the procedure was carried out only episodically, and it fell into disuse after Hyperbolos's ostracism in 418 or 417. Plutarch even claims that the people, indignant at the unnatural alliance between Alcibiades and Nicias on that occasion, renounced ostracism and abolished it. Indeed, we find no evidence of it occurring after this point, but it had already become quite uncommon. The political combat had shifted to other grounds, particularly legal ones. Pericles had still managed to have his principal rival, Thucydides, son of Melesias, ostracized in 443, but nothing indicates that he himself was ever threatened by this procedure; in contrast, he had to confront, directly or through the intermediary of his friends, a number of judicial procedures for various reasons (such as corruption or impiety), and fourth-century Athenian politicians, deprived of this recourse to the *vox populi,* went from one trial to another before the tribunal of the Heliaia, or before the assembly.

Who were the targets of ostracism? The first known victims were friends of the tyrants driven out in 510, for we know that Hippias took refuge in the Persian Empire and accompanied the Persian troops that landed at Marathon. The aim was thus clearly to get rid of individuals—at least for a time—who were politically dangerous, or considered so, in the context of the war with the Persians. In the aftermath of the victory at Marathon, the victims of ostracism were men who could not be brought to justice for want of adequate evidence, but who were suspected of duplicity or conspiracy. Before long, however, other milieus were affected, and the victims were often highly prominent individuals. Indeed, after the tyrants' friends, the next to be ostracized were Alcmaeonids, relatives of Cleisthenes. It is surprising to find the Alcmaeonids among the enemies of democracy, even if some indications suggest that we should not dismiss Aristotle's assertions on the subject; after all, some Alcmaeonids had been caught signaling the Persians from the ramparts of Athens at a time when the news of Marathon had not yet reached the city. In fact, we have too little information about the details of Athenian political life between Cleisthenes' mysterious disappearance and the Greco-Persian Wars to appreciate with any precision the factors that led to ostracisms. We have seen that Aristides' ostracism was based on his opposition to Themistocles: two conceptions of democracy, two external policies were in confrontation, until one of the adversaries was removed from the scene.

After this more or less foundational period, ostracism appeared only episodically. Themistocles was a victim in his turn, in 472–471, before being accused of the worst crimes by the Spartans and by the Athenians, which obliged him to go into complete exile. In 461, Cimon, the unchallenged leader of Athens after Themistocles' exile, the brilliant conqueror of the Persians on several occasions and the true creator of the Athenian empire, was exiled (but recalled in 457). The ostracisms of Thucydides, son of Melesias, and that of Hyperbolos have already been mentioned. It is obvious from this inventory that ostracism aimed high. Men of lower rank could be rendered harmless by judicial means, or could simply be ignored; in contrast, for men of great prestige who could be reproached for nothing but their politics, ostracism alone would do, because it required no justification.

We may also wonder whether the invention of two new procedures set up in 460–450 might have made ostracism superfluous. These dealt with illegal proposals *(graphe para nomon)*, on the one hand, and high treason *(eisangelia)*, on the other. The first made it possible to prosecute anyone who proposed a decision contrary to the existing laws; the second, more vaguely worded, was aimed at anyone who proposed a measure that turned out to be detrimental to the city-state. These procedures presumably left a great deal of latitude to judges, who were in reality just citizens among others, chosen by lot. And all these procedures were undertaken on the simple initiative of a citizen. There were safeguards, of course, and anyone who initiated suits lightly might lose his property, his rank as citizen, or even his life. But the principle of proceeding on the initiative of an individual clearly indicated that safeguarding the city-state's laws and its security was the direct responsibility of every citizen.

On the whole, ostracism was thus used only a little, over a century, and many of its victims returned to Athens before the ten years were over. This was the case for all those ostracized in 488–481, who were summoned back to confront the new Persian invasion, but also for Cimon in 457, after the Athenians were roundly defeated at Tanagra in Boeotia. In the face of a threat from outside, the city-states managed to calm their internal quarrels, and they counted on all their members. The fact remains that ostracism occupied a symbolic position of the first order, for, as Aristotle says, it symbolized the population's awareness of its own strength. After Marathon, a victory won by citizen-hoplites, the latter translated their military success into the political realm: just as they had driven back the Persians on the battlefield, so they expelled the Persians' friends from the assembly. Without having to answer to anyone.

CHAPTER TEN

Complaints of a Bastard,
or Pericles' Law on Citizenship

Peisthetaerus: Come aside here, I want a word with you. Your
uncle's out to cheat you, poor fellow. Of your father's estate
you don't get a single penny, that's the law. You see, you're a
bastard, illegitimate.

Heracles: Me, a bastard? What are you talking about?

Peisthetaerus: That's exactly what you are, your mother being
an alien. Why else do you think that Athena as a daughter
could be called The Heiress, if she had legitimate brethren?

Heracles: But couldn't my father at his death still leave me his
property as a bastard's portion?

Peisthetaerus: The law won't let him. Poseidon here, who's
now getting your hopes up, will be the first to dispute your
claim to your father's property, declaring himself the
legitimate brother. I'll even quote you the law of Solon: "A
bastard shall not qualify as next of kin, if there are legitimate
children; if there are no legitimate children, the next of kin
shall share the property."

Heracles: You mean I have no share in my father's property?

Peisthetaerus: Absolutely none! Tell me, has your father
inducted you into his phratry yet?

Heracles: Not me he hasn't, and that's always made me
wonder.

> Aristophanes, *Birds*, in *Aristophanes*, ed. and trans.
> Jeffrey Henderson (Loeb Classical Library, 2000), vol. 3,
> pp. 237–244 (1646–1670)

And two years after Lysicrates, in the year of Antidotus, owing
to the large number of the citizens an enactment was passed on

the proposal of Pericles confining citizenship to persons of citizen birth on both sides.

Aristotle, *The Athenian Constitution*, trans. H. Rackham,
in *Aristotle* (Loeb Classical Library, 1984), vol. 20, p. 79
(XXVI, 4)

ATHENS, EARLY 414. Aristophanes entered a new comedy in the Great Dionysia contest. The subject was quite remote from current local preoccupations, at least on the surface. The heroes, two Athenians, Peisetaerus and Euelpides, have decided to leave a city-state where they find life impossible because of their compatriots' absurd behavior. They have taken refuge in the forest and have made contact with the Bird people, with the hope that their leader Hoopoe will let them settle in some peaceful spot. After getting beyond their initial deep suspicion of these members of a hated race, the Birds not only adopt them but take them on as advisors and leaders. They then decide together to go off and found an ideal city-state, Cloudcuckooland. But they soon have to defend themselves against various threats to their community: a half-starved poet, someone who tells oracles, someone who sells decrees, and even the gods themselves, jealous of this place where happiness reigns. A wall has to be built to hold them back, and the gods begin to starve to death in their redoubt. The play ends with the reception of a divine embassy that has come to negotiate: Poseidon, a clever negotiator who is determined not to be sidelined, Heracles, who thinks only about eating (Peisetaerus just happens to be preparing some delicious brochettes!), and a god of the Triballi—a Thracian people reputed for their savagery, the most barbaric of the barbarians—who is more or less idiotic and does not speak a word of Greek. In a delirious scene in which Peisetaerus keeps on raising the stakes (he has already obliged Zeus to hand over his scepter and his daughter), Poseidon decides to break off the talks when Heracles pleads, on the contrary, in favor of giving up, because he is so hungry. Poseidon in effect tells him he's crazy, "it's you yourself you are ruining"; by giving up, according to Poseidon, Heracles will be selling off his own inheritance on the cheap. Zeus is indeed his father, and Heracles will inherit all Zeus's property when Zeus dies! For Immortals, talking this way is obviously absurd, but Peisetaerus takes a different tack: pulling Heracles aside, he whispers to

90

him that Poseidon is talking through his hat: by virtue of the existing laws, Heracles has no rights to anything, because "you're a bastard, you're not heir." A bastard, Heracles? But by virtue of what law? Knowing Aristophanes, we can guess that he is seeking to make his fellow citizens laugh about a situation they know well, and that what he locates in the world of gods and heroes is actually an Athenian reality that he is denouncing.

But first, what is a bastard? The word is no longer used much in our societies, owing to its profoundly pejorative character: a bastard is a child conceived outside of marriage (Christian societies would come to specify "a child of sin"), an illegitimate child. This was the term for a child a master had with a slave, with a concubine, with a prostitute, without consequences for anyone but the child, who, in Athens, following a law introduced by Solon and recalled by Aristophanes, was excluded from the paternal legacy. But "bastard" was also the term for a child a free woman had outside of marriage, an object of shame for herself and her family—which could thus get rid of the child, and, depending on circumstances, of the mother as well. Not that the Greeks attributed capital importance to women's virginity, or even to their fidelity, but irregular birth introduced into the family an individual of undetermined origin who thus needed to be excluded by any means available.

This notion of bastard, which is present in most societies, was enriched in Athens by a supplementary dimension starting in the mid-fifth century. In 451, Pericles put through a law that defined as citizens only males born of a legitimate marriage between a male citizen and a female citizen (the latter being a legitimate daughter of citizens). By this token, every child born of a marriage, even a legitimate one, between an Athenian and a foreign woman became a bastard. Alongside bastards born outside of marriage, *nothoi,* Athens thus had a second category of bastards, children of foreign mothers, *metroxenoi.*

On close examination, Heracles turns out to fall into both categories. The product of a love affair between Zeus and Alcmene, he was born outside of marriage (like all Zeus's children except for Hephaestus, born to Hera, and even here Zeus's paternity is doubtful), and born to a foreign woman, in this instance a mortal, a foreigner to the world of the gods. This is why Zeus's son is not a god himself, but simply a hero. As for his father's inheritance, Heracles must not count on it, if the laws of Athens are to be applied. The idea of applying an Athenian law on succession to the immortal gods must indeed have made the spectators laugh—even as it reminded them of an Athenian specificity of which they were proud.

A contemporary citizen may be astonished at Athenian "avarice" (Philippe Gauthier's word) where citizenship rights were concerned, when the city-state saw itself as a model of democracy.[1] For us today, democracy is coupled with generosity, even if the realities are not always in alignment. The evolution of our societies has also integrated illegitimate children (called "natural" children, in France, out of a linguistic prudishness that would have us imagine that they are something like an unexpected gift from Mother Nature, unless it is meant to suggest that other children are fruits of artifice!) and has suppressed the very notion of bastardy by various means, at least on the legal level. The fact that Periclean Athens limited citizenship, excluding children and young people already born, in short that it manifested extreme protectiveness toward access to civic rights, is something that may be surprising and calls for an explanation.

To this end, we need to go backward a bit in time, back to the end of the sixth century, when Cleisthenes was restructuring the internal organization of the city-state in a fundamental way. We are told that a number of foreigners who were living in Athens received citizenship on this occasion: they were inscribed in the demes and in the phratries. Moreover, according to Aristotle, it was in order to mask the origin of these new citizens that Cleisthenes decided that each Athenian would henceforth be designated by his own name and that of his deme, excluding the name of his father. No sign of belonging to a lineage would betray an individual's (sometimes foreign) origins. This indication, whose real importance we cannot measure, proves in any case that the isonomic city-state created by Cleisthenes tended to be welcoming to outsiders.

It is also true that an aristocratic tradition led sons of prominent families to marry outside the city-state. Cleisthenes himself was a descendant of the tyrant Cleisthenes of Sicyon, on his mother's side. During the first half of the fifth century, a number of Athenian political leaders—for example, Miltiades, Themistocles, and Cimon—also married foreigners. These were legitimate marriages, needless to say, and the children of these marriages had the customary rights of legitimate children. A father's citizenship was transmitted unproblematically to a son, and a daughter could marry an Athenian with complete legitimacy, if her father did not decide to use her for a more profitable matrimonial alliance outside of Athens.

The matrimonial politics of the Athenian aristocrats probably had few effects on the demographic level. In contrast, there must have been a good number of new citizens born of marriages between an Athenian, male or female, and a foreigner living in the city-state during the first half of the fifth century. It is impossible to estimate the population growth in numerical terms, and even less possible to say what that growth owed to mixed marriages. But it is conceivable that the civic population of Athens, that is, the population of free males over age twenty who enjoyed civic rights, could have doubled between Cleisthenes' era and the middle of the century, increasing, roughly speaking, from twenty thousand to forty thousand. The exact figures are not important, but a doubling in size still represents a nontrivial change. When it was time to give out free wheat, or silver, each share would have been reduced by half!

In addition, and in my view this is at least as significant a factor, this whole period was accompanied by an upheaval in the distribution of the population across the territory. Let us recall that Cleisthenes had set up tribes in relation to individuals' places of residence at the time (Chapter 7). Everyone thus had a spot on the registers of the phratry and the deme of his place of residence. Now, in the wake of the wars, but probably also owing to marriages, changes of occupation, or economic or familial needs, citizens often changed their place of residence. To be sure, the tie with their place of origin was not broken, because succeeding generations continued to be enrolled on the same registers. But the ties were weakened. Moreover, new citizens, born of marriages to foreign women or men, were enrolled, although we do not always know who they were. Were there also fraudulent enrollments, as have been noted in the fourth century? Perhaps, but we have virtually no information on this point.

Rightly or wrongly (but in this area, the way individuals felt about a situation is more significant than the reality of the phenomena being denounced), many Athenians must have had the impression that the city-state was growing disproportionately by absorbing foreigners whose origin was obscure. They were leaving behind a "face-to-face" society in which everyone knew everyone else and in which children grew up under the watchful eye of the whole community. When a son was born, his father went to show him off to the other members of his phratry, who could then attest to his legitimacy and his identity. They watched the boy grow up until he himself was inscribed in the phratry at age sixteen. When the young man married, he invited the members of his phratry and offered them a banquet; here again, he took care to have the necessary witnesses to prove who he was. For in case of a challenge, there could be no proofs but the testimony of others, those closest to the concerned party—that is, those with whom he shared membership in the same civic structures.

But the situation was modified by the displacement of families and the inscription in rural demes of new citizens who actually lived in Athens. To be sure, the father would go to his deme to present his newborn son, but who could prove that it was the same son who came years later to make the offering of his first beard and ask to be inscribed in the phratry? The old native-born Athenians were lost as they were confronted by so many new citizens whose origins were unknown to them, people whose families they did not know and whose family tombs they had never seen.

At a time when democracy was becoming more generous for those who had rights, pressure from at least some members of the public, especially from the poorest citizens, must have been insistent. The political situation in Athens had evolved considerably since the end of the Greco-Persian Wars. The establishment of the Delian League in 478 had provided Athenians with important revenues, for the military alliance was quickly transformed into a hegemonic empire; those city-states that thought they could leave the alliance, such as Naxos or Thasos, found this out the hard way. Some impoverished individuals profited from the situation, such as oarsmen or cleruchs—soldiers who were allotted parcels of land in certain of the Aegean Islands (Lemnos, Imbros, Skyros, Chalcis of Euboea). Politically, the change took longer, for Cimon, master of Athenian political life, seems not to have made up his mind to make new rights available to the poorest citizens. However, in 462, profiting from Cimon's absence and from a group of well-to-do citizens serving under his command as hoplites in Messenia, a certain Ephialtes—about whom we know nothing else—succeeded in getting powers formerly held by the Areopagos Council transferred to the people. Now, the Areopagos Council included only members of the wealthiest classes, because it was constituted by the archontes who had completed their service, that is, Athenians who belonged to the two highest census classes. These new rights gave primary control over the magistrates to the Council of the Five Hundred, to the popular assembly, or to the tribunal of the Heliaia, formed by a daily lottery of citizens taken from the ten tribes. Ephialtes' reform marginalized a consummately aristocratic institution and charged the population with executing the policies that it adopted during the assemblies. The power thus transferred was considerable.

In addition, starting in 457 the archontes were also drawn by lot from among the Zeugitae, the third census class; this broadened the base for recruitment. Finally, and this is perhaps the essential factor, Pericles, who began to play a leading role after Cimon's ostracism in 461, had daily indemnities paid to certain citizens who carried out specific tasks: judges serving on the Heliaia tribunal, and councilors *(bouleutai)*. Contrary to the claims of the ancient tradition, which was very hostile to such "salaries" *(misthoi)*, it was not a matter of paying citizens to carry out their duties, but a matter of compensating those who were drawn by lot (with very rare exceptions, those selected did not have the right to refuse) and who would thus lose one or more days of work to community service. These indemnities were rather small, less than an artisan's daily earnings, but they may have been a way of ensuring a minimum income for the poorest citizens. Should we believe Aristophanes when he shows, in *Wasps,* the old Philocleon ("Who loves Cleon") waiting before dawn for the lottery that will determine his income for the day, and then putting the power that is granted him to tyrannical use? The fact that Aristophanes was a committed adversary of Periclean democracy ought to put us on guard against the accuracy of his testimony, which is a burlesque and even grotesque accusation designed to amuse, not to testify in the eyes of history.

In addition, the citizens had the right to various distributions: public banquets after sacrifices (which for many constituted a rare opportunity to eat meat), distribution of free or inexpensive wheat, allocation of unexpected windfalls from the city-state (booty, or the products of mines). Had it become obvious that the number of citizens had recently grown out of all proportion? Was there more-insistent pressure from citizens belonging to the old families? Were there other underlying causes that escape us? In any case, Pericles proposed a new law, adopted in 451–450, that limited access to Athenian citizenship to male children born of a legitimate marriage between two Athenian citizens (the wife being the legitimate daughter of a male Athenian citizen). And the opportunity to apply this law arose very quickly, in the form of a large-scale cleansing of the civic lists.

According to Plutarch, as a way of thanking its ally Athens for its help in its revolt against the Persians, in 445–444 the Egyptian Psammetichos dynasty sent a ship loaded with wheat to be distributed among Athenian citizens. Plutarch describes a lively free-for-all:

And so when the king of Egypt sent a present to the people of forty thousand measures of grain, and this had to be divided up among the citizens, there was a great crop of prosecutions against citizens of illegal birth by the laws of Pericles, who had up to that time escaped notice and been overlooked, and many of them also suffered at the hands of informers. As a result, a little less than five thousand were convicted and sold into slavery, and those who retained their citizenship and were adjudged to be Athenians were found, as a result of this scrutiny, to be fourteen thousand and forty in number.[2]

Thus the law had an immediate retroactive effect. A great many people who had enjoyed the rights of citizenship lost them and were then sold into slavery for having usurped citizenship, if we are to believe Plutarch; young people who, born to a foreign mother, could have hoped to be enrolled on the civic lists, became bastards *(metroxenoi)* from one day to the next, like Heracles. Well before Pericles' law, Themistocles, who was born to a foreign mother, had succeeded in convincing *nothoi* like himself to meet in the Kynosarges gymnasium, which was located outside the walls of Athens and devoted to Heracles; this is evidence that bastardy had not constituted a handicap and that many people had been able to claim it without fearing for their civic status. Under Pericles' law, the bastards continued to meet at Kynosarges, but this was henceforth the sign of their exclusion from the city-state.

According to Plutarch, as we have seen, the number of citizens abruptly dropped to 14,040, which seems to be very few.[3] But if five thousand people really were excluded, this means that more than a quarter of the citizenry of Athens was suddenly written out of the civic lists. That is a considerable proportion. When we remember that Athens needed five hundred bouleutai a year, and if we estimate that the career of a citizen lasted on average forty years, from age twenty to age sixty, during that period twenty thousand bouleutai had to be recruited, which means that every citizen had the possibility of becoming a *bouleutes* at least once, and for many there could have been a second opportunity (possible only after a ten-year interval). Similarly, the judges of the Heliaia tribunal numbered 501, 1,001, or even 1,501, for every day the tribunal met, which means that every Athenian must have been chosen by lot several times a year. Participatory democracy was becoming a reality, not a remote theory!

The rule did not prevent the citizenry of Athens from growing; on the eve of the Peloponnesian War there are said to have been forty thousand citizens, perhaps even sixty thousand, according to some scholars. Yet by the end of the war this figure had been reduced by half. Taking wartime losses into account, the figure must have been much lower. In fact, during the war, the application of the law of 451 was suspended, in order to allow the civic body to be reconstituted, on an initiative of Pericles himself, it seems, thus quite soon after the beginning of the war, and it was not promulgated again until 403.

Thanks to the surviving speeches of Attic orators, we know that controlling access to citizenship continued to preoccupy Athenians. A number of cases were brought to trial throughout the fourth century with the purpose of excluding individuals deemed suspect. Holding citizenship was advantageous, because in addition to the indemnities for judges and bouleutai there was now another for those who participated in the people's assembly. At the same time, though, foreign residents sought the privilege for different reasons: these were often well-to-do individuals who were not chasing after indemnities (misthoi) but who wanted to participate in public life, acquire land and a house, or have free access to the tribunals in case of a dispute with a native Athenian.

Yet Athens remained strangely possessive regarding its citizenship. Even the metics who had actively fought at the end of the Peloponnesian War (432–404) to help restore democracy received only limited rights (the right to own property, the right to pay the same taxes), and until the Hellenistic period citizenship was granted rarely. We know of a few exceptions (such as the bankers Pasion and Phormio: Chapter 16). But it was only starting in the third century and especially in the second that the city-states—and Athens did not stand out in this regard—began to grant citizenship more generously. Not, as has sometimes been said, because citizenship had henceforth lost all real content, but because it was granted above all to foreign benefactors who made no practical use of it because they lived elsewhere. Now, Greek citizenship could not be virtual; it had meaning only for those who actually resided in the city-state that had granted it. Hence the reticence of city-states to attribute it to entire groups that actually lived within their territory, as the Alexandrians consistently refused to grant it to the Jews who had been their fellow citizens for three centuries. This happened only in cases of extreme necessity: thus in 133 the city of Pergamon granted citizenship to all noncitizens on its territory to help in the struggle against Aristonicus, the Attalid pretender who rejected the decision by Attalos III to bequeath the kingdom to Rome. Another case in which an entire group was added to the civic register came up in Miletus, which granted across-the-board citizenship between 234 and 228 to Cretan mercenaries whom it had been employing for some time. Here again, the city-state faced threats and was short on citizens; reinforcing the civic body was thus an urgent task.

As we can see, the city-states remained protective of the privilege of citizenship. Thus Pericles' law may have pushed the rules for transmission of citizenship to an extreme, but it was not as isolated a measure as it might have appeared. And the city-state was able to relax the rules when necessary. According to tradition, Pericles himself was a victim of the law he had originated. Finding himself without an heir after the death of his legitimate sons, he had to ask the people, as a favor, to legitimize the sons he had had with his concubine, Aspasia, so he would not die without heirs.

CHAPTER ELEVEN

Hippolytus's Prayer to Zeus,
or Women in the City-State

Hippolytus: O Zeus, why have you settled women, this bane to
cheat mankind, in the light of the sun? If you wished to
propagate the human race, it was not from women that you
should have provided this. Rather, men should put down in
the temples either bronze or iron or a mass of gold and buy
offspring, each for a price appropriate to his means, and
then dwell in houses free from the female sex . . . The clear
proof that woman is a great bane is this: her father, who
begot and raised her, sends her off by settling a dowry on her
in order to rid himself of trouble. But her husband, who has
taken this creature of ruin into his house, takes pleasure in
adding finery to the statue, lovely finery to worthless statue,
destroying by degrees the wealth of his house . . .

   That man has it easiest whose wife is a nothing—although
a woman who sits in the house in her folly causes harm. But
a clever woman—that I loathe! May there never be in my
house a woman with more intelligence than befits a woman!
For Cypris engenders more mischief in the clever ones. The
woman without ability is kept from indiscretion by the
slenderness of her wit.

   One ought to let no slave have access to a wife. Rather one
should give them as companions wild and brute beasts so
that they would be unable either to speak to anyone or to be
spoken to in return.

   Euripides, *Hippolytus*, in *Euripides*, trans. David Kovacs (Loeb
   Classical Library, 1995), vol. 2, pp. 185–187 (616–648)

ATHENS, 428 B.C.E., Dionysia contests. Euripides entered a tragedy
titled *Hippolytus*, which won first prize. This was actually his
second play on the subject, for the first was badly received; it
painted too dark a picture of the heroine, Phaedra. This is one source,
among others, of Euripides' reputation as a misogynist.

The excerpt from the second version chosen here hardly pleads to the contrary, for Hippolytus poses with brutality a question inspired by his mother-in-law's amorous passion: how can one do without women? But let us not yield to the illusion. Hippolytus's complaint is not a rejection of women, but of a particular woman: prey to Phaedra's incestuous desires, he unburdens himself to Zeus about his torment and, in his pain, ends up regretting the existence of the entire species. If there were no women, there would be no Phaedra.

Hippolytus's prayer, even read in its particular context, takes to the extreme a question raised by the Greeks: what place should women hold in the city-state? On this subject, about which the ancient sources offer contradictory testimony, historians over a long period of time have chosen clear-cut and opposing positions. Some, invoking Demosthenes, the authors of tragedies, or Pericles' *Funeral Oration,* have seen the classical Greek woman as one example among others of the Mediterranean—or even the "Oriental"—woman hidden away in her home (the mythical gyneceum), seeing no one but her (female) servants, her husband, and some members of her immediate family, going out only for serious or imperative reasons, such as to attend one of the religious festivals specific to women. This is wrong, other scholars have replied, sometimes invoking the same authors but citing different passages: Greek women were free women who participated in economic life; consider Aspasia, Pericles' partner, they have said, and Diotima, whom Plato puts on stage in *The Symposium,* not to mention all the women who sold products in marketplaces to earn their living. To be sure, there has been general agreement as to women's ineligibility to participate in political and legal matters, but concerning all other matters there have in fact been two opposing visions of Greek women.

This debate reached a peak during the years 1930–1960, that is, at a time when feminism was gaining strength in the West. Conservatives saw the retiring role of Greek women as the condition for healthy management of society as a whole; progressives found it inconceivable that a democratic society could have confined its women to a subaltern state. As is often the case, the debate over a problem of ancient history was inflected by the burning issues of the day and by the participants' own convictions: it has always been hard to separate the study of social questions from our personal concerns.

Have we a clearer vision of these matters today, and can we choose between such divergent views? Studies carried out by many historians, male and female, over the last thirty years have shifted the ground of the debate and seem, above all, to have at once reduced the underlying passion (it is no longer necessary to invoke Athens in order to defend women's rights) and changed the perspectives on the issue. First, because no one today would dare speak of Greek women "in general": the documentation does not allow this. We know nothing at all about the legal status of women in most of the city-states, and what we do know about women in a few city-states does not authorize any degree of extrapolation: the rights of Gortynian women in Crete in the sixth century have little to do with those of Athenian women in Pericles' day, and it would be very presumptuous to establish a parallel between the roles of Spartan women in the fourth century and Ephesian women in the imperial era. Not only did conditions evolve over time (Chapter 30), they differed from one city-state to the next. Euripides' text invites us to turn toward fifth-century Athens, so it is here that we shall begin, although it may be necessary to introduce comparisons, nuances, and divergences later on.

It seems to me that we have to take into account a variety of levels—social, legal, political, and mythical—to examine the place of women in a given city-state. Taking these angles of approach in combination will probably allow us to see a little more clearly. But first of all, let us specify which women we are talking about. We are concerned neither with slave women nor with foreign women (metics), who were slaves and metics before they were women. When we speak of Athenian women, we are referring to free women, daughters and spouses of citizens, the only women who would have had the right to call themselves "Athenian" had such a designation existed.

We have already looked at the debates that stirred up the historians, Anglo-Saxon historians in particular, in the first half of the twentieth century. All the texts they cited in support of their theses have to be taken into consideration, but they have to be examined in context, and it is important not to confuse ideals with realities. The discourse about women remains exclusively a man's discourse: the pictures that authors paint of the social status of Athenian women reflect above all, positively or negatively, their own ideal of the feminine status. The ideal for a woman in a well-to-do milieu consisted in not overly exposing herself in public. But please, let us dismiss once and for all the idea of the gyneceum as a place of seclusion for women. No one has ever been able to offer archaeological evidence that a separation existed within the home between women's rooms and the others. To be sure, wealthy households had reception rooms and private rooms, but there are no signs that women were confined to one part of the house. In contrast, the ideal remained that "honest" women should show themselves as little as possible in public and, when they had to go out, should do so with their heads covered and in the company of a female servant. This ideal of discretion even meant that women's names should not be known outside the family: for Demosthenes, honest women were the ones whose names one did not know. It is quite remarkable that in the entire corpus of Demosthenes' speeches (or speeches attributed to him), we find the names of more than five hundred men and only twenty-seven women—and of these, fourteen were prostitutes!

But this ideal of discretion could hardly be attained by all. Women in modest circumstances often worked alongside their husbands, whether helping in the fields or selling in the agora. We know something about the orator Aeschines' mother, who sold fruits and vegetables; this earned her mockery from Demosthenes, who was quick to use anything at hand against his adversaries. But in a speech for the defense that has come down to us under Demosthenes' name ("Against Eubulides"), a speech delivered during a citizenship trial, the orator ardently defended his client's mother, a widow, explaining that necessity alone had made her hire herself out as a wet nurse before she became a ribbon seller; but out of respect for her, the orator avoided citing her by name (Nikarete) as much as possible, using her name only in the concluding sentences, whereas she had been in question from the start. Thus we see how the ideal of reserve was imposed and how, in the case of a woman who showed herself in public, the orator would draw from this fact, according to the needs of his cause, either proof of her degradation or on the contrary proof of her courage in adversity. I find it hard to believe that this testimony can be taken as proof that Athenian women benefited from a favorable social status giving them a certain freedom of action. Even Aspasia must not be allowed to mislead us: as a foreigner (from Miletus), the mistress of a citizen, and perhaps a former prostitute and madam, she did not represent an ordinary Athenian woman in any way, and at all events she lived unconventionally.

The discretion that men wanted women to manifest did not completely deprive the latter of any role in private life, however. In his *Oeconomicus*, Xenophon entrusts to the wife of Ischomachos, the model landowner

102

whom he casts as his hero, a primordial role in managing the household. Keeper of the hearth and manager of the food supply, she has absolute control over the organization of the servants' work. A little earlier, Aristophanes translated a similar situation in his burlesque manner as an opportunity for women to give themselves over to their two real passions, drinking and sex. Even when Aristophanes seems to count on women to make men give up their follies—such as the Peloponnesian War—he cannot keep from turning their own enterprise into a fiasco. When the women decide to go on strike against sex in order to force men to make peace, they themselves are the first to give in. When, in imitation of the men, they meet in an assembly to decide what punishment to impose on Euripides, who is guilty of revealing their depravity over and over in his plays, they cannot keep from devising measures that would let them "tipple" as much as they like and win them the support of young men:

> If anyone . . . is a mistress' go-between slave who
> spills the beans on the master, or when sent on a
> mission brings back false messages; or is a lover who
> deceives a woman with lies or reneges on promised
> gifts; or is an old woman who gives gifts to a young
> lover, or is a courtesan who takes gifts from her
> boyfriend while cheating on him; or is a barman or
> barmaid who sells short pints or liters: put a curse on
> every such person, that they perish wretchedly and
> their families along with them![1]

Women clearly belonged to the private sphere, while men divided their time between the private and the public spheres. This is the source of their differing legal and political status. Legally, Athenian women remained eternal minors: throughout their lives, they passed from one guardianship to another, from one master (kyrios) to another, from father to husband, possibly from one husband to another, from husband to brother or son in the case of widowhood or divorce. Marriage obliged women to pass from one household to another without having a say in the matter; in any case, marriage was a private act, a contract between two families to which the spouses could do nothing but consent. This does not mean that fathers never consulted their sons or daughters, but nothing obliged them to do so.

Because she was legally a minor, a woman had no power in the legal sphere. She could be present in that sphere only through the intermediary of her kyrios: he received compensation if she had been harmed, and he delivered punishment if she were found guilty. Let us not conclude from this that women represented mere property belonging to the master, as slaves did, for women's independent existence was legally acknowledged in certain respects. A woman married off by her father received a dowry that her husband had to return in case of divorce; that dowry belonged to her as her share in the inheritance, because she could not claim a share in it otherwise.

The ineligibility of Athenian women to inherit paternal property obliged the city-state to create an institution that has often been misunderstood, one designed to ensure the transmission of property when the only heirs of the deceased were female: the epiclerate. A woman who was her father's only direct heir was called an *epikleros*. The goal, for the city-state as for the family, was to ensure that ownership of the property remained in the paternal line. Now, by definition, a daughter, married or engaged to be married, had to leave the paternal household for another *oikos*. It was thus appropriate to offer the epikleros in marriage to a member of the paternal line so that she could produce the male heir that was lacking. She was thus offered in turn, in a predetermined order, to her paternal uncles and their sons. The one who accepted could break off a previous marriage for this reason, just as the girl's marriage would be broken off if she were already married to someone outside the paternal oikos. No man was obliged to marry an epikleros (the practice was not equivalent to the Hebrews' levirate marriage), and this probably was not a concern unless the prospective marriage entailed a legacy of some importance. But in cases where a previous marriage was dissolved, it was the duty of the happy spouse of a wealthy epikleros to find a new husband for his previous wife; this would often be a close relative or a friend.

Eligible to transmit family property but not to profit from it herself: this, then, was the fate of the Athenian woman. And the same was true of political rights, starting with Pericles' famous 451 law on citizenship (Chapter 10). For a long time, citizenship had been transmitted through one of the two parents; in practice, this meant the father, because by definition an Athenian woman who married a foreigner had to go off and live under his roof, abroad. A number of prominent politicians in Athens in the first half of the fifth century were sons of foreigners: Cleisthenes (son of the Megarian Agaristes), Cimon, Themistocles, and many others.

But Pericles' law suddenly limited the possibility of gaining citizenship exclusively to children born of a legal marriage between a male Athenian citizen and a female Athenian "citizen." The term for female citizen existed in Greek *(politis)*, but it did not possess the same political and legal content as the masculine term. A female citizen was only the legitimate daughter of a male citizen and a female Athenian who was herself the legitimate daughter of a male citizen and a female Athenian, and so on. The woman gained nothing in terms of rights, but, excluded from all political rights (the first comic thrust of Aristophanes' *Assemblywomen* was the association between the two nouns of the title), she became indispensable to the transmission of citizenship. Whereas women elsewhere were content to produce children, women in Athens gave birth to citizens! Yet Athens seems to have offered women fewer rights than certain other city-states, such as Crete or Sparta, where women had access to a share in the inheritance and they owned their own property—not to mention that, in the case of Spartan women, they enjoyed a liberty bordering on license. The situation of Athenian women was thus paradoxical; it required an appropriate treatment that only myth and imagination could supply.

In his prayer to Zeus, Hippolytus reduces women from the outset to a biological role from which none of them can escape: making babies. In this realm alone, they are irreplaceable. And yet the Greeks singularly reduced even this role, as if, in this realm as in all others, the only goal were to exclude the women of Athens. In fact, the Greeks still did not know with any precision how the mechanisms of procreation worked. Let us consider the birth of the first Athenian, Erichthonius (who took the name Erechtheus when he became king). Hephaestus, consumed with love for Athena, pursued the goddess in vain; she barely escaped his grasp. But the god's desire was so strong that his sperm burst forth and sullied the goddess's leg. Ge (Gaia), Mother Earth, thus received the god's seed and from this the first Athenian was born, of the soil of Attica, autochthonous in the most literal sense. But let there be no mistake about it: Erichthonius was not the fruit of the loves of Hephaestus and Ge. The latter was only a womb, a receptacle, an incubator, as one prefers: the god's sperm alone engendered. In reality, ancient Greek scholars hesitated a long time before abandoning the belief that children were conceived from a mix of masculine and feminine sperm. Aristotle showed that the notion of feminine sperm was a false trail, an incorrect interpretation of vaginal secretions that played no role at all in impregnation. While he was right on this point, he nevertheless simultaneously introduced the false idea that male sperm alone produced children.

Indispensable for birth, women still found themselves excluded from this most indisputable of functions. Thus the first Athenian was born without a mother: women were set aside from the outset. What is more, the child in the myth, taken in by Athena, was thus reared by a goddess who had been born without a mother, because she emerged fully armed from the thigh (or skull) of her father, Zeus, after the latter had swallowed her mother, Metis. The choice of Athena as tutelary divinity for Athens entailed paying homage, not to a woman, still less to a mother, but to a virgin. How could this have failed to influence the myths of the city-state?

A myth remains a myth, that is, a story invented to provide an explanation for the world, and we may wonder about its real impact on Athenian daily life. It seems nontrivial to me, for the negation of the biological role of women was echoed over and over in fifth- and fourth-century Athenian speeches, often in an indirect way. Pericles, for example, pronouncing the funeral oration for citizens who died during the first year of the Peloponnesian War (431), expressed pity for fathers who had lost sons and encouraged them to give other sons to the city-state: not a word for the grief of mothers, as if they did not even exist (it is true that they were absent from the official ceremony). Demosthenes, for his part, declared that every man had two parents, his father and his city-state! And there was the way individuals were named: So-and-So, son of Such-and-Such, from a given deme; the mother's name was never mentioned. Countless occasions of daily life provided reasons to exclude women, to forget them, to erase them from the landscape.

Still, we must not extrapolate from the situation of women in classical Athens. Nowhere in the ancient world were women equal to men, of course, but there were nuances across both space and time. We shall look later on at the role played by a wealthy woman in Asia Minor in the second century B.C.E. (Chapter 30), but even if we remain within the classical era, the differences between Athens and Sparta are striking. Differences in education, in social status, in economic role. To be sure, in Sparta, too, women were wombs first and foremost. The only people who had the right to epitaphs were warriors killed in combat and women who died in child-birth: the parallel speaks for itself. The city-state took seriously the need to prepare women for these "combats" in which many probably succumbed, through an education that other Greeks mocked: with skirts split high up, these "thigh-revealers" in fact received athletic training and did not hesitate to appear naked in public.

> But even to the women Lycurgus paid all possible attention. He made the maidens exercise their bodies in running, wrestling, casting the discus, and hurling the javelin, in order that the fruit of their wombs might have vigorous root in vigorous bodies and come to better maturity, and that they themselves might come with vigour to the fullness of their times, and struggle successfully and easily with the pangs of child-birth. He freed them from softness and delicacy and all effeminacy by accustoming the maidens no less than the youths to wear tunics only in processions, and at certain festivals to dance and sing when the young men were present as spectators . . . Nor was there anything disgraceful in this scant clothing of the maidens, for modesty attended them, and wantonness was banished; nay, rather, it produced in them habits of simplicity and an ardent desire for health and beauty of body. It gave also to woman-kind a taste of lofty sentiment, for they felt that they too had a place in the arena of bravery and ambition.[2]

In addition, the eugenicist concerns of the Spartan authorities introduced possibilities of sexual exchange that surprised other Greeks: any husband could ask another man whom he admired for his moral or physical qualities to make his wife pregnant so as to have the most beautiful possible children. The notion of adultery lost all meaning. Beyond this, the militantism required of Spartan citizens at all times and the taboos placed on the acquisition of wealth led women to manage the family properties and to hold in their own names what their husbands could not officially possess. Thus Spartan women owned carriages that raced at Olympia or Delphi. The luxury of the houses discovered by Theban soldiers during the first invasion of Laconia by foreign troops in 370–369 stunned the invaders. During that same period, as it happens, both Aristotle and Plutarch confirm that Spartan women held a considerable part of the country's wealth: two-fifths, according to Aristotle.

Without going into greater detail, we can see that the situation varied from one city-state to another, and that any extrapolation would be dangerous. With the terms of the discussion carefully circumscribed, it becomes clear that the image of an eternal and universal Greek woman does not correspond to any tangible reality. Even in the heart of a given city-state, at a particular period in time, it is appropriate to take the milieu into account and especially to distinguish between what arises from masculine fantasies and what really constituted the lived reality of the women in question. Most critically, we shall probably never be able to hear what the women of Athens and elsewhere had to say on the subject themselves.

CHAPTER TWELVE

The Story of a Broken Sigma,
or Athenian Imperialism

As for the council's oath, let the secretary of the council and of the people inscribe the following as well: if someone mints silver money in the city-states or does not use the money of the Athenians, or their weights or their measures, but rather foreign coins, weights, or measures, that he shall be prosecuted for high treason [*eisangelia*] before the council, in conformity with our decree, the one that Clearchos has proposed.

Translated from the text established by E. Erxleben,
Archiv für Papyrusforschung 19 (1969): 136–137, §8

ATHENS, AROUND 450 or 420. This brief excerpt from an Athenian decree sums up the overall meaning of the text fairly well: Athens had voted to forbid the use of coins, weights, or measures other than its own in all the allied city-states (the ones that for convenience we call the Delian League). Various arrangements were made for the Athenian magistrates to withdraw all non-Athenian coins in circulation and carry out an exchange that procured a nontrivial benefit to Athens. This was an imperialist measure of unusual violence; it gives us a good sense of how far Athens had extended its dominion over states that it officially called its allies but that were designated by many as its subjects. The content and import of the measure leave little room for doubt, but the text poses one daunting problem: its date. For the very nature of Athenian imperialism changes, depending on the date retained. If the text dates from 427–424, that is, from the first phase of the Peloponnesian War, it can be seen simply as an emergency measure to fill the city-state's treasury and to force the allies to contribute to the war effort. But if the date is pushed back toward the middle of the fifth century, it has to be acknowledged that Athenian imperialism was not the consequence of a state of war but the initial goal

109

of Athenian policy. Now, this text has been vigorously debated for a long time, with each participant contributing philological, historical, ideological, and above all epigraphical arguments. The story is worth telling.

This Athenian decree has the peculiarity of being known through several fragments, none of which comes from Athens itself. The beginning is not complete, but the places where the various fragments overlap suffice to establish a definite and consistent meaning. The dispersal of copies of the decree proves at least that it was widely distributed and posted in the city-states that belonged to the Delian League. Indeed, it has been found on Cos, the big island located south of the coast of Asia Minor, on Syme, a very small island near Cos and Rhodes, in Siphnos, at the center of the Cyclades, and in Aphytis, located in Chalkidike on the Pallene Peninsula; in addition, a fragment lost today was recopied in Smyrna (Izmir), and one more fragment is in a museum in Odessa. This last was thought to have come from some Greek city-state on the banks of the Black Sea, but it is much more probable that it originated on an Aegean island and was brought to Odessa by a ship in the Russia imperial fleet, which frequently visited Aegean ports during the eighteenth and even early nineteenth centuries.

The text has lost its heading, which deprives us of any indication of the date through the mention of the eponymous archon, but its content seems to place it among the decisions of the imperialist type made by Athens when it was beginning to experience the first hardships of the Peloponnesian War. After a few years of a difficult war, which Athens had undertaken on its own, the city-state had exhausted its financial resources and undergone several reversals; it was time to call on its allies, who had had little direct involvement in the war. However, a vigorous polemic arose over the dating of our text, as with several others. The various surviving fragments found are all written in an Ionian script that cannot be dated with precision on the basis of the form of the letters, with one exception: the Cos copy is written in fine Attic script. We have enough texts originating from Athens to know with considerable accuracy how the form of the letters evolved; in principle, this ought to make a firm dating possible. However, the form of one letter posed an obstacle to the late dating (430–415) attributed by the early editors, who were not yet acquainted with the Cos text. In the Cos fragment, the sigma has only three branches; it is a broken line similar to the symbol for lightning, a form that disappeared in Athens around 445 at the latest. It seemed that the Attic script of the Cos text could be explained only if the text had been engraved in Athens itself, because Cos, a Dorian city-state, normally used a different script.

A polemic thus developed between those who maintained that a date at the beginning of the Peloponnesian War had to be excluded for paleographic reasons and those who, going beyond these considerations or challenging them, deemed that other arguments had to be taken into account. At first the latter group denied that the script had evolved everywhere at the same pace: might not the broken three-branched sigma have remained in use in Cos while it had disappeared from use in Athens? It was suggested that the text had been engraved in Cos by an Athenian who had left Athens before the 440s and did not know how the script had evolved there! The marble was then analyzed to see whether it came from Attica or not, for it was important to know whether the engraving had been done in Athens or in Cos. The best specialists in mineralogy were called upon, and they were decisive: the marble is not from the Athenian Pentelikon, but from the Cyclades, probably from Paros. Under these conditions, the likelihood that it was engraved in Cos rather than Athens increased. But why would an engraver, whether from Cos or from Athens, put a letter in a form that had fallen into disuse, when nothing in the rest of the text shows any particular attachment to archaic features? The very small number of fifth-century texts from outside of Athens made it impossible to settle the paleographic question with certainty. Other arguments thus had to be invoked.

One obvious approach was to try to see how and when the measure had been applied. If the Athenian decree had been in effect in other city-states, there ought to be evidence of an abrupt interruption in minting in the allied city-states on the date of its promulgation. Alas, this proved to be hard to verify. In reality, most city-states did not mint coins, or did so only irregularly, for minting was a costly enterprise, and it was better to use existing coinages, in particular those of Athens. For many city-states, especially small ones that did not have ready access to metal, the decree had no practical effect, because they were already applying its provisions. At the very most, the Athenian authorities were going to be able to go ahead and exchange other coins in circulation for their own. The application of the decree could thus be verified only for the small number of city-states that had actually minted their own coins continuously beyond the 450s. Yet there were practically no such city-states except for the big islands, Chios and Samos, the ones known as the naval allies, the rare members of the Delian League that were not subject to tribute because they contributed to the war effort with their own ships and troops. We are thus not certain that the measure proposed by Clearchos applied to them, especially because their coinages are hard to date and their classifications have often been problematic. Minting in Samos seems to have been interrupted around 440, but precisely in 440 a political revolution brought the adversaries of Athens to power; the intervention of the Athenian fleet brought the city-state back into the Delian League. While Athens did not drag its democratic allies back into the fold by force, it imposed heavy obligations on the new masters of Samos, including payment of the costs of the war: might not the interruption of minting be accounted for by this particular situation alone? Moreover, this dating is contested, and some scholars locate the beginning of one series of coins in 428 while others place it in 459. There remains the question of minting in Chios: this appears to constitute two series separated by an interval in which there was a single issue, in small quantity, of a stater made of electrum—a metal not targeted by Clearchos's decree (which involved only silver coins). Should this not have been seen as a reflection of the decision by Athens? Perhaps, but this single issue is dated only approximately in the middle of the fifth century; we cannot know whether this dating was determined on the basis of independent criteria or whether it must be attributed to the opinion that numismatists had already formed about the date of Clearchos's decree.

As we can see, the numismatic argument, which appeared at first glance to be the only disqualifier, turned out to be almost unusable. Scholars were then brought back to the starting point, the historical context, but they were unable to use it because doing so would have involved stereotypical circular reasoning: dating coin issues in relation to the presumed date of the decree, then dating the decree in relation to the dates of issue. Now, the weapon of common sense alone is the weakest available to historians. They had to try to find other arguments.

An English scholar, Harold B. Mattingly, went on the offensive very skillfully against early dating by pointing out two things. First, that the formulas used in the text were found repeatedly in decrees from the 420s, denoting a habit of writing proper to those years; he accumulated parallels, although his arguments were not truly convincing, for while the parallels established may not have been inexact, there were no points of comparison with earlier, midcentury decades, a period poor in official texts. Were these not formulas already in use in the years 450–440? Next, he noted that, in *Birds,* in 414, Aristophanes clearly alluded to Clearchos's decree: the decree-seller attempts to sell the following text: "The Cloud-cuckoolanders are to use the selfsame measures, weights, and decrees as the Black-and-Bluesians."[1] Why would the playwright have referred to a text a quarter of a century old, when he was always quick to comment on contemporary affairs? The argument was strong, but not conclusive. In fact, Mattingly's theses met with a good deal of hostility for reasons that were not all scientific. He could certainly be criticized for wanting to move all the decrees from the middle of the fifth century forward into the 420s as a group, including texts that seemed well established as dating from midcentury, such as the decree through which Athens imposed draconian surveillance conditions on Chalcis of Euboea following his revolt in 446. Above all, Mattingly was going against the grain of the prevailing opinion among historians of Athenian imperialism. In the 1960s and 1970s, at the high point of the third-world and antiimperialist movement in the West, it was being discovered that imperial violence in Athens was not a belated convulsion of a policy in the process of failing, but that it was in some sense consubstantial with the very origins of the Delian League. Scholars stressed the way Athens had prevented Naxos from leaving the alliance as early as 470, had done the same with Thasos five years later, and had severely punished both city-states for their abortive attempts; they also stressed the way Athens had gradually reduced the number of those who were called "naval allies," that is, those who had a fleet intended to support the Athenian fleet but capable on occasion of opposing it. The transfer of the Delian League's treasury to Athens in 454, even though it was justified by the Persian threats against the island of Apollo, was clearly part of this same strategy of domination, as was the fact that Athens alone set the amount of the tribute, and to its sole profit. Accountants noted that Athens spent far less than it collected from the allies—in the form of silver and various supplies—on collective defense. Moreover, Plutarch affirms that the grandiose program launched by Pericles in 450 for reconstructing the monuments of the Acropolis—burned down by the Persians in 480 and never rebuilt—was largely financed by the surpluses of the Delian League.

All arguments that pointed in this direction were thus welcomed. By placing Clearchos's decree in the early 440s, scholars were contributing an important piece to the construction: by delaying it to the 420s, they were weakening its impact, or rather, the decree could be seen to provide excuses for financing a war whose costs Athens had been bearing almost alone. Mattingly's theses thus went against the tide, even if they did not actually pose any fundamental challenge to the dominant thesis of Athenian imperialism that was developed at the very outset of the Delian League. But they did not succeed in convincing the scholarly community, and Clearchos's decree continued to vacillate between extreme dates, around 449 for some, a good quarter of a century later for others, with still others choosing a median date, though there was not the slightest argument to support this averaging approach. And then the polemic ran out of steam, and people lost interest.

Today the earlier date continues to have its partisans, but there is a barely perceptible slide back toward a later date. What is most striking is that the precise dating of Clearchos's decree no longer seems to be a scholarly priority, probably because everyone has understood the futility of making an effort without the discovery of a new, better-dated fragment. It also has to do with the fact that the ideological stakes have weakened, and that a certain consensus reigns as to the nature of Athenian imperialism. Several elements, in fact, attest to the authoritarian behavior of the Athenians as early as the years 470–450 (repression of the revolts in Naxos and Thasos, brutality toward the Chalkidians, massive settling of Athenian colonists in the cleruchies or on allies' territories), so that scholars are not searching for supplementary arguments. Even the shift of the Delian League treasury from Delos to Athens, in 454 or a little later, no longer looks like an imperialist measure; it may have been a mere precaution. In fact, the official name of the alliance alone suffices to display the nonegalitarian character of the association: "Athens and its allies." It was Athens that established the tribute to be given every four years during an Athenian festival, the Great Panathenaea, in honor of the tutelary goddess of Athens. The allies were associated with the festival in spite of themselves, for they had to give Athens, as a first installment, a sixtieth of the amount of their tribute. These payments are inscribed in long lists on Attic marble; the texts allow us to reconstitute the sum paid by each party and even to determine the allies' names. Under these conditions, it does not much matter whether Athens added one more imperialist measure as early as 459 or not until 425–420. Only the strength of the ideological confrontations among historians in the third quarter of the twentieth century gave the contrary impression.

CHAPTER THIRTEEN

Two Thousand Helots Gone!
or Slaves in the City-State

[The Lacedaemonians] made proclamation that all Helots who claimed to have rendered the Lacedaemonians the best service in war should be set apart, ostensibly to be set free. They were, in fact, merely testing them, thinking that those who claimed, each for himself, the first right to be set free would be precisely the men of high spirit who would be the most likely to attack their masters. About two thousand of them were selected and these put crowns on their heads and made the rounds of the temples as though they were already free, but the Spartans not long afterwards made away with them, and nobody ever knew in what way each one perished.

> Thucydides, *History of the Peloponnesian War*, trans.
> Charles Forster Smith (Loeb Classical Library, 1919),
> vol. 2, p. 351 (IV, 80, 3–4)

Thucydides reports in his *History of the Peloponnesian War* that helots, selected by the Spartans by virtue of their bravery, believed that they had been freed; they put crowns on their heads and walked around the temples of the gods, but soon afterward they all disappeared, more than two thousand men, and no one could say, either then or later, how they had perished. Aristotle even asserts that the ephors themselves, as soon as they took over their positions, declared war on the helots, so that the latter could be killed without sacrilege. In any case, they were treated harshly and cruelly: they were forced to drink great quantities of pure wine, then they were presented to the syssitias to show the young people what drunkenness looked like. They were forced to perform indecent and grotesque songs and dances, and they were forbidden to perform those of free men. It is also said that later on, during the Theban expedition to Laconia, the helots that had been taken prisoner were invited to sing the poems of Terpander, Alcman, and the Laconian Spendon but refused to do so, saying that their masters had forbidden it. That is why those who assert that in Lacedemonia the free man is freer than elsewhere, and the slave more enslaved, have truly understood the difference.

Plutarch, *Lycurgus*, in *Plutarch's Lives*, trans. Bernadotte Perrin
(Loeb Classical Library, 1914), vol. 1 (XXVIII, 6–11)

SPRING 424. The war between Athens and Sparta was bogging down. Neither side was managing to bring off a decisive victory. Rather than confronting each other directly, the adversaries multiplied diversionary actions. When the Athenians devastated the Peloponnesian coasts, the Spartans sent an expedition to Thrace to attack Athens's allies and penetrate the region that supplied Athens with both wood and income from the mines of Mt. Pangaeus. According to Thucydides' account, the Spartans seemed to be more afraid of a helot revolt than of enemy attacks. It is true that the city-state had undergone a real humiliation the year before. A Spartan contingent had found itself trapped by the Athenians on the island of Sphacteria, across from Pylos, on the west coast of Messenia; 294 Spartan citizens had been taken prisoner, despite efforts to help them, and 128 had been killed in the fighting. Helots in particular had risked their lives in an attempt to resupply them, swimming at night across a harbor guarded by the enemy fleet. In military terms, the episode was of little importance, but its psychological repercussions were enormous: Spartans had not only been killed in the war, which would have been glorious, but had been taken prisoner without fighting, which was shameful. Now, every time the city-state felt itself weakened, the fear of a helot revolt resurfaced. Such a revolt had already taken place in Messenia in 464, after an earthquake, and Sparta had had to call on Athens for help. A contingent led by Cimon had left Athens, but the Spartans ended up sending it back home for fear that the troops might side with the rebels. In reality, the Messenian rebels were not helots like the others; they were inhabitants of Messenia who had been reduced to the rank of helots after the conquest of their country by Sparta in the second half of the eighth century. Their demand for freedom was based on a tradition of independence that remained in the Messenians' collective memory. In any case, the unjustified rejection of their aid left the Athenians profoundly bitter.

118

The idea of danger from helots ran throughout Sparta's history, whereas in actual fact the only attested revolt was the one in 464. Why such an obsession, which could lead all the way to collective crime, as in the mysterious disappearance of two thousand men pointed out by Thucydides? Individual Spartans never seemed to be free of the obsession, if we are to believe Critias, cited by Libanius: "Out of mistrust of the helots, the Spartan, when he is at home, removes the handle of his shield. As he cannot do this when he is on a campaign (for in that case it often happens that there is urgency), he does not move about without his spear, sure to win out, in case of revolt, over the helot armed with the shield alone. They have also fitted their doors with locks, thinking that these would protect them against their attacks."[1] To understand this, we have to understand the meaning and function of helotism.

The origin of the helots remains largely mysterious, and the meaning of the word itself is uncertain: "prisoners of war" or "people of Helos," that is, people from the Marsh, an area south of Sparta. The hypothesis of pre-Dorian populations subjugated during the Lacedemonians' conquest of Laconia was proposed only belatedly and is not based on any serious argument. On the contrary, the Greeks outside of Sparta were shocked that the Spartans used people of the same origin as themselves as slaves. It was better to think that the populations involved were those that had refused to join the vast *synoikismos* that led, during the ninth or eighth century, to the creation of the Spartan city-state, or that had sought to separate from it and had been defeated. The only ones whose origin was known were the Messenian helots, collectively enslaved when their country lost its independence, and this continued to give them a distinct status among helots. What counts is that the helots formed a cohesive group that was constituted at a given moment and that reproduced itself naturally rather than by additions from the outside. Helotism was thus a form of collective enslavement twice over: on the one hand because the helots had been subjugated collectively, on the other because they were slaves of the city-state as a community, and not as the private property of individuals. This did not prevent the city-state from putting some of them at the disposal of citizens, in particular for the cultivation of the allotments of civic land *(cleros)* that allowed every Spartan to pay his share to the group with which he took his meals (his *syssitia*). But the Spartan who profited this way from a helot's labor was not the helot's owner; he could neither sell him nor kill him nor free him. In short, he had none of the customary rights of a master over a slave, not even on the economic level; indeed, curiously, the citizen did not have to provide minimum subsistence to the helot at his disposal, but it was rather the helot who had to provide the citizen with an annuity set by law, keeping the remainder himself. This explains how, according to the ancient authors, certain helots managed to become quite rich. At the beginning of the second century B.C.E., when the tyrant Nabis offered helots who desired their freedom the opportunity to purchase it, six thousand turned up to take advantage of the opportunity (Chapter 21).

But this is not the aspect of the helots' status about which Thucydides' text invites us to reflect. The cold-blooded killing of two thousand men who represented a non-negligible workforce seems as strange as it is appalling, but carrying this off without anyone knowing how it was done augments the horror still more. Now, Thucydides' text belongs to a set of traditions attesting that the Spartans feared the helots and applied to them a systematic policy of what Jean Ducat has rightly called "contempt."[2] Here is something that calls for explanation.

We have seen that fear of revolt, constantly invoked and never realized, served to justify the helots' elimination. A carefully targeted culling: the false announcement of the imminent liberation of those who judged that they had served Sparta well was intended to unmask the boldest of all, those who were aware of what the city-state owed them. It was thus not a matter of eliminating just any helot for the fun of it, but only those who corresponded least well to their status as slaves, morally or physically. For the ones selected were not only those who claimed what was due them, but also those of outstanding physical strength. Plutarch spells this out: during the *krypteia* (Chapter 14), the young men killed the sturdiest and strongest of the helots working in the fields. This indication is confirmed by Myron of Priene, who writes: "If there are any who surpass the degree of strength that befits slaves, they are punished by death, and their masters are fined for failing to restrict their development."[3]

It is obvious that the Spartans were determined to terrorize the helots. But these individual or collective assassinations ordered by the city-state cannot be isolated from the overall set of civic practices directed at helots. On this point, Plutarch's text provides a catalog (completed by a few additional texts) of discriminatory measures that we need to try to understand.

A helot stood out first of all by his dress, in particular a cap made of dog skin and clothing of animal skins. Not fur, which was an aristocratic luxury, but the raw pelt, which relegated men to the status of animals. Every occasion to humiliate helots was seized: they were made to get drunk, to perform indecent dances, and to sing ridiculous songs, whereas they did not have the right to perform the songs or dances of free men. Similarly, homosexual relations were forbidden them, as was training in the gymnasium. Everything converged to make helots look like the opposite of citizens, in other words, like beings lacking in moral value. But the point was not solely to use helots for pedagogical purposes, by showing young Spartan men the ravages of alcoholism or immodesty, as Plutarch believed. The point of this treatment was above all, it seems to me, to justify in the eyes of the Spartans and other Greeks the legitimacy of the enslavement of a group that was as Greek as the Spartans themselves. According to Plutarch, the practice of treating helots with scorn and cruelty took hold in Sparta fairly late, after the Messenian helot revolt in 464; Plutarch represents this as if it were in some sense a response to the fright that the helots had given the citizens. It is hard to know whether the gestures of contempt actually did originate in the archaic period, but I very much doubt that they were introduced as a form of reprisal. In contrast, they can easily be explained as a response to the general feeling on the Greeks' part that slavery was natural for barbarians, exceptional for Greeks. To be sure, any Greek could be reduced to slavery as a prisoner of war or, in certain city-states, as an insolvent debtor. But this was always a temporary status, and no one could refuse to free a prisoner for whom a ransom was paid, or a debtor who had been delivered from his debt. For the helots, on the contrary, liberation was rare; it depended exclusively on the good will of the Spartan state, and we have seen that an announcement of liberation could turn out to be a trap.

"Contempt for helots" constituted one of the ideological pillars of Spartan society, and it operated at several levels. It maintained the helots in a state of fear, or even terror, of their masters: any helot who stood out in any way at all risked death, especially at the hands of the krypteia during the period of initiation. But it also contributed to the moral, political, and physical education of young men, who saw the helots as the inverse image of the ideal to be attained. Helots constituted legitimate targets at every moment, if it is true, as Plutarch notes, that every year at the beginning of their term of office the ephors of Sparta declared war on the helots. But murdering helots was not an element in the training of hoplites for regular warfare; on the contrary, it was combat based on cunning that figured in the initiation of young men (Chapter 14). Finally, contempt for helots helped establish the necessary distance between two groups of the same origin, one of which nevertheless dominated the other for all time. In order to justify the exorbitant privileges on one side and the total absence of hope on the other, the gap between the two groups had to be widened; it had to be demonstrated that one group stood for virtue and strength while the other represented only degradation and weakness. Although the helots' behavior was imposed from the outside, it ended up being internalized by the individuals themselves: the helots taken prisoner by the Thebans in 369 staunchly refused to sing the songs of Terpander of Lesbos, Alcman of Sardis, or Spendon of Sparta, hymns that accompanied citizens on parade or marching to battle. This is evidence of the undeniable success of the Spartan policy, for the victims had internalized their inferiority and claimed it in standing up to their masters' enemy.

CHAPTER FOURTEEN

Naked and Unarmed in the Dark, or Training and Initiation of Spartan Youth

This [*krypteia*] was of the following nature. The magistrates from time to time sent out into the country at large the most intelligent of the young men, equipped only with daggers and such supplies as were necessary. In the day time they scattered into obscure and out of the way places, where they hid themselves apart and lay quiet; but in the night, they came down into the highways and killed every Helot whom they caught. Oftentimes, too, they actually traversed the fields where Helots were working and slew the sturdiest and best of them.

Plutarch, *Lycurgus*, in *Plutarch's Lives*, trans. Bernadotte Perrin
(Loeb Classical Library, 1914), vol. 1, pp. 289, 291
(XXVIII, 2–3)

SPARTA, SEVENTH TO fourth centuries B.C.E., at least; a strange institution, the *krypteia,* based on the verb *kruptein,* "to hide, to conceal oneself, to dissimulate," which also induces trickery and lies.

Plutarch saw the ritual of the krypteia as one of the cruelest practices in Spartan training; he was reluctant to attribute such an abominable practice to Lycurgus, moreover, for it seemed totally contrary to the spirit of justice that he saw as predominant in the work of the Lacedemonian legislator. However, by isolating the krypteia from the rest of the training given to young men, Plutarch condemned himself to seeing only its morally unacceptable aspects and not its internal logic. Now, this custom was inscribed within a process that might be better characterized not as training but as initiation. Thanks to the mix of astonishment and admiration that the Spartan system aroused, we have a good deal of information on the subject, and we can thus embark on a relatively precise analysis of its various aspects. The comparison with other city-states—with those of Crete in particular, but also with Athens—allows us to grasp the goals of a seemingly surprising education.

123

Sparta's ambition was to control the life of its citizens at every instant, from the cradle—or even from conception!—to the grave. Before age thirty, a young husband could rejoin his wife only in secret, for he was obliged to sleep with the members of his age cohort; thus Plutarch notes that he may well have had children without ever seeing his wife in broad daylight! From birth on, the elders of the tribe examined all children and decided whether to let them live or not according to their physical characteristics; the ones they deemed it possible to keep were given back to their families, and boys were reared in that context up to age seven.

Then began the system of *agoge,* Spartan-style "training," in which every boy shared his life, day and night, with others of his own age. In this rigorous program, physical endurance and the acquisition of moral principles came far ahead of intellectual development. Plutarch shows the young boys attending citizens' banquets, where they could hear about the great deeds of the ancients and listen to countless stories intended to show them which models to follow and which to avoid. This education was highly traditional by its very nature, in that it relied exclusively on repetition and imitation; it was far removed from what the sophists in Athens were defending in the late fifth century, for the latter advocated individual apprenticeship, experimentation, and the questioning of received ideas. To be sure, the sophists did not have a good reputation, and they were victims as much of the fact that certain of their disciples turned out badly (we find examples in particular among the Thirty Tyrants in Athens in 404) as of Aristophanes' ferocious mockery of their pedagogical methods. But with the excesses stripped away, their educational principles were in some sense the basis for modern education, in that they incited all students to think for themselves and to innovate. The Spartan model was clearly at the opposite extreme.

But it is not so much the education of young Spartans that is of interest here as the way in which they were integrated into the society of men. Before describing the krypteia, Plutarch alludes here and there to several features of behavior that do not mean much taken in isolation. Thus he indicates that, once they reach a certain age (he does not specify, but it seems to be around age twenty), young men are sought out by lovers *(erastai).* Plutarch remains rather evasive on this point, and he eliminates all sexual connotations while attributing a certain pedagogical and moral dimension to the relationship: the *erastes* shares the good or bad reputation of his *eromenos* (the name given to the younger of the two, literally "the one who is loved"), and can be punished in his place. Thus he is seen to play a quasi-paternal role in education; this should not be surprising, given that fathers, in Sparta even more than elsewhere, appear to have been completely absent from family life and education alike.

An excerpt preserved by Strabo from Ephoros, a fourth-century historian whose work has been almost entirely lost, contributes elements of primary importance that help us understand the place of this pederastic (or rather homosexual, for the eromenos is no longer exactly a child) relation in the formation of young citizens, although the customs described are those of the Cretan city-states rather than of Sparta. It is worth lingering over this material before returning to Sparta and then to Athens.

According to Ephoros, young men in the Cretan city-states were the object of abductions by grown men. But each abduction was organized in advance and to some extent codified. Someone who planned to kidnap a child announced this to his friends, who did all that was required to let the family know the day and the place of the planned event. The eromenos cooperated in the "kidnapping," in fact, if his family deemed that its author was of equal or higher rank. At the moment of the abduction, a semblance of combat took place between the erastes and his friends on the one hand and members of the young man's family on the other: "The friends pursue him and lay hold of him, though only in a very gentle way, thus satisfying the custom; and after that they cheerfully turn the boy over to [the erastes] to lead away; if, however, the abductor is unworthy, they take the boy away from him."[1]

All this had an obviously ritual character, and what followed was no less ritualized. The erastes and his eromenos, accompanied by friends who had participated in the abduction, withdrew to the countryside to enjoy a two-month period of banquets and festivities ("for it [was] not permitted to detain the boy for a longer time"), then went back down to the city.

The boy is released after receiving as presents a military habit, an ox, and a drinking-cup (these are the gifts required by law), and other things so numerous and costly that the friends, on account of the number of the expenses, make contributions thereto. Now the boy sacrifices the ox to Zeus and feasts those who returned with him; and then he makes known the facts about his intimacy with his lover, whether, perchance, it

125

has pleased him or not, the law allowing him this privilege in order that, if any force was applied to him at the time of the abduction, he might be able at this feast to avenge himself and be rid of the lover.[2]

As we can see, such abductions and all the events that accompanied them were strictly codified. It was not a matter of unbridled amorous passion, and Ephoros indicates clearly that the most coveted children were not the most attractive, but rather those who stood out by their courage and their proper behavior. Morality appears safe and sound. Still, whether or not it pleases those admirers of ancient Greece who have sought to see these relations between erastes and eromenos as purely Platonic, the words speak for themselves, and the pederastic Greek iconography is sufficiently abundant in explicit scenes to rule out any possible doubt. The word *erastes* designates the active lover, *eromenos* the one who submits, and the texts do not conceal the sexual nature of the relationship.

Nonetheless, this is not what really matters here. In Ephoros's text, anthropologists have had no trouble recognizing the description of a rite of passage resembling those found in all societies. In the early twentieth century, Arnold van Gennep described this process well, with its three successive phases: exclusion, inversion, and integration. The initiate was first separated out, cut off from his family, from the rest of his group, or from the population as a whole. In Crete, young men were abducted and sent off to the countryside for two months. In Sparta, the *kryptes* was sent off to live alone in the Laconian countryside. During this period of exclusion, the life of the initiate was the opposite of the life of the citizen he would presumably become. As we have seen, in Sparta a kryptes was active at night and hid during the day; living in the countryside was already the opposite of the normal life of a citizen, whose time was spent in the city-state and in the agora in particular. In Sparta, where the official ideology had every citizen living under the constant surveillance of the others ("like bees, they were to make themselves always integral parts of the whole community, clustering together about their leader"), the kryptes lived alone.[3] Even his occupations seem to have been just the opposite of those awaiting ordinary citizens. The kryptes assassinated helots through trickery, without showing himself; this is at the opposite pole from the honorable combat of the hoplite whom he will later become. The kryptes subsisted on what he could steal in fields or granaries, or on the product of his own hunting. But, lacking suitable weapons, he had to hunt by stealth, with traps. In Crete, the young man and his companions spent two months feasting, and there too they hunted. It is pointless to try to justify these practices in terms of their formative value on the physical level: the Greeks never claimed to constitute commando forces skilled at trickery. We must instead see them as part of an effort to plunge boys into a sort of upside-down world. Sexual relations with their lovers were part of the same process of ritual inversion, for a homosexual relation was never conceived as an apprenticeship for the heterosexual life that every Greek was destined to have later on. The eromenos made a foray, as it were, into the world of the opposite sex. An Athenian custom indicates this clearly: when the young men who had completed their two years of *ephebia* returned to the city, two of them led the procession dressed as girls. Conversely (but the meaning is the same), in the prenuptial ceremony that marked the passage of a Spartan girl to the status of married woman, she was rigged out in a beard. In each case, the initiate took on the appearance of the opposite sex as if the better to affirm his or her own sexual identity.

Next came integration into the civic group. In Athens, the end of the period of ephebia was the moment when a young man became a citizen and could participate in the meetings of the assembly. In Crete, he received highly symbolic gifts: military equipment, which marked his entry into the group of citizen soldiers; a steer, which signaled his capacity to sacrifice; and a drinking cup, which authorized him to take his place at the banquet or *symposium,* the masculine civic feast par excellence. Other gifts, not explicitly provided for by law, stemmed from social exchanges unrelated to the initiation process properly speaking.

Not everyone seems to have gone through these rites of passage. Plutarch asserts that in Sparta the krypteia constituted an elite ("the most intelligent of the young men"). In Crete, abductions involved only the upper levels of society, for the ritual required leisure and considerable resources; the abductor's friends gave him financial assistance to pay for the gifts, and the young abductees drew glory from this:

> But the parastathentes (for thus they call those who have been abducted) receive honors; for in both the dances and the races they have the positions of highest honor, and are allowed to dress in better clothes than the rest, that is, in the habit given them by their lovers; and not only then,

but even after they have grown to manhood, they wear a distinctive dress, which is intended to make known the fact that each wearer has become "kleinos," for they call the loved one "kleinos" and the lover "philetor."[4]

Nor did the ephebia bring together all young people of the same age group in Athens, it seems, except perhaps for a brief period after the process was reformed by Lycurgus in 338. In reality, this rite was reserved for a social elite that played its role in the name of an entire age group but that reaped the accompanying glory and prestige for itself alone.

The maintenance of such "primitive" rites in developed societies such as those of the Greek city-states may seem surprising. But Fr. Jean-François Lafitau, a Jesuit from Bordeaux who knew his classics well and who had been in contact with Indians in Canada, observed in the early eighteenth century that the Greeks, after all, had been savages too.[5]

CHAPTER FIFTEEN

Nicocles of Salamis in Cyprus,
or Foreigners in the City-State

And though Hellas was closed to us because of the war which had arisen, and though we were being robbed on every side, I solved most of these difficulties, paying to some their claims in full, to others in part, asking some to postpone theirs, and satisfying others as to their complaints by whatever means I could.

Isocrates, *Nicocles*, in *Isocrates*, trans. George Norlin (Loeb Classical Library, 1928), vol. 1, pp. 95–97

CYPRUS, AROUND 370–368 B.C.E. The big island across from the Syrian coast represented a curiosity in the Greek world: it had long been shared by Greeks and Phoenicians. This was not a north–south or an east–west divide; instead, some of the city-states scattered all around the island had Greek kings, others had Phoenician kings, and although on occasion a city-state might pass from Greek to Phoenician control or vice versa, they generally got along well. On the east coast, Salamis, a little north of today's Famagusta, went through several changes. A dynasty of Greek origin was removed from power by a Phoenician minister in the late fifth century; the minister was in turn toppled by a Cypriot adventurer of Phoenician origin, Abdemon of Citium (before 415). Exiled, the old Greek dynasty regained power in 411, thanks to the energetic action of Evagoras, of whom Isocrates left a quite striking portrait in the form of a eulogy. Despite an agitated life in which "the disorders of a court impregnated with Asian mores," as his French translator Georges Mathieu put it, may not have been the primary factors, Evagoras held on to power until his death in 374–373.[1] He was assassinated, perhaps at the same time as his oldest son Pnytagoras; he was replaced by his youngest son, Nicocles, to whom Isocrates addressed an exhortation *(To Nicocles)* around 370 before placing a rather strange speech in his mouth *(Nicocles,* around 368) in which the sovereign presents both a picture of his own actions and a list of his subjects' duties. During this entire period, Cyprus was of course under the authority of the Persians, to whom it supplied a number of battleships, but like their counterparts in Phoenicia, the Cypriot city-states retained considerable administrative autonomy.

By virtue of its location, the city was well placed to serve as a relay station in trade between the Levantine coast and the Aegean basin. Yet at a certain point that role appeared to be forbidden to its merchants. To be sure, there was the war, which had raged on in Asia Minor until 400, had started up again in Greece scarcely ten years after the end of the Peloponnesian War (the Corinth War, 395–386), and had continued almost unabated ever since. Sparta, the big winner in the conflict with Athens in 404, lost its hegemony after the battle of Leuctra (371) to the benefit of Thebes of Boeotia, but peace still did not reign. All this did not favor exchanges, but that was not what worried Nicocles. He focused on another phenomenon that had seriously hindered Salaminian trade. According to Nicocles, the Salaminians were subject to confiscation of property everywhere. What was going on? Why such relentless discrimination against the unfortunate Cypriots? Here is an opportunity to look back at the progress of the rights of foreigners in ancient Greece and discover unexpected situations in a world in which exchanges appeared indispensable to all.

In archaic Greece, a foreigner passing through was not the object of any provision in civic law. In principle he did not have the right to any protection, unless he presented himself as a suppliant in a sanctuary or unless he were a pilgrim going to some Panhellenic sanctuary at the moment of the truce decreed for the contests. But these were exceptional situations; they were of little use to merchants or travelers of any sort. The only defense against the theft of goods, the only personal security, was of the private order: a citizen of the city-state where a traveler found himself might offer his hospitality, his *xenia*, which went well beyond room and board. The host protected the passing foreigner against any attack on his person or his goods and served as his representative in case of trouble. Hospitality was sacred, and anyone who violated it was guilty of sacrilege. But the system had its limits, for it seemed to work almost exclusively in favor of important individuals, those who had a vast network of intercivic relations, sometimes through the intermediary of family relations. This was of no use to anonymous merchants, sailors, or travelers, who thus enjoyed no legal protection at all and had to beseech the gods that the inhabitants of the city-states they were passing through would not take everything they had.

For there was another Greek practice that further aggravated the situation, that of reprisals *(sulan)*. The Greeks considered that, in a case of conflict of interest between two citizens of different city-states, the right of confiscation applied to all the citizens of the opposing city-state. Let us take an example. A citizen of Miletus judged that a citizen of Smyrna owed him money following a commercial transaction. Despite the former's demands, the Smyrniot had not paid his debt, or even contested it. In principle, our Milesian could have the property of any Smyrniot who happened to be in Miletus confiscated, and could take the Smyrniot to court to claim his rights. If just a few Milesians who had many external dealings were thus in conflict with a few individuals of various foreign cities, that was enough to make the territory of Miletus essentially off limits to all citizens of the city-states involved; as soon as the potential adversaries of our Milesians maintained that these were the ones who owed them money, Milesians in turn were confined to their homeland, or severely limited in their travels.

This was exactly what happened with the Salaminians. Some merchants from Salamis found themselves entangled in business disputes with partners from a number of different city-states. In the absence of any tribunal capable of settling the disputes, or in the absence of a transactional agreement, everyone applied the right of confiscation or reprisal and, by the same token, the Salaminians, including those who had nothing to do with the conflicts in question, could not go anywhere. For a commercial city-state such as Salamis, this was a real disaster. Nicocles, concerned with the well-being of his citizens, thus undertook a vast campaign in the city-states with which certain of his fellow citizens had financial disagreements and tried to settle them at his own expense: by paying the amounts due when his compatriots had been condemned by the tribunals, by obtaining delays in payment when the sums were too large or when the matter had not yet gone to court, or by pushing the adversaries to compromise whenever possible. The goal was to dispel all conflict and thus to reopen the city-states to Salaminian traders. The very primitive character of this legal situation may seem astonishing, but it was not an isolated case. In *Oeconomicus*, attributed to Aristotle, the author mentions how the city-state of Chalcedonia, in order to procure resources, exercised a right of confiscation on all the ships that crossed the Bosporus and that belonged to citizens of any city-state with which one or another of its citizens had a business conflict. And a fourth-century inscription from Mantinea, in the Peloponnesus, lists the city-states with which a compensation agreement had been signed. For that very continental city-state, one would expect the list to include neighboring city-states for the most part; however, Cyrene of Libya is also among those mentioned. All this proves that until the fourth century the old right of sulan applied broadly throughout the Greek world. Yet over a long period of time, measures were already being taken to put an end to it and to facilitate the circulation of people and goods.

A treatise between two minuscule city-states of western Locris, Chaleion and Oiantheia, located on the north bank of the Gulf of Corinth west of Delphi, is the oldest example of an agreement between city-states to limit the right of reprisal. Dating from the middle of the fifth century, the text provided that a city-state could not seize the person or property of citizens from a neighboring city-state on its own territory, or within the bounds of the port. A citizen of Oiantheia could thus circulate freely and do business in Chaleion without difficulty, even if there were a dispute between one of his fellow citizens and a Chaleian, and vice versa. But curiously, the agreement did not apply on the open seas, probably because it was considered that neither city-state had the practical means to control what happened at sea; in contrast, the activities of all parties were subject to the scrutiny of the magistrates when they took place on the city-state's territory or inside its port.

This sort of agreement proliferated in the fifth century, and Athens seems to have signed many such treaties with maritime city-states belonging to its alliance. *Symbolai* were in fact legal agreements that provided recourse to the tribunals of one of the signatory city-states if conflict arose between their citizens, in place of the procedures of confiscation that had been operative previously. This represented major progress in rights, in that foreigners were now protected from being singled out at random, and had recourse to the courts on the same basis as citizens; by the same token, the protection of individuals was guaranteed without need for a *proxenos* or for the protection of some powerful person. But these conventions seem to have concerned little more than the allies and their commercial affairs. During the fourth century, there was new progress with the creation in

Athens of commercial actions *(dikai emporikai)* that authorized any individual, whatever his origin, to bring a commercial dispute that had arisen in Athens between himself and an Athenian before an Athenian tribunal; moreover, the Athenian tribunal was obliged to render its judgment within one month, which was the legal length of time a foreigner could stay before being obliged to pay the metic tax.

But there was more, and visibly, in Athens at least, there was concern for protection that would go beyond the framework of commercial affairs alone. In fact, Athens then signed conventions *(symbola,* agreements presumably making it possible to settle all types of conflicts and not only commercial disputes, as the *symbolai* did), sometimes with quite modest city-states; the field of application of these agreements seems to have been broad, "a veritable penal code valid for their citizens in a reciprocal manner."[2]

As attached as they were to the notion of citizenship and the privileges it entailed, the Greeks seem to me to have evolved considerably over time in this area. But this may be, at least in part, only an optical illusion based on the ferocious protectiveness of the Athenians in this respect during the classical period, for nothing indicates that the Athenians' exclusiveness was the rule in the other city-states. I believe that we can find signs of evolution in several areas.

In the Hellenistic period, the city-states seemed less jealous of the privilege of citizenship, and they seem to me to have granted it somewhat more readily to foreigners. We have several examples of this in the city-states of Asia Minor, where granting citizenship to foreign benefactors became more common. It sometimes happened, on the one hand, that a city-state granted citizenship to an entire group residing on its territory. We see this in Miletus, which gave citizenship to groups of Cretan mercenaries living in Miletus and serving the city-state. We also see it in Pergamon, during a period of crisis, to be sure, when it was useful to mobilize all available energy against an adversary: the city of Pergamon promised citizenship to all foreigners and noncitizen natives residing on its territory. The granting of citizenship en masse nevertheless remained extremely rare, and responded to a practical necessity, the decrease in the number of citizens. Thus it may not be evidence of greater generosity on the part of the city-states.

On the other hand, we see a proliferation of bilateral agreements that amount to granting equal rights to the citizens of the two contracting city-states. By *sympoliteia,* or joint citizenship, two city-states agreed to merge, which amounted to granting the same rights to all citizens originating from either one. More interesting for the evolution of legal rights seems to me to be *isopoliteia,* an agreement through which two neighboring city-states decided to grant each other's citizens the same rights their own citizens had: the right to own property, the right to marry, the right to engage in commerce, civic and political rights, and access to the tribunals. This did not entail a fusion of rights (each community retained its own rights and laws), but the foreigner ceased to be a foreigner, as it were.

To be sure, such agreements remained fairly rare, but generally speaking the practice of reprisals (sulan) regressed considerably to the extent that agreements of *asulia,* or nonreprisal, proliferated. City-states and sanctuaries obtained such privileges from kings, and got them recognized by the greatest possible number of city-states. This was a way for a city-state to protect its territory, or part of it, and to offer it as a refuge. Among the advantages granted to benefactors, it was not uncommon to guarantee them security in times of peace and war alike. More significantly still, more and more foreigners became property owners in city-states other than their own, especially after the Roman conquest. To be sure, this was a consequence of the indebtedness of individuals or city-states to wealthy Roman businessmen, because land served as security. In cases of nonreimbursement, a creditor had to be able to claim his land and take possession. But historians have never been concerned with the upheavals that this introduced in the laws of the Greek city-states, which were generally very protective of property rights. On the topic that concerns us here, it suffices to note that, under the influence of indebtedness to the Romans, the barriers raised to property ownership by foreigners in a given city-state seemed to fade away.

We are far removed from the situation described by Nicocles in the mid-fourth century. In the absence of a common law for all, the multiplication of bilateral agreements ended up relegating the procedures of confiscation to the storehouse of accessories from the past. To be sure, even in the Roman period a unified legal system was never achieved, but at least legal procedures became the rule where forced confiscations had prevailed earlier. It is hard to deny that this was progress, even if there was still a long road ahead. But does law ever cease to evolve along with society?

CHAPTER SIXTEEN

Pasion Bequeaths His Wife,
or from Slavery to Freedom

Socrates, the well-known banker, having been set free by his masters just as the plaintiff's father had been, gave his wife in marriage to Satyrus who had been his slave. Another, Socles, who had been in the banking business, gave his wife in marriage to Timodemus, who is still in being and alive, who had been his slave. And it is not here only, men of Athens, that those engaged in this line of business so act; but in Aegina Strymodorus gave his wife in marriage to Hermaeus, his own slave, and again, after her death, gave him his own daughter. And one could mention many other such cases; and no wonder. For although to you, men of Athens, who are citizens by birth, it would be a disgrace to esteem any conceivable amount of wealth above your honourable descent, yet those who obtain citizenship as a gift either from you or from others, and who in the first instance, thanks to this good fortune, were counted worthy of the same privileges, because of their success in money-making, and their possession of more wealth than others, must hold fast to these advantages. So your father Pasion—and he was neither the first nor the last to do this—without bringing disgrace upon himself or upon you, his sons, but seeing that the only protection for his business was that he should bind the defendant to you by a family tie, for this reason gave to him in marriage his own wife, your mother.

Demosthenes, "Friend Pleading for Phormio, a Special Plea,"
in *Demosthenes,* vol. 4, *Private Orations,* trans. A. T. Murray
(Loeb Classical Library, 1936), Oration 36, pp. 343–345
(28–30)

ATHENS, AROUND 350 B.C.E. A matter of inheritance in the well-off milieu of bankers. At least we call them bankers, although they had little in common with today's bankers, except perhaps for their fortunes. These were first and foremost money lenders, people who knew how to make the money of others (and their own) grow; they were also involved in maritime trade, which could bring in big profits (and costs as well). Their activity was not glamorous, and Athenian citizens practiced it very little, or else did so without talking about it. The bankers we know of were in fact mostly metics, or even slaves. This is the case here. The plaintiff is Apollodoros, son of Pasion. This Pasion had an exceptional career: he was a slave who had succeeded his former masters at the head of their bank, probably after having been freed. At the very beginning of the fourth century, his bank was known for its activity and its reliability. Pasion had even rendered enough service to the city to be awarded Athenian citizenship. Upon his death, in 370, he left two sons, Apollodoros, age twenty-four, and a ten-year-old minor son, Pasicles. Perhaps because he had little confidence in the abilities of his elder son, Pasion had taken the precaution of renting his property—and thus his bank—to his own freed slave, Phormio. And when he died, he gave Phormio his widow, Archippe, in his will. A fine social ascension, which seemed to reproduce the one Pasion had experienced himself.

The trial that led to Demosthenes' intervention took place some twenty years later. Apollodoros, who had had to acknowledge on two occasions that Phormio's management was impeccable, but who seems to have lived the high life, undertook to claim a sum of twenty talents from Phormio, on the pretext that his fortune arose from the placement of a sum of eleven talents bequeathed by Pasion that Phormio had never given back. The affair is complicated, and the details are of little importance here, but it shows that money handlers dealt in large sums and knew how to make them bear fruit.

After what has been said about the possessive attitude of Athenians—and Greeks in general—about citizenship, the promotion of these former slaves may be surprising. Demosthenes stresses that in this milieu in particular the practice was not exceptional, and he puts forward several examples, in Athens (Socrates, Socles) and also in Aegina, the big island nearby. In each case, a banker had bequeathed both his wife and his bank to a freed former slave. In Aegina, Strymodoros must have yielded his wife while he was still alive, because she died after becoming the wife of Hermaios, his former slave, and Strymodoros then gave the latter his own daughter as a new wife. There was a reason for this: preserving a hard-earned fortune. It was as if the banker, before retiring or dying, confided his business not to his children, who were outsiders in the banking world, but to his trusted right-hand man, a former slave, who knew all the ins and outs of the enterprise, all his master's secrets.

Phormio's story, like Pasion's before him, remains exceptional, despite the examples proffered by Demosthenes, who was doing his best to do his duty as a lawyer. Citizens actually made up a minority of the population, and access to citizenship remained rare for those who were not citizens by birth. Pericles' law of 451 only made access more difficult, because the marriage of a foreign woman to an Athenian became illegal, or at least could not produce future citizens. The application of the law had been suspended during the Peloponnesian War, at least toward the end, for the demographic void created by the war had to be filled, and new soldiers had to be recruited. But as early as 403–402, a certain Nikomenes seems to have proposed to restore the law of 451 in its full force. At most, it was specified that the legitimacy of children born "before Euclid's archontate," that is, before 403, was not in question, which meant that the decree had no retroactive effects. Several events that took place after 403 and a series of trials during the fourth century show to what extent the city-state remained sensitive on this essential point and sought to establish a strict barrier between citizens and noncitizens.

The debate over slavery in antiquity has continued to be enriched, even if it has sometimes strayed into secondary ideological confrontations. The questions that remain unresolved are numerous; they concern the total number of slaves in a given city-state, their origin (and especially the possible evolution of their recruitment over time), and their place in the economy. One point seems to me to have been settled: there is a clearly established difference between slaves bought and sold individually as merchandise and slaves who constituted a unified group. The latter are attested in several regions of Greece (Thessaly, Laconia, Asia Minor); they formed recognized groups, integrated to a certain extent into the city-state, as were, for example, the helots in Sparta (Chapter 13) or the *penestai* in Thessaly. This is not the place to go into detail about their status (which varied, moreover, from one city-state to another), but it is considered certain that these were indigenous groups (that is, Greeks in Greece proper, non-Greeks in Asia Minor such as the Mariandynians of Heraclea Pontica) who had been enslaved collectively. This type of slavery was not at all

the rule, and in the city-states where it existed it probably did not preclude the parallel existence of merchandise-slavery. The latter was the ordinary form of slavery: a free man bought a slave, who could be Greek or
barbarian, on the market or from another master. He could sell him at
will, or free him, and he could treat him as he liked, even if unjustified in-
humane behavior toward slaves was punished. Contrary to what is too
often said, the Greeks did not view their slaves as machines or as two-
legged animals; they were perfectly aware that slaves were human beings
like themselves. There is no shortage of texts to this effect. That fact did
not lead the Greeks to question the system, which they saw as perfectly
natural. At most, in the fourth century, one sees greater reticence about the
enslavement of Greeks, but we must not be misled: this was the normal
fate of prisoners of war, and Greeks had been held as slaves for a very long
time, if not from time immemorial. To be sure, slavery for indebtedness
was abolished fairly early in Athens (except for debts to the state), and the
practice of paying ransom allowed citizens who had been made prisoners
of war to avoid festering in slavery. The concern each city-state had with
protecting its fellow citizens led little by little to a drastic reduction in the
enslavement of Greeks.

We thus witness a barbarization of the servile group, a phenomenon
already perceptible in a few scattered inventories of the late fifth century. It
was accentuated in the fourth century, though it perhaps should not be
viewed as prevalent everywhere, even if Aristotle gives a sort of justification for the enslavement of barbarians by considering them as people born
to be slaves. We must not overlook, either, the number of slaves born in
households, whether from couplings between slaves duly authorized by
the masters, or from relations involving the master or the free men of the
household. Even without taking into account the Greek blood that might
run in the veins of many slaves, birth and life within the family meant that
a number of these "barbarian" slaves had never known anything but the
household of their Greek masters.

This obviously does not settle the still-open question of the number of
slaves, even for Athens, the city-state that has perhaps the best documentation on the subject: here, we have two figures! But what can be made of
them? In 413, during the occupation of Attica by the Spartiate troops,
20,000 slaves are said to have fled; according to a census taken in 317,
Athens had 400,000 *oiketai*. The first figure is practically useless, because

we do not know which slaves would have been able to flee: those of the Laurion mines, perhaps, or others who worked the fields, a few artisans? But what proportion of those who might have profited from the occasion did they represent? The mystery remains intact. As for the figure of 400,000, it has often been understood to represent the slaves, and consequently it has been denigrated in all sorts of ways, rather amusingly when we realize that historians of antiquity have complained endlessly about not having figures at their disposal. More seriously, it is probable that this figure does not represent the number of slaves (even though that is one of the possible meanings of *oiketai*), for then women and children would be completely absent from the census. It has thus been suggested that we see this as the number of "households": in other words, once the citizens and metics have been accounted for (we have separate figures for these groups), this figure would represent the inhabitants of their houses—women, children, and servants included. If we assume that there were as many free women as free men (21,000 citizens and 10,000 metics), and that there could have been two or three children per family, we would have to subtract from 400,000 around 30,000 women and 90,000 children, or 120,000 persons, which still leaves 280,000 slaves. The figure is unverifiable, perhaps excessive, but at all events it leads to the conclusion that, in Athens, slaves were roughly as numerous as free men.

It is perhaps more interesting to note that every Athenian owned one or several slaves, or, if they were among the poorest, at least dreamed of owning some. If we can characterize Greek societies as slaveholding, it is because slavery appeared irreplaceable to them; it occupied a place in the collective imagination that no one thought of calling into question. To be sure, slavery also played a major economic role, for it is certain that slaves were responsible for an important share of production in all sectors of activity. They were almost the only ones who worked in the dangerous or grueling trades, such as mining; they were undoubtedly a majority among artisans, and surely a very important presence in agriculture. Still, we must not envision Athenian citizens as unburdened of all activity, living in idleness with the support of their slaves. A large number of texts give the lie to such a picture, and it suffices to read speeches for the defense from fourth-century Attica to see how many free men and women, citizens, worked, sometimes at modest, unglamorous trades.

But although I do not want to paint too rosy a picture of the everyday situation, which must not have been very satisfactory for the majority, there were also slaves who led freer lives than others—in particular, those who lived apart from the master's household, or who had managed to make themselves indispensable by virtue of some special talent. Pasion must have been one of these in his master's bank. This is what earned him his freedom, just as he himself freed his own slave Phormio.

Beyond being bought out by a fellow citizen (which was hardly possible except for Greek prisoners of war), being liberated was the only way a slave could attain freedom. The practice is attested decisively as early as the end of the sixth century, but it may have existed earlier without leaving any formal traces. However, in the interest of the benefactor, the granting of liberty needed to enjoy the broadest publicity possible, and people thus adopted the habit of making a proclamation during a festival (for example, at the theater), and having the name of the freed man engraved on some public monument. This liberation depended exclusively on the will of the master, and the slave almost always paid a sum that was supposed to represent his own price, a sum that he managed to put together, that his master lent him, or that was provided to him by an association set up for the purpose. The procedure varied: sometimes it brought a god into play, sometimes it remained purely civic. In the case of liberations before a god, either the slave was consecrated to the god or else he was sold to the god on condition of being liberated (we have many examples of this at Delphi, where the acts are engraved on the supporting wall of the temple of Apollo). But freedom was also granted by testament, or by a declaration before the magistrates. It seems probable that the freed man in most cases remained in the city where he had served. In principle, the freed man, liberated from all obligations, could do as he pleased, go where he liked, and dispose of his own property. However, over time, more and more restrictive clauses were imposed; for example, the master could announce that one of his slaves was to be freed upon his own death, but with the obligation of remaining in the service of the master's wife or some other family member until that person's death.

Liberation remained rare, even if we know of quite a number of acts of liberation in Thessaly and Delphi. There was clearly a strong reticence in this regard, for liberation, which only people who had a large number of slaves could afford, appeared to modest folk as a form of waste or perhaps of parading one's wealth. Although Xenophon and Aristotle advised masters to make liberation a brilliant affair in order to motivate the best of their slaves, public opinion appears to have been reserved. In Athens, during the fourth century, proclaiming liberations at the theater had to be forbidden, because such proclamations had provoked unrest.

Even in exceptional circumstances, the city-state remained grudging in this area. Thus after the fall of the Thirty Tyrants in Athens, the slaves who had fought in the ranks of their adversaries received freedom only gradually. Moreover, it is rather surprising that the Greeks did not envisage a special legal status for former slaves who were freed. They did have a word for it, *apeleutheros*, "liberated," but not a status, as Rome did later on. A freed man, in Athens, shared the fate of a resident foreigner or a metic.

Pasion and then Phormio thus became metics. This status was recognized by the city-state and as such was somewhat advantageous in comparison to that of foreigners, who had no rights (Chapter 10). Viewed as permanent residents, metics had a light tax burden, one drachma a month for men, half that for women; the tax was not intended to exploit them fiscally, but to remind them of their status. In exchange for this symbolic sum, the city-state granted them the right to live in the country, to pay the same taxes as all others who were subject to taxation, to fight alongside citizens as hoplites or as light infantrymen (though they could not join the cavalry), and to have access to the tribunals under the protection of a citizen who represented them (the *prostates*). Metics thus enjoyed relatively extensive rights and, most importantly, they benefited from a legal recognition that was in principle lacking to passing foreigners. However, they were also subjected to limitations and prohibitions. Naturally, they had no political rights and did not participate in the political life of the city-state in any way; they could not own land or houses in Attica, which excluded them in practical terms from agriculture and hampered those who did business, because they could never own their own workshops, stores, or homes. The situation, in short, was awkward: they were neither wholly excluded nor wholly included. To be sure, metics enjoyed great freedom of action in the economic arena, and the examples of Pasion and Phormio show that they could be involved in important business, could grow rich and attain a social rank in no way inferior to that of the most well-to-do citizens. But their activity had the limits imposed by the interdiction on owning real estate and the obligation to be represented by a prostates.

Forbidden to speak out politically and to vote, the metics nevertheless had a certain relative capacity to intervene. As sophists, metics unquestionably trained a number of Athenian politicians in the late fifth century. In particular, as victims of the Thirty, who tried to strip them of their property, many metics took up the cause of the "democrats" in 404–403 and took up arms to fight for the reestablishment of Athenian democracy in 403. Nor were they totally excluded from civic religious life, for they participated in the most celebrated and the most emblematic festival of the city-state, the Panathenaea. Perhaps nothing sums up the metics' ambiguous situation better than a remark made in passing by Aristophanes in *Acharnians* (502–508) where he is defending himself for always criticizing the politicians of his city-state in the presence of foreigners: "This time Cleon will not accuse me of defaming the city in the presence of foreigners," he has his hero say, "for we are by ourselves; it's the Lenaean competition, and no foreigners are here yet; neither tribute nor troops have arrived from the allied cities. This time we are by ourselves, clean-hulled—for I count the resident foreigners as the bran of our populace."[1]

For most people, this awareness of the proximity between metics and citizens did not make the barrier between the two any easier to cross. Pasion and Phormio alike were remarkable exceptions. Both became citizens, undoubtedly because of their exceptional service, that is, their considerable expenditures to the benefit of the city-state. Beyond that, they both came out of slavery, and may have been Greek in origin, or at least born into Athenian families. For many other metics, it was impossible to become citizens. This was clearly apparent after the return of peace in 403–402, when a certain Thrasybulos proposed to thank slaves and metics who had fought for democracy by granting them citizenship. The assembly refused, and settled, a little later on (401–400), for granting freedom to the first group, fiscal equality to the second, and citizenship to a handful of others. Generally speaking, throughout the fourth century we see a great reluctance to grant full citizenship, and freed men often had to be content with more modest privileges, fiscal equality *(isotelia)* or the right to own real estate *(enktesis)*.

This "avarice" doubtless had many sources, and we can refer back here to what has been said about the law of 451 (Chapter 10). What applied to half-foreigners applied all the more logically to complete foreigners or to liberated former slaves. But I wonder whether the Athenians' close-fistedness in the matter did not find part of its justification, more profoundly, in the Athenian myths of autochthony. The Athenians believed that, alone among the Greeks, they had been born of the very soil of Attica. Now, precisely at the end of the fifth century in the Hippocratic treatise *Airs, Waters, Places,* which seems to have had an immense influence on later authors and from which Aristotle borrowed and popularized numerous elements, the author developed the idea that any displacement or mixing only weakened peoples, provoking a sort of degeneration of their original qualities. Indeed, the idea is expressed by many other authors, and from these texts one could easily make a number of deductions regarding naturalization. In a play of which only fragments remain, Euripides had already put the following words into the mouth of a heroine:

> To begin with, I consider it impossible to find a city-state better than this one [Athens]. In the first place, its people did not come from outside: we sprang up from our own soil. As for the other city-states, their inhabitants move around as pawns are moved on a game board, and they get new ones in exchange. Whoever leaves his city-state to live in another one is like a peg inserted into a piece of wood, but too loosely; he is a citizen in name, but not in fact.[2]

Demosthenes expresses the same idea in different terms when he contrasts citizens by birth to the others.

Thus we see the exceptional character of the honors granted Pasion and then Phormio. It must not have been common to traverse the entire path from slavery to citizenship in this way. There were certainly some disadvantages, for families of metics who had been settled for a long time, completely integrated into the city-state of Athens, might have had the impression that they were deliberately being kept on the sidelines. Moreover, being placed under guardianship and deprived of certain rights must have been a hindrance for their businesses. Xenophon saw the problem clearly, and in a treatise composed around 355 *(Ways and Means),* he proposed to grant the metics broader rights: the right to fight in the cavalry, the right to own land and build a house on it. His goal was to increase the resources of the city-state by attracting as many active foreigners as possible. But from another standpoint his proposal also showed how difficult it seemed to integrate the metics completely, metics who in increasing numbers were not Greek. There is no doubt about it: Pasion and Phormio remained exceptions.

CHAPTER SEVENTEEN

An Arabian Owl,
or Greek Trade and Culture
in the Near and Middle East
before Alexander

Arab imitation of an Athenian coin,
4th c. B.C.E. Cabinet des Médailles

G AZA, FOURTH CENTURY B.C.E. The city, at the entrance to the
coastal route that leads from Palestine to Egypt through the Sinai, has traditionally been viewed as the Arabs' port. In fact,
throughout its history it has never ceased to appear as the Arabs' outlet to
the Mediterranean, probably because it is the destination point of the
shortest routes between the base of the Gulf of Aqaba and the Mediterranean, or for the caravans that came up from Arabia Felix. Gaza was a
Philistine metropolis (Deuteronomy 2:23; Joshua 13:3); although the Hebrews occupied it in Judah's time (Judges 1:18), it almost always remained
beyond the reach of the inhabitants of Judaea (Samson in Gaza, a Philistine city: Judges 16:1; Gaza, at the frontier of Solomon's kingdom: 1 Kings
5:4). During the Persian period, it was the seat of an important Achaemenid regiment that was governed by the eunuch Batis at the time Alexander came through. From there, the Persians controlled the Arab tribes of
the Negev, ancient Idumea.

A silver coin of a well-known type: on the face, an owl, Athena's owl,
and the emblem of Athenian coins; on the obverse, a Janus-faced mascu-

line head but, on other coins of the same provenance, a feminine head, which could be Athena. This one was found in southern Palestine, but others came from Egypt. This provenance is insignificant in itself, because we know that Athenian owls circulated everywhere and served as the coinage of reference; it was the only coinage accepted everywhere without being weighed, for users trusted it. However, it is clear that this coin was not issued in Athens; numismatists view the coin in question as a free interpretation of an Attic coin, produced in Gaza in the fourth century. It is not counterfeit, for the alloy and weight conform to Athenian requirements. But why copy Athenian coins? If the Gazans wanted to mint coins, why did they not adopt their own model, which would have made their city-state known elsewhere? Let us note at the outset that they were not alone. "Owls" of similar appearance were issued in Egypt during the fourth century; they can sometimes be identified thanks to an Aramean inscription.

Athens was not the first city-state to mint coins (Chapter 3), but it began to do so fairly early among the city-states of Balkan Greece, and thanks to its silver mines it could regularly mint pieces of good quality and constant weight. When the city-state imposed itself as the greatest maritime power and the most active business center in the eastern Mediterranean, its coins were accepted everywhere as instruments of reference. Most city-states minted coins only sporadically, if they did so at all. For minting was expensive: it was necessary to have metal, which few city-states did; the engraver had to be paid, the mint had to be organized, and its operations had to be overseen very closely. Under these conditions, well before Athens imposed the use of its own weights, coins, and measures on its allies in the Delian League (Chapter 12), a good many city-states used essentially nothing but Athenian coinage for important exchanges.

The same was true for the Phoenician city-states, which had not yet started to mint coins but had quickly discovered the advantages of money. We may be astonished that neither Tyre, Sidon, Byblos, nor Arados followed the examples of the city-states of Asia Minor as soon as coinage was invented, or at least in the course of the sixth century, by minting coins in their turn. Did they not see the advantages? Was minting prohibited by the Achaemenid sovereigns? The latter allowed the circulation of croeseids, the coins of Croesus of Lydia, until Darius I undertook to have properly Persian money produced for the western part of the empire. The mint, located in Sardis, then produced silver shekels bearing the image of the Great King as an archer. A little later, gold coins, called darics, were issued in the eastern part of the empire. If Persian shekels appeared to find their place in the monetary circulation of the Greek city-states of Asia Minor (we must recall that these city-states were under Persian domination after 546), in contrast none of the Achaemenid issues seem to have been actually used for monetary purposes in the rest of the empire. The treasuries of archaic coins from the Levant and Egypt included cut-up pieces of silver, proof that the metal was weighed for want of confidence in the minted silver.

Nevertheless, during the fifth century, the ease of use provided by Athenian coinage must have gradually become apparent to Phoenician merchants. For a long time, Greek coinages, and especially that of Athens, in which these merchants had confidence and which were abundant, met all their needs. It was thus not before the second half of the fifth century at the earliest that the first issues from the Phoenician cities of Tyre, Sidon, and Arados began to appear. These cities adopted their own standards, lighter than the Attic version, and they decorated the coins with their own emblems, proceeding exactly as the Greek city-states had done before them.

But these coins had the disadvantage of novelty. For users located more to the east or to the south, in Arabia and in Yemen, who were used to owls and knew nothing else, the Phoenician coins inspired mistrust. Now, the production of owls was drying up. In fact, with the occupation of Decelea (a small town in Attica) by Spartan troops in 413, Athens found itself unable to exploit the Laurion mines that supplied its metal. Foreign coins could be melted down and the metal re-struck, but the volume of issues was declining. The disturbances in the exchanges between Phoenicia and Aegean Greece introduced by the Peloponnesian War further reduced the arrival of owls in Phoenician cities. A solution had to be found: it was to develop local versions of the owl, such as those issued by Gaza for its exchanges with Arabia Felix.

Are we to see Phoenicia and Gaza, then, as relays of Hellenism in the direction of Mesopotamia and Arabia Felix? This would be going too far. But the history of the "Phoenician" or "Arabian" owls attests to close relations between the two shores of the eastern Mediterranean, and indicates that people had not waited for Alexander's conquest to discover one another. From the time when the Phoenicians traded in the Greece of the "dark ages" (dark only for us, though less and less so), when the Greeks borrowed their writing system and perhaps, in part, a mode of political organization, the city-state, exchanges had never ceased. Whether the Phoenicians were under the control of the Assyrians (until 612–609), the Babylonians (until 539), or the Persians, trade with the Aegean world was never really hindered. To be sure, Greeks and Phoenicians found themselves on opposing sides in some conflicts, but we cannot forget that during the Greco-Persian Wars there were as many Greeks on the Phoenician side as on the other!

Generally speaking, from the fourth century on, Greeks frequented the Persian Empire in large numbers, its western regions in particular (not to mention the zones populated by Greeks, such as Asia Minor and Cyprus). It may be worthwhile to take a rapid look around in order to see what the Greeks could have known about the empire on the eve of Alexander's conquest and, conversely, what the peoples of that empire could have known about the Greeks.

A Greek presence in the Persian Empire, leaving aside the Greeks of Asia Minor, appeared as early as the middle of the sixth century, that is, starting with the foundation of the dynasty by Cyrus the Great. Archaeologists have observed that certain architectural and decorative achievements of Pasargadae, Persepolis, and Susa were the work of Greek artists or artisans. At Susa, the charter of the foundation of the palace mentions the Ionians specifically as those who brought cedar wood from Babylonia to Susa, but also as stonemasons. At Persepolis, in the ruins of the palace burned down by Alexander, among the thousands of tablets charred in the fire that have to do with the construction accounts, there is only one mention of Ionians working in the colonnaded hall in 483, but specialists recognize a type of stonecutting characteristic of the Greeks (who used a toothed chisel) in several sections of the great terrace. There was also a Greek inscription in the archaic Ionian alphabet in a quarry near Persepolis, reading "I belong to Pytharchos." In Pasargadae, the capital of Cyrus the Great, the use of toothed chisels also betrays a Greek presence. Among these artisans there may have been a number of prisoners of war (many earned ridiculously low salaries, which surely would not have attracted free artisans from Greece or Asia Minor), but we know of at least one Greek sculptor, Telephanes of Phocaea, who had been invited to work at the court of Xerxes and Darius II, in the middle of the fifth century.

Artisans and artists were not the only Greeks at the court of the Great King; we also find doctors, such as the celebrated Ctesias of Cnidos, the only one who left us a description of the empire, in *Persica*, his history of the Persians, unfortunately preserved only in part. But there were many others after him, from the era of Darius I to the end of the sixth century and the beginning of the fifth (Democedes of Croton), and throughout the entire fifth century (Apollonides of Cnidos, Polycritos of Cos), and we have the impression that Greek doctors alternated with Egyptians at the bedsides of the royal family. We also find soothsayers (and even a Greek sibyl under Cyrus the Great), explorers (Scylax of Caryanda, who explored the Oman Sea and the coasts of the Persian Gulf), a dancer (Zeno the Cretan), counselors of all sorts, and sometimes political refugees. But these Greeks at court were not confined to the royal palaces; others frequented the satrapic courts in the provinces of the empire, or those of the kings of Phoenicia.

We need to set apart three categories of Greeks settled in the Persian Empire. First, mercenaries, who were numerous starting in the fourth century. The expedition of Greek mercenaries in the service of the Achaemenid pretender Cyrus the Younger in 401–399, recounted in Xenophon's celebrated *Anabasis*, touched northern Syria only lightly, between the Syrian Gates and the Euphrates. But after the failure of the enterprise the Great King hired a number of mercenaries to lead his campaigns to reconquer Egypt, which had been chronically in revolt since the mid-fifth century. These mercenaries thus assiduously frequented Phoenicia, the point of departure for all royal expeditions to Egypt. At the time of Alexander's conquest, many Greek mercenaries thus found themselves in Persian armies.

There were also voluntary exiles who were threatened in their own city-states and preferred to take refuge at the court of the Great King. Themistocles, Sparta's regent Pausanias, and its king Demarates, the Gongylides, an Eretrian family believed to have opened the city's gates to the Persians in 490, and still others who left no traces settled in the empire, sometimes in proximity to Asia Minor, where the king gave them the income from a piece of land or a city for their support, but others at court, in the immediate royal entourage.

Finally, there were the deportees, Greeks punished for rebelling or resisting the king. These included, first of all, residents of Priene and Magnesia on the Meaender, who were deported because they had participated in a revolt right after the conquest, in 545. After the Ionian revolt, there were the Milesians, who were deported onto the banks of the Persian Gulf, at Ampe; the Eretrians, who settled after 490 in Arderikka, in Cissia, north of Susa; and the inhabitants of Barca in Cyrenaica, sent to the remote Bactrian region in 514. When Alexander passed through Susiana and Bactria, he freed unhappy Greeks who had been deported generations earlier, and urged them to return home. These populations formed small clusters of Greeks dispersed throughout the empire, but it must not be imagined that they transmitted the slightest Greek legacy to the surrounding populations. At most, they may have known what Greeks were!

But apart from these Greeks, whether they were passing through or settling in for the long haul, other Greeks frequented the Persian Empire under very different conditions. First, there were the ambassadors from the city-states, especially numerous in the second half of the fifth century and during the entire fourth century, when the Great King appeared as the arbiter of Greek conflicts. We know that Persian gold helped Sparta win out over Athens, and that the Great King imposed the dissolution of the Leagues during the peace of Antalcidas in 386, rightly called the "King's Peace." In the city-states, then, there were people who were well acquainted with the Persian Empire from the inside. It is all the more regrettable that, apart from Ctesias of Cnidos, none of these Greeks left the slightest account, the briefest description, of what they had seen in the empire.

One region experienced more intense exchanges with the Greeks than the others, especially in the fourth century, to the point that we can speak of cultural exchanges going beyond the sort that customarily accompanied trade: this was Phoenicia. Exchanges involving men were naturally more numerous at first: Greek mercenaries in Phoenicia, Phoenician merchants in Greece. Closer relations were woven between Athens and Sidon, whose king Strato was honored with the title *proxenos* as early as the 360s. But archaeological discoveries in Sidon show that cultural Hellenism penetrated into Phoenicia as early as the late fifth century. Its precise impact remains to be measured.

In Sidonian necropolises, several sarcophagi of exceptional quality have been discovered, dating from the late fifth to the late fourth centuries. The most recent, known as "Alexander's sarcophagus," can be left aside: it is agreed today that this was the sarcophagus of the last king of Sidon, Abdalonymos, after Alexander's conquest. The oldest may be the one known as the satrap's, finished around 430 (though some scholars situate it around 380–370); after that we have the Lycian sarcophagus and that of the Weeping Women, from the late fifth and the mid-fourth centuries, respectively; these are masterpieces of Greek sculpture. It is clear that this art corresponded to the tastes of rich Sidonians, although we cannot assess with precision the cultural impact of this undeniable change in aesthetic choices. Moreover, what are we to conclude when all the monuments come from a single city, Sidon, and perhaps from a royal necropolis, which is by definition exceptional? But a series of anthropoidal sarcophagi carved in marble from Paros by Ionians and their eastern students must correspond to the demands of a group larger than the royal family alone. To be sure, in overall appearance these sarcophagi seem foreign to Greek customs, for they take roughly human forms, following the Egyptian tradition; nevertheless, the heads are sculptured in the Greek style, with realistic faces and coiffures with carefully wrought curls. Such a mix of influences is found only here; it must correspond to a specific local demand. Thus there was a category of Phoenicians who were sensitive to the charms of Greek, and more specifically Ionian, art.

More precious still, because more revealing of popular taste, are the objects found in a *favissa* in Amrit, on the continent across from the island of Arados. Hundreds of fragments of Hellenic or Hellenized objects come from this repository, where they must have been buried at the beginning of the Hellenistic period. The vast majority come from Cyprus, which confirms this big island's role as a relay station. In a way, the attraction of Greek style among the wealthiest people, as attested both by the sarcophagi in Sidon and the taste attributed to Sidon's King Strato for Greek dancers and singers, is echoed even in more modest milieus. Thus at the time of the Alexandrian conquest, Phoenicia was already sensitive to certain aspects of Hellenism, including its cultural form. It was probably no accident that the culture of the new masters penetrated the Phoenician elites so quickly after 332, even if many nuances have to be brought to bear on this point (Chapter 25).

The converse is probably much less true. To be sure, the Greeks had known the Phoenicians for a long time, and had integrated them into certain of their myths—for example, that of Europa and Io (Chapter 20).

They knew that they owed them their writing system, but it is still surprising that so little information was transmitted by ancient authors before Alexander. Even a man such as Herodotus, who surely visited Phoenicia, gives very little specific information about the country. He knows the Greek myths about the Phoenicians, and he supplies some details about their navigations in the Mediterranean and about their colonial enterprises (especially in Carthage and Sicily). He is well acquainted with their role in the Persian fleet during the Greco-Persian Wars, but he never takes the trouble to describe their cities, their political institutions, their gods, either because he considers all this to be well known to his readers or because he views it as without interest. All in all, Herodotus tells us less about these Phoenician neighbors than about the Egyptians, the Scythians, or even the Arabs.

Under these conditions, it is hard to evaluate what the Greeks and the Phoenicians knew about one another on the eve of Alexander's conquest. We cannot go wrong in assuming that Greek culture had already penetrated certain governing milieus, at least through specific artistic forms. A number of merchants must even have known the Greek language. But everything else escapes us, and it is very difficult to say whether we are seeing the effect of a passing fad or a veritable infatuation with a seductive art form. By placing Phoenicia under the domination of the Macedonians, Alexander created entirely new conditions that could only accelerate and amplify a movement that had been initiated long before.

CHAPTER EIGHTEEN

The Susa Weddings, or Alexander, Iran, and the Greeks

Then he held also weddings at Susa, both his own and for his Companions; he married Dareius' eldest daughter Barsine, and, as Aristobulus says, another wife besides, the youngest daughter of Ochus, Parysatis. He had already taken to wife Roxane, the daughter of Oxyartes the Bactrian. To Hephaestion he gave Drypetis, also a daughter of Dareius, sister to his own wife, for he desired that Hephaestion's children should be his own nephews and nieces; to Craterus, Amastrine daughter of Oxyartes, Dareius' brother; to Perdiccas a daughter of Atropates, the satrap of Media; to Ptolemy the officer of the bodyguard and Eumenes the royal secretary, the daughters of Artabazus, Artacama to Ptolemy, Artonis to Eumenes; to Nearchus the daughter of Barsine and Mentor; to Seleucus the daughter of Spitamenes the Bactrian, and similarly to the other Companions the noblest daughters of Persians and Medes, to the number of eighty. These weddings were solemnized in the Persian fashion; chairs were placed for the bridegrooms in order; then after the health-drinkings the brides came in, and each sat down by the side of her bridegroom; they took them by the hand and kissed them, the King setting the example; for all the weddings took place together. In this, if ever, Alexander was thought to have shown a spirit of condescension and comradeship. Then the bridegrooms having received their brides led them back to their homes, and to all Alexander gave dowries. Any other Macedonians who had married Asian women Alexander ordered to be struck off the army list, and they proved to be more than ten thousand, and to all Alexander gave wedding gifts.

Arrian, *Anabasis of Alexander,* trans. E. Iliff Robson (Loeb Classical Library, 1933), vol. 2, pp. 215–217 (VII, iv, 4–8)

Susa (iran), february 324. Alexander had been marching toward home for nearly a year and a half—since the fall of 326, when his troops had refused to go farther and cross the Hyphasis, the eastern branch of the Indus River. They were expecting to see the end of the inhabited lands, and instead they found immense, seemingly limitless plains spreading before them. At that point, the old Macedonians, who had been campaigning for eight years, refused to follow, and what could the Conqueror do without his troops? And Alexander gave in. But there was no question of going straight back by the shortest route. The army went down the Indus Valley, engaged in battle (Alexander was seriously wounded), conquered the Sindh, and reached Patala, in the Indus Delta. Alexander had a port and a fleet built, because he wanted to have Nearchos, a good navigator, explore the coasts of the Persian Gulf. While Crateros was bringing back some of the troops by way of Kandahar and the center of Iran, Alexander, with the rest, would take a more southerly route, through Baluchistan, in order to follow Nearchos's itinerary to some extent. Alexander left India in August 325; Nearchos set sail in September. In December, the two groups managed to meet in Carmania before pursuing their own routes, one by land toward Persia, the other by sea to the mouth of the Euphrates. The return was hard on the weakened troops, who were obliged to traverse hostile, almost desertlike lands. A little later, Crateros met Alexander inside Carmania (Khanu), and it was an exhausted army that finally reached Persia and passed through the three ancient Persian capitals in turn, Pasargadae (where Alexander had the tomb of Cyrus the Great restored), Persepolis, and, finally, Susa.

Susa, a capital well known to the Greeks! In the era of Achaemenid splendor, embassies from the city-states came one after another to ask for aid and assistance against other Greeks. This was the framework Alexander chose for a spectacular ceremony designed to make an impression on people and, perhaps, to establish a clear political line for the future. Arrian alone reports, with the details we have just seen, what tradition has called "the Susa weddings." Neither Diodoros of Sicily nor Quintus Curtius, important historians of Alexander's reign, say a word about them, though it should be noted that the part of Quintus Curtius's text concerning this sojourn in Susa is lost. This is not critical, however, for it is highly unlikely that Arrian would have invented such a staging, and the episode must be basically authentic. Still, it needs to be understood and interpreted.

The decision to hold the Susa weddings is among those that have most fostered the image of a visionary Alexander. Might the Conqueror not have had in mind a fusion of races or cultures, in which there would be no more Greeks or Persians? Or, in the absence of such a cosmic vision, might the event not have been the expression of a Greco-Persian Empire that Alexander would command? Thus Ulrich Wilcken, the great German papyrologist, did not hesitate to see this episode as the beginning of a project aimed at blending Persians and other Iranians with the Macedonians in order to forge "a dominant people, to whom he could entrust the defence of his Asiatic Empire,"[1] to the exclusion of the Semites, the Anatolians, and the Egyptians.

It is very difficult to know what Alexander's projects may have been, for we do not have any memoirs. Moreover, is it appropriate to credit him with preconceived projects when his policies seem, by and large, to have been dictated by circumstances? This does not preclude a great ability to react, and, ultimately, a long-term vision that was modified in relation to new conditions. From this perspective, the Susa weddings take on major importance, for they embody the grounding of a policy that had been adopted much earlier, and they probably mark, behind the festivities, a point of rupture between Alexander and the Macedonians.

As of 331, Alexander had already enrolled in his service Persian leaders of the highest rank, doubtless judging that their knowledge of the country was irreplaceable and could help him avoid many missteps. This came about as soon as he believed his power was assured, that is, after the victory at Gaugamela and the entry into Babylon. It was at this point that he named Mazaeus satrap of Babylonia and Mithrenes satrap of Armenia (a province that Alexander had not conquered); a few weeks later, Aboulites, satrap of Persia, retained his command after Alexander's conquest of his province. This policy was pursued throughout the march through Iran and Central Asia, even if the satrap was often paired with a commander in chief of the Macedonian or Greek troops. We can understand why certain Macedonian leaders might have taken umbrage at a policy that seemed to invite them to share power, and thus honors. That was probably an exaggerated view of the situation, however, for these leaders did not all rally to Alexander; far from it. On the contrary, Alexander encountered vigorous resistance during his stay in Persepolis in the spring of 330. He had to face incessant, exasperating guerilla warfare. The burning of the Persepolis palace, which ancient historians of Alexander's reign could explain only by way of anecdotes, is quite likely to have been Alexander's response to that unexpected resistance. Not the order of a drunkard, still less the whim of a courtesan, but a logical decision. By burning the Persepolis palace, symbol of Achaemenid power (all the peoples of the empire were represented on the steps of its monumental staircase), Alexander clearly signified that the Achaemenid Empire had ended, that there was no justification for continued resistance on the part of the Persian nobility, and that he alone embodied the new power. This did not prevent him from assuming power in his own way without a break a little later on, after the death of Darius III.

The fire at Persepolis cannot mask the pursuit of a policy favorable to the Persian elites. The assassination of Darius III by people close to him allowed Alexander to appear as the king's avenger, and thus in some sense as his legitimate heir. The Persian elites, henceforth deprived of their leader, rallied in large numbers just as the Macedonians were beginning to grumble at the duration of the adventure. It was no accident if at that very moment Alexander began to adopt certain practices of the Achaemenid court, such as *proscynesis,* or the constitution of a harem of 365 concubines. The Macedonians complained, and Alexander experienced the first serious crisis within his entourage, and resolved it with maximum brutality, through assassination (he eliminated Philotas, head of the elite cavalry, and his father Parmenion). Whereas the war was growing more and more difficult (Alexander encountered very strong pockets of resistance in Sogdiana), his marriage to Roxana, the daughter of a noble Bactrian, Oxyathres, in the winter of 329–328, attested to a new rapprochement with the Iranian elites and to his desire to collaborate with the former Achaemenid administration.

Necessity drove Alexander to go further in this respect. The long campaign begun in 334 had exhausted the Macedonian troops, and the appeal for reinforcements from Greece, Macedonia, and Asia Minor scarcely sufficed to fill the gaps. Having arrived in central Asia, Alexander also had to take into account the length of his lines of communication. He knew he could not hold on to regions as remote as these forever by using recruits from Europe and the Aegean basin. He thus began to call on indigenous contingents. Better still, he formed an elite corps of young Persians who had been educated in the Greek manner and equipped like Macedonians. Thirty thousand troops were to be incorporated this way into the royal army.

The arrival in Susa in February 324 marked the end of a trying trip back; Alexander could not have avoided drawing lessons from it. To be sure, he had given the end of the expedition the air of a Dionysiac procession, punctuated with binges of drinking reminiscent of the Dionysiac cortege returning from India, but Alexander's lucidity did not allow him to forget that this inglorious return had been imposed on him by the Macedonians' refusal to proceed any farther. It was their fault that he had not been able to go beyond the limits of the Persian Empire. The Susa episode marked his visible determination, if not to create a Greco-Persian elite, at least to anchor his entourage deeply in an empire of which Iran and Mesopotamia were to constitute the center. The Susa weddings were carefully orchestrated, the choice of spouses calculated with precision: Alexander himself, a polygamist, married both a daughter of Darius III and a daughter of his predecessor, Artaxerxes III, thus bringing together a double royal legitimacy. His companions married, on orders, women chosen by Alexander as a function of their rank. Arrian does not mention the slightest resistance on the part of the companions, but these forced marriages may well have helped fuel the dissatisfaction that was brewing.

For at the same time Susa was taking in the thirty thousand young Persians who were to form an essential element of the new army. What is more, to fill the gaps provoked by the return of the veterans to Macedonia, Alexander incorporated more than twenty thousand Persian archers, rebels brought in by Peukestas, one of the very rare Macedonians to play the game of Greco-Persian fusion openly, for he had learned the Persian language.

Alongside the marriages celebrated at the highest level, we also need to look at the regularization of the unions of Macedonian soldiers with native women, prisoners of war, and others. According to Diodoros, it was at Susa that Alexander took an interest in the matter; he then sought out all those who had had children under these conditions (and in ten years of military operations, they must have been numerous); he found some ten thousand children, whom he freed, legitimized, and provided with Greek masters so they would be reared in the Greek manner.

All these factors unquestionably have to be taken together as a whole, but how much stress should be placed on the Iranian aspect? Arrian specifies, to be sure, that the Susa weddings were celebrated according to Iranian rites; this was no doubt a token concession to the brides' fathers and brothers. But the description of the accompanying festivities, according to

Chares of Mytilene (who was Alexander's high chamberlain and thus attended the event), shows that the organizers called on a constellation of Greek artists, players of flutes, lyres, and cithares, and comic and tragic actors. In the same spirit, I note that the young Persians were educated in the Greek manner and that the soldiers' legitimate children were provided with Greek masters. If there was a fusion of the elites, Hellenism found itself in first place, and there was no question of infusing either the army or the society with Persian culture.

However, these gestures aroused the ire of the army, undoubtedly driven by one of its leaders. Alexander, who was contemplating an expedition to Arabia, first had to confront the Macedonians' rebellion. When he announced to the army gathered in Opis on the Tigris that he was sending the veterans, soldiers who had been wounded or were otherwise unable to serve, back to Macedonia, the army revolted: could it be that from now on the conquerors had become useless and that the king was going to replace them with these soldiers drawn from the subjugated and conquered peoples? It took a good deal of skill on Alexander's part to bring the movement to a halt and persuade the Macedonians that they still occupied first place in his entourage. After withdrawing to his tent for several days while waiting for the rebels to come ask for his clemency, he offered a great banquet where, in very symbolic fashion, the Macedonians occupied the front rank, while the Persians were placed toward the rear.

On the eve of Alexander's death, the tension between the two elements on which the survival of the empire depended reached a climax. Was the death of the conqueror not going to lead to a radical change in policy on the part of his successors? If some Iranians managed to save their positions at the head of their satrapies during the successive distributions of 323 and 321, let us note that only one of the companions kept his wife from Susa: Seleucus, husband of Apame. Is it by chance that Seleucus was also the heir to Alexander's Iranian possessions in 312?

CHAPTER NINETEEN

A Hymn for Demetrios Poliorcetes, or New Kings, New Gods

The highest and dearest of the gods are come to our city. Hither, indeed, the time hath brought together Demeter and Demetrius. She comes to celebrate the solemn mysteries of the Daughter, but he, as is meet for the god, is here in gladness, fair and smiling. Something august he seemeth, all his friends about him, and he himself in their midst, his friends the stars, even as he is the sun. O son of the most mighty god Poseidon and of Aphrodite, hail! For other gods are either far away, or have not ears, or are not, or heed us not at all; but thee we can see in very presence, not in wood and not in stone, but in truth. And so we pray to thee. First bring peace, thou very dear! For thou hast the power. That Sphinx which crushes, not Thebes but all Hellas—the Aetolian who sits upon the cliff, even as the Sphinx of old, and snatches up and carries off all our men—against it I cannot fight. For it is the Aetolian way to carry off the things of their neighbours, and now even the things more distant. Best were it that thou thyself punish him; but if not, find some Oedipus who shall either send him hurtling down, or turn him to rock.

Duris of Samos, cited in Athenaeus, *The Deipnosophists,* trans.
Charles Burton Gulick (Loeb Classical Library, 1967), vol. 3,
pp. 143–145 (VI, 253 d–f)

ATHENS, 291 B.C.E. King Demetrios Poliorcetes landed in Athens for the second time: he had already come in 307, and his behavior caused a scandal. But in 291, the city feared an invasion by the Aetolians above all else. This people from central Greece, until then somewhat scorned by most Greeks because they had kept an ancient political structure, knowing nothing of city-states, was able to organize itself into a powerful league that gradually came to dominate all of central Greece, including Boeotia, at the gates of Attica. Duris makes a direct allusion to this and recalls the memory of Oedipus, who had rid the region of the Sphinx that had been interrogating travelers on the route to Thebes. Athens had been occupied since 322 by a Macedonian regiment; the Athenians had no way to defend themselves, and they did not know to what god they should turn. As Duris notes somewhat insolently: "For other gods are either far away, or have not ears, or are not, or heed us not at all; but thee we can see in very presence, not in wood and not in stone, but in truth." So the 307 visit, when Demetrios had insisted on being housed in the Pantheon, was forgotten. And the poet paid by the city-state to sing the king's praises did not fear to establish a parallel between King Demetrios's entrance into the city-state and the procession that was at that very moment leading the goddess Demeter of Eleusis to the Acropolis in Athens.

But the hero of the moment needs to be presented a little more fully. Demetrios Poliorcetes, son of Antigonus the One-Eyed, a companion at arms of Philip of Macedonia, whom Alexander had left to guard Asia with the title Satrap of Magna Phrygia, at the beginning of his expedition to the east. The son remained in his father's shadow, but given the latter's age (he was around sixty when Alexander died), Demetrios served as his father's secular arm, even if Antigonus did not give up going to war himself when necessary. Demetrios won his nickname during the siege of Rhodes, in 305, which he led on his father's behalf: despite the failure he experienced there, the importance of the poliorcetic means deployed earned him the nickname "Besieger of Cities," and his final failure did not call this back into question. It was a little earlier, when Demetrios had just crushed the Seleucid fleet off Salamis of Cyprus, that Antigonus took the royal title, thus positioning himself as Alexander's confirmed successor, and he associated his son with this move, attesting to his intention to found a dynasty.

When Alexander died, in June 323 in Babylon, his chief generals and companions had resolved to recognize the only legitimate heir to the Macedonian crown, Alexander's half-brother Philip Arrhidaeus, despite his well-known incompetence and the ambitions several of them probably had for themselves. There were actually at least two reasons for this. One may have been operative only for a short time: Roxana, Alexander's Persian wife, was pregnant; if she bore a son, the succession would be assured in the most incontestable way. To be sure, there would have to be a regency, but the wisest course was to wait. The second could not be acknowledged openly: the ambitions of some thwarted the projects of others, and while waiting until one or the other should find himself in a position of strength, it was no doubt best to distribute roles among themselves, without giving anyone a preponderant position.

Roxana gave birth to a son, Alexander (IV), who was thus proclaimed king with his uncle Philip (III) Arrhidaeus. But the power clearly lay elsewhere, according to the successive arrangements that need not be spelled out at this point. Rather quickly, some names emerged that were also at the origin of the principal Hellenistic kingdoms. These are the ones we shall focus on here.

In the first rank, there was Antigonus the One-Eyed. Although he did not participate in Alexander's march into Iran and India, as the master of western Asia he controlled the lines of ground communication between Macedonia and Alexander's new empire. He wasted no time in asserting himself as the chief claimant to the succession. He had rapidly become the master of Macedonia, Asia Minor, most of Syria, and the upper satrapies, that is, of all the space stretching from Iran to the Indus and central Asia. He was unquestionably the most powerful military leader from 319 on; when the empire was divided up in Triparadeisos in 321, his colleagues entrusted the command of the army to him and gave him control over finances. This explains why all the others readily banded together to put obstacles in the way of his ambitions. Ptolemy, son of Lagos, one of Alexander's closest companions after the death of Hephaistion, had taken over Egypt after Alexander's death; he clashed with Antigonus in Syria, for Ptolemy believed, like all the pharaohs before him, that the place to defend Egypt was not the Delta but Syria. To weaken his rival, he did not hesitate to form an alliance with an officer who had not played a major role immediately after Alexander's death: Seleucus, leader of the *hypaspistai*, elite troops in the Macedonian army. Ptolemy helped Seleucus establish himself in Babylonia, which could have deprived Antigonus of all contact with the upper satrapies.

But whatever the assorted ambitions may have been, there could be no question of succeeding Alexander as long as legitimate and recognized kings still existed. The assassination of Philip III Arrhidaeus in 317 on the order of Alexander's mother, Olympias, followed by her condemnation to death for the crime, began to thin the ranks of the legitimate lineages. As young Alexander IV approached the age of majority, several people were worried. Cassander, who had the king and his mother under his protection in Macedonia, took the initiative to have them assassinated (310). There were open expressions of indignation, secret sighs of satisfaction; everyone took precautions, for it must not look as though one of the Diadochs sought to create a situation of legitimacy for himself. For a sister of Alexander the Great remained, Cleopatra. A fine match, for someone with ambition! Olympias, her mother, had succeeded in marrying her to Perdiccas, Alexander's chiliarch—a rank second only to the king—in 323–322, but Perdiccas's assassination in 322 left her free again. Ptolemy tried to marry her in 309–308, but Antigonus, who governed Asia, where Cleopatra had taken refuge, saw the danger and preferred to have her assassinated. While awaiting an uncertain outcome, Alexander's generals administered a kingdom without a king. For how long?

Antigonus the One-Eyed was the first to make a move, in the wake of his son's victory at Salamis of Cyprus, at the conclusion of a carefully prepared staging. The messenger bringing the news of the victory presented himself at the palace with an expressionless face; he agreed to speak only in the presence of the king, who was frantic with worry. Then the messenger greeted him with the title "King Antigonus," a title that the latter did not refuse and that he also granted his son, who became "King Demetrios." Failure to react would have signified, for his rivals, that they recognized Antigonus as Alexander's de facto successor. That was obviously out of the question, and in the months that followed, Ptolemy, Seleucus, Cassander, and Lysimachos all proclaimed themselves kings. They did not all succeed in founding dynasties, but Antigonus, Ptolemy, and Seleucus in fact launched the three most important Hellenistic dynasties, those that established their seats in Macedonia, Egypt, and Syria, and reigned from there over the greater part of Alexander's empire.

Alexander had unquestionably inaugurated a new type of monarchy. By birthright he was "king of the Macedonians," and this obliged him to respect certain rules, such as having himself acclaimed by the Macedonian popular assembly. But from the time of his passage through Asia, Alexander had seemed to go beyond that traditional framework. Not that he neglected the duties that were his as "king of the Macedonians"; on the contrary, he was often careful to submit to them. But victory gave another dimension to his rule. For the Greeks, it was not so much "Alexander, king of the Macedonians," as "King Alexander," as if the royal quality were attached to his very person. This exceptional character was what allowed Alexander to be honored as a god by the Greeks of Asia Minor, moreover, as early as 334. This is the origin of the cult of sovereigns that was to prosper during the Hellenistic period, and there is no point in pursuing the long-standing efforts to find its origins in the Orient. The Greeks of Asia deemed that Alexander deserved both to be king, as conqueror, and to be god, as savior, for he had delivered them from Persian domination. These two notions, victory and salvation, were the basis for the legitimacy of new kings from that point on.

It was in fact in the wake of a victory that Antigonus was greeted as king, and the others responded rapidly by emphasizing their own victories. Moreover, for the dynasties that were founded in Hellenistic Asia a little later, it is almost always possible to establish a direct relation between the claiming of the royal title and a striking victory. Thus at Pergamon, from the late 280s on, a certain Philetairos manifested his independence with respect to the Seleucids. To be sure, that independence remained threatened, but neither Philetairos nor his nephew and heir Eumenes I ever dared to cross the line, even though doing so would have been a way to signal their obvious pretensions. Attalos I had to win a striking victory over Antiochus Hierax (a Seleucid usurper) and his Gallic allies around 230 in order to include the royal title on his coins: it is true that his victory saved the kingdom itself from disappearing. Similarly, the king of Bithynia, Zipoites, seemed to have waited to achieve victory over Lysimachos before adopting the royal title in 297. We could find additional examples in Cappadocia and Pontus.

Treatises "on royalty" were increasingly in fashion in the third century, and they confirm this analysis. What grounded the legitimacy of a king was above all victory, a manifest sign of divine favor. To be sure, there was no shortage, later, of defeated kings who held on to power, but the strength of the dynastic idea ended up, over time, counterbalancing the original principle of legitimacy. Nevertheless, this principle was never completely forgotten, for it was probably no accident that incompetent, weak, defeated kings saw usurpers stand up against them, challenging their titles. The dynastic quarrels that poisoned the last century of Lagid history and especially Seleucid history originated in part in the military weakness of sovereigns.

However this may be, the personal character of royalty remained constantly affirmed. But the reason for this did not always lie in an imitation of Alexander, even if we are obliged to see this as the essential cause. In fact, when Antigonus the One-Eyed proclaimed himself king, unless he had wanted to declare himself "king of the Macedonians," it is not clear of what country or of what people he could have claimed sovereignty. To the extent that his ambition was to recuperate the entirety of Alexander's empire, it goes without saying that he could not set any limits to his royalty. Thus he could only be "King Antigonus," whose kingdom would be as vast as possible. Even a king such as Ptolemy, who had obviously chosen to rely on Egypt, had not given up hope of dominating other regions: Syria, Cyprus, the coast of Asia Minor, the Aegean Islands. No territorial or ethnic definition of his power would have made any sense at all, short of a long and laborious enumeration.

This new conception of royalty helps us understand the development that the cult of sovereigns underwent starting with Alexander. The notion is important, for it strongly marked the Roman Empire, which borrowed from the Greeks this concept of kings assimilated to gods and adapted it only marginally.

Historians refused for a long time to believe that the Greeks, models of intelligence and political reflection, could have adopted a practice that is at first glance so shocking. Thus for a long time the Greek practice of divinizing kings was attributed to imitation of the Orient (without specifying too clearly what Orient). Fortunately, such theories have been abandoned by now, for there was no need for the Greeks to imitate the kingdoms of the Near East in this respect. First, because the peoples of the Near East who viewed their king as a god were rare: neither the Phoenicians nor the Persians nor the Babylonians subscribed to that idea, and only the Egyptians characterized pharaohs as "sons of Re," that is, sons of the sun god. The Greeks were doubtless aware of this, but nothing suggests that they borrowed the idea from Egypt. Above all, this would be to forget that the initiative for the divinization of Alexander did not follow the conquest but preceded it: we have already seen that the Greeks of Asia voted divine honors for Alexander as early as 334.

Nevertheless, the idea did not please everyone. In 324 when Alexander asked the Greeks to award him divine honors in all the city-states, people laughed at the notion, in Athens as elsewhere. But the Athenians prudently waited for the king to die before condemning to a fine of ten talents—a colossal sum for a private individual—the orator Demades, who had spoken in favor of introducing this "new god"; the accusation of impiety even cost him his civic rights, for he was unable to pay the fine. Yet these same Athenians commissioned Duris of Samos to write the hymn cited above, in which vain flattery and political lucidity are conjugated in an inimitable style. In the intervening time, the exception had become the rule.

The divine honors adopted by vote for Alexander were justified, in the Greeks' eyes, by the extraordinary divine protection he enjoyed, but even more by the salvation he brought to the city-states and peoples. The idea of a savior king *(soter)* is one of the ideas most solidly anchored in mentalities as of the late fourth century. The salvation expected from a king could take multiple forms: avoiding the domination of an enemy army, sparing the ravages of war or banditry, returning or buying back prisoners of war, supplying the necessary wheat in case of a grain crisis. It could go as far as the refoundation of the city, if the king took the initiative to undertake important constructions that gave the city-state a new appearance; at that point, the city did not fear to honor the king as a new "founder" *(ktistes)* on the same level as the hero (or the god) responsible for the original foundation. This image of the king as the source of salvation is found over and over in literature as well as in inscriptions in honor of the kings.

Under these conditions, the divine quality of kings imposed itself. Did not kings dispose of prerogatives that belonged to the gods: the power to act, the power to save? A late epigram sums up the situation well: "What is a god? The one who exercises power. What is a king? The equal of a god!"[1]

Duris of Samos had already said the same thing. Between a powerless god and an all-powerful king, it is not hard to see where the source of salvation lies! The real soter was much more the king than the god. Does this mean that the Greeks—and the Romans after them—really began to view the sovereigns as gods? It would be doing them an injustice to think that they made no distinctions—if only because, unlike gods, sovereigns proved to be mortal. Indeed, if we read the anonymous maxim cited above carefully, we do not find an assertion that the kings are gods, but only that they are "equivalent to the gods" *(isotheoi)*. And the sovereign-gods were often associated in their temples with the traditional gods, sharing honors with them without being precisely their equals. Other indications attest to this slightly subordinate character; people did not fear to offer the gods sacrifices for the health of the king, which gave the latter human stature. Similarly, people spoke of the "god Antiochus" or the "god Ptolemy"; the specification was unnecessary when referring to an Olympian god. A sovereign was sometimes identified with a god by being called a "New Dionysus" or a "New Helios." In contrast, a temple could be erected in honor of a divinized king; he was granted epithets characteristic of the gods ("savior"); contests were organized in his honor. And the Greeks never took the trouble to make the distinction in their vocabulary, as the Romans did later on. The Romans, when they adopted the cult of sovereign, reserved for dead emperors the title *divus,* "divine," and not *deus,* "god," whereas in the same situation the Greeks spoke of *theos,* "god." This is more than a nuance.

This cult of sovereigns, accepted if not sought after by the first Hellenistic sovereigns, did not take long to spread. In reality, it developed in two forms that need to be distinguished. On the one hand, the Greek city-states, wherever they were located, were free to decide to honor some particular king with a cult, to dedicate a temple to him, to organize festivals, to give his name to a month of the year or to a civic tribe. Only the city-state itself was bound by such measures, even though it had the king's agreement. It did not fail to inform him by an official embassy, and if it was not already a matter of thanking him for benefits received, there is no doubt that the city-state hoped to profit in some way from the measure.

On the other hand, the kings had the idea of organizing a cult of the state, which would regroup the members of the court and the administration around the dynasty and the king in place. The first to have had this idea seems to have been Ptolemy II, who instituted a cult for his deceased parents, Ptolemy I and Queen Berenice. After the death of his own spouse, Arsinoe, he divinized her in turn, and shortly thereafter, as the spouse of a goddess, he found it normal to proclaim himself a god. After him, all the Lagid rulers did the same, forming pairs of god-kings associated with deceased and divinized sovereigns. Nothing was better suited to founding dynastic legitimacy.

The Seleucids acted in the same way, although we have very few details. We know only that in the time of Antiochus III (223–187), there was a sanctuary of sovereigns in every satrapy of the kingdom, and the high priest and priestess were chosen from among the most prominent officials—such as the strategos (governor of the satrapy) in Phoenicia, or the

Seleucid king's own daughter in Media. Others acted differently. For example, the Attalids of Pergamon never divinized living sovereigns, only the dead, and the Antigonids never organized an official cult of sovereigns. This did not prevent either group from being honored as gods by city-states that were so inclined, either in their own kingdoms or elsewhere.

The irruption of Roman power in Greece and then in Asia Minor caused changes that show to what extent the idea of associating power with the notion of divinity had become powerful among the Greeks. In fact, when the kings disappeared, the Greeks no longer knew exactly whom to honor as gods. There could be no question of transferring honors that were valid for eternity to the Roman consuls, who changed every year. So a new goddess began to be honored: *Roma*, an allegory of power par excellence, sometimes associated with the Senate. Greek-style contests were created for her, such as the *Rhomaia* of Xanthos (Lycia). But this solution was not entirely satisfactory either, for it amounted to honoring an abstraction, which went against the deep reasons for the cult of the sovereigns. Let us recall Duris's words: "thee we can see in very presence, not in wood and not in stone, but in truth." Thus the Greeks transferred to prestigious Roman leaders (Flamininus, Sulla, Pompey, Caesar, Antony), and to governments that were particularly benevolent toward them (Mucius Scaevola in Asia), the honors that they had until then granted kings. Power was embodied in men; these men were to be honored like gods. This shocked the Romans initially, and some (such as Cicero) refused; but they rapidly came to understand the political advantages, and ended up going along with the practice. At the same time, wealthy Greeks, remarkable for their generosity toward the community, benefited from the same honors: Theophanes of Mytilene, who had obtained freedom for his city-state from Pompey, was identified with Zeus Liberator; in Pergamon, Diodoros Pasparos (around 69) and, in Cnidos, Artemidoros (around 50) also received isotheoi, honors "equivalent to those accorded the gods," after having won important political and fiscal advantages for their city-states owing to embassies taken to Rome at their own expense. Appearances notwithstanding, the framework here had not changed: all power was shown to be divine in nature, and the power of benefactors who "saved" their city-states through political interventions and their own generosity was certainly equivalent to that of the kings of yesteryear, the Roman governors, or the *imperators.*

167

One last avatar of the cult put an end to this proliferation of divinized powers. In 29 B.C.E., Greeks from the Roman provinces of Asia and Bithynia asked Octavius for the right to render him divine honors as they had had the habit of doing for other benefactors. Once again, let us note that the initiative came from the Greeks of Asia Minor. Octavius hesitated, fearing that in Rome he would be mocked, or accused of angling for royalty. He nevertheless accepted, on condition that he would be associated with Roma and that the Roman citizens settle for participating in a cult of the divine Julius, his father. Asia and Bithynia thus set the example for a cult that was gradually organized in all the provinces where Greek was spoken, except Egypt and Judaea. But above all, fairly rapidly, the provincials understood that henceforth the emperor and the members of his family would be the only ones who could benefit from such honors. Ordinary individuals—even munificent benefactors—and provincial governors would be ineligible, lacking special authorization from the emperor. As it happened, the cult of sovereigns returned to its source, honoring power in the person of the one who embodied it henceforth all alone.

CHAPTER TWENTY

In Io's Footsteps, or Greek Settlement in Alexander's Empire

Furthermore, Antiocheia is the metropolis of Syria; and here was established the royal residence for the rulers of the country. And it does not fall much short, either in power or in size, of Seleuceia on the Tigris or Alexandria in Aegypt. Nicator also settled here the descendants of Triptolemus, whom I mentioned a little before. And it is on this account that the Antiocheians worship him as a hero and celebrate a festival in his honour on Mt. Casius in the neighbourhood of Seleuceia. It is said that he was sent by the Argives in search of Io, who disappeared first in Tyre, and that he wandered through Cilicia; and that there some of his Argive companions left him and founded Tarsus, but the others accompanied him into the next stretch of seaboard, gave up the search in despair, and remained with him in the river-country of the Orontes; and that Gordys, the son of Triptolemus, along with some of the peoples who had accompanied his father, emigrated to Gordyene, whereas the descendants of the rest became fellow-inhabitants with the Antiocheians.

Strabo, *Geography,* trans. Horace Leonard Jones
(Loeb Classical Library, 1928), vol. 7, p. 243 (XVI, ii, 5)

ANTIOCH (SYRIA), 300 B.C.E. Usually known as Antioch on the Orontes, or Antioch near Daphne, it became the capital of Seleucid Syria, then of Roman Syria. Strabo, the great geographer of the Augustan era, surely visited the city, one of the three largest in the entire Orient in his day, along with Seleucia on the Tigris (near contemporary Baghdad) and Alexandria. In his narrative, he deemed it useful, after a brief description of the city and the conditions of its founding, to go back in time and integrate into the history a series of legends that fit perfectly, from his standpoint. But let us retain from this account first of all that in Strabo's time the three most populous Greek city-states in the ancient world were located in the new Greek world that had emerged from Alexander's conquest, and that each had been founded ex nihilo, one by Alexander (Alexandria) and the other two by Seleucus Nicator, the first of the Seleucids. The situation was hardly an ordinary one, in reality, even if little attention was paid to it thereafter; it invites questions about the role of the Greeks in the major phenomenon constituted by the urbanization of the Hellenized Near East. Why so many new foundations in a land that already included many large and beautiful cities? Were all these foundations successful? And how were they viewed in relation to the old city-states of the Greek world, rich with a history going back several centuries that gave them immense prestige?

Alexander set the example, as he did in many other areas, by founding along his route what the ancient authors called "city-states." From Alexandria in Egypt to Alexandria Eschate ("Extreme": modern Khujand) and Alexandria in Opiane on the Hyphasis (Beas) River, the easternmost branch of the Indus, he multiplied foundations of cities and named them after himself, for example Alexandria in Aria (Herat), Alexandria in Arachosia (Kandahar), Alexandria in the Caucasus (Bagram, north of Kabul), after creatures he held dear (his horse Bucephalos is associated with him in an Alexandria Bucephala in India), or after some geographical or functional peculiarity (Aornos, "without birds," e.g., inaccessible). Sowing kernels of Greek and Macedonian populations everywhere along his route, he seemed in the eyes of the ancients to have spread the model of the city-state to the outer limits of the ancient Achaemenid Empire.

In reality, there were probably relatively few "city-states" in the technical sense of the term, that is, cities endowed with the specific political institutions characteristic of a *polis*. Alexander left behind very small groups of men, Macedonians for the most part but occasionally Greeks, who had to find wives locally and had to cohabit with an indigenous population that outnumbered them. It may be that all these settlements aspired to become city-states one day, but it remains doubtful that they all were such from the outset. There were some exceptions, such as Alexandria in Egypt, to which Alexander gave a certain importance by making it much more than a military colony organized around a garrison. But at the time of Alexander's death the city was not yet ten years old, and it must have still been a vast construction site.

However this may be, the model provided by Alexander as founder, in a way relaunching colonization as the Greeks had practiced it in the archaic period (Chapter 2), was followed by a number of his successors. Some of them, such as the Lagids, showed prudence in this area. Alexandria was completed, but the masters of Egypt were only modest founders of city-states: just one in Eygpt (a Ptolemais), a few in southern Syria and in Phoenicia, more through promotion of indigenous cities than through creation ex nihilo—for example, Philadelphia (modern Amman), Berenike (Aqaba), Ptolemais (Akko), and especially the ancient Phoenician city-states (Chapter 25)—and others, finally, in their possessions in southern Anatolia. Thus a decree from the small, ancient Cilician city-state of Nagidos has been found explaining how the king created the new foundation of Arsinoeia on land cut off from its territory. Others were more active, such as the Attalids of Pergamon, who colonized their own small realm intensively starting in the first half of the third century, and pursued their policy of foundation when they had grown considerably after the peace of Apamea in Phrygia in 188, founding Attaleia (modern Antalya), for example, on the coast of Pamphylia. Diadochs such as Antigonus the One-Eyed and Lysimachos were also founders of several new city-states, Lysimachos on the Straits and Antigonus in Syria.

But the undisputed champions of this policy were certainly the Seleucids, who inherited the largest part of Alexander's empire, and who had the time required. In fact, most of their foundations were carried out by their first two sovereigns, Seleucus I (312–281) and Antiochus I (281–261). After that, only Antiochus IV (175–164) refounded a few indigenous city-states as Greek city-states, such as Epiphaneia (Hama in Syria) or Antioch-Jerusalem, at the request of the Hellenized inhabitants (Chapter 28). As for the foundations of the first two kings, it would be tedious to list them all; instead, let us look at the situation in broad terms.

In the first place, the new foundations were very unevenly distributed. Seleucid Syria, that is, central and northern Syria, had most of them, and the largest ones, such as the four "sisters" of the Syrian Tetrapolis, Antioch-by-Daphne, Seleucia Pieria, Laodicea-by-the-Sea, and Apamea on the Orontes. There were far fewer in Mesopotamia (Seleucia on the Tigris), in Iran (Laodicea in Media, modern Nehavend, Seleucia on the Eulaios, ex-Susa); as for central Asia, Alexander had already founded so many Greek settlements there that little remained to be done. We must add Asia Minor, where the Seleucids implanted a number of new colonies.

These foundations can be divided into two main groups.[1] A great many of them were foundations ex nihilo, or virtually so—in the latter case they replaced an indigenous village, or an ancient city that had fallen into such a deep decline that the foundation could look like a thorough-going creation. This was the case of the four city-states mentioned above, although Apamea replaced an ancient Persian military colony, Pharnake, which had itself been refounded under the name Pella by Antigonus the One-Eyed. To this list we would need to add a large number of other Seleucid foundations, such as Seleucia on the Tigris and Dura-Europos on the Euphrates. Others, perhaps as many, were founded on previous indigenous settlements, large or small but so profoundly transformed that a name change seemed justified: Apamea in Phrygia was none other than the ancient regional capital Kelainai, Seleucia on the Eulaios the ancient Achaemenid administrative capital Susa, Edessa the ancient Orhai, Antioch in Mygdonia the city of Nisibis, and so on. According to John Malalas, a Syrian from Antioch who lived in the sixth century C.E. but who relied on an older source, Pausanias the Chronographer, Seleucus I alone founded seventy-five new city-states and Appian, a generally well-informed Greek author from the second century C.E., attributes fifty-nine to him; some forty have been identified for the first two Seleucids, and many cities remain simply names for us. This does not mean that they were invented by the Ancients, but that we still have a great deal left to discover. Thus, while some foundations have not been localized, in contrast we know of some Hellenistic settlements whose ancient names remain unknown (Jebel Khalid on the Euphrates, Ras Ibn Hani near Laodicea-by-the-Sea).

As with Alexander's foundations, it is very doubtful, despite the terms used by the ancient authors, that all these cities were "city-states" in the institutional sense of the term. We can even be sure of the contrary for most of the colonies founded in Asia Minor, but also for Dura-Europos, a military colony. The question remains open even for as important a city as Apamea on the Orontes, conceived as a gigantic garrison (this is where the Seleucids kept the elephants they used as weapons of mass destruction). To be sure, over time, Dura, Apamea, and many other cities also achieved the rank of polis, but this may have happened only gradually, as the foundations came to shelter enough colonists to make civic institutions viable.

For we must not imagine that all these cities sprang up in a few months or years, like the new cities created on the periphery of our own metropolises. On the contrary, it was a slow process, as we can tell from the recent excavations at Apamea and Dura-Europos. Both founded around 300, neither really began to develop until the middle of the second century, when Dura adopted a regular urban layout. And we can be certain that others vegetated, faded away, disappeared. We know of at least one city-state that was developed and then abandoned. Apamea on the Euphrates was located on the left bank of the Euphrates, across from Seleucia-Zeugma. A major river crossing was located there, and the twin cities shared guard duty, as it were. When the Parthians seized the eastern part of the Seleucid kingdom, they reached Apamea on the Euphrates, which for unknown reasons struck them as without interest. The city declined, and even though it was located on the border between the Seleucids and the Parthians, then between the Romans and the Parthians, it was abandoned; only Seleucia-Zeugma prospered, growing rich from its position as a border city, as became clear with the discovery of sumptuous houses covered with paintings and mosaics during the salvage efforts undertaken in the 1990s in connection with the construction of the Birecik dam. If Apamea on the Euphrates nevertheless existed for three centuries—not a negligible period, after all—we must not overlook the fact that foundations could fail much more rapidly, and thus we shall probably never find all the cities mentioned by the ancient authors, who did not distinguish between the ones that succeeded and those that failed.

But city-states for whom? And for what purpose? In somewhat older works, which make Alexander and—on occasion—his successors sound like propagandists for a civilizing Hellenism, the foundation of the Greek city-states is represented as a privileged way to spread Greek culture among the natives. This viewpoint, marked with the seal of the triumphant colonialism of the period between 1880 and 1940, has been vigorously contested since, and rightly so, for nothing authorizes such conclusions. First, because the new foundations—let us speak of cities, whatever their real status at the outset—were destined for Greeks and Macedonians, who alone would reap the advantages attached to the settlement. The new cities were colonies to be populated, destined to receive Greek or Macedonian colonists (there was little distinction between these groups on the cultural level). Their territory was thus divided into parcels attributed to the colonists: an allotment of agricultural lands, and a plot of land in the city for a house and garden. Recent studies of ancient land surveys, made on the basis of aerial photographs taken during the French Mandate, show a clear coherence between the urban network and the way the territory near the city was parceled out in both Antioch and Damascus. According to Malalas, Antioch was divided into fifty-three hundred lots, which gives an idea of the size of the early city. In Dura, regulations governing successions provided for returning allotments to the king if there were no heir, so that the king could install a newcomer there and keep the city from declining.

It cannot be repeated too often that the foundations of Greek city-states were above all intended to provide Greek colonists with a framework for the way of life to which they were accustomed. Both military colonies and colonies destined to be populated thus included agricultural land that allowed for the support of the new inhabitants, whether they themselves farmed or were owners renting out their fields. All other aspects were secondary in the beginning, even if some rapidly took on importance. To be sure, it is probable that the founding kings did not choose the sites at random and that they set some particular goals for each settlement. We saw earlier the role played by Apamea on the Orontes as the kingdom's principal military camp and the place where elephants were kept. Similarly, Dura was a military outpost on the Middle Euphrates, well situated on the edge of the plateau to keep watch over a large territory. Seleucia Pieria and Laodicea-by-the-Sea were indispensable ports for the Seleucids on the part of the Syrian coastline that they controlled, and Seleucus I may have considered making this Seleucia his capital before he conferred that role on Antioch. Moreover, the success of each of these cities attracted new inhabitants, especially natives drawn by the possibility of setting up shop as artisans or tradesmen. A prosperous city saw an influx of all sorts of merchandise, especially when it was a royal residence or when it harbored well-to-do individuals such as soldiers and royal agents. It is clear that several of these cities became important economic centers, creating in northern Syria and Anatolia alike a new urban network that modified earlier patterns of circulation. But this was the consequence of the success of the city-states, not the original goal. Kings did not found cities in order to make markets of them, or production centers; cities evolved in these directions in proportion to their success.

In the same way, populated by Greeks, these cities were foyers of Greek culture in the broadest sense: people spoke Greek there, frequented gymnasia, lived in the Greek manner. In northern Syria, for example, to a considerable extent the colonists reproduced a new Greece, as evidenced even in place names. Apart from the dynastic toponyms such as Antioch, Seleucia, Apamea or Laodicea, a number of cities bore names drawn from Greek toponyms (Tegea, Chalcis), and still more had Macedonian origins (Europos, Gindaros, Amphipolis, Edessa, Beroia, Kyrrhos), even in names of regions (Pieria, Mygdonia, Kyrrhestis). This amounted to transforming northern Syria into a new Macedonia, where the colonists felt at home. The parallel with the colonization of North America is not completely unjustified, on this point at least.

These Greek foyers attracted natives, and it is certain that some of them were drawn to Greek culture, out of interest or taste. The tradition holds that prominent natives were the first to adopt some or all of the practices of the new masters, as the only way they could keep their status as heads of their communities. It is thus probable that some portion of the Syrian, Anatolian, Babylonian, and Iranian elites merged fairly quickly into the new settlements, spoke Greek, and shared in the Greek lifestyle sufficiently to appear "Greek" themselves in the long run (Chapter 25). The culture of the masters could not help but attract prominent natives, but this in no way implies that the city-states were founded *in order* to Hellenize the locals. The kings were largely unconcerned with this prospect; it held virtually no interest for them. Without reducing the Hellenistic sovereigns to somber brutes, military men thirsty for blood and wealth, shamelessly pillaging the occupied lands, as in the image Victor Hanson seeks to impose, there is no doubt that their goal remained primarily the regular collection of tribute, the indispensable means behind their military and diplomatic action.[2] That prominent natives became "Greek" represented no advantage for the kings in this respect. In contrast, and it is undoubtedly in this way that the Hellenistic world differed profoundly from later colonial societies, any man could become Greek as completely as he wished, and could thus blend into the mass of Greeks in Syria or elsewhere without having to abandon his language, his ancestral customs, or even his lifestyle (Chapter 25). We must not overlook the fact that a number of philosophers in the Hellenistic period were Hellenized Phoenicians, not Syrian Greek descendants of colonists, even though we do have examples of the latter, such as Posidonios of Apamea.

175

These new foundations thus met different fates. Many became important cities and remained so for centuries. They suffered nevertheless from what can be called a deficit of history, hence a deficit of prestige and glory. The fact that they were of relatively recent origin put them in a position of inferiority with respect to the old city-states of Greece. Few had the good fortune of Sidon, characterized by Greek myths as a colony of Argos and a metropolis of Thebes (Chapter 25). Those that were entirely new city-states, without even an indigenous past, had to resign themselves to appearing as recent creations. However, many were not content to do so. Antioch offers exemplary testimony on this point; we do not know to what extent it was followed by others, although we do know of an identical practice in Apamea on the Orontes. First, the narrative of the historical foundation was embellished. John Malalas, himself a native of Antioch and proud of his city-state, left a long narrative full of marvelous episodes that belong to an official tradition, a sort of national legend. After having founded Seleucia Pieria in a site designated by an eagle sent by Zeus Casios, Seleucus is said to have solicited divine aid in the same way to found a city in the plain up the river from Seleucia. The question was whether Seleucus was to take over a recent foundation by Antigonus the One-Eyed, an Antigoneia, or on the contrary proceed to a new foundation. An eagle brought the answer (the same thing happened for each of the four cities of the Syrian Tetrapolis), and it was thus decided to found a new city-state:

> When the priest, the augurs and Seleukos saw the wonder, they said, "It is here that we must settle: we must not settle in Antigoneia nor should it become a city, since the gods do not want this." Then he discussed with them where to place the city to make it secure. Since he was afraid of the streams from Mount Silpios and the torrents that came down from it, it was there on the floor of the valley, opposite the mountain near the great river Drakon, renamed the Orontes, on the site of the village known as Bottia, opposite Iopolis, that they marked out the foundations for the wall. Through the agency of Amphion, the chief priest and wonder worker, he sacrificed a virgin girl named Aimathe, between the city and the river, on 22nd Artemisios[-May], at the first hour of the day, at sunrise.[3]

But above all, numerous mythical elements were integrated into the history of the new city, falling naturally into place. Thus in the case of Antioch, Strabo and Malalas both begin with a perfectly historical and dated element, the existence near Antioch of a foundation by Antigonus the One-Eyed, Antigoneia. There were indeed already Greeks and Macedonians in the region before Antioch was founded. The ancient authors are simply mistaken on one point: Seleucus did not in fact destroy Antigoneia, for we know that the latter still existed in the first century B.C.E., probably in the form of a village dependent on Antioch. But as soon as that first indication is in place, and on the same level as this verifiable piece of historical information, Strabo and Malalas report that Seleucus installed in his new city-state Greek colonists who had been living in the region from time immemorial: companions of Triptolemos, the Argive hero who had set out to find Io, the heifer plagued by a horsefly that was running along all the banks of the eastern Mediterranean. Malalas specifies that they inhabited the city-state of Iopolis and that Seleucus installed them while making them sacred and noble citizens. But other groups were there also, Cretans "whom Kasos, the son of Inachos, had left to live up there"—that is, on the acropolis of the future Antioch (Inachos was Io's father)—but also Cypriots: "They had migrated to Antioch with the Cypriots, since the [king] Kasos married Amyke, also known as Kitia [Amukia Kuntinyna], daughter of Salaminos, [king] of Cyprus. Cypriots came with her and made their homes on the Acropolis. Amyke died and was buried 100 stades from the city; because of her the country was called Amyke."[4] (The Antioch plain is called the Amuq plain—meaning "being deep"—still today).

Thus recently founded Antioch was endowed with remote origins; to be sure, its foundation as a city-state did not go back further than Seleucus, but it integrated into its national legend a host of mythico-historical episodes that invoked a timeless Greek presence and allowed Antioch to rival the city-states of the Aegean world in terms of age.

Antioch was not the only one to exploit this vein, and we have multiple indications showing that this was a generalized practice. The city of Rhosos claimed to have been founded by Kilix, son of Agenor, the Argive who founded Sidon. Apamea on the Orontes, heir to a Pella founded by Antigonus the One-Eyed (who was a native of the Macedonian city of the same name), identified the swampy valley bordering the city as the locus for a new version of the founding myth of the Macedonian Pella, adapting it only a little to local geographic conditions (Chapter 25). The entire toponymy was transposed to the new site, not only Pella but also the river, called Axios in both cases (for the name Orontes is only one of the two Greek names for the river), and an erudite poet was charged with shaping what constituted the city-state's founding myth.

This capacity to create national legends must not be judged childish or artificial; on the contrary, historians draw many lessons from it. First, for the new colonists this was a way to appropriate the Syrian space for themselves, by transposing both place names and myths that evoked their original homeland. They reproduced a New Macedonia, a New Greece on Syrian soil, which helped them sustain the idea that they were indeed at home; this was probably a way of inscribing Greek colonization for the long run. In addition, the development of founding myths that integrated marvelous episodes connected with Zeus's loves, Perseus's exploits, or the return of the heroes of the Trojan War also helped expand the field of the exploits of Greek gods and heroes to the dimensions of the new world. What had been for a long time consigned to the realm of the imagination, the idea of traveling outside the world known to the Greeks, was henceforth inscribed in a landscape populated by Greeks. To be sure, there still remained exotic lands where Greek gods had traveled, such as India and Arabia, where Dionysus had led his cortege, but that world was shrinking and appeared to be within reach. Moreover, a city-state such as Scythopolis, in Galilee, refounded as a Nysa by Antiochus IV in honor of his daughter, cleverly used this new name to establish a link with the Dionysian myth, which made far-away Nysa the context for one of the god's adventures, in Ethiopia, Libya, India, or Arabia. The use of myths helped complete what Alexander's military conquest had only sketched out, making Greek the vast spaces of the Achaemenid empire in which the Greeks were after all so few in number!

CHAPTER TWENTY-ONE

Long Live Poverty! or Revolutions in Sparta in the Third Century

Agis, therefore, thinking it a noble achievement, as it was, to equalize and restore to full numbers the body of citizens, began to sound the inclinations of people. The young men, as he found, quickly and beyond his expectations gave ear to him, and stripped themselves for the contest in behalf of virtue, like him casting aside their old ways of living as worn-out garments in order to attain liberty. But most of the older men, since they were now far gone in corruption, feared and shuddered at the name of Lycurgus as if they had run away from their master and were being led back to him, and they upbraided Agis for bewailing the present state of affairs and yearning after the ancient dignity of Sparta.

Plutarch, *Agis*, in *Plutarch's Lives*, trans. Bernadotte Perrin
(Loeb Classical Library, 1914), vol. 10, p. 15 (VI, 1–2)

S PARTA, 246 B.C.E. The brilliant city-state that defeated Athens in 405–404 was no more than a shadow of its former self. And here came a young king, new to power, who threw himself into a program of bold reforms. If Plutarch is to be believed, Sparta's young people were enthusiastic about his plans, while the older generation was terrified. This would hardly be surprising if the proposed reforms had not meant reinstituting the iron discipline that the city-state had once known, and restoring Lycurgus's laws to a place of honor. One might expect that such a program would not inspire young people, though it might please those of the older generation who were inclined to regret the prevailing moral decadence and long for the good old days. Yet just the opposite happened, and we witness a genuine role reversal in the city-state: while the opposition between young and old is a time-honored one, it is quite unusual for the young to be the ones demanding a return to the old order. This odd situation calls for an explanation, and leads us into the convulsions of a prestigious ancient city-state that was a prisoner of its own past and incapable of adapting to a profoundly changed world.

Without going back to the epoch of the legendary Lycurgus, under whose patronage Sparta situated the origin of its laws and its entire social and political system, we know that the Sparta of the classical era prided itself on being a model egalitarian society. Each of its citizens had an equivalent plot of ground that was worked by the public slaves, the helots, who returned fixed revenues to the masters. Brought up together, living communally up to the age of thirty, Spartans hardly ever deviated from this perpetually collective life: they took their meals together and participated in a host of diverse obligations such as athletic and military training, religious ceremonies, assembly meetings, supervision of young people, and so on. As Plutarch says, everyone lived continually under the community's watchful eye.

This system was based both on relative economic equality and on the absence of work for all. Plutarch tells the story of a Spartan who arrived in Athens just when a citizen had been condemned there for idleness. Surprised by such an accusation, the visitor was eager to have the honor of meeting that free man. For in Sparta the absence of economic activity was not synonymous with idleness, with the freedom to pursue a leisure activity of one's liking. On the contrary, it was the condition for constant participation in public life, and one might almost say without paradoxical intent that Sparta took the concern for wholesale democracy further than Athens did by offering each citizen the possibility of spending every moment in the service of the city-state.

But the official image corresponds to the reality only in part, and this was true well before the difficulties of the fourth century began. To be sure, Sparta's citizens—who were called *homoioi,* a term closer to "alike" than "equal"—did not all live under the same conditions, far from it. It is true that, to be a *homoios,* one had to have received a *cleros,* a plot of civic land that provided material support for a citizen and his family. In the fifth century, Sparta's nine to ten thousand citizens could thus all be free to carry out their civic tasks. But for a long time the *cleroi* had not been the only source of landed wealth in Sparta. Alongside their civic cleroi, some families owned other lands, worked by slaves of the customary sort—that is, non-helots; for it is too often forgotten that alongside the exploitation of helots (Chapter 13), mercantile slavery was also common in Sparta. Moreover, although citizens could not devote themselves to any other activity, this was not true of women, or of the various categories of free men who were not citizens: inferiors (citizens deprived of their political rights for various reasons, such as cowardice in battle), *neodamodes* (males accepted in the educational system and eligible to become citizens one day), or *perioekoi* (free populations lacking political rights but living and working in Laconia and Messenia). We have no documentation to tell us what links may have united these groups, but it would be extremely naive to believe that citizens played no role at all in the economic arena, whether by way of their wives or by way of straw men belonging to other legal categories who were not subject to the same prohibitions.

In any event, it is certain that, from the archaic period on, there were significant differences in fortune within the group of homoioi. Large Spartan families could maintain chariots that competed in the contests at Delphi or Olympia. To escape sanctions, the owners often placed such property in the hands of women. Thus, despite the lack of a local currency, differentiation in terms of wealth was introduced to Sparta early on.

Plutarch, ever the moralist, supposes that "when once the love of silver and gold had crept into the city, [it was] closely followed by greed and parsimony in the acquisition of wealth and by luxury, effeminacy, and extravagance in the use and enjoyment in it."[1] He dates this phenomenon precisely to Sparta's victory over Athens in 405. It must actually have begun somewhat earlier, for it was around 410 that Persian gold began to arrive in Sparta in great quantities to support the war effort against Athens—the Achaemenids had clearly understood that the defeat of the Athenians would bring Asia Minor under their control. Sparta still refused to mint coins; its citizens had to use *oboloi,* awkward iron spindles without intrinsic value. But certain families had unquestionably accumulated real coins of standard weight minted elsewhere.

The situation was further aggravated at some point during the fourth century, according to Plutarch, by a modification of the ancestral laws. Plutarch reports that a certain Epitadeus, about whom we know nothing else, succeeded in getting a law passed that allowed citizens to give or bequeath not only their land but also their cleroi to persons of their own choosing. The measure must have existed, for Aristotle seems to allude to it in a passage of *The Politics*, where he approves of Lycurgus's prohibition on the sale of lands but regrets the law authorizing unrestricted donation or bequeathal, which amounted to the same thing in the end. Thus during the fourth century there was a massive trend toward concentration of real estate that involved even the civic lots. And because owning a cleros was indispensable for the enjoyment of civic rights, there was a steep decline in the number of homoioi, or citizens with full rights. The number of citizens, which had stabilized at around nine thousand during the fifth century, fell to around fifteen hundred before the middle of the fourth century, and Plutarch speaks of seven hundred toward the end of that century; of these, perhaps a hundred owned both a cleros and other lands. This means that austere Sparta was no more than a plutocracy in which all wealth was concentrated in the hands of roughly a hundred individuals. Under these conditions, we can understand why "the ordinary throng, without resources and without civic rights, lived in enforced idleness, showing no zeal or energy in warding off foreign wars, but ever watching for some opportunity to subvert and change affairs at home."[2]

The concentration of land holdings, in which women seem to have played a major role, according to Aristotle, was only the most visible aspect of the transformations in Sparta. For the minority of citizens engorged with wealth, Lycurgus's severe laws seemed somewhat outdated. Plutarch explicitly connects the influx of gold and silver with the abandonment of ancestral practices. The Spartan system of education, or rather training, was no doubt preserved in a formal sense, but it lacked the necessary rigor. In short, Sparta had become a city-state like any other (it even began to mint money around 280, during the reign of Areus I), probably more inegalitarian than most. But fidelity to the laws of Lycurgus remained the official ideology. It was around this program that the new king, Agis, attempted to mobilize Spartan youth in 246. And at first he seemed to succeed.

In reality, Agis benefited from favorable circumstances. To be sure, he could not count on any support from the other king, Leonidas, because "for a long time [Leonidas] had frequented oriental courts and had been a servile follower of Seleucus [I], and now sought to transfer the pride and pomp which prevailed abroad into Hellenic relations and a constitutional government, where they were out of place."[3] Moreover, he overtly rejected the ancestral ways. But Agis could rely on the youth, who had been influenced by his own cousin, Hippomedon: these young men were seduced by change without having a clear sense of where it might lead. In addition, Agis received help that was not exactly disinterested from three powerful individuals: a certain Lysander, the most respected man in Sparta, who probably was quite sincere in his support for a return to the old order; Mandrocleidas, the most skilled in intrigues and the most devious, according to Plutarch; and finally Agesilaus, the king's uncle, "effeminate and avaricious,"[4] but who saw what benefit he might be able to draw from a revolution that would be manifested, like every Greek revolution, by debt cancellation and land redistribution. Heavily indebted himself, he had everything to gain on the first point, assuming that he could use all his influence to make sure the second point in the program was never enacted.

And the revolution began on a cheerful note, with the help of the women in the king's family: it took time to convince them, but they eventually threw themselves into the adventure and drew in their husbands. For, according to Plutarch, nowhere were husbands more subservient to their wives than in Sparta. But most wives opposed the change, not without reason, because they held the greatest share of the wealth and because that wealth was the basis for their power in Sparta.

Lysander, appointed to serve as ephor, thus proposed a law that would both forgive debts and authorize a new division of civic lands. To meet the goal of repopulation, that is, of reconstituting a body of citizens commensurate with the city-state's ambitions, Sparta had to go through this new distribution, for it was not prepared to give up the indissoluble bond between land and citizenship. Thus forty-five hundred lots were marked off in the heart of Laconia, while fifteen thousand others were created in more distant sectors and were to be distributed to the perioekoi, free men who were not citizens but who had always lived on the periphery alongside Spartans. Perioekoi or even foreigners who had been educated as free men were granted the status of citizen in order to be provided with civic lots. But the military objective of the reform becomes clear from two details: Plutarch asserts that the perioekoi's lots were given to those of an age to bear arms, while the new homoioi were chosen among men who were "of vigorous bodies and in the prime of life."[5] For the rest, the ancestral customs were restored: common meals within the *phiditia* (or *syssitia*), groups of two hundred or four hundred men linked by a common way of life.

Despite the enthusiasm of the young people, there must have been a great deal of resistance, for those who had built their fortunes both by making interest-bearing loans and by accumulating lands had a great deal to lose. But popular pressure was strong, and King Agis set the example by announcing that he was dividing up his own fortune (a large amount of land, but also six hundred talents in cash); his mother, his grandmother, his family, and his friends all followed suit. The opposition of the wealthy crystallized around the other king, Leonidas, and the new law was rejected by a single vote in the Council of Elders, which had full power to decide whether or not a proposal would be presented to the popular assembly for a vote. A major crisis arose at the very heart of Sparta's dual monarchy.

Defeated by so little, Agis chose cunning, reviving an old law from Lycurgus's time that forbade members of either of Sparta's royal families to have children with foreign women and condemning to death any one of their members who should leave the city to go live elsewhere. Now Leonidas had had two children with the daughter of a Seleucid satrap (whom he had abandoned before returning to Sparta), and he had lived at the court of Seleucus I! Leonidas was demoted from kingship in favor of his son-in-law Cleombrotos. As new ephors, hostile to the reforms, were taking office, the two kings deposed them by force and named others who favored the reforms. Their young partisans spread terror to such an extent that Leonidas and others chose to go into exile in Tegea, a small city-state in Arcadia, north of Sparta. The implementation of the reforms could now begin.

The leaders cheerfully proceeded to abolish debts, burning the relevant documents in public, while wealthy citizens and creditors hid out at home. But Agesilaus, Agis's uncle, who had become an ephor, managed to keep the leaders from proceeding immediately to the anticipated land distribution. The new army had to go to the aid of other Peloponnesians who feared an invasion of the Aetolians via the Isthmus of Corinth. An army made up of poor young men who were supposed to receive lots and full citizenship on their return set out in the summer of 241 under Agis's command; in all the city-states they passed through, they were admired by the local citizens, who had the impression that they were at last seeing anew the Spartan army of the glorious era of Leonidas the Elder (the one who was defeated at Thermopylae in 480).

However, the situation was suddenly reversed. On the one hand, the other city-states in the region did not look favorably on the reconstitution of a powerful Spartan army, which recalled the time when Sparta had obliged virtually the entire Peloponnesus to be its ally. On the other hand, the wealthy had everything to fear from the social revolution that was under way and that could spread rapidly, for inequality of fortunes was just as great in most of the Greek city-states. In any case, the Achaeans whom the Spartans had gone to help ultimately pulled back from a confrontation with the Aetolians, for reasons that are unclear. Thus the fine Spartan army went back home without having won the glory it had hoped for; it had, however, given rise to many fears in the lands along its route.

At the same time, intrigues were thriving in Sparta itself, and the two kings soon took refuge as suppliants in a temple; meanwhile, Leonidas returned from exile and took the kingship back from Cleombrotos, who was himself condemned to exile in turn. This somewhat curious reversal can be explained by the loss of popular support, for Agesilaus's maneuverings succeeded in continually postponing the redistribution of lands. Agis, isolated, was finally caught, condemned to death, and strangled, along with his mother and grandmother. The adventure seemed to be over: the power of the wealthy had defeated an attempt to restore the former grandeur which the reference to Lycurgus had not sufficed to impose.

However, the struggle was revived a little later. Leonidas had obliged Agis's widow, Agiatis, to marry his own son, Cleomenes, even though the latter had scarcely reached manhood. For the former queen found herself the head and sole heir of a considerable fortune. Now, Agiatis had retained a deep admiration for her first husband, and she transmitted his reformist zeal to Cleomenes. Becoming king upon Leonidas's death in 235, Cleomenes did not repeat Agis's mistakes. First of all, he seems to have understood that the context of an external war could facilitate his plans, by ensuring that they would have the necessary popular support. He managed this fairly quickly by confronting the Achaeans, Sparta's neighbors to the north, who were trying to force all the peoples of the Peloponnesus into their confederation. On the strength of his successes, and relying henceforth on a powerful troop of foreign mercenaries (even while leaving some homoioi who might be hostile to the mercenaries in a garrison outside of Sparta), Cleomenes brought off a veritable coup d'état by quickly removing the ephors from office and putting them to death (just one escaped, miraculously) and by condemning eighty citizens to exile. And he proceeded at once to enact the reforms that Agis had only begun to introduce: putting all wealth in common, redistributing land, introducing into the civic body the "most promising of the perioekoi."[6] An army of four thousand hoplites was formed and modernized on the model of the Macedonian phalanx, which had proven very effective in action. The earlier discipline was restored everywhere, including athletic training, education and meals in common, thanks to the action of a Stoic philosopher whom Cleomenes seems to have greatly admired, Sphaerus of Borysthenes. Finally, because the exiled king from the other royal family, Agis's brother, had been assassinated on his way back home, Cleomenes had his own brother named as the second king, flouting the rules according to which the two kings had to belong to the two traditional royal houses, the Agiads and the Eurypontids. For the first time, the two kings were both from the same family, the Agiads.

If Plutarch is to be believed, Sparta had returned to the old ways: an army entirely focused on training, citizens living in austerity, Cleomenes himself setting the example. Whereas the title of king was accompanied everywhere else by indecent sumptuous displays, in Sparta the king lived frugally, receiving his guests himself and inviting them to share his meager pittance. Plutarch may be painting a somewhat overly idyllic picture of this return to the good old days, but Cleomenes' revolution must surely have impressed people, for Sparta's neighbors became fearful.

Beyond its moral and properly Spartan aspect (the return to Lycurgus's rules), Cleomenes' program had what it took to seduce the poor and frighten the rich throughout the Peloponnesus. To complete what seemed to him a necessary restoration of Sparta's ancestral might, Cleomenes undertook to help all those in the area who rejected the domination of the Achaean League. Supported at once by those who were expecting him to lead a social revolution, by the Achaeans' adversaries, and by those of their allies the Macedonians, Cleomenes achieved some significant successes, but reversals followed in short order, and the Spartan army ended up being crushed in Sellasia, in Arcadia, in 222. Occupied by the Macedonian army, Sparta fell back under the sway of those who opposed the reforms, although we cannot say that everything Cleomenes had accomplished came to naught. But the impetus he had provided was destroyed. He himself fled to Cyrene and then to Alexandria, where he was rapidly placed under close surveillance by the new king Ptolemy IV, who did not trust this dangerous agitator. After an attempt to stir up the Alexandrian populace against Ptolemy's oppression, Cleomenes committed suicide along with all his companions, while in reprisal Ptolemy had all the members of their families executed, in particular Cleomenes' mother and his children. The adventure ended in a bloodbath.

The story of the failed revolutions in Sparta in the third century held Plutarch's attention, for it seemed to offer a good parallel with the double attempt of the Gracchi, in Rome, in the following century—they too tried to restore the Republic by a better distribution of land—but also because it abounded in particularly edifying moral anecdotes. For the historian, however, the episode leads to reflection on the underlying motivations of the reform-minded kings and on the causes of their failure. For it is surprising to see the wealthiest men in Sparta pleading in favor of austerity, and to see them fail when the large majority of inhabitants seem to have had everything to gain from the success of their enterprise.

It seems to me that the revolution instigated by Agis and Cleomenes constitutes, in the literal sense, a reactionary revolution, meaning that it was not a matter of adapting to a new situation—only the military reform tended in that direction—but of getting rid of the ills from which the city-state was suffering by a pure and simple return to the past, a mythic past that had never actually existed. This undertaking amounted to denying Sparta's entrance into the world of its time; it meant rejecting the Sparta that took part in the movement of exchanges, that was henceforth familiar with the use of money and that opened itself up to others. To be sure, many people had been losers in this evolution, for the concentration of lands, with its political corollary (a decrease in the number of citizens), reduced to a minimal core the number of free men who enjoyed full rights. The watchwords of land redistribution and abolition of debts had been seductive to some, but all in all the proposed revolution had brought about only minor changes. The mass of free men who were not citizens—perioekoi or inferiors—unquestionably far exceeded the forty-five hundred who were supposed to benefit from the reforms, for the fifteen thousand perioekoi who should have received lands from Agis found themselves subject to military service without having access to full citizenship. Agis did not imagine unifying the multiple statuses that divided Spartan society into antagonistic groups; on the contrary, he sought to reconstitute them. Furthermore, revalorizing the presumed austerity of former times could work for a while on an ideological level for a wealthy minority made indifferent by abundance; but what charm could it have had for those who had been tightening their belts for so long and who looked enviously at the wealth of the minority? Agis's revolution was seductive for privileged young people like himself, but the larger population must have quickly come to see its limits. Even the abolition of debts ended up benefiting indebted wealthy people more than the poor, who waited in vain for the always-deferred redistribution of lands. Cleomenes carried out his own revolution with more determination, but he proposed a return to Lycurgus's laws only to violate some of the essential ones at once, when he got rid of the ephors and named two kings from the same family. Moreover, his very success must have alienated all the Peloponnesian leaders, who feared that he would export his revolution (which he did not do, thus probably provoking the disaffection of poor citizens), and all the patriots who were not happy to see the reconstitution of a Spartan force that had left decidedly mixed memories. What good did it do to escape from the Achaeans and the Macedonians, the Argives, Arcadians, and other Messenians must have thought, if it only meant falling under the sway of the Lacedemonians. If we look closely, we can see that the adventures of the revolutionary kings bore the seeds of their own ultimate failure.

And Sparta's trials were not yet over. Two makeshift tyrants, a certain Lycurgus who claimed to be of royal descent, and then a Tarantine adventurer, Machanidas (killed in 207), left only fleeting traces, but shortly afterward someone named Nabis, he too claiming to be of royal descent, seized power and followed a revolutionary policy that Polybius sums up in a few sentences: "banishing the citizens who were distinguished for their wealth and illustrious ancestry, [he] gave their property and wives to the chief of his own supporters and to his mercenaries, who were for the most part murderers, rippers, highwaymen, and burglars. For such kind of people flocked sedulously to his court from all over the world, people who dared not set foot in their own countries owing to their crimes against God and man."[7] And Polybius added that Nabis sent assassins on the track of exiles, when he did not kill those who resisted him by an automaton constructed as an effigy of his wife: this device pierced the unfortunates through and through while embracing them in its arms. And as if that were not enough, he freed the helots, that is, the slaves![8]

A conservative aristocrat, Polybius could not help but be frightened by Nabis's policies, and his invectives against the "scum" may reflect the fear they inspired in the well-to-do. Did Nabis enjoy the support of prominent individuals, as Polybius's remark on the transfer of property might lead us to suppose? Livy indicates that the confiscated property was supposed to be attributed to indigents: this seems to be in alignment with the policy implemented unsuccessfully by Agis and Cleomenes. In a speech attributed to him by Livy, Nabis aims to reestablish a civic body of small landowners, the only way to reconstitute a civic army. To stand up to oliganthropy, he freed some helots (surely not all of them, for we learn that he had some massacred again in 195). The novelty lies more in the massive character of the measure than in the measure itself, for such liberations had been carried out before. Moreover, the marriages with wives and daughters of exiles were perhaps intended to place these new citizens in control of patrimonies, given that, since the fourth century, women had held a large percentage of land-based wealth.

Nabis belonged to a dual tradition. First, that of the tyrant who does violence to laws and institutions, because he was the sole king, whereas Sparta had always had two, and because he suppressed the control formerly exercised by the Council of Elders and the ephors; in a sense, he found himself king in the manner of a Hellenistic sovereign, and it is not impossible that he sought in this way to modernize a system of government that he deemed outdated. Next, he illustrates the tradition of the reformer king represented by Agis and Cleomenes, with all the accompanying reactionary implications (the return to a relative equality of fortunes), but probably with some audacious moves that his predecessors had not made, such as the massive liberation of slaves; similarly, he does not seem to have had as a goal the return to frugality advocated by Lycurgus. Which could have been to his advantage.

His failure came from outside: the Achaean League, which bordered Laconia to the north and counted as Rome's best ally in Greece at the time, managed to block his policy of conquest. Rome had just defeated the king of Macedonia and solemnly proclaimed the freedom of the Greeks; Nabis's enterprises ran counter to such commitments. In the wake of dubious alliances and despite initial successes, Nabis ended up assassinated by his own allies, during the summer or fall of 192. He was the last great figure in the history of Sparta. Behind the unfavorable portrait painted by his adversaries, we sense a man concerned with modernity and greatness. But he came too early, or too late. Sparta's greatness had long since become a thing of the past.

CHAPTER TWENTY-TWO

A Capital on the Banks of the Amu Darya, or the Greeks in Bactria and India

Wooden Ionic capital, charred

AI-KHANUM (AFGHANISTAN), third century B.C.E. On a terrace overlooking the Amu Darya and its tributary on the left bank, the Kokcha, a vast city spreads out, dominated by a triangular acropolis. The site is superb, easy to protect simply by closing off access from the east with a rampart whose outline appears clearly between the Amu Darya and the northeast corner of the acropolis. On the edges of the plateau, rising some fifteen meters above the river, there is a gymnasium and a fountain. On the fountain, one of the spouts represents a dolphin. Crafted by Greeks, naturally! Right alongside, a gymnasium with an inscription, a dedication to Hermes and Heracles. Here, on the border between Afghanistan and Tajikistan, the spectacle is surprising. But these are only two of the surprises that this exceptional site was to reveal. And since these initial discoveries, many others have come along to give us a somewhat clearer picture of the outer limits of the Greek world conquered by Alexander and quickly lost by the Seleucids, perhaps, but a world in which the fortunes of Hellenism were far from ephemeral.

Ai-Khanum, a city on the banks of the ancient Oxus River, was discovered in 1963. By 1965 the French archaeological mission headed by Paul

Bernard was uncovering one surprising element after another. Not only a gymnasium, a clear affirmation of Greek presence, but also a palace, a sanctuary, and a *heroon,* a monumental tomb devoted to the founder. All this was built for the most part in the local style—baked brick at the bottom of the very thick walls, raw brick above—and laid out in a way that was not especially Greek. But elements that were visibly imported signaled the Greek character of the construction: Corinthian capitals in one place, a wooden Ionic capital (charred) in another, pebble mosaics elsewhere. And then a highly typical theatrical mask, and a silvered medallion featuring Cybele on her chariot drawn by wild beasts. And elsewhere, suddenly, the first Greek inscription: the maxims of the Sages copied at Delphi and engraved on the occasion of a visit to Bactria by the Aristotelian philosopher Clearchos of Soli! A dedication to Hermes and Heracles, the gods of the gymnasium, offered by Triballos and Strato, sons of Strato. And many other Greek inscriptions, and accounts, in Greek, in the palace treasury. And, in the same building, a manuscript of plays in Greek, and even fragments of one of Aristotle's lost philosophic dialogues, on Ideas!

All at once an unknown Greek city appeared, one whose name we still do not know (Alexandria on the Oxus?), one that may have been founded by Alexander himself or shortly after he came through, the first such city that could be excavated with care. And the Hellenism of central Asia, which scholars had tended to view as marginal and ephemeral, took on an unprecedented consistency. Everyone had of course read the accounts of Alexander's conquest, its difficulties and its successes; it was known that a number of Greeks and Macedonians had been left behind to settle and marry local women. What is more, they joined Greeks deported by the Persians, whom Alexander had rediscovered: people from Barca of Cyrenica residing in Bactria, perhaps the Branchids of Miletus in Sogdiana. There was even talk, around the time of the conqueror's death, of a revolt of the Bactrian Greeks: they must have represented a force of some importance, to be remembered this way. And then, for a long time, there had been coins, many of them, impressive in their aesthetic quality: they provided information about a number of the Greek kings who had reigned over Bactria, Sogdiana, and Margiana in the north, Arachosia and India in the south. Numismatists had reconstituted genealogies, delimited dynasties, and established relative chronologies. Apart from a few scattered texts, these were all the elements available for a history of Hellenism in central Asia. In 1951 the great British scholar William W. Tarn sketched out a stirring picture of this adventure, making Bactria and India new Greek territories: his work caused a sensation despite obvious weaknesses in the documentation. The Indian scholar A. K. Narain countered this picture tilted in favor of the Greeks with a no less appealing picture of a Hellenism rapidly submerged by the old indigenous civilizations, Indian in particular, that had been able to appropriate the most seductive aspects of the foreign culture. Historiography was translating, as it must, the preoccupations of an era.

The discovery of Ai-Khanum gave new impetus to the debate, for scholars now had in hand direct archaeological documents. The older digs had turned up nothing at Bactra, the capital of the northern regions, and those at Bagram, near Kabul, revealed later periods. Of course there were occasional discoveries in one place or another: edicts of the great Indian king Ashoka, engraved in Greek in southeastern Afghanistan, near Kandahar; treasuries of coins, sporadic discoveries on a few sites in Turkmenistan, Uzbekistan, or Tajikistan. But nothing to compare with what was revealed at Ai-Khanum. Until then, paradoxically, traces of Hellenism appeared where the Greeks had exercised only ephemeral control—in Arachosia, above all, more than in Bactria, which had been the heart of their most powerful kingdom. Similarly, more was known about the later repercussions of the Greek art produced in Hadda, Surkh Kotal, or Gandhara than about the productions that must have inspired it. Ai-Khanum turned the perspective upside down, and later discoveries only confirmed the conclusions that could be drawn from this site: there had indeed been original Greek art in Bactria, an inventive and vigorous Greek society whose cultural models influenced the neighboring regions and continued for a long time to irrigate the Hellenized milieus of the Greek Far East.

Alas! After fifteen years of digging at Ai-Khanum, the war in Afghanistan forced the archaeologists to pack up and leave (1979). Looting began. But a little later, the collapse of the Soviet Union opened up new fields of investigation to Western archaeologists. Foreign teams could finally work in the former Soviet Republics of central Asia, and major sites were developed in Samarkand (Afrasiab), Merv, and Termez. New discoveries confirmed what Ai-Khanum had revealed: the solidity and the durability of Greek culture in central Asia, despite the distance from the Mediterranean and the political rupture that came about in the middle of the third century.

And then, after the fall of the Taliban, archaeologists went back, timidly at first, to assess the extent of the disaster. To tell the truth, it was immense. A recent mission to Ai-Khanum discovered that the site had been completely devastated by clandestine digs. The Corinthian capitals had been reused as pedestals for pillars in a teahouse in a neighboring village: this is almost the only good news! But at the same time, new discoveries appeared, this time in the south of the Hindu Kush. (The most recent is a magnificent Greek inscription that originated in Kandahar; we shall return to it later on.) In short, despite the difficulties and the ravages of time, knowledge of the history of the easternmost regions of the Alexandrian Empire has progressed so far in a quarter of a century that nearly everything has to be revised.

We had known for a long time that the outermost regions of the ancient Persian Empire contained a large number of Alexandrian foundations, many more than in Mesopotamia or even Iran. The ancient authors supplied numerous details about the installation of Greek and Macedonian colonists in these cities, very few of which must have been city-states at the outset in the institutional sense of the term (Chapter 20). We know, for example, that intercommunity marriage agreements were made with the locals, so that children born of the union between Alexander's soldiers and indigenous women would not be considered bastards on both sides. It is impossible to know how many colonists Alexander left behind when he headed back toward the west, but we must not underestimate the number, for the strength of Hellenism in central Asia, as in Arachosia, argues for a strong community, even if it remained a tiny minority alongside the native population.

Shortly after the Macedonian army left, the situation of Alexander's conquests became precarious, especially in the south of the Hindu Kush. It is probable that India properly speaking (that is, the Indus Valley) and also Arachosia (the southeastern part of contemporary Afghanistan) were retaken by the Mauryas, who were building a powerful empire in northern India. Despite the remarkable qualities of the satraps Alexander appointed in the region, first Meno (who died of illness in 325), then Sibyrtios (of whom we know nothing after 315), the Maurya emperors took over the eastern part of the Alexandrian Empire. In any case, when Seleucus I undertook an expedition to reconquer the territory around 305, the Mauryas were the ones with whom he had to deal. He probably did not have a military confrontation with the one the Greek sources named Sandracottos, the Indian Chandragupta. For despite the testimony of coins issued following this repeat version of Alexander's expedition, coins on which Seleucus had elephants represented, the Macedonian king did not succeed in taking back the Indus Valley or even Arachosia, both of which had fallen under Maurya control before he got there. A treaty between Seleucus I and Chandragupta in 303 settled the fate of the provinces located in the south of the Hindu Kush; Seleucus acknowledged Indian domination in the region. Although some scholars have limited the territories ceded to Chandragupta to a narrow strip of land to the west of the Indus, it is probable that a much larger area was given up, and that it included at least all of Arachosia and the Paropamisadae (in the Kabul region), perhaps even Gedrosia (southwestern Afghanistan) and Aria (the Herat region). In any case, the discovery of edicts by the Maurya king Ashoka, the second successor to Chandragupta, in Arachosia, is proof enough that his power extended that far.

Does this mean that the Greeks were driven away and all traces of Hellenism banished? Surely not. The treaty of 303 already included an epigamy clause, that is, a clause recognizing the legitimacy of marriages between Greek men and local women; this would have made no sense if the Greeks had left the region. Moreover, two of Ashoka's edicts that were engraved near Kandahar were written in Greek! And these were not just summary translations made by some subaltern civil servant. The edicts dealt with the spread of the religious views that Ashoka was propagating, and the great historian Louis Robert has shown that they had been translated by an educated Greek, someone perfectly conversant with the concepts and vocabulary of Greek philosophy, capable of finding the most appropriate Greek words to translate the terms used in the Indian and Aramaic versions. Moreover, it is probable that the very Greek-looking coinage of a certain Sophytos, which for a long time was attributed to some satrap serving in the north of the Hindu Kush—that is, under Seleucid suzerainty—should be attributed instead to an Indian satrap (the name Sophytos itself is fully Indian with a Greek inflection) who governed Arachosia for the Mauryas. The choice of Greek coinage proved that Sophytos was taking pains to satisfy the Greek populations of his satrapy. In other words, not only had the Greeks of Arachosia, whatever their number (Alexander had left forty-six hundred troops in this province), not disappeared, but in fact they constituted a recognized group that was pampered, privileged, influential, and cultivated. One of the rare Greek inscriptions from Arachosia in the third century, apart from Ashoka's edicts, is a dedication in verse accompanying the consecration of a votive offering; it attests to a concern with fine language that is rarely found outside of cultivated milieus. In a certain way, flaunting one's Greek culture amounted to highlighting one's membership in the social elite of the province. And the recent discoveries at the site of the ancient Hellenistic city at Kandahar and its necropolis confirm the cultural importance of the Greek community in that city.

North of the Hindu Kush, Macedonian control was maintained without interruption after the Alexandrian conquest. A son of Seleucus I, Antiochus, moved into Bactra with the right to oversee all the satraps in the so-called "higher satrapies," that is, all the provinces located east of the Tigris. Bactra thus became a vice-capital for the eastern part of the empire, as Sardis was for Asia Minor. In this favorable political context, the Greek cities had time to take root and prosper. For a long time, Bactra revealed nothing of its Greek past, but things are changing: recent discoveries include Corinthian capitals similar to those at Ai-Khanum, tambours from columns, and an Ionic capital like those found in Tajikistan at Takht-i Sangin, where Russian archaeologists have brought to light a large Hellenistic sanctuary devoted to the god Oxus (early third century B.C.E.). The discoveries made at Ai-Khanum, Samarkand, Merv (Alexandria of Margiana), and elsewhere attest to the strength of the Greek implantation in the region. It is true that, everywhere they went, the Greeks had to adapt and adopt agricultural methods or construction techniques that were foreign to their own traditions. But the Greek character of their cities leaves no room for doubt.

Despite the uncertainties that cloud its history, Ai-Khanum offers a good example of rapid implantation of a Greek city. We cannot be sure whether the city was founded on the occasion of Alexander's conquest or only during Seleucus I's expedition at the very end of the fourth century, but by the first half of the third century the major outlines of urban development were set: the main east–west street at the foot of the acropolis, the principal public buildings, including the palace, the heroon of Kineas, the city's founder (who was of Thessalian origin), and a sanctuary. There may have already been a gymnasium, but the one whose vestiges have been found was built toward the end of the city's Greek period, during the reign of Eucratides I, around 150–145; the inscription quite probably dates from the third century, and thus attests to the presence of that characteristic Greek institution shortly after the city's foundation.

Around the mid-third century, an event took place in Iran that considerably modified the political situation. A nomadic people from the north, the Parni, settled first in the regions located southwest of the Caspian Sea, in Parthyene; they soon took control of the entire Iranian plateau. These Parni—who became the Parthians—established their capital at Susa, in imitation of the Achaemenid Persians. Despite the Seleucids' efforts to drive the Parni away, the regions east of Iran were henceforth cut off politically from the Syro-Mesopotamian part of the Seleucid kingdom. Bactria's Macedonian strategos Diodotos seceded, to some extent by force; he assumed the royal title and founded a new independent Hellenistic kingdom in Bactria over which he reigned for some fifteen years (ca. 250–235) before ceding the throne to his son Diodotos II (ca. 235–225). An expedition led by Antiochus III between 212 and 204, directed against Diodotos II's successor Euthydemos I (ca. 225–190) as part of an effort to regain control of the entire country, had no lasting results despite a long siege against Bactra (208–206). The Parthians, like the Greeks of central Asia and certain Indian princes, swore an act of allegiance and showered the Seleucid sovereign with gifts, but they reclaimed their independence as soon as the latter turned his back. Moreover, Antiochus III himself had acknowledged Euthydemos I's royal title and promised one of his daughters in marriage to Euthydemos's son Demetrios.

The break between east and west undoubtedly had practical repercussions, especially in that it stemmed the Greek emigration toward central Asia, but it by no means tolled the death knell for Hellenism in these regions. Very little of the political history of the kingdoms can be reconstituted, even if coins give us approximate indications of the area controlled by one sovereign or another. Thus between the death of Euthydemos I, around 190, and Eucratides' ascension to power in 171 or 170, six sovereigns of the Euthydemid dynasty reigned, in succession or simultaneously, north and south of the Hindu Kush. Then, starting in 190, these sovereigns not only succeeded in reconquering regions to the south of the Hindu Kush, that is, the Paropamisadae and Arachosia, but they also penetrated much farther, going even beyond the area of Alexander's conquests: Demetrios I was able to take possession of the region now known as the Sindh, and Menander unquestionably advanced all the way to the Ganges, to Pataliputra (modern Patna). The minting of Indo-Greek coins (square coins with legends in both Greek and Kharoshthi) by these sovereigns is explained by this extension of their kingdom to the detriment of the Mauryas. Eucratides' usurpation, which eliminated the legitimate sovereign Demetrios I, gave rise to the creation of a new era, echoes of which seem to be found as far away as southern India—a good indication of Eucratides' fame. The Greek presence in these meridional regions may have benefited as well from the fact that a certain number of Bactrian Greeks drew back after the conquest of the Oxus basin by the Sakas and Yue-Chi nomads, starting in 145–130.

For what the Greeks gained in the south did not prevent threats from materializing in the north. Thus, following the death of Eucratides I, who was assassinated by one of his sons after a reign of about twenty-five years, a period of uncertainty and unrest began, creating favorable conditions for incursions by nomadic tribes. It was at this point, around 145, that the Greeks definitively abandoned Ai-Khanum: they left the city when invaders burned the palace (which had just been partially renovated, splendidly, on Eucratides' orders). These nomads (mentioned most notably by Chinese sources under the name Yue-Chi) must have controlled the entire right bank of the Amu Darya at the time. Some fifteen years later, around 130, all of Greek Bactria fell to the invaders. It has occasionally been suggested that some Greek principalities subsisted until around 70 B.C.E. in the remote region of Badakhshan, on the grounds that coins of several sovereigns adopted the customary features of the Greco-Bactrian coins, that is, a Greek legend and an Attic stallion. But this hypothesis is not very plausible; these coins were minted by sovereigns reigning south of the Hindu Kush, and they were intended for trade with the former Greek Bactria.

After 130, the political domination of the Greeks was limited to the southern regions, those that had been taken back from Indian princes after 190. We have already seen how the period of Maurya domination had allowed the Greek community to prosper and to retain a privileged social rank. An exceptional document that has recently been discovered and published sheds additional and fascinating light on this community in the second century, or perhaps a little later. This is a long Greek inscription discovered in Kandahar, in verse, signed by an acrostic underlined by the repetition of the initial letter to the left of each line of the text. Here is a rendering of the text based on the French translation proposed by its first editors:[1]

Stele erected by Sophytos
For a long time the house of my ancestors had flourished
when the irresistible violence of the three Moirae destroyed it;
and I, quite young and deprived of the fortune of my fathers,
I, Sophytos—pitiful destitution—of the race of Naratos,
Having cultivated the talents of the Archer and the Muses
united with a noble wisdom, I then reflected
on ways to raise up my fathers' house once again;
and, having received money to invest from others,
I left my country resolved not to return
before I had amassed a great pile of riches;
that is why, devoting myself to trade and traveling to numerous cities,
I harvested, without experiencing any harm, a vast fortune.
Surrounded by praise, here I am back in my homeland after countless years,
    and my return was a joy for my friends.
And all at once, right away, I rebuilt my fathers' house, which was dilapi-
    dated, with new funds and much bigger than before,
And, since their tomb lay collapsed on the ground, I had another one built;
this stele, in my own lifetime, I placed on the path, so it could speak.
See how they are worthy of being imitated, these works I have accomplished;
may my sons, my grandsons preserve the house that they owe to me!
Acrostic:
By the care of Sophytos, son of Naratos.

This is an extraordinary text for its literary quality as much as for the adventure it relates. The author, Sophytos, son of Naratos (or Narates), has an Indian name, the same as that of the third-century satrap of Arachosia mentioned earlier. The editors do not rule out the possibility that he belonged to the same family, moreover; let us recall that Sophytos the satrap had issued coins of the Greek type. The inscription may date from any time between 200 B.C.E. and 100 C.E., but a date in the second or first century B.C.E. seems appropriate. If we understand correctly, Sophytos's family had undergone reversals of fortune that obliged the young man to flee. It may be that this ruin was related to the reconquest of Arachosia by the Bactrian Greeks at the beginning of the second century, especially if it is true that that family had connections to those who were administering the province on behalf of the Maurya emperors. However this may be, young Sophytos, who in Kandahar (and perhaps elsewhere) had received an excellent classical Greek education (he alludes to the Muses and to the archer Apollo, the Muses' director), found himself obliged to earn his own living. We get a sense of the once-wealthy young man who, burning with rage, swears to himself that he will come back one day as a conqueror. Thanks to money lent by some relatives or faithful friends, he turns to trade. A bad reading of the Greek text had at first made it appear that the young man had traversed "the numerous cities of the Chinese"—which would have been a tremendous "scoop"; however, a better reading eliminated the Chinese without diminishing the text's interest. In any case, Sophytos achieved his goal: wealthy once again, he went back home and rebuilt the house and the tombs of his ancestors. His stele in the form of a victory notice does a good job of expressing his pride at taking his revenge on an unjust fate.

But above and beyond the tale of a fascinating life, it is important to note here that this prominent young man of Indian origin gives evidence of an excellent Greek education; he writes regular elegiac couplets in elegant Greek (he makes only one error in meter), thus unmistakably attesting to the privileged place of Greek culture in second- or first-century B.C.E. Arachosia. This sheds new light on anecdotes that cultural historians had tended to take lightly and dismiss as without interest. For example, Ashoka's predecessor Bindusara was said to have written to King Antiochus II "begging him . . . to purchase and send him grape-syrup [wine], figs, and a sophist."[2] The Seleucid replied that as for the wine and the figs he would comply with pleasure, but that it was not customary, among the Greeks, to sell sophists! I retain from this the Maurya king's curiosity about Greek culture. The maintenance of Indo-Greek kings at India's northwest border until around the mid-first century B.C.E. unquestionably favored the development of Greek culture in "white India"—this is how Isidoros of Charax designated Arachosia at the beginning of the Common Era, adding that Alexandria of Arachosia was still a "Greek city"—and its dissemination among the Indian elites.

Much remains to discover, but what arises from the soil of central Asia and Afghanistan almost every year helps us understand better the intellectual and artistic substratum that underlay the birth and development of the mixed art, known for a long time and highly appreciated by collectors, that we know as the Greco-Buddhist art of Gandhara.

CHAPTER TWENTY-THREE

Gymnasium: Keep Out! or Education and Citizenship in the Hellenistic World

Those who must not participate in the gymnasium. Not to appear naked in the gymnasium: slaves, freed men, their sons, *apalaistroi,* prostitutes, or (one) of those who practice a trade on the agora, nor anyone in a state of drunkenness or dementia. If the gymnasiarch allows one of those to apply oil to his body even though he knows or someone informs him [of the intrusion] and has shown him [the intruder], he will pay a fine of one thousand drachmae.

Inscription, in Philippe Gauthier and Miltiade B. Hatzopoulos,
La loi gymnasiarchique de Beroia (Athens: Centre de
Recherches de l'Antiquité grecque et romaine, 1993), p. 31

BEROIA, MACEDONIA, BEFORE 167 B.C.E., perhaps around 190–180. The city-state adopted a law pertaining to gymnasia. Despite damage to the stone, the essential text remains, enough for us to understand what close attention a city-state paid to the operation of its gymnasium and, indirectly, to the education of young men. The law was adopted with only one dissenting vote. One would like to know the reasons behind that one opposing voice, but they are lost forever; our bad luck!

Like every Greek city-state, Beroia had a gymnasium. In the early second century, it was first and foremost the place where young men and boys were trained. One passage in our text is clear on this point: the gymnasium was frequented by people under the age of thirty. Beyond that age, special authorization from the gymnasiarch, the director of the establishment, was required. Perhaps he granted it to experts who were capable of training the boys and young men, offering educational demonstrations. But it is clear that an effort was made to avoid contacts between the young people and anyone who might disturb their training. Even among those who had access to the gymnasium, strict separation was maintained: the "young men" were not to associate with the "boys." It is hard to see this as intended merely to keep everyone fully focused on training, or to avoid disputes or brawls. One senses a moral preoccupation, which the passage cited seems to confirm. The fact that athletes trained in the nude had long marked the gymnasium as a place frequented by men attracted to good-looking boys. Not that civic morality frowned on such liaisons, which were prestigious for the one who was their object. But the gymnasiarch was entrusted with the specific mission of training young people, and he did not want his charges to be distracted by amorous adventures that could just as well take place elsewhere and at other times.

From the classical period on, the gymnasium was a privileged place for the civic community. Just as citizens were also simultaneously soldiers, so sons of citizens had the duty of preparing themselves for their future role through intensive training. The prohibition recalled by the Beroia law regarding slaves, freed men, prostitutes, and others excluded from the arena *(apalaistroi)* can be explained by the eminently civic character of the gymnasium: those who were not citizens or who were under some restriction in the wake of a dishonorable penalty (prostitutes) or owing to some degrading activity (people who worked on the agora) were barred from access. Or at least they could not frequent the same gymnasium as the elite among the citizenry: in Athens, after the implementation of the 451 law on citizenship, bastards fell into the habit of meeting at the gymnasium of Kynosarges, proof that they were free to engage in sports (unlike slaves)—provided that they did not mingle with citizens.

In the early second century, the civic role of the gymnasium had not disappeared, and it goes without saying that the young men who went there virtually every day to practice wrestling, javelin throwing, and archery did not do so solely for pleasure. In Macedonia, before the Roman conquest (167), the city-states still had to supply contingents for the royal army, and thus they had to prepare young men for their future mission. Similarly, in the city-states of Asia Minor, until the creation of the Roman province of Asia in 133 B.C.E., the city-states often maintained civic armies to defend themselves against their neighbors; it would have been unthinkable not to prepare future citizens for the task, even if recourse to mercenaries often proved to be indispensable.

The quasi-military discipline that the gymnasiarch imposed is thus not surprising. First, because it was in the interest of the gymnasiarch himself. Elected by his fellow citizens as head of the gymnasium, he spent considerable sums there, for he himself very probably had to pay, at least in part, to heat the baths associated with the athletic facilities (where these existed), oil distributions, and building maintenance. Oil presumably represented the greatest expense; in any case, in decrees in honor of benefactors, this aspect was often stressed. Sports were practiced in the nude; bodies were oiled to soften the skin and for self-protection. In the Beroia text, one passage specifies that people were not to get undressed until a signal was raised, indicating that the distribution of oil had begun; as soon as the signal was lowered, it was no longer possible to get oil, and the gymnasium was considered closed. Other texts praise gymnasiarchs for showing munificence by lowering the signal late in the day, or even not lowering it at all, which meant that oil could be had at any time.

Oil was very costly, especially if it was of good quality. Certain gymnasiarchs had perfumed oil distributed, and were publicly thanked for it. But the Beroia inscription is precious in that it is not a statement thanking a benefactor, only a statement of everyday regulations. It does not contradict the honorific decrees, but it completes them. Thus a passage concerning the guardian of the gymnasium, a slave, specifies that the person who held that position would be the one who bought the right to sell the *gloios*. The term *gloios* designates "the mixture of oil and sweat and filth that was scraped off with a strigil or that floated on top of the bathwater."[1] Thus the city-state (or the gymnasiarch?) leased the right to recuperate this unappetizing mixture to an individual who must have profited by reselling it. For gloios was resold, according to Pliny the Elder, most often to the poor, who applied it to their bodies for want of oil, and even sometimes used it as medication! In exchange for that concession, for which he must have had to pay a fixed price, the guardian maintained the gymnasium, under threat of the whip (which proves that the position was indeed held by a slave).

The life led by those who frequented the gymnasium was not exactly fun and games. Helped by three men who were elected and probably also by an adjunct whom he had appointed himself, the gymnasiarch had to make sure the training was done seriously, and those who did not obey were beaten. Beatings for the youngest boys, fines for the oldest, for corporal punishment could not be applied to all, especially not to those who were old enough to have become actual citizens. I see this as proof that the discipline had not been relaxed, despite what Aristophanes said on the subject in the late fifth century, when he complained about the laxity to be found in the schools of his day; he was actually being humorous when he repeated the old saw about "the good old days," which were often idealized by the older generation and always by conservatives.

The strictness of the law in Beroia attests more generally to the Greek city-states' concern for the education of their youth. To be sure, this is only one aspect of education, athletic training for military purposes, but we find similar features in the few school regulations that have been preserved. One of these, concerning the small city-state of Teos in Asia Minor, dates from the second century and thus is fairly close in time to the Beroia text; it shows just as much severity toward children and great mistrust toward the adults who are in charge of them. The text refers to a school for boys and girls that was financed by a wealthy benefactor, Polythrous. It is worth citing a lengthy excerpt here, for we find many details that shed light on the Beroia text:

> in order that all children of free condition be instructed, as Polythrous son of Onesimos has solemnly promised the people to provide for this, erecting the finest monument to his zeal, and for this purpose has given 34,000 drachmae; that every year in the electoral assemblies after the election of the secretaries three masters of letters be designated to teach boys and girls; that each one who has been elected for the first level be given the sum of 600 drachmae each year, to those elected for the second level 550 drachmae, and to those elected for the third level 500 drachmae; that two gymnastics masters also be designated and that each be paid a salary of 500 drachmae each year; that a cithara or lyre master be designated and that the one who has been elected for the year be paid a salary of 700 drachmae; the latter shall teach music and the cithara or the lyre to children who can pass on to the following level and those who are one year younger, and he shall teach music to the *epheboi* (adolescent males); that the *paidonomos* shall determine the age of these children; and if we observe an intercalary month, that in addition to the annual salary the sum corresponding to one month's pay be added; that the

paidonomos and the gymnasiarch hire a master of arms and a master of archery and of javelin-throwing provided that this be referred to the people; that these latter [the masters] teach the *epheboi* and the boys to whom it has been decided that music will be taught; that a salary of 250 drachmae be paid to the master of archery and javelin-throwing, and 300 drachmae to the master of arms; the latter will teach no less than two months; that the *paidonomos* and the gymnasiarch will make sure that the children and the *epheboi* practice their lessons with care, as they are ordered to do in conformity with the laws; if the masters of letters disagree among themselves on the subject of the number of boys, that the *paidonomos* shall decide and that they shall respect his distribution; that the schoolmasters and the music master shall administer on the Council site the examinations that were to take place in the gymnasium.[2]

As we can see, the education in question is comprehensive, intellectual and athletic, even though girls are probably involved only in the intellectual component. The hierarchy of salaries also indicates the importance attributed to each discipline: the music teacher receives almost 50 percent more than the gymnastics teacher! But it also reflects the level of instruction: the curriculum was divided into three cycles or degrees, given here in reverse order. At the lowest level, a *grammatistes* taught children the rudiments of reading and writing; at the second level, a *grammatikos* perfected their literary education; at the third level, a sophist or a rhetor intervened.

The important place attributed to athletics—notwithstanding what has just been said about salaries—can be explained, of course, by the role of sports in Greek identity. To practice sports in heroic or athletic nudity seems to have been the distinguishing feature of a Greek man. The pious Jews of Jerusalem were not mistaken when they vituperated against those who rushed to the gymnasium as soon as the gong rang to announce the beginning of the distribution of oil (the equivalent of the signal raised or lowered in Beroia). In each new Greek city-state, the gymnasium appeared as the indispensable element, presumably the better to display the Greek identity of the place: in Jerusalem (Chapter 28), in Toriaion of Phrygia (Chapter 26), and on the banks of the Amu Darya (Chapter 22). In Jerusalem, this was even one of the rare innovations introduced by Jason, with the *ephebeion*; in Toriaion, it was one of the king's preoccupations. And in Ai-Khanum, the gymnasium occupied a privileged site on the plateau bordering the river. In Egypt, the Greeks dispersed throughout the countryside met at the gymnasium, and did not fear to call themselves "the people of the gymnasium" to distinguish themselves from the native Egyptians.

Does this mean that the gymnasium did not evolve? Certainly not, and between Beroia's Hellenistic gymnasium and those we see in any city in the eastern Mediterranean under the Roman Empire, the situation differed significantly. First, because the Roman conquest put a definitive end to any need for the city-states to train young men in view of integrating them into the civic army; there were no more civic armies, and those who wanted to enlist in the Roman army would be given the appropriate training in that context. Next, because the gymnasium was now just one element in a much broader complex. The bathing component had expanded considerably under the influence of Roman practices, for the Romans attached great importance to the bath, or rather to baths in the plural, with a succession of rooms at different temperatures. To be sure, Greek gymnasia usually had a hygienic component, for people had to clean themselves off after their exertions, but this was a marginal aspect that we glimpse only by chance (for example, in connection with the recuperation of gloios in Beroia). Under the empire, on the contrary, the arena became an appendix to the thermal baths. Moreover, the entire bath-gymnasium complex was enriched by connecting rooms that served as libraries and conference spaces. We must not visualize these as resembling the multipurpose rooms of our community buildings, but the gymnasium had become one of the cultural sites of the city-state. To be sure, not all educational activity took place there. Specialists are divided on this point, but there must have been schools that received children, especially girls, for basic intellectual education, and there is no evidence that young men frequented the gymnasium for educational purposes. However, the annexes that multiplied in gymnasia, sometimes including libraries, received the young men who were following the teachings of the rhetors, and this conferred an intellectual dimension on gymnasia that they had not had in the classical era. In this respect, they still stand unchallenged as witnesses to the Greek identity of a city-state. But more importantly still, the practice of sports or the mere spectacle of nude athletes in training belonged to the most easily identifiable Greek cultural patrimony; conforming to this norm visibly emphasized one's adherence to an entire culture.

A Wild Ass for the King, or Greeks, Jews, and Hellenism in the Transjordan

Toubias to Apollonios, greetings. As you wrote me to send (gifts to the king?) this month [Xanthicos], on 10 Xanthicos I have sent you Aineas, a member of my circle, with two horses, six dogs, a mule born of an ass, two white Arabian carriage asses, two colts from a half-wild ass, and a wild ass colt; they are tamed. I have sent you the letter I wrote on the subject of the gifts for the king and also a copy so that you would be informed. Goodbye. Year 29, 10 Xanthicos.

To King Ptolemy, greetings. I have sent you two horses, six dogs, a mule born of an ass, two white Arabian carriage asses, two colts from a half-wild ass, and a wild ass colt. Be well.

Papyrus, in Xavier Durand, Des Grecs en Palestine au IIIe siècle avant Jésus-Christ (Paris: J. Gabalda et Cie, 1997), pp. 179–184, no. 29

AMMAN (TRANSJORDAN) or its outskirts, 257 B.C.E. But the document was found in Fayyum, in Egypt. Three characters. First, King Ptolemy, that is, Ptolemy II Philadelphia, in the twenty-ninth year of his reign, the tenth day of the month of Xanthicos, or May 13, 257. Then, Apollonios, his *dioiketes* or minister of finances, manager of the royal treasury. An important person, to whom Ptolemy II manifested a deep attachment. Apollonios received from the king as a gift *(dorea)*, for his support, a domain of about twenty-five thousand acres in the Fayyum region. But these were not his only holdings; he also owned a large property in Galilee, which provided him above all with wine. We have the good fortune to be well acquainted with his private affairs thanks to the archives of his personal steward, Zeno of Caunos. These archives have been found in abundance in the Fayyum region near Philadelphia for the years 261–252. Zeno does not appear in the two letters cited, but it is he who archived them for Apollonios. Finally, the letters' author, Toubias (Greek) or Tobiah (Hebrew): he was a Jew, a member of a well-known Transjordanian family to which we shall return. At this point, he was the head of the family, and it was on this basis that he wrote to Apollonios. He informed him that, in keeping with his request, he had sent a certain number of gifts intended for King Ptolemy II. Another letter, written the same day, added that Aineas, Toubias's envoy, was also accompanied by a eunuch and four young slaves—two of them uncircumcised—who were surely intended to be offered to the king or to Apollonios himself.

The epistolary formulas did not get bogged down in circumlocutions. The writer named himself first, except when he addressed the king, but this exception was not obligatory. The niceties were reduced to a minimum: "Greetings!" "Be well!" "Goodbye!"

The matter was a simple one, but it must be situated in a broader context. Between 261 and 259, Apollonios's steward Zeno had made a lengthy tour of the Lagid province of Syria and Phoenicia, that is, the southern part of Syria, which had been dominated by the Greek kings of Alexandria since the end of the fourth century. He seems to have gone on business (at least this is the impression we get from his archives), but we may wonder whether he was not also seeking to evaluate the situation as the Lagids were about to launch the second Syrian War. We shall never have any proof of this, of course. But in settlements along the margins of the Lagid province, Zeno visited a number of local leaders, including Toubias, who played a role of the first order in the Transjordan. Might Zeno not have been seeking to verify the state of mind of the people who held the region on the king's behalf?

Toubias's letter came after Zeno had returned to Egypt, while the second Syrian War was under way in Asia Minor, and the Lagids were unquestionably suffering defeats. Ptolemy II might well have feared a Seleucid offensive in southern Syria. Was this not the moment to verify the loyalties of those who controlled the province? Apollonios, one of the principal members of the royal entourage, had been charged with checking out Toubias. For Toubias indicates clearly in his letter that he was acting at Apollonios's invitation. Had there been frictions with the king, or simply doubts as to Toubias's loyalty? In any case, the latter acceded to Apollonios's request and sent the king horses, dogs, and above all original gifts, white asses and colts of wild or half-wild asses (though the colts themselves were tame). It was probably more a matter of curiosity than of using the animals for some particular purpose. Scholars studying at the Alexandria museum were trying to establish an inventory of knowledge, and they would presumably have been interested in observing these rare creatures.

This is obviously not the main interest of our text, which allows us above all to see how the Greeks administered regions far away from their kingdom, and what relations were developed between Macedonian kings, colonists, and natives. Starting in 319, Ptolemy had tried to seize the greater part of Syria; as a good heir to the Pharaohs, he had understood that Egypt was not to be defended at the eastern limit of the Delta, but rather as far as possible to the northeast, at the entrance to the Sinai, in Galilee, or, better still, north of Lebanon, or even on the Euphrates and in the Anti-Taurus. Unable to establish his frontier that far north, he had nevertheless succeeded, around 302, in seizing all of Palestine and the Transjordan across from it, extending the frontier to the north as far as the Eleutheros, today the Nahr al-Kebir, which serves as the border between Syria and northern Lebanon. This set of territories was much more composite than it appears, for it grouped together, among others, the Phoenician city-states, long accustomed to contacts with Greeks, the Jews of Judaea, placed under the authority of their high priest, and the Aramean farmers of southern Syria, around Damascus and even in the Transjordan, where they already mingled with groups of Arab nomads. We do not know much about how the Lagid administration in the region was organized, but it is certain that various peoples enjoyed relative autonomy; this was true of the Jews, whose settlements seem to have harbored neither Lagid regiments nor government officials. Beyond the Jordan, Ptolemy I had kept an indigenous structure that existed while the Achaemenids ruled the region and that may have gone back to the Assyrian period, in the eighth and seventh centuries. At the center was a Jewish family known as the Tobiads: whoever the master of the region happened to be, this family administered the Amanitis on the king's behalf.

At the time of Zeno's visit, the master of the place was thus Tobias or Toubias, a namesake of the family's founder. His place of residence is designated in certain texts as the *birtha* of the Amanitis, that is, the fortified castle in the Amman region, which doubtless corresponded to the city of Amman itself, called Rabbatamana in antiquity. Enjoying considerable autonomy, Toubias had to maintain order and probably had to bring the king any help he requested. For maintaining order, he relied on troops, whom he may have recruited himself or who may have been sent by the king. In any case, these troops had lands for their support, according to the well-known cleruchy system: in exchange for military service, the king gave each of his soldiers a plot of land, larger or smaller depending on rank and corps (more for a horseman than for an infantryman, who himself received much more than an Egyptian auxiliary). We know something about a few of Toubias's soldiers: some were Persian, some Arab, some Greek, that is, they were a mix of the various populations of Alexander's former empire, as was typical for mercenaries in Hellenistic armies.

Toubias behaved like a member of an indigenous dynasty, but he had to demonstrate his loyalty to the king, hence the gifts mentioned in the text, which look almost like gestures of submission, the payment of a voluntary tribute. Moreover, perhaps around the same time or a little earlier, the birtha, Toubias's residence, became a Greek city-state, a *polis,* owing to a decision by Ptolemy, who named it Philadelphia in his own honor. Did that oblige Toubias to settle elsewhere? This is not certain, for a city-state could serve as capital for a local prince, but a little later we see that one of Toubias's successors had a sumptuous palace built at the heart of an agricultural domain some twenty kilometers west of Amman, at Iraq al-Emir. This was probably a way to distance himself a little from the capital, especially because, in the interim (around 200–198), Rabbatamana had fallen into the hands of the Seleucids, who had installed a governor and a regiment there. There was hardly room for two authorities, even complementary ones, in the same city.

The Tobiads draw attention to a phenomenon that is poorly documented but probably not as uncommon as the documentation we have would suggest: the place of prominent indigenous families in administration, and also in the process through which Greek culture spread into the kingdoms. The Tobiads, a leading Jewish family, had settled beyond the Jordan, probably very early, as we have seen, at the border of the Promised Land. Powerful by virtue of the lands it owned, the clan was always positioned on the margins with respect to the priestly aristocracy in Jerusalem, with which it inevitably maintained ties. Thus when Seleucus IV's chief minister came to ransack the Temple in Jerusalem, the high priest made it known that the four hundred talents of silver and two hundred talents of gold belonged in part to Hyrcanos the Tobiad.[1]

Their direct relations with the Lagids and later the Seleucids made the Tobiads privileged interlocutors, intermediaries with the administration. In this connection we have a text by Flavius Josephus, presented as an excursus attached to his great history of the Jews from their origins to the revolt of 66 C.E., *Jewish Antiquities,* which historians call "the Novel of the Tobiads." This text unquestionably includes a great deal of historical information about the relations between the Lagids and the Seleucids and about the Lagid fiscal system in Syria, but its use poses almost insoluble problems owing to the chronological contradictions that it presents: historians disagree in particular over whether it deals with the period of Lagid domination, around 220–200, or only with the era of Seleucid domination, after 195. There is no need to go into a detailed scholarly demonstration here, but my hypothesis is that Josephus's history essentially has to do with the period after 195.

When the peace of 195 was concluded, sealing the end of five years of war during which the Seleucid troops had defeated the Lagids of Syria-Phoenicia and claimed all their possessions in Asia Minor, King Antiochus III gave his daughter Cleopatra (I) in marriage to the young King Ptolemy V. As a dowry, he gave her the income from the former Lagid Syria-Phoenicia. The situation was paradoxical: whereas this region had just been wrenched away from Lagid domination, the fiscal revenues—at least the tributes—were to come back again to Egypt! In keeping with Lagid customs, the taxes were leased out to the highest bidder. Although the innumerable episodes of Flavius Josephus's account cannot be taken as wholly reliable, it does seem that a certain Josephus, the son or perhaps the grandson of the Toubias whose letter is cited above, had obtained the right to collect all the taxes payable in the province under the terms of Cleopatra's dowry. This tells us a great deal about his fortune; above all, it makes Josephus look like one of the court Jews of whom we have many examples—real or fictional—from Esdras and Nehemiah to Mordechai and Daniel. Josephus had offices in Alexandria and stored up a colossal fortune there; his son Hyrcanos participated in court life and offered sumptuous gifts to the king, despite reproofs from his father and older brothers. Moreover, Hyrcanos's attitude led to a break and open war between him and his brothers.

Victorious, Hyrcanos settled in his turn in the Transjordan, and had a palace built there, the atypical monument described above that scholars were slow to identify. Even today, some continue to see it as a temple rivaling the one in Jerusalem. French archaeological investigations have definitively shown that it was indeed the palace of the Tobiad Hyrcanos, the one Josephus discusses and describes as decorated with wild animals in bas-relief; these animals can be seen today, recessed in the walls. Probably for political reasons, Hyrcanos chose to commit suicide at the beginning of Antiochus IV's reign. Scholars have speculated on the reasons for his fears, but these can best be explained if, as I believe, Hyrcanos had taken over from his father the job of collecting Lagid taxes in Syria-Phoenicia. This would indicate that he was closely connected to the Lagids. Now, Antiochus IV seems to have put a brutal end to the donation made by Antiochus III under the terms of Cleopatra's dowry; the donation was no longer justified because the queen mother had died, in 176 apparently, not long after her husband's death (Ptolemy V died in 180). For Antiochus IV, who was always short of money, recuperating the tribute of a province that belonged to him seemed natural, and it was the occasion for renewed tension between the two dynasties. Hyrcanos, as the chief Lagid agent in the region, had everything to fear from the policies of Antiochus IV.

After Hyrcanos's suicide, the Tobiads—Hellenized Jews, local dynasts who relied on non-Jewish troops—disappeared from the regional scene, at a time when the construction of one of the most beautiful witnesses to Hellenistic art in the region was barely completed. Curiously, whereas the Greek city-state of Philadelphia remains enveloped in mystery up to the first century B.C.E., and none of its Hellenistic monuments are known, we must turn to a Jewish aristocrat of the Transjordan to seek out the earliest testimony regarding the spread of Hellenism beyond the Jordan, on a great domain that appears to be both the heir to the Achaemenid earthly paradises, realms of leisure and experimentation where kings or their satraps spent their time hunting, and an example of the Hellenistic *doreai,* great properties set up as fiefdoms to provide for the support of high-ranking royal agents.

Hyrcanos gave that function brilliant luster by building a palace that Josephus describes in detail:

> He built a strong fortress, which was constructed entirely of white marble up to the very roof, and had beasts of gigantic size carved on it, and he enclosed it with a wide and deep moat. He also cut through the projecting rock opposite the mountain, and made caves many stades in length; then he made chambers in it, some for banqueting and others for sleeping and living, and he let into it an abundance of running water, which was both a delight and an ornament to his country-estate . . . In addition, he also built enclosures remarkable for their size, and adorned them with vast parks.[2]

The palace itself was on a little butte in the middle of a vast flat space supported by a dike, and there must have been a lake or a pond nearby. The wild animals sculpted on the walls are still in place. The artificial grottos have been found in the nearby cliff. Better still, above the cliff in question a hydraulic arrangement has recently been discovered, a vast basin surrounded by a colonnade, which must have been used to make a waterfall. Such quasi-royal luxury may well have aroused envy. In any case, the palace of Iraq al-Emir is the finest example of a Hellenistic palace, the best preserved, that we have today. What a paradox that it should have been built by a Jewish prince!

CHAPTER TWENTY-FIVE

An Epigram from Sidon, or Hellenism in Syria in the Third and Second Centuries B.C.E.

The city of the Sidonians honors Diotimos, son of Dionysios, a judge, who was the victor in chariot racing in the Nemean contests.

Timocharis of Eleutherna made the statue.

The day when, in the Argolic Valley, from their seats, all the competitors drove their fast horses forward for the contest, the people of Phoronis awarded you a fine honor, and you received the crown, eternally memorable. For, first among citizens, you brought back from Hellas the glory of a hippic victory in the house of the noble Agenorides. The holy Cadmean city-state, Thebes, also exults at seeing its metropolis made illustrious by victories. And as for your father, Dionysios, his wish on the subject of the contest was fulfilled when Hellas made this clamor ring out: "it is not only in ships that you excel, O proud Sidon, but also in harnessed chariots, bringing back victory."

> Inscription, in E. J. Bikerman, "Sur une inscription grecque de Sidon," *Mélanges syriens offerts à monsieur René Dussaud* (Paris: Geuthner, 1939), pp. 91–99

SIDON (LEBANON), around 200 B.C.E. A Cretan sculptor known from other sources (this moreover is what allowed us to establish an approximate date for the text above) was commissioned to make a statue in honor of a winner in the chariot race in the contest at Nemea, in the Argolid. A perfectly ordinary undertaking, one that must have provided the artist with some of his resources. The statue has been lost, but the dedication remains, a real mine of information for anyone who knows how to observe and decode it.

The place where it was discovered warrants attention first of all: Saida, in Lebanon. The city is laid out over the vestiges of the ancient Phoenician city of Sidon, the secular rival of its neighbor Tyre, less prestigious perhaps than the metropolis of Carthage, but nevertheless rich in history and in legends that it knew how to put to good use. During the Persian occupation of Syria (from 545 or 525 to 333), it harbored the Achaemenid administration, and the Great King had one of his prestigious residences there, a "paradise." When Alexander arrived in Phoenicia, this was the only city where the conqueror deemed it necessary to replace the ruling king; it is true that the latter had been enthroned by the Achaemenids without respect for any of the local dynastic traditions, following a revolt by the city some years before. Alexander reestablished a member of the legitimate dynasty, a certain Abdalonymos, who was said to have been getting by rather meagerly as a gardener. This may be a pious legend, but it hardly matters.

When Timocharis was called upon, Sidon had thus been Greek for more than a century. As we do not have a precise date for the text, we do not know whether the city belonged to the Lagids of Alexandria (before 200) or to the Seleucids of Antioch (afterward). Only one thing is certain: Sidon had become a Greek city-state, a *polis*, probably fairly early in the third century, and it no longer had a king after the death of Philocles, a Greek or Macedonian friend of Ptolemy I. Philocles had been given this position of trust—which only confirms the city's strategic importance—in the years 300–290, probably after Abdalonymos's death.

What is important, first of all, is that Sidon was Greek. Not that it had been populated by Greek colonists and reconstructed from the ground up. Had Greeks and Macedonians settled in the city? Probably, for it would be very strange if no one had been attracted by the prosperity of the large port and the multiple opportunities it represented for an enterprising man. But there had not been—as there had not been in other Syrian cities, new or old—any deliberate colonization on the part of the king, no land distributions to veterans of the royal armies or to colonists who had come from Greece, Macedonia, or the Aegean world to seek their fortunes (Chapter 20). And yet the city was nevertheless Greek. The proof: a Sidonian was admitted to compete in one of the most prestigious Panhellenic contests, those of Nemea, in the northeastern Peloponnesus, one of the four great competitions, along with those of Olympia, Delphi, and the Isthmus of

216

Corinth, that formed what the Greeks called the *periodos*. A victory in one of these four contests established the athlete as one of the greatest, rather like a victory in one of today's Grand Slam tennis tournaments. Now, from the time they were founded, the contests were reserved for Greeks. And if a Sidonian was able to compete, it was because the Greeks considered him as one of their own, because he was a citizen of a polis. This is a living illustration of what Isocrates declared in his praise of Athens in 380: "the title 'Hellenes' is applied rather to those who share our culture than to those who share a common blood."[1]

The first sign of this Hellenization, for the term has to be used despite all the ambiguities it entails, appears with the name of our champion: Diotimos, son of Dionysios. The name and patronymic are Greek. Diotimos is thus not a first-generation Hellenized Phoenician; that was his father's position. Does the Greek name mask a Phoenician original? Historians have long been systematically searching for indigenous names translated by the Greek names borne by Hellenized natives. The effort strikes me most often as illegitimate. To be sure, an individual occasionally bears a Greek name in a Greek inscription and an indigenous name in a Semitic inscription. The most convincing example comes from Palmyra, where the son of Zenobia, Wahballat ("gift of Allat") was also called Athenodoros ("gift of Athena"); now, the great Arab goddess Allat was called Athena in Greek, and the statue erected in her temple at Palmyra was only a copy of a very classical Athena, with her helmet and shield. But the case of Wahballat is actually quite unusual, and of some hundred bearers of double names identified in Syria, almost all have a Greek name lacking any relation to the Semitic one, as if the individual really had two names, probably for use in two different contexts.

Thus Diotimos may have been called only Diotimos, as his father may have been known only as Dionysios. One thing is certain: they figured among the prominent members of the city-state. Dionysios, the father, was a "judge" *(dikastes)*. The title is completely Greek, and yet quite unexpected. For while the word is an ordinary Greek term, it never appears as the title of a function following the name of an individual. To be sure, in Athens during the classical era, judges were citizens selected by lot, but none of them ever fastened onto the label as a claim to glory. What was indicated following the name of a citizen was a magistracy, an executive function such as *archon*, strategos, *agoranomos* (the magistrate in charge of the marketplace), or, during the period we are interested in here, a prestigious *leitourgeia* such as the gymnasiarchy. But never a judgeship—except here. Why? Probably because the "judge" in Sidon was a magistrate: this is indeed the most appropriate translation of the traditional title *suffete*, well known in the Phoenician and Punic city-states. And this sheds light on the nature of the transformations undergone by Sidon when it became a polis instead of a Phoenician city-state: the function of king was eliminated, and the titles of existing functions were translated into Greek, with a few others created as needed. The Phoenician city-states already had magistrates and a council; it sufficed to give them Greek names, for there was no unique Greek institutional model that every new city-state had to follow. Everyone was quite aware that the titles of magistrates varied from one city-state to another, and there was thus no reason to be surprised that the Sidonians were governed by a dikastes rather than by an archon, a *stephanephoros*, a *brabeutes*, or a strategos. Around 175, when the high priest Jason undertook to transform Jerusalem into an Antioch-Jerusalem, a new polis, he behaved no differently: even his most determined adversaries (I am thinking in particular of the author of the second book of Maccabees) found nothing to reproach him for on the institutional level, probably because he made no changes in this realm.

But, one may ask, among native-born Greeks, the Greeks of the Aegean basin or the old colonial world, were there no signs of mistrust toward these recently minted Greeks? For people who readily divided up humanity between Greeks and barbarians, people whose racist thinking has been well brought to light by Benjamin Isaac's recent work, might not a Sidonian—but this would apply equally well to a Tyrian, an Egyptian, or any other barbarian—remain, no matter what, a barbarian, or at best a "mixo-Hellene," a "blended Greek"?[2] To vanquish such prejudices, the Sidonians had a formidable weapon at their disposal: Greek mythology. And Diotimos made stunning use of it: this is the meaning of the epigram that follows the official dedication of the statue.

This brief epigram adopts the most classical form for praising victors in Greek contests: it suffices to read, or reread, the many poems that Pindar, the master of the genre, devoted to victors, in order to note the perfect comparability of structure between our epigram and those of the Boeotian poet. Praise for the victor, praise for the father or for his lineage, and, finally, praise for the city-state where he was born and educated. But everything here is calculated to emphasize the close kinship between Sidon and Argos. Even though the contests took place not in Argos but in neighboring Nemea, the writer recalls that the race was held in the Argolic Valley, and that the people of Phoronis were the ones who crowned the victor. Phoronis evokes Phoroneus, the first inhabitant of Argos, father of Niobe and son of Inachos, the Argive river-god. The reminder of the noble house of the Agenorids may appear incongruous: why recall the name of the royal Sidonian line when the city-state had gotten rid of its royalty? It is because Agenor, the founder of the line, was an Argive: as a colony of a Greek city-state, Sidon could thus claim a much longer history as a Greek city (without being a polis) than its recent history might have suggested. And for this it had no need to invent new legends, as other city-states did in Syria and elsewhere. It had only to draw upon the mythic traditions of the Greeks themselves, who in fact considered Sidon as having been founded by the Argive Agenor, but also as the homeland of Cadmos, the founder of Thebes in Boeotia. This is recalled by the epigram immediately afterward, which associates the name Thebes with that of Cadmos. A colony of one Greek city-state, the metropolis of another, and an important one at that, how could Sidon fail to be prestigious among the Greeks? No mention of the recent promotion to the status of polis, no allusion to the dubious reputation of the Sidonians as merchants who are more or less honest, more or less piratical (a frequent motif in Homer). The last sentence of the epigram has no purpose but to reverse or at least to complete the traditional image of the city; Sidon no longer shines solely owing to the reputation of its navy, but also by virtue of what counts most in Greek eyes, the quality of its athletes! The fact that Diotimos was the owner of his team and not just the chariot driver (though he could have been both at once) takes nothing away from his glory or from the glory that spills over onto the city-state as a whole. In any case, the erection of the hero's statue in the city and at the expense of the city-state was very much an official act, undoubtedly authorized by a decision of the council and the magistrates.

There are many parallels with Diotimos's adventure, even though Diotimos's glory was enhanced by the fact that he was the first of the Sidonians to win a victory at Nemea. We know what importance the Greeks attached to the notion of "first," a term found in stadiums and in civic activities: the city-state praised a benefactor as much for being the first to carry out a given act of generosity as for what he actually gave. Other athletes who were natives of Phoenicia were admitted, like Diotimos, to Greek contests in the Hellenistic period, Tyrians in particular. We shall look more closely into the contests and their importance later on (Chapter 32), but the epigram from Sidon illustrates marvelously the way the new Greeks were able to use myths to insert themselves into a Greek world that had been constituted long before they entered it.

The question of recognition as a Greek city-state, as a polis, arose for ancient cities like Tyre, Sidon, or Damascus, but even more for the new urban foundations disseminated more or less everywhere from northern Syria to the Indus. For very old cities, we might have thought that they would valorize their age as such. The Phoenicians are mentioned by Homer, who refers to them as Sidonians on several occasions. But age was of no use, if it was not in a Greek context. We have seen what skillful use Sidon was able to make of Greek traditions. It used many others as well; after all, the Greeks had made Europa a Sidonian princess. Similarly, Io's wanderings allowed the group of Greeks who had set out to find her to pass through a number of existing Greek cities or sites of new ones. Thus Antioch, founded in 300 B.C.E. by Seleucus I, could boast of having taken in Greeks who had settled on its site centuries earlier, the descendants of Triptolemos and his companions, who had gone off in search of Io and were worn out from all their traveling. Elsewhere, other legends were used. Thus in Iamnia (Iavne, near Tel Aviv), people pointed to rock formations bearing traces of the irons that had bound lovely Andromeda when she was delivered by Perseus. In another city in Asia Minor, famous for its marble, one could see the very blood of the god Attis in the reddish striations that ran through the stone. Elsewhere, a similarity to a Greek or Macedonian city in name or geographic situation could be used to transport myths belonging to an ancient city-state into a very recent one. Thus Apamea on the Orontes, in Syria, was first founded, perhaps around 307, under the name Pella. Like its homonym in Macedonia, it was located on a plateau overlooking a swampy plain traversed by a sluggish river. The locals did not fail to name the river Axios, like its counterpart in Macedonia, and they explained the landscape by Axios's passion for a local nymph, Meliboia. Indeed, Axios, in love with Meliboia, did not manage to leave the place, lingering near the object of his affections to the point of creating swamps, then a lake, and even threatening the ramparts of the city. By chance, Heracles passed through and used his club to cut through the circle of mountains and create a breach through which the Axios could rush out toward the north (this is the narrow pass that currently stretches from Jisr al-Shoghur to Darkush) before veering west and rejoining the sea. Now, a similar story was told about Pella in Macedonia, located near a swampy lake fed by the Axios River. According to the legend, the nymph Periboia held back her sinuous waters to avoid rejoining her aquatic spouse, the Axios, which flowed at some distance to the east! The parallel is striking, and leaves little room for doubt, despite some adjustments required by slightly different topographical realities.

Sometimes legendary kinships were invented, like those of the Jews with Sparta or Pergamon.[3] Elsewhere, people were content to develop etymologies that appear totally fantastic to our philologists' eyes, but that seemed to the Greeks perfectly justified nonetheless. Thus Damascus, in Greek Damaskos, was said to owe its name to the fact that it was the place where Hermes, an ally of Dionysus, flayed the giant Askos (from *derma,* skin, and *Askos*); but there are variants on the story, such as the one that attributes the foundation of the city to one Damaskos, son of Heracles and an Arcadian nymph, Halimede; this Damaskos was said to have been flayed there by Dionysus, whose vines he had cut down. Or else that was the place where Dionysus subjugated *(damazo)* his enemy Lycurgus (the god who did not drink wine) by sprinkling the opposing army with wine drawn from a wineskin *(askos)!* Gaza was said to have harbored the treasure *(gaza)* of Zeus. Even the obscure Bostra of Arabia was said by the Neoplatonic philosopher Damascius to owe its name to the fact that Io the heifer was pursued there by the sting of a horsefly *(boos oistron);* this put the city in the company of the famous places Io had passed through in her flight, such as the Bosporus, "the bovine passage," an allusion to Io, according to many commentators.

The importance of these legends has too often been neglected; they have been rejected as erudite digressions. Some reconstructions may indeed have been amusing inventions by local scholars. But many were adopted by city-states on a quite official basis. The epigram for Diotimos was engraved on the official monument that the city-state erected for him. In Iamnia, according to Josephus, they really did put Andromeda's rock on display. Elsewhere, coins preserved the memory of Heracles or some other Greek god or hero. In Apamea, the official legend was shaped at the request of the city-state by a learned scholar, Euphorion of Chalcis, the royal librarian of Antioch in the era of Antiochus III. Jerusalem sent embassies to Sparta to renew the bonds of friendship, and it was to Sparta that the high priest Jason fled when he was expelled by his cousin Menelaos—who perhaps did not choose his own name at random!

Thus the new Greek city-states tried as best they could to invent a Greek past for themselves that would bring them closer to their oldest counterparts; they sought to fill the gap created by time so as to appear as Greek as their elders, and as prestigious as the legend would permit, if the history were lacking. Diotimos's victory allowed Sidon to put on public display, before all visitors, the national legend and the city-state's claim to fame! That certainly warranted a statue.

CHAPTER TWENTY-SIX

The Promotion of Toriaion,
or How to Become a City-State

With good fortune King Eumenes to the inhabitants of Toriaion, greetings. Your men, Antigenes, Brennos, Heliades, whom you sent to congratulate us for having accomplished everything and for arriving in good health at this place—on account of which, while giving thank-offerings to the gods, you offered the proper sacrifices—and to request, because of the goodwill you have for our state, to grant you a city constitution [*politeia*] and (the use of) your own laws and a gymnasium, and other things consistent with those, (these men) have spoken with great enthusiasm, and after declaring you are most eager to do everything advantageous to us, they asked for (our) assent; as (they spoke) befitting expressions of gratitude to me on the part of your people that will remain forever, and that you will not diverge from what is advantageous and necessary for me. I could observe that it is no small matter for me to grant your demands, since it is directly concerned with many affairs of great consequence; indeed, any (favor) bestowed upon you by me at this moment would be durable as I have full powers by virtue of receiving these from the Romans who prevailed both in the war and in treaty; that would not be so with powers decreed by someone without authority for such would be condemned by all as empty and deceitful. But because of the goodwill you have for us as you have shown at the right time, I grant both you and those with you to organize yourselves into one polity and to make your own laws; if you are satisfied with some of these, submit them to us that we may inspect them for anything contrary to our interest; if not, let us know and we will send you the men capable of appointing officials and a council, of dividing people and assigning them to tribes, of building gymnasia and giving oil for youth. Also, that your city is officially recognized, I myself have (already) declared this at the beginning of the second letter. After having received such great honors from me, try to show your true goodwill by your deeds on all occasions. King Eumenes to the council and the people of Toriaion, greetings. Since we have granted a polity to you and a gymnasium, we want to make clear our goodwill by increasing our grant, and we give you for the (purchase of) oil the revenue coming from the market director, until Herodes, "One and a half," examines the matter and earmarks other revenue, from an estate, some land, or anything else he might choose that a tenth of all produce is collected (thereof). On balance, be assured that if you preserve your goodwill toward us, you will receive many times the privileges.

Inscription, in Lloyd Jonnes, *The Inscriptions of the Sultan Dagi* (Bonn: R. Habelt, 2002), pp. 87–88, no. 393

T ORIAION, PHRYGIA, between 188 and 159 B.C.E. The interior of Asia Minor, in a zone that had long been in contact with Greeks from the coast, but where Greeks and Macedonians had come to settle only after Alexander's conquest. A few city-states dating from the late fourth century, chiefly indigenous cities of some importance, such as Sardis, Pergamon, and Apamea of Phrygia, the former Kelainai, and the satrapic capital of Antigonus the One-Eyed. There were many new foundations, but mostly modest ones, certainly not city-states, but *katoikiai*, settlements of colonists *(katoikoi)* lacking civic status, military colonists in some places, perhaps civilian settlers elsewhere. Toriaion must have been among these royal foundations in the third century; whether the Seleucids or the Attalids were responsible we do not know.

The text cited above was discovered only a few years ago in a small village, Mahmuthisar, just south of the city of Ilgin in Turkey (about sixty kilometers northwest of Konya), near the site of ancient Toriaion or Tyriaion in eastern Phrygia. The document caused an immediate sensation, because it illustrated exceptionally well a phenomenon that must have been repeated countless times: the transformation of an indigenous village into a new Greek city-state, a *polis*. Only two other texts could be compared to this one. On the one hand, an inscription from Cilicia mentions the creation of a city-state called Arsinoeia near Nagidos, at the initiative of the Lagids, in the second half of the third century B.C.E.; the territory in question had been seized from Nagidos. On the other hand, a letter from an emperor notifies a governor that the status of city-state has been granted to the town of Tymandos, in eastern Phrygia, perhaps around the mid-second century C.E. (the emperor was probably Antoninus Pius). But these two texts present obvious differences. In the first case, colonists sent from elsewhere had settled on part of the territory of an existing city-state; in the second case, we are in the era of the Roman Empire, under conditions that can be viewed a priori as quite different. In our case, on the contrary, we witness the birth of a Greek city-state "live," under the reign of Eumenes II (197–159), in the regions of interior Asia Minor that Eumenes had recently received from Rome after Antiochus III had been defeated at Magnesia ad Sipylum (189) and had had to abandon the region under the terms of the peace of Apamea (188). Eumenes II, a faithful ally of Rome since the beginning of his reign, had been rewarded by a considerable territorial increase that gave him control of nearly all of Asia Minor, with an outlet to the Mediterranean to the south, where he founded the city of Attaleia (now Antalya). But this kingdom hardly constituted a uniform whole. Although Greeks were present everywhere in large numbers, they cohabited in the interior regions with numerous indigenous populations that had been more or less touched by Hellenism: Lydians, Phrygians, Pisidians, Pamphylians, and Mysians, not to mention the Galatians, Gauls who had come in throngs around 270 and who ended up settling in the center of the Anatolian plateau in the region known from then on as Galatia. The troubles and devastation for which the Galatians were responsible were still fresh in memory: in 189, the Roman consul Manlius Vulso had had to mount a campaign against them under difficult conditions.

This was the context, then: a recently enriched king, an expanded kingdom, mixed populations. The lengthy inscription presented above actually included three royal letters, which were no doubt written in the order in which they were engraved: indeed, in the first, the king addresses the katoikoi of Toriaion, that is, the residents or colonists, whereas the second and third are intended for the council and the people of the new city-state. There is little to be learned from the third text (not reproduced here), because only the address and opening words remain. The first two are thus the ones that warrant our attention.

We learn that Toriaion—let us retain the original form transmitted by the text, even if historians are more accustomed to calling it Tyriaion—had been populated up to that point with katoikoi. The term poses some problems, but it has to be viewed as the equivalent of *colonists*. We can presume that the embassy was sent not by native villagers but by Hellenized residents who had arrived in Toriaion long before, either as settlers who were to exploit the land for agricultural purposes or, more probably, as military colonists who were to ensure its security. Other katoikoi are attested in Asia Minor, often in a military context. Some had been installed by the Attalids of Pergamon, others by the Seleucids. Here, the Seleucids are viewed as the founders, because Toriaion had only recently been given to the Attalids.

Who were these katoikoi? Greeks, at least in part, but also probably Hellenized natives, Phrygians, Pisidians, Thracians, or other peoples quick to enlist in royal armies. Here, among the ambassadors, we can readily guess the origin of one of these katoikoi: Brennos is unmistakably Galatian. The Greek names of the others—Antigenes, Heliades, Orestes—may conceal almost any origin: Greek, Macedonian, or indigenous.

The colonists from Toriaion had sent an embassy to Eumenes II to ask him to grant the katoikia the status of polis. It was never spelled out in these terms, but the fact that the city lived according to its own laws was precisely what characterized a city-state. Thus there is no room for hesitation about what lay behind the request, all the more so because in addressing the second letter to "the council and the people of Toriaion" the king uses precisely the vocabulary appropriate to a city-state. The king shows in his rather convoluted response that he has hesitated quite a bit, not knowing whether the advantages to him would outweigh the disadvantages. For the king was bound to lose in terms of both authority and money. If Toriaion became a polis, the king could no longer give it the sort of direct orders he could give to a military colony that was entirely subject to him. There was actually little risk that the new city-state would prove to be unfaithful or disobedient, but it would escape from direct administration by royal agents. On the fiscal level, it would no doubt continue to pay tribute, but the king would no longer be the sole beneficiary of all the income from the territory, for the city-state would need to have its own resources so its institutions could function. We find an echo of this in the second letter, where the financing of a gymnasium is discussed.

The king had nevertheless decided in favor of Toriaion's request. In a newly annexed region, he may have had an interest in creating solid friend-ships against the day when the Seleucids might return. Was this not what the ambassadors meant by the assertion the king recalls when he says that "you will not diverge from what is advantageous and necessary for me"? The political advantages must have won out over the material disadvan-tages. Thus the king granted Toriaion a *politeia,* that is, both a govern-ment and a constitution.

It is particularly interesting to look closely at the material aspects of this creation. First of all, the king recognized the city-state's control over a territory: the favor applied to "you and those [natives living] with you" in villages. Toriaion thus had its own territory, a *chora,* whose inhabitants shared the same advantages. It would then be appropriate to begin by list-ing the civic bodies, the *demos,* or rather, here, the *politeuma,* the group of citizens. Should we assume that certain inhabitants were excluded? Per-haps, but we do not know which ones. Once the list was drawn up, the new citizens would be divided into tribes, as in all the city-states. We do not know how many tribes there were; that would doubtless be the object of a specific law later on. Nevertheless, the king must have anticipated dif-ficulties, because he announced that if the people of Toriaion did not suc-ceed in setting up the requisite institutions, he would send someone to do it for them.

For, in order to adopt laws, the body of citizens first had to be consti-tuted. It would be up to this body to meet in order to elect magistrates and make all the institutional arrangements that, taken together, formed what could be called the politeia. Some laws may already have existed; others remained to be adopted. In any case, the king did not want to take any risks: when a law had been approved by the people, it was to be sent to him so that he could ascertain that it was not contrary to his interests.

Perhaps the most surprising element lies in the insistence with which the matter of the gymnasium and oil for the young men (the *neoi*) is addressed. In the first letter, the granting of civic status boils down to a politeia, the right to live according to the city-state's own laws, and the right to build a gymnasium; the other advantages do not need to be spelled out. At the end of the same letter, the king returns to the point: it is appropriate to have a gymnasium built and to supply oil for the young men. This insistence can-not be accidental; it has to be seen as a fundamental preoccupation of the new city-state.

The example of Toriaion is not an isolated one. When the Jewish high priest Jason obtained from Antiochus IV the right to transform Jerusalem into a polis (Chapter 28), he hastened to build a gymnasium and an *ephebeion*. One might suppose that his adversaries—our only sources of information about his policies—were the ones who emphasized the gymnasium, for they were unquestionably scandalized by the nudity on display there, but this would be a mistake. It is probable, as we shall see, that Jason did not make many changes in the traditional Jewish institutions, and that the creation of the polis was largely limited to the foundation of a gymnasium. In Egypt, where many Greeks lived outside of Alexandria and the two other city-states of the country (Naucratis and Ptolemais), they called themselves "the people of the gymnasium."

Why was the gymnasium viewed as so important? We can say without risk of contradiction that the gymnasium constituted the very symbol of life "in the Greek manner," that is, civilized life. We shall see what role the contests played (Chapter 32), but already we must retain the fact that the Greeks viewed the practice of sport, with its accompanying nudity, as what distinguished them most surely from the barbarians. A barbarian could learn Greek (and he had to, to meet the needs of daily life), he could take up wine drinking (the Gauls were quite fond of this), he could begin to cook with olive oil and wear Greek clothing, but only nudity in the stadium would show him to be fully Greek! So much so that, in the new city-states founded in the Hellenistic period, education in the gymnasium became the normal way for young men to attain citizenship. In Alexandria, under the empire, the *epicrisis,* or examination of young citizens, was founded on this sole criterion: anyone who did not have access to the gymnasium could not claim to be an Alexandrian. Associated as it was with the ephebeion, that is, the place where the *epheboi* were taught, the gymnasium guaranteed the Hellenism of those who frequented it.

Under these conditions, we can see why the people of Toriaion, just like Jason the Jew, were determined above all to build a gymnasium, the most visible sign of the change of status on both the cultural and the political levels. What good was it to be a Greek city-state if its residents did not live like Greeks? We have seen what an important place was reserved for sports in the education of young men (Chapter 23); here is a concrete illustration, in the founding act of a new Greek city-state.

Toriaion is the only Hellenistic city, except for Jerusalem and Arsinoeia of Cilicia, for which we have a text mentioning its creation. And yet, from Alexander's era on, the practice was widespread. Even if we leave aside the new foundations (Chapter 20), we find that a number of indigenous cities sought to obtain this particular status. The observation leads necessarily to a first conclusion: far from being an empty shell, an institution devoid of meaning and power, the polis struck Greek or Hellenized populations as an enviable status. And all these populations went to some lengths to acquire the status of polis, which only the king—or, later, the emperor—could grant. To be sure, the city-state had changed since the fifth century B.C.E., but change does not signify decline. At all events, we see the indigenous communities of Asia Minor and Syria making serious efforts to obtain the status of polis from the king. This is the case for a number of ancient cities became city-states one by one during the third century B.C.E. (Sardis, Tyre, Sidon, Berytos, Byblos, Arados) and sometimes later (Hama, Damascus, Jerusalem). The movement went on unabated and continued through the empire: tribes that were organized in villages and sanctuaries, too, obtained the status during this period. We have numerous examples in Asia Minor, where village or tribal communities formed a single city-state (the Charakenoi became Charakipolis, for example) or several (the Milyades community splintered into five city-states). In Syria, the movement was less clear-cut, but indigenous communities were still being promoted to the rank of city-state in the first century C.E. (Palmyra), in the second (Bostra, Dionysias, Adraha, Petra), in the third (Philippopolis, Neapolis on the Euphrates, Marcopolis), and even in the fourth (Maximianopolis, Constantine). To insist on the "decline" of the city-state thus appears to be going against the documentation. At least the contemporaries did not seem to be aware of such a decline. There were good reasons for this.

The city-state remained attached to the image of Hellenism. Although in all periods many Greeks lived outside of civic structures, the city-state was nevertheless the form of political organization that appeared most characteristic of the Greeks. To adopt it was thus to enter, as it were, into the camp of the masters. It was also a way of manifesting one's adherence to Greek culture, whatever adaptations it had been made to undergo. In fact, nothing designated someone as Greek better than the fact of being able to display a Greek *ethnikos*. This was the only way one could have access to the Greek contests or organize them oneself.

Still, the political advantages should not be neglected. To be sure, not very many city-states remained totally independent of the kingdoms during the Hellenistic period, even if Rhodes, Sparta, Athens (usually), and a few others could claim that they were. But after all, the situation was not so different from that of the classical period, when most of the city-states belonged, more or less voluntarily, to a military league that was hegemonic by nature: the city-state members of the Delian League could hardly boast of their "independence" (Chapter 12). From that point on, most city-states found themselves situated within relatively large kingdoms or states (the Achaean or Aetolian Leagues, for example). It was within this framework that they had to find their own reasons for being. There was no question of total freedom: we have seen that the people of Toriaion were committed to respecting the interests of the king. But there were many other stakes in the life of a city-state beyond foreign affairs. Living according to one's own laws and not according to the king's law was perceived as an immense privilege: it meant recognition of the city-state's political capability. Moreover, set up as a city-state, the community could send ambassadors to the king, negotiate the amount of tribute to be paid or try to obtain new privileges. The negotiation was one-sided, of course, but in the Greeks' eyes there was a gulf between giving in without any possibility of discussion and accepting one charge or another after discussion. There was a big difference between barbarians who submitted to a monarch and citizens who accepted the authority of a king.

To live in a city-state was thus to enjoy a large degree of self-administration. The royal taxes themselves were undoubtedly distributed by the city-state's magistrates. It meant deciding independently which gods to honor, in what form, and when; it meant the possibility of participating officially in the Panhellenic contests. It meant being integrated into the immense community of Greeks.

It also meant that the urban center located at the heart of the new city-state had to adopt the essential characteristic features of a city-state. The citizens thus had to finance (or get the wealthiest among them to finance) not only the indispensable public buildings, like the bouleuterion for council meetings, the theater for the meetings of the demos, an *archeion* for the public archives, the sanctuaries for the city-state's gods, the ephebeion and the gymnasium, but also what made a city-state stand out: paved streets, public fountains (and aqueducts to bring in water), thermal baths, an agora, a sewage system, sometimes ramparts, and a library. All this was costly, and someone had to pay for it (Chapter 23).

But the new city-state leaders also had to assume all the responsibilities that had earlier fallen to the king's officers: they had to maintain order and security by creating a police corps *(diogmitai)* placed under the direction of an irenarch, watch out for the constancy of weights and measures and the proper functioning of markets, ensure a regular supply of wheat and oil, maintain the public buildings, and oversee public behavior (especially in the gymnasium: Chapter 23) and the education of children. Who would dare claim that civic life had become pointless?

231

Steles of Mercenaries from Sidon, or the Army and the War in the Hellenistic World

Painted stele from Sidon
(The text is translated as no. 3 , below.)

1. The *politeuma* of the Caunians (honors) Hippolytos (?)
   and Apollonides, son of Hermagoras, Zeno son of Zeno,
   [—] of Zeno, Isidoros son of Athenodoros, Hermonax son
   of Artemidoros, their fellow citizens.
2. Hekataios son of Menogenos, of Thyatira, his companions.
   Excellent Hekataios, greetings.
3. Salma mo[—], native of Adadea, excellent, greetings.
4. Dioscourides son of Exaboas, Pisidian of Balbura, standard-bearer of the auxiliary troops, excellent, greetings.
   Keraias his brother has erected (this stele).
5. Saettas, son of Trocondos, *symmachos,* Pisidian native of
   Termessos near Oinoanda, the *politeuma* of the residents
   of Termessos near Oinoanda (honors) their excellent fellow
   citizen. Greetings.
6. The *politeuma* of the Pinareans honors Kartadis, son of
   Hermactilibos, Lycian, excellent and lamented; greetings.

233

7. To Diodotos, son of Patron, Cretan from Hyrtakina,
   Athabous, worthily, to her husband. Excellent Diodotos,
   greetings.
8. Aristeides, son of Aristeides, Lacedemonian of Gytheium;
   his friends and tent companions Alexon and Tetaridas.
   Excellent (companion), greetings.
9. Stomphias, son of Apollonodas, of Euromos, excellent
   man, greetings.
10. Eunastides, son of Nicanor, Perrhaebus.
11. The *politeuma* of [—]ndeans (honors) Hermolaos (?), son
    of Demetrios (?), [—], their fellow citizen. Excellent man,
    greetings.

Inscriptions, in Theodore Macridy, "À travers les nécropoles
sidoniennes, I: Stèles peintes de Sidon," *Revue biblique* 13
(1904): 547–556

IDON, PHOENICIA, during the third century or perhaps the beginning of the second century B.C.E. In a necropolis in the Sidonian
countryside, a series of lovely steles with pediments, each with an
inscription. Several have painted motifs, in hollowed-out frames above the
texts. When they are viewed as a series (and this is justified by their style),
they turn out to be of great interest, despite the brevity of their texts. They
merit a moment's reflection.

The texts are banal in appearance, but an attentive examination brings
to light some features common to the entire set. A first observation: these
are all steles commemorating men. The Greeks did not hesitate to decorate
women's tombs with engraved epitaphs, often with handsome ornamentation sculpted in bas-relief; recently, just south of Sidon, a painted stele has
been found bearing a portrait of a woman, with her name, Robia, dating
from the same period as the steles illustrated above. The absence of wom-
en's steles in the Sidon necropolis must therefore have a specific historical
significance. This first remark needs to be extended by a second observation: the dead are accompanied by the wishes and solicitude of companions; only one epitaph was erected by a spouse (no. 7) and one other by a
brother (no. 4). We are clearly in a masculine environment. The key is supplied by two of the texts and by the painted image below the pediment in
other cases, probably justifying the extrapolation: we are dealing with soldiers. In text 4, Dioscourides is identified as the standard-bearer of the

auxiliary troops; in text 8, we learn that the companions who shared a tent with Aristeides chipped in to honor him with an epitaph. The painted images confirm this analysis. Thus on stele no. 1 we see "two warriors wearing big plumed Greek helmets and armed with shields" (Macridy, p. 549), and one of the two seems also to be holding a lance. On steles 2 and 3, the warrior stands alone. On stele 4, one of the best preserved, the painter represented "a beardless warrior, in combat posture, dressed in a short tunic, belted at the waist, which leaves his arms bare . . . on his head he is wearing a bell-shaped helmet decorated with a plumed crest; the cheek protectors are pulled down . . . in his left hand, the warrior is holding a long light-colored oval shield, and in his raised right hand a big grey-blue sword with a triangular blade whose sheath is attached to a harness in sling position" (Macridy, p. 551). With some variations, all these steles carry the same principal motifs: one or several soldiers bearing arms. The variants are not unimportant, for they attest to a concern for realism: the soldiers were not all equipped in the same way.

We are thus in the presence of a community of soldiers from the Sidon garrison. But in the service of whom? Lagids or Seleucids? This depends on the date, for Sidon was Lagid until 200–198, Seleucid after that, but the date cannot be established by the text itself, because no inscription bears any such indication. Attentive readers will have noted that all the deceased are foreigners. A rapid inventory of their places of origin may put us on the right track. If we proceed by large geographical sectors, we note a strong representation from southern Asia Minor. In fact, we find three soldiers who came from Greece proper: a Cretan, a Lacedemonian from Gytheium, Sparta's port, and a Thessalian (Perrhaebus). We are clearly dealing with mercenaries, for neither the Lagids nor the Seleucids dominated those regions politically, and they could not have raised troops there. All the others come from Asia Minor. One is from Thyatira, in Lydia, a city-state long dominated by the Seleucids before it fell under the control of the kings of Pergamon. This is the only city-state represented from the northern half of the Anatolian Peninsula. All the others are located in the south, mainly in Caria (Caunos, Euromos), Lycia (Pinara), and Pisidia (Balbura, Adada, Termessos near Oinoanda). And all these regions were under Lagid domination during most of the third century, until its conquest by Antiochus III in 197. Although these soldiers were mercenaries who might have gone off to enlist in the service of anyone at all, it seems more plausible that Caria, Lycia, and Pisidia constituted a recruitment pool for the Lagids, and we can deduce from this that the painted steles of Sidon may well have belonged to soldiers from the Lagid garrison in Sidon, before the city fell into the hands of the Seleucids in 199. The strong presence of Pisidians is no accident: these fierce mountain people, feared for their looting, were known for their courage and aptitude for combat. Enlisting as mercenaries must have been an outlet for many of them.

Before broadening our scope, we need to look closely at one more word. Several steles were offered by an association called *politeuma* followed by an *ethnikos:* politeuma of the people of Caunos, Pinara, Termessos, and a city-state whose name is mutilated (–ndos or –nda). The meaning of the word *politeuma* is controversial and probably multiple. In the letter from Eumenes II to the inhabitants of Toriaion (Chapter 26), the word clearly designates the group of citizens of the new city-state, those who would be called the *demos* elsewhere. The word stems from the same root as *polis* (city-state) and *politeia* (civic constitution), and it has sometimes been understood to designate an association of the civic type that allowed people with a common origin to form a group within a city-state that was not their own in order to lead a life of the civic type. The politeuma of the Caunians of Sidon would thus be, in Sidon, a grouping of all the residents originating in Caunos who, not being citizens of Sidon, did not have access to the civic institutions of that city-state; they formed their own civic group, probably electing their own magistrates and forming an organized community. After the discovery of the archives of a Jewish politeuma in Heracleopolis of Egypt, it seemed that this interpretation would have to be revised. In the Hellenistic kingdoms, when the word *politeuma* does not refer to the demos of a city-state as it does in Toriaion, it refers to a military unit serving as an auxiliary to the royal army, founded on the principle of homogeneous ethnic recruitment. The Jewish politeuma of Heracleopolis of Egypt was in effect the local garrison, and it is clear that in Sidon we are dealing with soldiers in every case. There are other examples of politeuma formation in Egypt—for example, by the Boeotians of Xois in the Delta, the Cilicians in the Fayyum, the Cretans in the Arsinoite nome, or the Idumeans in Memphis—all clearly made up of soldiers. Sylvie Honigman, who proposed this very convincing interpretation, sees it as a reason to take seriously an affirmation by Josephus that has often been dismissed as propaganda. Josephus asserts that Alexander had offered the Jews the possibility of joining his army while continuing to respect their own customs, and that Ptolemy I had hired Jews as soldiers to guard Egypt. Scholars have assumed that in this passage Josephus was simply supporting the cause of the Alexandrian Jews, who made the claim in the first century C.E. that they had been present in the city-state from its foundation and consequently demanded rights equivalent to those of the Greeks (Chapter 35). Now the Alexandrian Jews, or at least some of them, formed a politeuma. To be sure, at the time Josephus was writing, this could not have been a military unit, which would have been useless under Roman domination. But it is probable that the Jewish politeuma of Alexandria was a successor to the Jewish military unit established in the city by Ptolemy I shortly after its foundation. That would explain why, in Josephus's day, not all Jews belonged to the politeuma, but only those who descended from old military families.

Whatever may be the case regarding this controversial point, it is clear from the findings in Sidon that there was a certain communal solidarity, expressed by the erection of steles for the deceased. The politeuma substituted for the absent or nonexistent family. Only one of the deceased in our sample was married; one other had a brother, who was clearly in the same military unit. A soldier, like so many other individuals in the Greek world, belonged to a network of solidarity that left a trace, for us, at the time of death, but that must have been expressed similarly when its members married, or on the occasion of religious festivals.

The soldier is one of the emblematic figures of the Hellenistic era. Products of a far-reaching military operation, the Alexandrian conquest, the Hellenistic kingdoms were based on strength. When Antiochus I designated what constituted the two pillars of his power, he spoke of his troops and his friends (philoi). We have seen that victory justified the royal title of the Diadochs. In a world in which war was a permanent fixture, military power was the basis for their authority. Hence the extreme solicitude of kings for their troops, their concern with recruiting soldiers who were both experienced and reliable. But the armies evolved over some three centuries before they started to disappear along with the kingdoms they had to defend.

Alexander's army was mainly a Macedonian army. It did include contingents from elsewhere, but the Macedonian phalanx was at its heart.

Even after the troops that had participated in the expedition to India were let go, the Diadochs' armies remained Macedonian for the most part, and Greek, although some "exotic" contingents (archers, rebels, elephant drivers) were recruited to do the specialized work for which they were famous.

During the course of the third century, the composition of the armies changed considerably. It is hard to know the precise makeup of the royal armies for at least two reasons: first because we have access to only a small number of rolls, and then because these lists do not really distinguish between the soldiers' origins and their weaponry—in other words, a soldier fighting with the "Macedonians" may be either a Macedonian himself or a non-Macedonian equipped in the Macedonian fashion. Despite these reservations and difficulties, specialists have used all available sources—including lists, graffiti (for example, those left by the mercenaries at Memmonion of Abydos, where the Greeks of the archaic period had many successors [Chapter 4]), and descriptions of some of the expeditionary corps—to give us a good picture of Antiochus III's army at the battle of Raphia (217) and at the battle of Magnesia ad Sipylum (189), although in each case we see only part of the army (the infantry in 217, three contingents in 189), or the battle of the Lagids in 219.

We can conclude that there was relative stability in recruitment, but also that these armies had put down increasingly strong local roots. Throughout the entire third century, continental Greeks, Cretans, and Macedonians appear in large numbers in the records of all the Hellenistic armies, but their numbers drop abruptly after 200; indeed, except for the Macedonians, they practically disappear. Similarly, the number of Thracians and Greeks and natives of Asia Minor, very considerable until around 200, tends to diminish fairly rapidly, although probably less sharply than that of the continental Greeks. During the same period, Semites and Egyptians appear in large numbers. As for the Lagid army, the massive mobilization of Egyptian contingents to confront Antiochus III in the battle of Raphia (217) was a real revolution. The kings of Alexandria had carefully avoided falling back on Egyptians before then, but necessity prevailed, and twenty thousand Egyptian infantry participated in the victory. Similarly, Arabs, Jews, and Idumeans were numerous in the Lagid army, which is better known than the Seleucid one; but the latter must not have been very different, for by the middle of the second century the Seleucids could no longer recruit in Iran or in the Zagros region (in Kurdistan), where they had gotten so many battle-tested soldiers earlier.

These soldiers were spread out over the entire territory, and through texts we know the placement of a number of garrisons. We noted above the *politeumata* of various localities in Egypt; these undoubtedly constituted the garrisons in those cities. The same holds true for the soldiers buried in Sidon. The army was thus intended not only to defend the borders, but also to keep the country under control, to keep watch and prevent any uprisings. However, the kings needed expeditionary corps for their distant campaigns as well. Some soldiers were probably directly supported by the king, like those of the garrison in Apamea on the Orontes, in the third century, who were responsible for maintaining the elephants used in combat. But a considerable percentage of soldiers lived off their lands under the cleruchy system, a borrowed term and practice of which the Athenians had made much use during the time of the Delian League and on into the fourth century. It consisted, as we have seen (Chapter 24), in granting each soldier, according to his rank and weaponry, a plot of land intended for his support. Whether he cultivated it himself with his family or rented it to a farmer, he drew his subsistence from it year-round. This was a temporary concession, in exchange for military service, and it came to an end as soon as the titleholder was no longer in a position to render that service. In reality, the system must have broken down early on, and the king no longer took back the lots *(cleroi)* whose titleholders were dead or elderly. This was justified in certain cases where the soldier had a son who could replace him; in a way, the cleruchy system encouraged the hereditary transmission of functions within the army. But in Egypt we see the system slowly drifting off course. During the third century, it seemed to work more or less correctly: even if a *cleros* fell into the hands of a woman without sons to fulfill the family's military obligations, the woman could find a man who could take over that task, for a fee. But as time passed, the cleros became detached from all military obligations when there were no more men, and it came to be viewed as private land, subject to the same taxes and fees.

The cleruchy system was used by the Lagids in Egypt itself, but also in the Transjordan, where the troops of Tobias the Ammonite (Chapter 24) were made up of cleruchs from very diverse regions: in particular, we find Greeks, Persians, and Arabs side by side. But the system also existed in the Seleucid kingdom, in Dura-Europos, where a law governing succession provided for the return of the cleros to the king in the absence of a male heir. Above all, we know from a text by Josephus that Antiochus III settled two thousand Babylonian Jews in Phrygia (with their families) to maintain order in the country. And a letter from the king to his viceroy in Asia Minor provides expressly for distributions of land, seed, and food supplies: "When you have brought them to the places mentioned, you shall give each of them a place to build a house and land to cultivate and plant with vines, and you shall exempt them from payment of taxes on the produce of the soil for ten years. And also, until they get produce from the soil, let them have grain measured out to them for feeding their servants."[1]

The weakening of royal authority alone was responsible for the monopolization of the cleruch lands by individuals who no longer rendered the services that had been expected of them. At the same time, however, the shrinking of the military horizons of the last Seleucids and the last Lagids meant that they no longer required large armies. The king needed only to have a small, committed troop at his disposal to protect him from his rivals. Finally, the gradual annexation of the kingdoms by Rome put the soldiers of the royal armies out of work. Not all of them, however: some elements of royal armies were incorporated into the Roman army, like that of King Deiotarios of Paphlagonia, which formed Legion XXII Deioteriana; certain Nabatean troops were transformed into cohorts of the Petraeans, and some of Herod's were incorporated into the cohorts of Sebastenoi. After many mutations, the last remnants of the Hellenistic armies took their places within the army of the conqueror.

CHAPTER TWENTY-EIGHT

Jason the Impious, or Hellenism
in Jerusalem

When Seleucus had departed this life and Antiochus styled
Epiphanes had succeeded to the kingdom, Jason, brother of Onias, usurped the high-priesthood by underhand methods; he approached the king with a promise of three hundred and sixty
talents of silver, with eighty talents to come from some other
source of revenue. He further committed himself to guarantee
another hundred and fifty if he was allowed to use his authority
to establish a gymnasium and a youth centre [*ephebeion*], and
to [list] men in Jerusalem as [Antiochenes]. When the king gave
his assent, Jason set about introducing his fellow countrymen to
the Greek way of life as soon as he was in power. He suppressed
the existing royal concessions to the Jews, granted at the instance of John, father of that Eupolemus who was later to be
sent on the embassy of friendship and alliance with the Romans,
and, overthrowing the lawful institutions, introduced new us-
ages contrary to the Law. He went so far as to plant a gymnasium at the very foot of the Citadel, and to fit out the noblest of
his cadets in the petasos [Macedonian hat]. Godless wretch that
he was and no true high priest, Jason set no bounds to his impiety; indeed the hellenising process reached such a pitch that the
priests ceased to show any interest in the services of the altar;
scorning the Temple and neglecting the sacrifices, they would
hurry to take part in the unlawful exercises on the training
ground as soon as the signal was given . . .[1] They disdained all
that their ancestors had esteemed, and set the highest value on
Hellenic honours. But all this brought its own retribution; the
very people whose way of life they envied, whom they sought to
resemble in everything, proved to be their enemies and execu-

tioners. It is no small thing to violate the divine laws, as the period that followed will demonstrate.

2 Maccabees 4:7–17, in *The Jerusalem Bible,* ed. Alexander Jones (Garden City, N.Y.: Doubleday, 1966)

JERUSALEM, 175 B.C.E. Could one be Jewish and Greek at the same time? Put differently, would the Jews be the only ones among all the peoples conquered by Alexander and his successors whose leaders were to remain scrupulously apart from the new customs? The question is not at all theoretical, for there is no example in history or in culture, in the broadest sense, of political masters who did not end up penetrating the dominated peoples, to a greater or lesser extent. Yet did not the all-encompassing character of Jewish Law, in the sense that the Law governed both religious life and daily life, and the monotheism that was well established by this point, rule out any contamination by Hellenism? This is exactly what was at stake in the violent crisis triggered in Jerusalem by Jason's reform. The fact that we know it only through accounts by its adversaries, the authors of the two books titled "Maccabees," gives historians a remarkable advantage: for once, we can see Hellenism from the viewpoint of a conquered people, and we know in detail on what grounds pious Jews reproached the "Hellenists," as Jews who supported the reform were labeled. We can set aside 1 Maccabees here: written toward the end of the second century, it is limited to a rapid analysis of the underlying causes of the revolt, neglecting even the primordial role of the Hellenists, and it attempts in particular to use their heroism to justify the power that the successors of Judas Maccabaeus had acquired in Judaea. In contrast, 2 Maccabees, the source of the short excerpt cited above, supplies essential keys for understanding.

Drafted even before the war of the Maccabees against the Seleucid kings was over, around 160, the work of a certain Jason of Cyrene, probably a Jew of the Diaspora, has survived only in the form of a summary produced toward the end of the second century by an abbreviator more concerned with warning his compatriots against the temptations of Hellenism than with writing a complete history of the conflict. Drawing on the work of Jason of Cyrene, he excerpted the most edifying passages and, by good fortune, deemed it useful to go back to what he believed was the cause of all the trouble: the desire of the high priest Jason to introduce new customs into Jerusalem and, in the long run, to abolish Judaism. We shall see that the actual reality was somewhat different, but by highlighting the role of the Jews themselves, the writer transmits information of prime importance.

What actually happened? The year was 175. King Seleucus IV, son of the great king Antiochus III, had just died. His legitimate heir, Demetrios, was a hostage in Rome, where he had just replaced his uncle Antiochus; the latter was on his way home. Seleucus IV had another son, also called Antiochus, but the latter was a still a child. The boy probably did proclaim himself king, but as soon as Antiochus the uncle (Antiochus IV) returned, he too proclaimed himself king, entering into a temporary association with his minor nephew before getting rid of him altogether. This atmosphere of dynastic crisis must not be overlooked in an effort to understand Jason's initiatives.

While this difficult and, in sum, illegal succession was under way, Onias III, the high priest of Jerusalem, found himself in Antioch, where he seems to have been summoned by Seleucus IV. He was there to explain the Temple authorities' refusal to make a financial contribution to the royal treasury, which the principal minister, Heliodoros, had come to demand in person.[2] The Jews had related that Yahweh himself had driven Heliodoros from his Temple, but the king had presumably been unwilling to settle for this response. The cause of Onias III seemed to be indefensible.

At the same time as Onias, his brother and rival Jason was also in Antioch. The latter's Greek name, probably chosen because of its assonance with his Hebrew name, Yeshua, unquestionably denoted a man who was not put off by Greek culture. Profiting from Onias's difficulties and the fact that Antiochus IV needed money (an enormous war debt from 188 remained to be paid to the Romans), Jason presented a double request that Antiochus IV had no reason to deny. He asked him, on the one hand, to name him high priest in place of his brother, and, on the other hand, to authorize him to transform Jerusalem into a city-state, a *polis,* in exchange for which he agreed to pay a considerable sum of money. Setting aside the first request and the financial considerations, let us focus on the foundation of the new city-state.

The author of 2 Maccabees did not explicitly say that Jason founded a polis, and this has given rise to countless commentaries and hypotheses, but I believe there is no room for doubt on the point. The text says that Jason asked for authorization to "draw up a list of the Antiochenes in Jerusalem," which means nothing less than establishing a list of the citizens of the new city-state, named Antioch in honor of the king, the only legitimate founder, although the name Jerusalem was probably kept as well to distinguish it from the countless other cities of the same name. Why did the author of 2 Maccabees not speak of a "city-state"? Probably because, given the passage of time, it did not even occur to him that Jason's reform consisted in founding a polis. He thus pointed out the visible effects of the reform: the registration of citizens' names, the foundation of a gymnasium, the establishment of an *ephebeion*.

For to found a city-state was first of all to constitute a civic body. Unlike what was taking place around the same time in the small city-state of Toriaion in Phrygia (Chapter 26), where the king granted the right of citizenship to all Greeks and Macedonians in the city along with all the natives living nearby, it is probable that Jerusalem's civic body was more limited, excluding Jews who did not speak Greek. But apart from this innovation, which unquestionably created a dangerous legal cleavage within the heart of the Jewish community itself, there was probably no institutional modification, in any case none that had shocked our informant: had there been any, we can be certain that he would not have failed to reproach Jason for it. Besides, why change the institutions? We have seen how, in the previous century, Sidon and the Phoenician city-states were content to abolish royalty. Here, the high priest would serve as magistrate and the politico-religious agencies that had administered Judaea since the Jews' return from exile in Babylonia (539–538) would remain in place within the new framework.

What struck our abbreviator most of all was the creation of a gymnasium and an ephebeion. And, if we think about it, this proves that he had perfectly understood where the danger for the future lay. An ephebeion? This was the place where young men destined to become citizens were trained. The *ephebia* was an old Greek civic institution that combined political and military training and allowed young men in the same age cohort to become full participants in the city-state. The training—including its military component—continued into the Hellenistic period, but it seems to have been reserved for an affluent elite. However this may be, we can rest assured that in Jerusalem the ephebia would have served to separate young Jewish men into two groups, future citizens of Antioch of Jerusalem on one side, noncitizens on the other, perpetuating the cleavage already noted above. Did Jason's adversaries also fear that the teachings delivered at the ephebeion were contrary to the Law? This is possible, but dressing in Greek clothing, participating in sports, using weapons, and speaking Greek exclusively seemed to pious Jews to indicate a dangerous adherence to a foreign way of life.

The creation of the gymnasium, which was unquestionably frequented by ephebes, is even stronger testimony to this adherence. Priests flocked there, even at the expense of Temple service, according to the author of our text. Apart from this specific reproach, the writer does not indicate in what respect he is scandalized by the presence of Jews in the gymnasium. He settles for allusive formulae about practices contrary to the Law, about the extreme importance granted to "Hellenistic glory," no doubt victory in contests, or the excessive attention paid to the body and its appearance. But a passage in 1 Maccabees is more explicit, for just after mentioning the foundation of the gymnasium, the author adds: they "removed the marks of circumcision" (I, 15). For here is the real paradox of this innovation intended to turn Jews into Greeks like all the rest: the nudity of the athlete disclosed the fact that he was a Jew! Thus Jews were seen to practice on themselves an operation *(epispasmos)* intended to mask their circumcision, while parents gave up the practice of circumcising their newborn sons. From adherence to an apparently anodyne Greek cultural practice, these Jews suddenly crossed over into impiety, for circumcision constituted the visible sign of the alliance between Yahweh and his people.

This drift may have appeared only in a marginal way, but it was enough for Jason's adversaries to accuse him of seeking purely and simply to abolish Judaism. Can we reasonably accept his detractors' views? I do not think so, and the fact that our document stresses the massive participation of priests in the exercises at the gymnasium strikes me as proof of the contrary. Can we really imagine that the throng of priests and other Temple servants, whose power and wealth rested on these functions, wanted to eliminate their source of income? This is improbable, to say the least. Thus we have to seek a different explanation. Readers have too often been obsessed by the disastrous end of the adventure, the revolt, the edict of persecution, and the difficult war of liberation, without wondering about Jason's real objectives and the reasons for his failure.

Who was Jason? A highly prominent citizen, brother of Jerusalem's high priest, and thus like all leaders of peoples in the Seleucid kingdom a man in contact with Greeks, at least with the royal agents. Did he speak Greek? Probably. As for the actual extent of his Hellenism, we cannot tell. All that appears in his desire for reform is the wish to insert Hellenized Jews like himself more fully into the society of his day. A little belatedly, the results he sought closely resembled what had happened in Phoenicia a century before—and in Babylonia and central Anatolia as well. In other words, Jason wanted nothing other than to be modern. And he clearly did not see how that could imperil his religious practice. Nothing in the Greek way of life seemed to him to contradict the Law. No one asked him to sacrifice to Greek gods, even when he participated in Greek festivals. The author of 2 Maccabees himself was obliged to acknowledge this. His indignation was aroused when an official delegation of the new Antiochenes was sent from Jerusalem to the contests in Tyre in honor of Heracles, but he noted nevertheless that the delegates had spent the money they had been given, not to sacrifice to the idols, but rather to buy equipment for their boats. For Jason, as for those who followed, there was no doubt that one could be Greek even while remaining a Jew.

And yet Jason failed. Why? The temptation to become part of the surrounding world must have been just as strong among the Jewish elite as in all governing milieus of conquered peoples. After more than a century and a half of coexistence between Greeks and Jews, the latter had been able to see that Greek domination did not threaten the application of the Law any more than Persian rule had done. Moreover, some members of this elite had probably understood that certain behaviors proper to Hellenism sufficed to make them look Greek; they would not have to give up the fundamental aspects of their own religion.

But Jason and his partisans neglected some essential points. First, they may have overestimated the number of Hellenized Jews, those who were capable of supporting the foundation of an Antioch of Jerusalem. By establishing a list of citizens, Jason was creating one more cleavage within the Judaean population, between citizens and those who were excluded from citizenship in the new city-state. To the traditional gap between rich and poor was added a political and legal gap between Jews who were Hellenized citizens and Jews who found themselves deprived of rights in the new city-state and excluded from the activities characteristic of Hellenism. This could give rise to frustrations; not only that, but it helped make the elite look like outsiders, foreigners. And this is where Jason's mistake proved to be most serious. He had not understood that ordinary people, who had remained largely outside the cultural processes at work since 331, could not grasp the difference between a Jew who called himself a citizen of Antioch—even of Jerusalem!—and a Greek from any other city-state. In the eyes of pious Jews, a Jew who became a Greek became a pagan. How indeed could one explain that a Jew who dressed (or undressed) like a Greek, who frequented the gymnasium, who spoke Greek, could at the same time remain faithful to Yahweh? To be sure, sports were not forbidden a priori by the Torah, and it could be objected that nudity was not debauchery. But nudity was shocking, for it was foreign to Jewish tradition. Furthermore, nudity revealed circumcision, which Hellenized Jews proceeded to stop practicing or else to disguise.

And here the people who cried sacrilege must have been not only the ordinary folk but also the scribes. For circumcision was not a hygienic custom; it was the sign of an alliance between Yahweh and his people. When Antiochus IV proscribed the Torah, one of the practices most severely repressed was circumcision: the king had surely been informed of its central character in Jewish practice.

Jason found himself in a tragic situation. In step with the Hellenized elites of the Seleucid kingdom, he thought he could integrate Judaea—at least its governing classes—into an acculturation process that would have allowed it to lose its foreignness without having to renounce its fundamental religious practices. Overwhelmed by elements no doubt less concerned than he with preserving the Torah (his rival and successor Menelas, for example), he opened up a Pandora's box without seeing all the consequences of an updating that would ultimately affect Judaism at its deepest level. The tempest he unleashed unintentionally ended up carrying him off in its wake.

CHAPTER TWENTY-NINE

Amphora Stamps from Rhodes and Elsewhere, or Exchanges in the Mediterranean Region and Beyond, Third to First Centuries B.C.E.

Amphora handle from Sinope, first quarter of the third century B.C.E.

MARISA (IDUMEA), third century B.C.E. A small city on the border between Palestine and the Negev desert, an astonishingly cosmopolitan city, to judge by the names on its tombs: Arabs, Arameans, Jews, Phoenicians, and Greeks lie side by side. It was not a large city, but it was an administrative center of some importance. And it has the advantage, for us, of having been destroyed brutally at a precise, known date, in 110, and then rapidly abandoned after 108–107. Digs have thus offered up a rich Hellenistic documentation, something that is fairly rare in the Near East. But it is not the city of Marisa (modern Maresha) that holds my attention here, but only the type of discovery that serves as a point of departure, which I could have chosen just as well in Alexandria, Tyre, Dura-Europos, Athens, or countless other places: an amphora handle. Because the name of a particular *astynomos* (the magistrate responsible for security and sanitation) appears on the stamp, we can affirm that the one reproduced here, found in Sinope on the Black Sea, dates from around 283–280, but its place of origin remains unknown.

249

Everyone is familiar with these large, very heavy ceramic vessels used in the ancient world to transport wine, oil, pickled fish, and also grain, cheese, honey, olives, and a great deal of other merchandise. It always seems surprising that the Ancients should have used such inconvenient containers: not only were they almost as heavy as the product they contained, but most of them did not stand upright on their own, and had to be either embedded in sand, supported by a metal framework, or at best placed against a wall with others for mutual support. Their size meant that it was almost out of the question to use pack animals to transport them, for a donkey or a mule could hardly carry more than two at once, so a whole herd would have been required for transporting large quantities. Amphorae were almost exclusively moved on carts drawn by a powerful team of oxen—provided that the terrain was not too rough—and above all on ships.

But amphorae presented advantages as well as disadvantages; otherwise their success over more than a millennium would be impossible to explain, for even before the invention of the wooden barrel other recipients existed, such as wineskins. The advantages of amphorae were in fact not inconsiderable. First, they could be produced everywhere, as long as clay of middling quality and skillful potters were available—and these could be found throughout the Mediterranean. Thus amphorae were not expensive, and they could be made in immediate proximity to places where the merchandise to be transported was produced. In addition, they provided good conditions for preserving foodstuffs, once waxed stoppers were correctly inserted: wine, oil, olives, and so on were protected from insects and vermin, and they did not take on bad odors, while the more or less porous ceramic material allowed for atmospheric exchanges between the inside and the outside of the amphora, as is the case with corked wine bottles today. The same results could not be obtained from containers made of animal skins, which require a lengthy tanning process and always retain an odor. Transportation took a long time, and upon delivery the merchandise could remain in its original container. Leather skin bags were thus used only for merchandise that could be easily decanted or that did not absorb odors. Some of these are mentioned, for example, in the price list for the municipal distribution in Palmyra, in the second century C.E., where camels carried both oil and animal fats in wineskins; but the buyer had to transfer the oil thus purchased into an amphora right away.

However, it is a different aspect of the question that interests me here. In fact, the amphora handle that is our point of departure bears a trademark stamp, a mark that makes it possible to identify its provenance and even, with relative precision in this case, its date. Not all city-states followed this practice, and many did not put any marks on the amphorae produced on their territory. It is thus only after lengthy comparative studies of the shapes and analysis of the chemical composition of the clay itself that we can attribute the provenance of specific amphorae to certain city-states with relative certainty. But other city-states put distinctive marks on all or a portion of the amphorae produced, and this simplifies the task of archaeologists and historians today. The question that everyone raises at the outset concerns the purpose of that mark. It consists in a symbol representing the city-state (a rose for Rhodes, the archer Heracles or a dolphin—among others—for Thasos), sometimes the name of a magistrate (here, the astynomos). But there is no indication of measure, which tells us that the stamp is in no sense a mark of quantity control; it has been calculated that the capacity of amphorae of the same provenance varied from the mean by more or less three liters, which represents a variation of 5 to 10 percent, depending on the capacity of the amphorae. This may have been an acceptable margin, but in a cargo of a hundred or so amphorae the seller or the buyer could nevertheless experience a real loss in profits. It must be acknowledged that even today we do not know why amphorae were stamped.

The observation remains: the Rhodians stamped practically all their production, on both handles; those of Cos, Chios, Cnidos, Thasos, Heraclea Pontica, and Sinope did so somewhat less regularly; those of Samos did so rarely, on a single handle, and for a variable portion of the production. Thus if we tally the finds on a given site, it is hard to make reliable comparisons. To begin with, the number of Rhodian amphorae (more than 80 percent of the stamps attested) must be divided by two, because finding a stamped handle is twice as likely. Then it is impossible to establish a parallel between the amphorae of a city-state that stamped all its production and those of a city-state that stamped only some of it. For example, according to an already ancient inventory, more than eighty thousand Rhodian amphorae had been found at Alexandria, as compared to fewer than fifteen hundred originating from Cos. It would be absurd to deduce that there were fifty times as many imports from Rhodes as from Cos, or even, taking the double stamping into account, twenty-five times as many, for we do not know what proportion of the Cos amphorae were stamped. The only possible conclusion is chronological: Rhodian imports were abundant in the third century, reaching an apex around 200 and continuing during most of the second century, while those of Cnidos achieved their peak distribution during the first century.

All quantitative questions aside, the amphorae offer very precious information about the circulation of merchandise. To be sure, what we learn from them can be completed by other sources, such as the customs statements preserved in the archives of Zeno of Caunos, Zeno being the steward of the properties of Apollonios, who was finance minister under Ptolemy II. Unsurprisingly, we note that typically Greek products such as wine and olive oil were imported into regions that did not produce them or where Greeks had settled and found productions of poor quality. This was the case in Egypt, but also along the shores of the Black Sea, especially in the Caucasus and on the border of the Sea of Azov, and in the interior of Anatolia. Luxury products such as wines of good quality naturally occupied an important place. Although Greeks had acclimatized grapevines and olive trees in Syria and had brought with them their procedures for producing wine and olive oil, a strong demand remained for imported products, recognized as of superior quality. This demand must have increased all the more as natives adopted the Greek way of life: the multiplication of gymnasia led ipso facto to the use of olive oil for the care of the body.

But the circuits were not as simple as they appear. One might imagine direct exchanges, with Alexandria and the Egyptian ports importing everything that was necessary to the Greeks living in the villages of the Delta and the Nile Valley. However, even though this must have been the pattern in a good number of cases, it was not the only one. In fact, the customs records in Zeno's archives give a very different picture. In 259, Zeno went on an inspection tour for his master in Syria-Phoenicia. He visited Tyre, Sidon, and Ptolemais as well as the outer regions of the country, the Hauran, the Transjordan, the Negev. He profited from his travels by acquiring local products: young slaves from the Arabs, and Phoenician artisanal products (candelabra, beds, mattresses), which is logical. But in addition to these local products, he acquired every other type of merchandise that struck him as opportune. A statement from May–June 259 evokes

252

a real Prévert-style inventory: wines from Chios and Thasos, white oil, dry figs, honey from Theangela (Caria), Rhodes, Athens, Lycia, Coracesium (Pamphylia), and Chalybon (location unknown), cheese from Chios, salted fish, tuna, tuna filets, grey mullet, wild boar meat (presumably dried), venison, goat meat, sponges! Nothing that came from Phoenicia, actually, and all merchandise that could have come just as well directly from Alexandria. But Zeno, finding himself at the moment in Phoenicia, bought whatever he found, as if he feared falling short on supplies, or as if he were saving money this way. He behaved, as it were, like residents of countries in which endemic poverty reigns, people always equipped with a shopping basket or bag who stand in line without knowing what is for sale, and buy whatever products are available for fear of not finding them the next day.

But historians draw several conclusions from all this. First, the Greeks of the new world that emerged from the Alexandrian conquest may not have lived in a society of abundance so far as imported products were concerned. Not that they lacked anything in particular, but products from remote places arrived irregularly, by fits and starts; they were subject to the unpredictability of navigation, which remained hazardous. Second, prices could vary considerably from one port to another, even within a single kingdom, as a function of supply and demand; Zeno, a zealous steward, must have bought what struck him as of interest for his master. Third, the demand for products from the Aegean region was not limited to wine or olive oil, for which there existed a great variety of vintages; cheese, pickled fish, dried or salted meats were equally sought after. Finally, the Phoenician ports—like others, without question—played an important role in the redistribution of goods. A Rhodian amphora found in Alexandria might have transited by way of Sidon; another unearthed in Petra might have come from Alexandria via Gaza or Ascalon.

Alexander's conquest unified the eastern Mediterranean politically for a long time, even if rival kingdoms divided up its banks throughout the Hellenistic period. But the fact that Greek settlements were spread from the First Cataract of the Nile to the Caucasus, from Iran to Phoenicia, did even more: it helped disseminate a way of life and at the same time it helped distribute the products that were the indispensable complements of that way of life. No gymnasium without oil, no Greek without wine. Despite the abundance of local production, where staple items (wheat, vegetables, fowl) were concerned, despite the adoption by the Greeks of certain products that had been virtually unknown before (beer, dates), the spread of Hellenism led to an acceleration and an amplification of exchanges among all parts of the Mediterranean, along more or less complex circuits. Amphora handles provide one element in the analysis of the phenomenon; the rare customs records we have supply another element that at least allows us to put a finger on the complexity of the circuits of exchange.

CHAPTER THIRTY

Let Us Pray for Archippe's Recovery! or Women and Euergetism

Decree on the subject of the sacrifice for Archippe. It has pleased the council, upon the proposal of the strategoi, the phylarchs and the synedroi. Given that Archippe, daughter of Dikaiogenes, fell ill with an uncertain and dangerous malady, the people are in anguish, so attached are they to her, the faithful one, the wise one, worthy of her fine conduct and that of her ancestors, and who has given numerous and great proofs of her benevolence and her love of the good for her fatherland. Given that, thanks to the foresight of the gods, she now finds herself in a better state, the people rejoice greatly in her recovery and they hold it good and in keeping with its good will toward Archippe to pay its debt to the gods for all this in suitable actions of thanksgiving.

That is why, with good fortune, may it please the people. That the *strategoi* offer a sacrifice to the gods for Archippe's recovery and health.

Date (decree of the council): in the month of Zeus, under Athenaeus, son of Zeno.

Date (decree of the people): all the *strategoi* made the proposal, on 5 Terpheios, under Athenaeus.

> Inscription, in Helmut Engelmann, *Inschriften von Kyme*
> (Bonn: Habelt, 1979), no. 13

K YME (AEOLIS), toward the end of the second century B.C.E. A small, undistinguished city-state. The heroine: Archippe, daughter of Dikaiogenes. The excerpt from the decree cited here is somewhat astonishing, for the entire city-state has mobilized to thank the gods for saving the life of this woman when she was ill. In a Greek society reputed to be misogynist, what a strange attitude! The fact is that Archippe was not an ordinary woman, and that, since the era when the Athenians had done everything possible to exclude women from the political arena (Chapter 11), times had changed. Only the dossier of Archippe's honors sheds light on this woman's situation, for she remains otherwise completely unknown. However, a collection of eight very precise and detailed texts allows us to understand who she was and why she benefited from exceptional honors in her city-state.

Archippe was born in a small city-state in northern Asia Minor, Kyme of Aeolis, near Phocaea, which was the point of departure for Marseille's founders, around 600 B.C.E. This was not one of the recent city-states that proliferated in Hellenistic Asia (Chapter 26), but an older one that traced its history back to Greek settlements in Asia around 1000 B.C.E. Nevertheless, it had always remained rather modest: a few thousand inhabitants, perhaps slightly more than a thousand citizens. In other words, everyone knew everyone else: this society had maintained the face-to-face relations whose disappearance Athenians regretted in the mid-fifth century (Chapter 10).

Archippe belonged to a good family from the city, surely a wealthy family, or at least one that had been prominent for a long time. Her father, Dikaiogenes, son of Lakrates, who had no doubt died by this time, had warranted an honorific statue; but two of the texts at our disposal mention that Archippe proved worthy of her ancestors, allowing us to suppose that Dikaiogenes was not the first in his family to be a benefactor of the city-state. Archippe seems to surpass them all, by tireless activity. The texts deserve to be looked at in some detail.

A first decree reveals that Archippe had proposed to restore the roof of the bouleuterion, the room in which the city-state's council, or boule, met, at her own expense. The city-state had actually been concerned for some time about the regrettable state of the building, for we find references to lack of security, inappropriate use of the premises, and studies commissioned from several architects. Archippe was thus not proposing something fanciful; rather, seeing the city-state in a difficult position, given the costs of the repairs, she decided to take them on herself. She scrupulously followed a rule-governed procedure by referring to the citizens as a whole, as the decree stipulates. She asked in exchange, however, to have control of the construction project, ownership of the land, and the right to store construction materials on public land. The city-state agreed, and offered her in thanks the right to have any honorific decree already adopted in her honor engraved on the marble walls of the bouleuterion. This was thus not Archippe's first act of generosity. And it was not the last: for the inauguration of the bouleuterion she had a sacrifice celebrated at her own expense. On this occasion she offered a banquet to the entire council, complete with fifty measures of old wine, plus the same quantity of wine given to the tribes and the *paroikoi,* that is, to the residents who were not citizens, and then an additional glass of sweet wine apiece to all the citizens and residents of the city-state in the completed bouleuterion. All this is carefully documented with figures, so we know how much the benefactress spent.

According to another decree, Archippe also donated a piece of land that she owned in a neighboring locality and that would revert to the people after her death. With the income from these lands, the people were to erect "votive monuments on the agora, that is, a temple of *Homonoia* (Concord), an altar, porticoes, and shops." Administrators were named, with Archippe's agreement.

So much generosity deserved a recompense, and the city-state did not skimp on this point. A bronze statue of Archippe was erected, accompanied by a colossal statue of Demos—the citizenry personified—in the process of crowning its benefactress. A statue of her father would be added to complete the group. In addition, during the next festival in honor of Dionysus, Archippe was to be crowned with a golden crown by the person in charge of the children's contests, and she would preside over the ceremony. And the same thing would happen at all future Dionysia celebrations. Upon her death, she would be crowned anew, and would be given a tomb in the square of the benefactors. Archippe must have been elderly and in poor health, for the people appeared to be in a hurry to carry out these projects, and her brother was asked to do what was necessary: in particular, to contribute the anticipated funds. This leaves us to suppose that the honors voted by the city-state were taken on financially by the family, unless the text signifies that the brother was urged to complete the contributions planned by Archippe, as if it were she who had decided on the benefits to be awarded but her brother who would carry out the resulting financial operations.

Whatever the case, once the honors had been approved by vote, it was

Archippe's turn to express thanks, and she gave exactly the same thing as for the inauguration of the bouleuterion:

> Since the statues approved by the people have been built, and since Archippe has been crowned by the people with a colossal statue, along with her father Dikaiogenes, after these statues have been erected in the *bouleuterion* built by Archippe, she has the intention of providing gifts in conformity with her generosity, and she has given for the sacrifice and the banquet to the council as a whole 50 staters and for the ox destined for the sacrifice 70 drachmae of Attic silver, and 50 measures of old wine, and the same quantity to each of the tribes and to the metics and the freedmen, and she has offered the citizens and the other persons residing in the city-state a glass of sweet wine in the *bouleuterion* completed by her good offices.[1]

Now we can understand why, when Archippe fell ill, the people were "in anguish," and then decided to offer thanksgiving to the gods when she found herself in better health later on. The well-being of the city-state rested in part on her generosity, and although she necessarily had heirs, most notably her brother, the people preferred to see a citizen on whom it knew it could count remain alive and well as long as possible.

Archippe thus takes place among the *euergetai,* those benefactors on whom the city-state's survival—or at least its standard of living—depended. Archippe's story sets two aspects of civic life in the Hellenistic era into relief: the essential role of benefactors and the new place of women. As we shall have occasion to return to the place and function of euergetism, or philanthropy, in the city-states, I shall make only a few general remarks on the first aspect in order to develop the second in more detail.

Euergetism—a word that does not exist in Greek, but which the moderns derived from the verb *euergetein* (to act well) and the substantives that derive from it, *euergetes* (benefactor) and *euergesia* (benefit)—was an ancient Greek practice that is not specific to the Hellenistic or imperial era. As early as the classical period, it behooved well-to-do citizens to demonstrate generosity toward the city-state. Not that the city-state had no resources of its own—on the contrary—but the fact remains that part of the financing for civic activities came, as it were, straight from the source. By this I mean that there was no general system of taxation feeding a budget that the city-state would then distribute in relation to its political and military options. A number of expenses were directly handled by wealthy citizens designated explicitly for this role: these were the *leitourgoi*. Thus one person had to pay the choruses and the expenses for a theatrical representation, another financed battleship gear, yet another the upkeep of the gymnasium. The costs of all these requirements were not always established in advance. The spirit of competition *(agon)* that inspired many wealthy citizens drove some of them to go beyond what was strictly necessary, and this was the beginning of euergetism. Strictly speaking, to be an euergetes was to do good (for one's city-state or for some other particular group) without being forced to do so. There was a voluntary aspect that was always highlighted in the honorific decrees, even when social pressure in fact obliged the wealthy to pay.

Although the phenomenon is well attested in the classical period, it did not bring euergetai any particular reward at the time, as if the rich benefactors were simply doing their duty. Only foreigners received honors, for in their case nothing obliged them to shower benefits on a city-state that was not their own. When Heracleides of Salamis in Cyprus sold wheat at a low price to Athens around 330, he received the privilege of being allowed to own land and a house in Attica. From the late fourth century until well into the second, the role of the wealthy grew, not so much because they were spending more freely than before but because city-states used their special relations with kings to obtain privileges from the latter or to escape, when the circumstance arose, from levies deemed abusive. In a way, then, we observe two sorts of benefactors: citizens who acted to influence kings and dynasts, and kings and dynasts themselves who took the trouble to extend their benefits to the city-states. But from the city-states' standpoint, only the latter were euergetai; these alone had the right to the title and to the honors that went with it, such as statues and crowns. The former remained citizens subjected to tight control by the city-states, even if the city-states were able to recognize their merits and quite prepared to adopt decrees of thanks.

With the weakening and impoverishment of the Hellenistic sovereigns, wealthy citizens were increasingly called upon to fill the breach: which meant that the city-states no longer asked them simply to intervene politically with outside powers, but asked them to pay for a number of public expenses out of their own pockets. Euergetism changed in nature at this point, for the city-state found itself financially dependent on its rich citizens, at least in part. At the same time, the practices surrounding thanks and honors were being codified. The Archippe text alludes to this at two points, when it mentions the crowning of Archippe's statue and the place of honor conferred on her during the Dionysia festivals, "as on the other *euergetai*," and by planning her tomb in the square devoted to the benefactors. The position of euergetes thus became a civic category in itself, and the city-states saw the creation of a caste of remarkable leaders who were distinguished by a series of specific honors that elevated them above the people as a whole: statues, crowns, inscriptions, titles (that of euergetes, henceforth even for a citizen), and soon heroization and divinization (in the first century B.C.E.). It is clear that the euergetai were substitutes for kings who had disappeared or lost their wealth, but also that by coming to constitute a specific class they entered into a system of social constraint from which they could not escape: who would dare depart from the family tradition by ceasing to shower the city-state with benefits? Archippe was firmly ensconced within this logic, and the decrees indicate at several points that she conducted herself in a way worthy of her ancestors. She already belonged to a dynasty of benefactors.

This evolution of euergetism, in which the financial aspects henceforth occupied an increasing place, thus explains why female benefactors began to appear. This is the second aspect, which I should like to develop more fully here. We recall the extent to which Athenian documentation from the fifth century suggests that women were relegated to the background, their presence denied, in a way, even in areas where men could not very well get along without them. To be sure, the documentation we have is almost exclusively Athenian, and we have no evidence that the same attitudes prevailed everywhere. Nevertheless, it is probable that the Hellenistic documentation available outside Athens reflects perceptible evolutions in a number of city-states.

Archippe's dossier teaches us, first of all, that a woman could have access to money and use it as she liked. For there is nothing to suggest that Archippe's will was expressed through intermediaries—a husband, a brother, a father. Her father was probably already dead; nowhere is there any reference to a husband, or children; only her brother is mentioned, in an accessory fashion. Thus we have to acknowledge that Archippe controlled her own fortune, whatever its origins. This seemed unthinkable in fifth-century Athens, but Athens may have been an exception. Cretan women had the right to a share in the paternal legacy (half the share of their brothers), and Plutarch asserts that during the fourth century Spartan women monopolized two-fifths of the real estate wealth in the country. The women in question were obviously well-to-do: they might have received inheritances, or concluded matrimonial alliances that consolidated or reconstituted fortunes. It is all the more remarkable that Archippe could spend as she pleased, and apparently without limits. She was not alone in this position, and many other texts point in the same direction. Thus, in a public subscription launched by Cos to finance the defensive measures taken by the city-state, volunteers were asked to announce in advance what they wished to give; among the volunteers, female citizens were mentioned immediately after the males, and before noncitizen residents and foreigners.

In addition, Archippe was spending for the good of the city-state. By having the bouleuterion repaired, she must have entered into relations with the sitting magistrates, negotiated the amount of her expenditures, perhaps discussed material details. To be sure, we may also hypothesize that she made it known that she wanted to spend money on the city-state's behalf and that the magistrates suggested that she pay for the bouleuterion, without leaving her anything to say about the construction itself or the building's ornamentation. The fact that it was up to her to choose the text of the dedication does not support the second hypothesis, for Archippe knew what she wanted. In any case, she was getting involved in an aspect of civic life that was hardly secondary, the maintenance of public buildings and the beautification of the city-state. Of course she had no official title allowing her to do this, but it is clear that money gave her rights that nature denied her: by choosing the text of the dedication, she imprinted her personal mark on a public building, one she had no hope of ever penetrating, except as a visitor! For a female *bouleutes* had never been seen, and never would be.

However, the exclusion of women from political life was not as thoroughgoing as during the classical era. From the Hellenistic era on, we know of women gymnasiarchs, whose role was not limited to managing gymnasia reserved for girls and women: they were in charge of ordinary gymnasia. In reality, the gymnasiarchy was not a magistracy, but rather a *leitourgeia*. It was ultimately a matter of financial responsibility: the person in charge presumably had an interest in keeping tabs on what was

261

happening in the gymnasium in order to avoid waste and unnecessary expense. But it is hard to imagine a woman going to the gymnasium and the adjacent thermal baths where nude men were running, working out, and bathing. We have to suppose that she simply paid the bills and had the gymnasium and the baths overseen by trustworthy men. The fact remains that women could take pride in the prestigious title of "gymnasiarch"! Henceforth, the city-state flushed out money wherever it was, even if it was in the hands of a woman.

But the evolution went further still. Women assumed magistracies in Asia Minor: they served as *stephanephoroi* and *prytaneis*. Naturally, like their male counterparts, these women were wealthy, and they were chosen on that basis. But, unlike the gymnasiarchy, which was first of all a leitourgeia, that is, a form of tax, before being a claim to fame, the magistracies were honors *(timai)* reserved to citizens alone. Conferring them on women meant privileging the financial aspect, which also existed in every magistracy, to the detriment of the honorific aspect.

A lot of questions have been raised about how women, who were obliged by decorum to show themselves in public as little as possible, could fulfill their obligations. In reality, the few magistracies occupied by women lacked any real political content. These were often eponymous, thus prestigious, magistracies that unquestionably entailed expenditures (sacrifices, banquets), but were devoid of any power over the affairs of the city-state.[2] A woman stephanephoros thus had to appear, at the very most, in official ceremonies, as she might have done if she were a priestess dedicated to a goddess; she did not have to participate in the debates of the boule.

This evolution, begun in the Hellenistic period, was accentuated under the empire, and the imperial legislation did not differentiate between men and women where liturgical obligations were concerned. The number of women euergetai, leitourgoi, and even magistrates multiplied. In Ephesus, women prytaneis belonged to the leading families of the city, and we know the names of their fathers, their husbands, their sons. Similarly, in Syllium of Pamphylia, a certain Menodora offered numerous gifts to the city-state when her son and her daughter took over their functions; like their mother, each became a gymnasiarch and a *demiurgos* (this latter function probably meant serving as the eponymous magistrate of the city-state). In reality, Menodora seemed to control the family fortune; it was from her own property that she offered the city-state the gifts required upon her children's accession to their new functions.

The Greek city-state remained a living organism, with an astonishing capacity to adapt to new times. To be sure, some evolutions never came about: women were never citizens on the same basis as men, and those who had public roles to play did so above all as holders of wealth—despite their sex, we might be tempted to say. But the classical Athenian model was far from the dominant one, in space and time alike. Though we cannot speak in any respect of a "decline" of the city-state, it is obvious that the functions assigned to that institution evolved over time, that the strictly "political" aspects shifted to the background (even though relations with the powers in place constituted an essential facet), and that the most concrete tasks (maintenance of the cults, of public buildings and roadways, and so on) ended up moving to the foreground. As they took on importance, the functions that required money pushed those who had access to it onto the center of the civic stage, whatever their status: citizens, foreigners, women, children. Archippe offers a marvelous illustration of the beginning of this phenomenon, which was destined to perpetuate itself as long as the civic model of antiquity kept functioning—that is, all the way into late antiquity.

CHAPTER THIRTY-ONE

"Kill Them All," or the Greeks, Rome, and Mithridates VI Eupator

Mithridates . . . wrote secretly to all his satraps and city governors that on the thirtieth day thereafter they should set upon all Romans and Italians in their towns, and upon their wives and children, and their freedmen of Italian birth, kill them and throw their bodies out unburied, and share their goods with King Mithridates. He threatened to punish any who should bury the dead or conceal the living, and proclaimed rewards to informers and to those who should kill persons in hiding. To slaves who killed or betrayed their masters he offered freedom, to debtors, who did the same to their creditors, the remission of half of their debt. These secret orders Mithridates sent to all the cities at the same time. When the appointed day came disasters of the most varied kinds occurred throughout Asia.

Appian, *The Mithridatic Wars*, in *Appian's Roman History*, trans. Horace White (Loeb Classical Library, 1912), vol. 2, p. 279 (IV, 22)

EPHESUS, 88 B.C.E. More than half a century earlier, the ancient kingdom of Pergamon had become the Roman province of Asia. In fact, when King Attalos III died in 133, his subjects discovered that he had bequeathed his kingdom to Rome. A surprising decision for which no reliable explanation has been found. Perhaps he had only been seeking insurance against a potential assassination attempt, while waiting for a legitimate heir. For the king was still young, and there had been no reason to expect an early death, especially because he belonged to a family known for the longevity of its members.

Whatever Attalos's reasons may have been, the fact remains that Rome found itself heir to a realm it had helped expand significantly. After conquering Antiochus III in Magnesia ad Sipylum in 189, and after imposing the disastrous peace of Apamea in 188, Rome decided against direct administration of the territories abandoned by the Seleucid king; instead, it entrusted one portion to the Rhodians, and the largest portion to the Attalids of Pergamon. Thus the kingdom that Rome received was an extensive one, spreading from the Sea of Marmara to the southern coast of Anatolia, from the Aegean Sea to the edge of the Galatian Plateau. Did Rome hesitate to accept? There was probably some discussion in the Senate about what should be done, but the decision to accept was finally made, especially given the existence of an heir, a bastard son of King Eumenes II, the father of Attalos III, a certain Aristonicus, who had had himself recognized as king under the name Eumenes III. He found enough support to sustain a lengthy war: Rome had to fight for three years in order to impose itself. In 129, it was all over, and Aristonicus-Eumenes was eliminated.

This marked the beginning of a somber period for the new province. Turned over to the appetites of the publicans, it was placed under strict controls. The Roman fiscal system—whenever it was put in place (133? 129?)—turned out to facilitate all sorts of excesses. The amount of tribute was set in Rome, and its collection was entrusted to agricultural societies that paid the total to the state in advance and then had to collect not only the amount they had paid but additional sums to cover their operating expenses and the interest they owed their shareholders. The actual amount of the tribute rose accordingly.

The residents of the province, of whom only a few (such as those in Pergamon itself) had been excluded by Attalos III's donation, rapidly came to feel that they were being systematically looted. And misfortunes were proliferating: armed robbers and pirates were running rampant during the same period, for want of troops to fight them—neither the Attalid fleet nor the Attalid army had been replaced. A few more scrupulous governors did try to limit the abuses of the agricultural societies—in 97–96, for instance, Q. Mucius Scaevola forbade the recapitalization of interests, and had some corrupt Roman equestrians executed—but this was the exception, not the rule, and the provincials' exasperation kept on growing.

While anger was on the rise among the Greeks in Asia, an ambitious young king ascended to the throne of Pontus, in northeastern Anatolia, on the Caucasian border. Mithridates VI Eupator was still a minor when he succeeded his father in 120; he did not really take the reins of power until 112. And he too had reasons to complain about Rome. His father, Mithridates V, had helped Rome in its struggle against Aristonicus, and had received some districts of eastern Phrygia as a reward. Yet as soon as the young king came to power, Rome revoked the donation and reattached the districts in question to the province of Asia. In the years that followed, a series of complicated conflicts opposed Mithridates to the neighboring kingdoms of Cappadocia and Bithynia; in any case, it turned out that Rome, which neither of those two kingdoms had the resources to disobey, did nothing to put a stop to the aggressions committed by its allies, and refused even to listen to Mithridates' complaints. Mithridates then installed his own client-king in Cappadocia (90) and repeated his complaints to Rome. He still met with rejection, for it was clear that the governor of Asia, Manius Aquillius, the son and namesake of the man who had organized the province in 129, sought to provoke a war that would open up the Pontus region to the financial activities of the knights.

An ancient tradition holds that around 109–108 Mithridates traveled incognito to Asia and observed the exasperation of the provincials firsthand. The information is unverifiable, but it is not impossible that the king of Pontus counted on the support of populations infuriated by the behavior of the Roman knights. In any case, facing yet another refusal on Rome's part to intervene with its Cappadocian and Bithynian allies, Mithridates invaded Cappadocia and then Bithynia (89); his army swept away the few Roman garrisons that were guarding Asia, while his fleet forced its way through the Straits. Manius Aquillius was taken prisoner and executed in Pergamon, an event greeted with widespread enthusiasm. The Pontic invasion was experienced as a liberation.

This was the context for the event that has been called the Ephesian Vespers, by analogy with the Sicilian Vespers, despite the obvious anachronism. As it happens, we have relatively little testimony about the way the planned collective assassination took place; it is as if the Greeks had tried to wipe out the memory of this notorious act.

If we are to believe Appian, one of the rare authors who supplies details about the event, the massacre was carefully prepared. Mithridates instructed the Greeks to massacre all the Roman residents, sparing no one. A plan was devised to ensure that the massacre would take place everywhere at the same time, so that the surprise factor would have its full effect. It was a success, for, according to the ancient authors, eighty thousand people fell victim to Greek hatred within just a few hours. To widespread astonishment, even sanctuaries that guaranteed safety to those who took refuge as suppliants there were violated. In Ephesus, Romans clinging to statues of Artemision were massacred. In Pergamon, arrows were shot at people who thought they had found protection in the arms of the statues in the temple of Asclepios. In Caunos, suppliants were dragged from the statue of Hestia that stood in the council hall; children were killed in front of their mothers, wives in front of their husbands, and men, finally, without remission; the action was all the more shocking in that Caunos had just regained its independence thanks to Rome, which had taken the city-state from the Rhodians. In Adramyttion, Romans who sought to escape by swimming away were pursued into the sea. In Tralles, some reticence was manifested: "The citizens of Tralles, in order to avoid the appearance of blood-guiltiness, hired a savage monster named Theophilus of Paphlagonia, to do the work. He conducted the victims to the temple of Concord, and there murdered them, chopping off the hands of some who were embracing the sacred images."[1]

A few weeks later, in a new massacre in Delos and the islands, twenty thousand Romans died.

Mithridates' plan seems to have succeeded beyond all expectations. Nevertheless, there were some pockets of resistance. It was to avoid having blood on their own hands that the residents of Tralles called on the mercenary Theophilos the Paphlagonian. Some city-states refused to follow orders: Stratoniceia in Caria, Laodicea on the Lycos, Aphrodisias, Magnesia ad Sipylum. Here and there Mithridates ran into opposition from prominent leaders who were friendly with Rome. He offered large sums to have them turned over to him, without success: a decree engraved after the war in favor of the Greek Chairemon of Nysa recalls that the king promised forty talents for his capture or that of his sons, twenty talents for each of their heads! It is true that the man was suspected of having helped the Romans win Rhodes, and of fostering resistance throughout the entire province. The apparent unanimity was thus only a façade. The horror of Mithridates' plan may have inspired repugnance in some, but, more importantly, despite its exactions, Rome did have some faithful friends.

What was Mithridates trying to accomplish by programming such a massacre? At bottom, he derived no personal benefit from it, given that he had defeated Rome militarily and that most Greeks had already rallied to his side. It seems to me that in his eyes these atrocities served as a test, and were aimed at definitively attaching the Greeks of Asia to his cause. If it had only been a matter of getting rid of the Romans, his troops could have done the job. By obliging the Greeks to massacre the Romans themselves, he killed two birds with one stone: he forced pockets of resistance to reveal themselves, and he compromised those who had obeyed him in such a way that there was no turning back. From then on, those who had participated in the atrocities of 88 knew that they could expect nothing but the worst punishments if the Romans made a victorious comeback. This was a very clever political calculation, but it nonetheless turned out to be wrong.

For Mithridates' policy toward the inhabitants of Asia fell far short of bringing about the liberation they would have liked. To be sure, the king took some initial steps that made him popular. Thanks to the seizure of Roman property, he could offer the gift of five years' tribute, and his acts of generosity proliferated. Some of them are surprising: he gave one hundred talents to Apamea of Phrygia after an earthquake, expanded the territory of the sanctuary of Artemis in Ephesus that was exempted from tribute, and even financed the Moukieia in Smyrna (these were contests established by that city-state in honor of the ancient Roman governor of Asia, Mucius Scaevola, who had struggled against the publicans' abuses). But for many, disillusion was not long in coming, given the violence of the Pontic troops and Mithridates' demands. The inhabitants of Chios were deported en masse to the Black Sea, for example, because they refused to pay two thousand talents. Abolishing the existing regimes, Mithridates installed tyrants in his pay in Tralles, Colophon, and Adramyttion, while a military governor brutalized the population of Ephesus.

While Asia began to look back on Rome's domination with some nostalgia, the Roman counteroffensive began to bear fruit in Balkan Greece, where Mithridates had succeeded in taking Athens. The prospect of a reversal in the situation must have led the Asian Greeks to think hard about their future! The Ephesians, who had been among the first to celebrate the Pontic invasion, rose up against Mithridates and called upon their neighbors to join in. A decree adopted by the Ephesians in 86 or 85 provides a highly polished model of political hypocrisy. Rewriting recent history (the events had happened two or three years earlier at most) solely as a way of preparing for the future, the Ephesians did not hesitate to present themselves as victims:

> He first took the cities situated on the way to Ephesus by surprise, and finally succeeded in taking control of our own city, which was stunned by the great number of his troops and the suddenness of his attack. But the Ephesian people, remaining faithful to their affection toward Rome, were only awaiting the opportunity to take up arms for the safety of all; they have now resolved to declare war on Mithridates in support of Rome's hegemony and the freedom of all; our citizens have all devoted themselves body and soul, in a common impulse, to this great struggle.[2]

The poor Ephesians thus represented themselves as victims of a surprise attack; abandoned to their own devices after the defeat of the Roman troops (which was true), they had no choice but to yield in order not to perish. This representation is not entirely false, to be sure, but it does not account for the enthusiasm that accompanied the massacre of the Romans in 88.

Once again master of Asia in 85 after a peace treaty restoring the status quo had been signed with Mithridates in Dardanos, the Roman general Sulla was not deceived by this belated about-face. The repression that followed was extremely severe. All the cities that had welcomed Mithridates were deprived of their freedom, except for Chios, owing to its later misfortunes. Conversely, those that had resisted received freedom and sometimes immunity, which meant that they were not only free from oversight by the provincial governor, they were also exempt from paying tribute; this was the case for Ilion, Aphrodisias, Laodicea on the Lycos, Tabae, Stratoniceia in Caria, and Magnesia ad Sipylum, while Rhodes, which had successfully resisted all those years, received new lands in Caria (the territory of Caunos). Collectively, the Asian city-states were required to pay a fine of twenty thousand talents, corresponding to the five years of tribute that had not been paid, plus an equivalent indemnity to defray the costs of the war. In addition, they had to cover the costs of the troops (forty thousand soldiers to be housed and fed, plus sixteen drachmae a day per soldier and forty drachmae per officer) and make various supplementary contributions. Yet when the peace of Dardanos was signed, Rome had imposed a fine of only two thousand talents on Mithridates. It was becoming clear who the real losers were in this adventure. The Ephesian Vespers came at a very high price.

CHAPTER THIRTY-TWO

Prizes for an Athlete from Miletus, or Competition and Greek Culture

(The city-state honors) [— son of [–]crates, a Milesian, who won:

—in the Olympieia, the double race [*diaulon*], in the 190th Year, the same day;

—in the Nemeia, among the men, the stadium race, the *diaulon*, and the armed race, one after another in the same year, the first of all to do so;

—in the Eleutheria held at Plataea by the *koinon* of the Greeks, among the men, the stadium, and the armed race from the trophy; and he was proclaimed "the best of the Greeks," the first and the only one of the Greeks born in Asia;

—in the Great Aktia Kaisareia, among the men, the stadium, the *diaulon*, and the armed race, in the same day, first of all;

—in the Nemeia, again the *diaulon* and the armed race;

—in Sebasta Rhomaia celebrated by the *koinon* of Asia, the armed race, first among the Ionians;

—in the Isthmia, the armed race, first among the Milesians;

—in the Pythian contests, again, the stadium and the armed race, first among the Ionians;

—in the contest celebrated by the sacred stephanite conquerors of the inhabited world, the *diaulon* and the armed race, first of all;

—in the Heraia, in Argos, the stadium, first among the Milesians, and the armed race;

—in the Halieia, in Rhodes, the stadium and the armed race;

—In the Eleutheria celebrated at Plataea by the *koinon* of the Greeks, again the stadium, the *diaulon*, the armed race, and the race in arms from the trophy, and he was proclaimed the second time "best of the Greeks," the first and the only one, he was honored by the *koinon* of the Greeks with a golden crown as the price for excellence;

—in the Isthmian contests, for the second time, the stadium (?), and the armed race;

—in the Great Eleusinia that the Athenian people celebrate, the

271

diaulon and the armed race, and he was honored by the
Athenian people with citizenship, a portrait and a crown of
olive leaves, because of his valor.

Inscription, in Louis Robert, *Hellenica*, vol. 7
(Paris: Librairie d'Amérique et d'Orient, 1949), pp. 117–125

MILETUS, ASIA MINOR, around 20 B.C.E. An athlete whose
name has disappeared—only the end of the patronymic remains—had brought such glory to his city-state that the latter
was determined to honor him by having the list of his triumphs engraved
in stone. This testimony, added to many others, helps us understand not
only how the Greek contests worked but also what was at stake in them
and what accounted for their prestige. This text gives us a good overview
of the topic.

Our athlete unquestionably belonged to the elite: the list of contests in
which he participated is evidence enough. Every contest bore a name that
evoked either the god to whom it was dedicated or else the name of the
god's sanctuary: the Olympieia for Zeus Olympios in Olympia, the Pythia
for Apollo Pythios in Delphi, the Heraia for the goddess Hera in Argos,
the Eleutheria for Zeus Eleutherios (the "Liberator") whose cult was celebrated at Plataea in memory of the Greek victory over the Persians in 479,
the Halieia for Helios in Rhodes (he is called Halios in the Dorian dialect
in use in that city-state), the Isthmia for Poseidon in his sanctuary on the
Isthmus of Corinth, the Nemeia for Archemoros in Nemea, and the Eleusinia for Demeter and Kore, the two goddesses of Eleusis near Athens.
All the contests were celebrated in a religious context. They were not spectacles to distract people from their boredom, but rather essential elements
of religious festivals, along with processions, sacrifices, banquets, and often the fairs that were held nearby and that profited from the crowds. But
the contests were not organized for just any religious festival, only for the
most important ones, at regular intervals. No contests took place annually; most were held every four years (the Greeks called them "penteteric,"
"every fifth year," for they counted the starting year as the fifth year of the
previous cycle), others every two years ("trieteric, "every third year").
This made it possible to avoid crowding the calendar and to alternate the
major contests. It took Nero's megalomania—for it goes without saying

that the emperor was eager to appear as a conqueror in all the important Panhellenic contests during his one trip to Greece—to spur the organization, in defiance of the rules, of the four great Panhellenic contests in a single year (Chapter 36)! Ordinarily, things were orchestrated so that the major contests did not impinge on one another, and gaps were scheduled between contests so that athletes and artisans would have time to get to the next venue.

These contests were not of equal importance. The Greeks distinguished first of all between sacred or "stephanite" contests and "thematic" contests. The first, more prestigious ones were distinguished in that the conquerors took home symbolic prizes, often crowns of leaves (hence the name "stephanite," from the Greek *stephanos*, crown). The second group carried less prestige, but prizes of silver were offered (hence the name "thematic," from the Greek *thema*, "sum of money"). But within the first group, a supplementary hierarchy was respected. The four great Panhellenic contests—held in Olympia, Delphi (Pythia), the Isthmus of Corinth, and Nemea—form a separate group, the *periodos*, by far the most prestigious of the lot. After Augustus founded contests in Actium to celebrate his victory over Antony and Cleopatra, the Actia were added to the four preceding venues to form a new periodos. At the center of this group, the Olympieia enjoyed the highest rank; every winner in a round of these contests indicated the fact at the head of his list of victories, whatever place this one might have held in the unfolding of his career. Let us recall that the only calendar system common to all Greeks, the counting of years by Olympiads, used the names of the men who won the stadium races to designate the various Olympieia.

Contests proliferated. In addition to all those that could be found dating back to the archaic and classical eras in Greece itself and in the colonial world, there were also, in the Hellenistic period, countless contests in new city-states founded by kings, or in indigenous cities that had been promoted to the rank of city-state. Thus we find important contests in Alexandria (Ptolemaieia), in Antioch (Olympieia), in Pergamon (Nikephoria), but also in Tyre and Sidon. The Roman conquest did not put a stop to this expansion, quite the contrary; in the imperial era, we witness a real explosion in the number of contests. There was no city in Syria that did not have one or several of these, except for Palmyra and Petra, where specific cultural phenomena must have come into play; a modest city-state

273

like Bostra held contests twice in the mid-third century, both times in honor of the great local native god, Dusares. In older cities, contests abounded, sometimes financed by private foundations; in Aphrodisias in Caria, in the mid-third century, we count no fewer than fourteen contests!

Our Milesian was a runner. Like many others, he had more than one specialty. He competed in both the stadium race (in which the distance varied between 180 and 200 meters) and the *diaulon* (twice the length of the stadium), and even in the armed race, a Greek specialty, although it was not included in all the contests. This latter was the most prestigious of the Eleutheria contests in Plataea, where it recalled the Greek victory over the Persians in 479. We do not know how long the race course was, but we do know that the contestants were equipped like hoplites. Generally speaking, racing had greater prestige than any other sport. In addition to the contests mentioned above, there was also a middle-distance race, the *dolichon*, whose length varied according to the city-state, from 1,350 to 3,000 meters. In contrast, there were no full cross-country races, and certainly no marathons; these are a modern invention by Pierre de Coubertin.

Alongside the racing contests, there were three involving combat and one combination contest. Combat sports were represented by wrestling, boxing, and *pankration*, a combination of the two. Boxing was practiced bare-handed, with only leather bindings around the hands, both to protect the joints and to injure more effectively. The difference between pankration and wrestling is not always obvious, but pankration was reputed to be more violent, for nothing was forbidden except blinding one's opponent by putting fingers in his eyes. In wrestling, the winner was the one who downed his adversary or made him leave the circle established for the fight. In pankration, the fighting took place mostly on the ground, and the winner was the one who held out longest against the pain inflicted by his adversary: the winner was indicated when the other contestant gave up, signaling his decision by tapping his adversary on the shoulder or back. Referees watched closely to make sure the rules were followed, and they had long pointed sticks with which they jabbed contestants who had committed faults. Finally, the pentathlon combined five contests, three of which never occurred in isolation: the javelin, the discus, the (triple) jump, plus the stadium race and wrestling. The victor had to win at least three contests out of the five. Some competitions also included equestrian contests, races on horseback, or chariot races with one, two, or four horses; here, the person proclaimed the winner was never the jockey or the driver but the owner of the horse or team: this was the only case in which women (we know of several wealthy Spartan women in this situation) could carry the day in a contest reserved for men.

The list of honors credited to our anonymous Milesian specifies on two occasions that he won "among the men." The Greeks distinguished among athletes by age group but not by weight. Thus there were typically three categories, men, young men ("beardless"), and boys. It is hard to be sure where the lines were drawn between them, and the distinction may even have been left to the judges' discretion, as a function not of a candidate's actual age but of his physical appearance and sexual maturity, which was easy to verify because all sports were practiced in the nude. In any case, athletes could always compete in the next higher category, and we know of winners who boasted of having won among the boys and the young men, or among the young men and the adult men, during the same contests, sometimes even on the same day. In contrast, competing against adversaries in a lower category was not allowed. The absence of any classification by weight was significant mainly for the combat sports, for it gave an obvious advantage to heavier contestants. And indeed, the images that we have of wrestlers or boxers on vase paintings or sculptures show massive men. As a result, when there was too great a difference in weight between the two athletes selected by lot, the slighter one sometimes withdrew. One statement of praise for an athlete of Magnesia on the Meander, in Asia Minor, points out that during one competition, this fellow defeated all his adversaries by default, because, the text says, when he took off his clothes, his competitors withdrew. The violence of the combat sports could lead to serious injuries that were difficult to treat; rather than remaining crippled for life, some contestants thus preferred to walk away before the fight.

All sports were practiced in the nude, and the Greeks even made this a distinctive feature of their contests. For while they were not the only people in the ancient world to practice sports, they were the only ones who did so without clothing. Various legends have circulated about the origin of this athletic nudity, but none of them is convincing. It is certain that nudity was not a matter of comfort, quite the contrary: there has been some discussion moreover as to whether nudity was really practiced during the contests, or whether the competitors wore some kind of jock-strap to hold their genitals in place. The nudity on display in the gymnasium actually had an ideological function above all: it distinguished Greeks from barbarians. This was not unproblematic for Hellenized Jews (Chapter 28). But the trainers, too, had to present themselves naked, after an incident in 404 B.C.E. when, we are told, a woman from Rhodes disguised herself as a trainer in order to help her boxer son in an Olympian contest, and gave herself away when she vaulted over the parapet at the moment of his victory.

However this may be, from the archaic period on the athletes were professionals. While all free men went regularly to the gymnasium and engaged in physical exercises there (although the moralists expressed regret that baths were increasing in importance to the detriment of the arena), participation in contests was reserved for professionals, whose lifestyle was not very different from that of athletes today: daily training, a strict regimen overseen by a trainer and often also by a doctor who prescribed a diet, and constant travel between contests. And not everyone made a fortune in the process.

We have been focusing up to now on sporting competitions, but we should not forget that there were also musical competitions, so named not because they were exclusively devoted to music but because they were placed under the patronage of the Muses. Moreover, a number of contests combined the two aspects, sporting and musical, during a single festival. The contests were numerous, and varied: they might include comedy, tragedy, singing with accompaniment, solo instruments (cithara, oboe) with or without chorus, trumpet, bugle, mime, pantomime, eulogies in prose or verse, poetry, and so on. Some great artists were just as famous as athletes.

But let us come back to our Milesian, whom the city-state was honoring by listing all his victories. This is not always the case: an athlete sometimes signaled that he had been admitted to compete in some prestigious contest, generally in a periodos, whereas all his victories had been won in more modest competitions. Here, on the contrary, the list stands out by the importance of the contests. The five contests in the new periodos are included, as well as some other prestigious ones such as those held in Plataea, Athens, the *koinon* of Asia, and Rhodes. Indeed, we can be certain that the list given here is only very partial, limited to victories won in sacred contests, the prestigious ones; victories in thematic contests are not mentioned. We have other lists that spell out victories in detail, listing those won in sacred contests first, along with the name of the contests and the host city, and then noting cities—without indicating the name of the contests—where the candidate won in competitions for prizes. One list, after enumerating the sacred victories, simply mentions the number of victories won in thematic contests, with no details at all. These practices highlight the difference in prestige between the two categories.

Victory had only one form: coming in first in a race, being the last man standing in combat sports, throwing the discus and the javelin as far as possible, jumping as far as possible. This is not very different from what we know today, with one exception: the notion of "record" is absent. No comparisons are made between contests, or from one year to another. This attitude can perhaps be explained by the absence of any way to measure time, for the races, and by the fact that the length of the stadium varied from place to place. But I do not think that is the underlying reason. The ideal of the Greek athlete was not to surpass himself, to break his own record (and all the more so that of others) but to be first, at the crucial moment.

The anonymous Milesian pushed that logic to the extreme. We know that he came in first in every contest mentioned, of course, because he was the winner. But his glory was augmented in almost every case by the fact that he was also the first to win in a given configuration of contests: "in the Nemeia, among the men, the stadium race, the *diaulon,* and the armed race, one after another in the same year, the first of all": in other words, never before had anyone won these three races in a row in a single celebration of these contests. He was also the first in the history of the contests to win the stadium race, the diaulon, and the armed race in the Actia of Nicopolis of Epiros on the same day. Without seeking to diminish his merit, we should note that this must have happened during the second or third celebration of these contests, which facilitated the acquisition of unprecedented titles. His triple victory must have been more prestigious "in the contest celebrated by the sacred stephanite conquerors of the inhabited world, the diaulon and the armed race, first of all," that is, in a competition reserved for athletes who had been victorious in sacred contests. From this, he derived supplementary glory, as if he had won an additional victory. Similarly, in the Eleutherian contests held at Plataea "he was proclaimed 'the best of the Greeks,' the first and the only one of the Greeks born in Asia." The innovation is less striking, for he is only the first of the Greeks from Asia. The decline in prestige continues as we come to the Sebasta Rhomaia, where he was only the first of the Ionians, or, less illustrious still, the Isthmia, where he was only the first Milesian to win; similarly, in the Heraia, in Argos, he was the first Milesian to win the stadium race, whereas for the armed race he did not even have that privilege.

This flattering enumeration shows what mattered to the athlete as well as to his city-state: to be the first of all. In lists of athletes' honors we find a notion that is put in abundant relief in the eulogies addressed to the benefactors of city-states. To be sure, the latter are praised for bestowing their gifts, but it is always emphasized that they were the first to have done so. Thus, in a decree from Gerasa of Arabia praising a *euergetes,* it was noted that he was the first to distribute perfumed oil in the gymnasium. To be at the head of the line, to be first, was to take place among the notables: those to whom we attribute this label were designated in Greek texts, after all, as *hoi protoi,* "the firsts."

The list of honors won by our Milesian remains silent about one aspect of his career: his earnings. By indicating only the sacred victories, it bypassed any reference to his monetary winnings, but everyone knew perfectly well what those victories had brought him: glory and symbolic prizes—crowns of olive leaves in Olympia, laurel in Delphi, pine in the Isthmus (and wild celery in Nemea), a shield in Argos, whereas other contests awarded the winners earthenware jars of oil (the Pan-Athenian contests in Athens), or a glorious title, such as that of "best of the Greeks," awarded to the winner of the armed race at Plataea.

From the archaic period on, these symbolic rewards were actually only the tip of the iceberg, like the gold, silver, or bronze medals won by our athletes today. The city-state of origin could give a monetary reward, sometimes a considerable sum: Solon is said to have established a scale in Athens that attributed five hundred drachmae to an Olympic winner and one hundred to a winner in the Isthmia contests, thus revealing a clear hierarchy between these competitions. These amounts, high as they were, still encouraged everyone to view the honor involved as more important than the money. Perhaps there was also a concern for limiting excesses and imposing the city-state's control.

Other more symbolic rewards could be added: the right to make a solemn entry on horseback into the city-state to the acclamations of the crowd (like parading down Broadway or the Champs-Élysées), the right to take meals at the *prytaneum* at the expense of the state, the right to be honored with a statue and a decree. From the Hellenistic period on, but especially in the imperial period, the city-state granted citizenship to the most brilliant winners in their contests, and sometimes also a seat as a member of their council. We also know of athletes who accumulated some fifteen different citizenships, a privilege that remained theoretical except for the city-state in which each one actually resided.

But, even though this was never stated, what enriched the winners were their victories in contests for prize money. These prizes were sometimes very high, a talent or a half-talent. It has been calculated that one athlete of the imperial period for whom we have a detailed list of honors had won, at the time the inscription was written, the equivalent of five hundred times the yearly pay of a legionnaire! It is not just in our own day that stars in sports and entertainment accumulate colossal fortunes.

Which raises the question of financing. We have very little information on this point, and it is probable that the contests were most often financed by the city-state, thanks to the god's treasury. The stephanite contests did not cost very much in principle, because there were no monetary awards. But the stadium and the gymnasium had to be maintained, training rooms had to be set up, oil and heat for the baths had to be paid for. It must have been necessary to draw either on the public treasury or else on contributions, voluntary or otherwise, from wealthy citizens.

The contests that offered monetary prizes were handled differently, for, in addition to the expenses noted above, money for the winners had to be found. Two privately funded contests in Asia Minor during the imperial era give us some indications of costs. In Aphrodisias, a certain Flavios Lysimachos bequeathed the city-state a sum for the organization of musical contests every four years. This sum was invested, but the returns were inadequate; it was thus increased little by little, no doubt by reinvesting the interest, until it reached 120,000 denarii, which seems to have been sufficient from that point on. This sum produced 31,839 denarii of interest (because drachmae and denarii were interchangeable, it came to a little more than five talents!); the curator of the foundation thus authorized the contests, with a prize of one talent "and the hope of performances worthy of the prize," he added. In Oinoanda, a small city-state on the border between the regions of Caria and Lycia, Iulius Demosthenes founded a pen-teteric competition in his own honor, with detailed indications as to how the contests would be financed and organized, and so on. For the first celebration, a sum of 4,450 denarii had been collected: 1,900 to be used to compensate the winners, 900 for the organization of the spectacles, 150 to be distributed to the citizens participating in the contests reserved for them, and the remaining 1,800 to be remitted to the referees and the *bouleutai* who acted as referees, with any remaining sums to be divided among other creditors. The prizes awarded to the winners were particularly low: 50 denarii for the winners of the bugle and trumpet competitions, 75 for the prose eulogy and poetry competitions, but 125 for the winner of the contest for oboe *(aulos)* with chorus and 75 for the runner-up. This practice of also rewarding the runner-up is found in the same contests for the competitions in comedy (200 and 100 denarii), tragedy (250 and 125), and singing with cithara accompaniment (300 and 150). The gradation in prizes probably also attests to the prestige of each discipline. But, once again, the Demostheneia were only modest contests, financed by an individual, in a small city-state, and the prizes were well below those given in the larger venues.

For a long time historians have consistently emphasized the popularity of the contests and their importance in the Greeks' value system. But they have less often drawn attention to the harsh criticisms of some thinkers who denounced the excessive honors granted to athletes. This tendency appeared with particular strength in the last third of the fifth century B.C.E., under the dual influence of circumstances (the Peloponnesian War) and the sophists, but it had begun much earlier. In the seventh century, the poet Tyrtaeus placed athleticism well below courage in war. Around 525, Xenophanes of Colophon deemed that the food provided to winning athletes at the expense of the city-state would be better used to compensate "intellectuals." Around 420, most strikingly, Euripides attributed to one of his heroes an extraordinarily violent tirade against athletes. To be sure, the fragment is isolated, and we cannot put it back in context, but at least it proves that a discourse hostile to athletes existed. One passage is worth citing:

Among the countless scourges with which Greece is plagued, nothing is worse than the breed of athletes . . . Dazzling in their youth and the glories of their cities, they strut about. But when bitter old age descends upon them, they go about casting off their tattered rags! I also blame the Greek custom of gathering in their honor, and of placing high value on vain pleasures as a pretext for feasting. This one is a brilliant wrestler, an agile runner, a good discus-thrower or jaw-breaking boxer: has any one of these ever done his city a service by winning a crown? Will these people ever fight the enemy discus in hand? Will we see them without shields, driving the enemy out of their homeland? . . . Wise and good men are the ones who should be crowned with leaves—whoever, being full of wisdom, most beneficially guides the city, and whoever, through his speech, averts misfortune by preventing conflict and civil strife.[1]

We must doubtless be cautious in our use of this text, but we can clearly see the breakthrough of a discourse—one that has never ceased—associating strong arms and small brains. In the fourth century, on several occasions Isocrates lamented the fact that the city-states did more to honor athletes than to honor wise men. But all this did not prevent the same authors from multiplying images borrowed from the world of sport, as they were sure of being well understood by their listeners.

The Christian authors had no choice but to denounce the contests forcefully by virtue of their connections with pagan festivals. Clement of Alexandria, whose flock surely participated enthusiastically in these spectacles, spoke of a "plague that has invaded [our] customs."[2] However, it was not until the year 393 that the contests were outlawed by Theodosius, along with any public celebration of the pagan cults. With their suppression, an essential aspect of ancient culture disappeared.

CHAPTER THIRTY-THREE

Epaminondas Offers a Banquet, or Civic Ruin and Philanthropy in Greece in the First Century C.E.

[—] (9 lines damaged) [—] he made a distribution of perfumed oil (?), something that none of the preceding gymnasiarchs among us had done [—] (10 lines damaged) [—] time when he fed the whole city-state, and again after offering a bull to Hermes and to Heracles, and to the Augusti an athletic contest for which he established shields as prizes for the winners, the first and the only one from all eternity to have imagined such a reward. He regaled the city-state the same day at lunch in the gymnasium, after a proclamation; he excluded no one, not among the residents and not even among the visitors passing through or the freedmen and the slaves of citizens, according to his habitual love of glory.

When he controlled the supreme magistracy, he bore witness to greatness of spirit. He sacrificed a bull to the Augusti and he offered the city-state a banquet lasting a whole day, celebrating the festival called [—] in the gymnasium, in such a way that the unsurpassable and uninterrupted flow of his expenditures was a subject of admiration not only here among ourselves but also in the neighboring city-states.

The resurfacing of the great dike that protects our territory had been neglected in the rental contract; confronting the situation by himself, he drew up plans and had repairs carried out and the entire work resurfaced; the repairs on twelve stadium lengths cost more than 6,000 denarii.

But since then he has extended his penchant for magnanimity to the Boeotian League.[1] During the meeting of the Achaeans and the Panhellenes in Argos, an effort was made to send an embassy to the new Augustus. Many people ranking among the first in dignity from several city-states refused to go there and encouraged others to participate. He put his own affairs in second place and quite willingly took on the embassy on behalf of the Boeotian League, and to the nobility of his proud attitude he added the magnanimity of a promise to cover the expenses of the embassy. Admired for all this and judged worthy of full approbation, he received honors among the Panhellenes and recognition also in the letter that they sent to our city-state.

When he had brought his embassy to a good end with the other peoples and had brought back the emperor's response, once again he received honors along with his colleagues from the embassy, and the Panboeotian Council (synedrion), which had been delighted to accept the favor and good will spontaneously offered, voted to award him suitable honors and sent a copy to our city-state. Then the other city-states and villages, also desiring to do something by way of thanks, hastened to honor him by issuing decrees, by granting citizenship, and by displaying his image.

Surpassing in generosity and merit all those who came before him and surpassing himself through love of honors and pleasure in doing good by his successive expenditures, thinking only about behaving as a patriot and benefactor, when he was designated as an agonothetes—whereas the Ptoia contests had not been held for thirty years—he eagerly accepted that charge in the hope of renewing the former splendor of the contests and he became the founder of the Great Ptoia and Kaisareia contests.[2] As soon as he assumed that charge, he carried out the sacrifices and the oracles of the god. Regaling the magistrates and delegates five times a year with magnificent banquets and supplying lunch to the city-state during his four-year term, he never postponed the execution of a sacrifice or an expenditure. The sixth year, at the beginning of the contests, he had a distribution made to the city-state in the name of the competition to come, giving a basket of grain and a half-measure of wine each to all citizens, to the foreigners present, and to those who had property in the country. He had the great ancestral processions and the ancestral Syrtoi dance restored, and, sacrificing a bull to the gods and to the Augusti, he offered gifts of wine, lunches, sweet wines, and banquets without interruption. Then, between the 20th and the 30th of the month, he invited to all the lunches the sons of citizens and the adult male slaves, by age cohort, while his wife Kotila regaled the citizens' spouses as well as their servants and adult female slaves at lunch. He did not exclude even the itinerants sleeping in tents, and these contributed to the brilliance of the festival. He regaled them at lunch, after a special proclamation, which no one before him had made, for he did not want anyone to be excluded from the favors he was granting.

While the spectacles of the musical competition were taking place, he offered a snack with sweet wine, in the theater, to all the spectators from here and to those who came from the other city-states, and he distributed great and costly gifts on a broad scale, so that his expenditures were talked about even in the neighboring city-states.

After the contests were over, after the popular banquet, he took charge once again and repeated the expenditure by a distribution of 10 denarii for each *triclinion,* and with the rest of the funds he gave an earthenware jar of vintage wine and six denarii to accompany the bread.[3] After the festivities, when he returned from the sanctuary to the city-state, the citizens went out as a body to meet him, as a testimonial of honor and gratitude. He did not discontinue his generosity; instead, he sacrificed a bull to Most High Zeus in the city-state and once again invited those who had all come together to a banquet of thanks.

It is for this reason that, after such acts, it is just that men of such generosity and such patriotism receive recognition in the form of honors and privileges. For all these reasons, the magistrates, councilors, and people have decided to award praise to the aforenamed Epaminondas for the immense devotion that he has manifested toward the city-state of his ancestors and his magnanimity toward the Boeotian League, for, with the embassy, he also rendered service to the city-state of his ancestors. In the second place, to honor him with a crown of gold and a portrait in bronze, with good fortune, one in the sanctuary of Apollo Ptoios, the other in the city-state on the agora, and, similarly, gilded portraits with the following inscription: "The people and the council honor Epaminondas son of Epaminondas because of his excellent and very just behavior as citizen and as magistrate"; and, fifthly, to have a copy of this decree engraved in the sanctuary of Apollo Ptoios and in the city-state on the agora.

Inscription, in *Inscriptiones Graecae* (Berlin: G. de Gruyter, 1892), vol. 7, 2712

ACRAEPHIA (BOEOTIA), mid-first century C.E. The hero of the day had a name that was famous in Boeotia: it was the name of one of the most celebrated politicians and generals of the fourth century B.C.E.—doubtless the period when Boeotia experienced an apogee of sorts.

Since then, despite rather favorable agricultural conditions that procured a certain comfort level, Boeotia had played only a marginal role in Greek affairs. The destruction of Thebes by Alexander in 335 deprived the region of its most powerful city-state, even if Thebes did come back to life from its ruins over time. But the Hellenistic era marked a period of profound decline for the region. Scattered among several small city-states, the population survived as best it could in difficult times. Roman businessmen settled there in the first century B.C.E., proof that the area was not without resources, but it would be inaccurate to speak of prosperity.

Acraephia was one of the small city-states that shared the rich Boeotian plain. Situated on the banks of Lake Copais, known throughout Greece for its eels, it was a modest town whose chief claim to fame was that it possessed a great sanctuary frequented by all Boeotians from time to time, that of Apollo Ptoios, known as early as the archaic period. But depopulation and widespread impoverishment had left the city-state and the sanctuary in a sorry state. Fortunately, an exceptional citizen named Epaminondas came forward and took matters in hand. The decree adopted by the city-state to thank him for his benefactions allows us to assess both the lamentable situation of the Greek city-states at the beginning of the early empire and the dependence of these city-states on all-powerful benefactors.

It would be absurd to claim that Acraephia's situation was emblematic of Greece as a whole, but much of the information supplied by this extremely rich text is confirmed by other information valid for different regions. What makes this text particularly interesting is that Boeotia was neither a remote region like Arcadia or Phocis nor a province favored by the presence of a major city, like Attica. In a way, it can be viewed as an average Greek region, neither poor nor rich, one that had suffered neither more nor less than others during the crises of the Hellenistic period.

Epaminondas's action allows us both to put a finger on some aspects of the misfortunes that had struck the city-state and to see how a small city-state might find itself entirely dependent on one of its wealthy citizens. On the first point, the text offers few details; of course the first part of the text, which might have been more explicit, is lacking. From the information that has survived, we know that Epaminondas's action was applied in two realms: maintaining the dike and renewing the festivals in honor of Apollo Ptoios. Acraephia had to be protected from Lake Copais, on whose banks it was situated; the lake was fed by a network of inland rivers and thus was subjected to wide variations in level according to the season. In order to keep water from invading arable land, the lake level had to be maintained by means of dikes. The dike in question in our text had clearly been abandoned or neglected for years, but the city-state had recently contracted for its maintenance. However, the rental contract turned out to be unsatisfactory, and Epaminondas undertook to complete the work at his own expense: the surface had to be recoated to ensure that it was waterproof. It is worth noting that we have here one of the rather rare cases in which a benefactor invested in an area where there were direct economic implications, but of course the safety of the populace was also at stake, for the city-state could have been flooded if nothing had been done.

As for the sanctuary of Apollo Ptoios, which constituted a non-negligible source of income for the city-state, for it was frequented by pilgrims from all over Boeotia and even beyond, the building was dilapidated and the great contests that had formerly attracted pilgrims had not been held for more than thirty years, for want of financial means. Here, too, Epaminondas acted: he took the initiative of restoring the former contests, while modifying their dedication. The festivals in honor of Apollo henceforth associated Apollo Ptoios with the divinized emperor: they were to be called Ptoia and Kaisareia. Epaminondas, a leading citizen if there ever was one, made himself a skillful propagandist for the imperial cult and thereby manifested his attachment to the Roman domination and his loyalty to the dynasty. It was one of Rome's great strengths that it was able to associate local dignitaries with the management of the city-states and provinces, and that it had gotten them to accept its interests as their own. Epaminondas offers a superb example of this in the first century of our era.

To celebrate a restoration that could give the illusion of a return to the golden age, as Augustus had given the example to Rome by inaugurating the *Ara Pacis* ("Altar of Peace"), Epaminondas multiplied the festivities. And in this he was probably giving the full measure of his generosity, but also of his real power over a city-state in distress.

Let us note first of all that Epaminondas acted within the framework of existing civic institutions. In the damaged part of the decree, the fact that he had the function of gymnasiarch—that is, administrator of the gymnasium—is mentioned. Later, he became supreme magistrate, that is, the eponymous magistrate, and it was as *agonothetes*, director of the contests, that he worked toward the restoration of the Ptoia. In principle, then, he submitted to the democratic designation that prevailed in the city-states, and agreed to be subject to the controls provided by law. The exemplary citizen he sought to be could not exempt himself, but this was not always the case. Many extravagant *euergetai* were accused of behaving like tyrants in their own city-states. Thus, in the middle of the first century B.C.E., the Carian city-state of Mylasa was governed successively by two orators, Euthydemos and Hybreas, about the first of whom Strabo said: "Even if there was something tyrannical about him, it was atoned for by the fact that it was attended by what was good for the city."[4] Euthydemos's successor, Hybreas, master of the city-state after the former's death, summed this up in a sentence reported by Strabo: "Euthydemos, you are an evil necessary to the city, for we can live neither with you nor without you."[5] There was henceforth such a disparity in fortune between the richest citizens and the general population, and such a bond of dependence, that even a good citizen who respected the laws enjoyed excessive authority, whatever the circumstances. The systematic mention of Epaminondas's functions highlights the extent to which this benefactor was determined to respect the laws of the city-state, when no one at all would have been in a position to oppose him.

The action of the *euergetes* took shape in particular around the festivals and the contests. As gymnasiarch, he supplied perfumed oil at his own expense (this is the most probable meaning of the passage), something that had never been done before. We have seen (Chapter 32) how much the fact of being the first to win a given victory or combination of victories added to the athlete's glory. Similarly, a benefactor gained special prestige from such an innovation. But, as gymnasiarch, Epaminondas did more than the minimum service required by his charge. He offered the requisite sacrifices to the gods of the gymnasium, Hermes and Heracles, but he also took advantage of the occasion to introduce (or further develop) the imperial cult in his city-state by creating athletic contests in honor of the emperor. Sacred contests, it seems, because the prizes awarded the winners were not sums of money, but shields. The decree acclaimed the innovative character of the reward, but the novelty was only relative, for shields had been awarded to the winners of the Heraia in Argos.

To celebrate the inauguration of this new competition, Epaminondas offered a banquet to the entire city-state. The banquet was an integral part of the festival, and it was an opportunity to consume the meat of the animals sacrificed to the gods: the latter received the homage of the skin and bones, whose odor was agreeable to the gods' nostrils, while the faithful shared the meat, boiled or roasted, according to the provisions of the ritual associated with the festival. In this, Epaminondas was conforming to tradition; nevertheless, he went further, and manifested exceptional generosity in that he did not limit the benefits of his liberality to citizens alone, as was the custom, but extended them to all residents of the city-state, to visitors passing through, and even to freedmen and to slaves belonging to citizens. The gesture may seem surprising, because it amounts to erasing a fundamental distinction at the heart of the civic community, not only between citizens and the others, but also between free men and those who were not free. By making them all recipients of his generosity, Epaminondas freed himself from the prevailing social and legal hierarchies, and marked a little more clearly the extent to which he himself was above the rank of ordinary mortals. Some were no doubt astonished, even shocked, but what could be said in the face of so much generosity?

The restoration of the Great Ptoia was a more far-reaching project. Suspended for thirty years, the great federal Boeotian contests had to be reestablished in all the more sumptuous a fashion in that they henceforth associated the cult of Apollo with that of the emperor. Once again, Epaminondas made himself the propagandist for the imperial cult, in an era when that cult did not yet exist at the provincial level in the province of Achaea, to which Boeotia belonged. It took a full six years to pull together the necessary funds, perhaps to restore the sanctuary and to build the facilities that were indispensable to the organization of the contests. These would include a musical competition, for which a theater was required, at a minimum. During the entire preparatory period, Epaminondas had the appropriate rites celebrated; these seem to have been largely neglected in recent times. Sacrifices, banquets, processions, ceremonies of all sorts (like the one during which the Syrtoi dance took place) were held one after another at Epaminondas's expense. On the occasion of the first celebration of the restored contests, he surpassed himself. He fed the whole city-state, men and women, citizens and visitors, people who were free and those who were not, for ten days without interruption. During the competition itself, light meals were served to the spectators, with sweet wine. And when the festival was over, he provided each group of revelers with vintage wine, bread, and a small sum of money. When the citizens came as a body to thank him, he organized another banquet to thank them! Epaminondas manifested a frenetic desire to feed his fellow citizens, to use banquets as manifest signs of his generosity. More than any other benefactor, he deserved the title *tropheus*, "nurturer," which the city-states occasionally awarded to generous *euergetai*. Emperor Hadrian himself received it from the Athenians after he had made various arrangements for sending them supplies.

Epaminondas thus supported his city-state and all the visitors drawn by the festival for days, even weeks. We may suppose that Acraephia must have appeared to offer a constricted framework to a man whose fortune placed him so high above his fellow citizens. In fact, Epaminondas's career as *euergetes* also flourished at the Boeotian federal level, thus extending his reputation beyond his own city-state. The occasion of this particular act of generosity was the advent of a new emperor, Caligula. According to custom, delegates from the provincial peoples were to carry their congratulations to the new Augustus. The decision to do so was made during a meeting in Argos (and not in Corinth, which was the capital of the province of Achaea) by the members of the provincial organization called the *koinon* of the Achaeans and Panhellenes, a group representing the Achaean city-states. It was probably decided that the common embassy would include representatives from the various communities along with those from the largest city-states of the province. For Boeotia, no volunteer came forward, and those who were solicited demurred. Not only were there risks involved in the expedition, but it was also costly, for the league gave very little money, if any, toward the mission. Epaminondas, neglecting his own affairs, offered to go, and he financed not only his own trip but the entire embassy, thus earning the gratitude of the koinon of the Panhellenes as well as that of his fellow citizens. With this gesture he placed himself at the outset, despite the obscurity of his homeland, among the provincial notables on whom the proconsuls of Achaea could count. Epaminondas's career as a responsible politician reached its apogee a little later, under Nero's reign: it is he who was charged with thanking Nero after the latter had proclaimed the freedom of the Greeks in 67 (Chapter 36).

Euergetism, which made great strides during the Hellenistic era, took on new amplitude under the empire. To be sure, historians rightly identify a pronounced shift between the early and late Hellenistic eras—however vague the boundary between these two periods may be—sometime around the middle of the second century B.C.E. The break occurred at the moment when the great Hellenistic kingdoms were weakening and then disappearing. As Polybius noted around 150, the kings of his time had become "skinflints," presumably because they had become poor and there was little political benefit to be reaped from generosity. In this context, immensely wealthy citizens took over where the kings left off. With the aggravated difficulties occasioned by the long Mithridatic Wars and then the Roman civil war (and we have to remember that this latter devastated Greece and Asia Minor at least as much as Italy), the ruined city-states had no choice but to turn to private fortunes. From the first century B.C.E. on, extravagant euergetai spent colossal sums for the benefit of their fellow citizens. Euthydemos and Hybreas of Mysala were cited above, but we could add several other names, such as Diodoros Pasparos in Pergamon, Chairemon of Nysa, Zeno of Laodicea, and Pythodoros of Tralles, who became privileged interlocutors of the Roman *imperatores*. Epaminondas situated himself right in the middle of this euergetistic tradition characteristic of the late Hellenistic era, a tradition that associated political influence with the expenditure of large sums for the citizens' benefit. By his actions, he allowed Acraephia to maintain its rank as a city-state, to live in conformity with what must have been the "Greek way of life." Thus the importance attached to the most emblematic manifestations of *civilized* life: a gymnasium, competitions, cults, banquets. Epaminondas was not concerned with finding work for those who had none, or with restoring abandoned fields to cultivation (even if the work on the dikes supported such efforts); his primary aim was to allow his fellow citizens to live like Greeks.

CHAPTER THIRTY-FOUR

"The Sun and the Stars," or Rome, the Client Princes, and the Provinces in the Eastern Mediterranean

During the time that Gaius Caesar was hipparch, on 9 Thargelion, it pleased the people; at the suggestion of all the archontes, Aiolos son of Aiolos of the Oinopis tribe, secretary of the council, during the second assembly, under the presidency of Menophon, declared:[1]

Given that the New Helios Gaius Caesar Augustus Germanicus willed that kings too, guardians of his dominion, should have their own rays shining along with his, so that the grandeur of his immortality should be more majestic in this respect too, the kings, although they thought about it constantly, unable to find by way of thanks to such a powerful god any gifts equal to those he had generously bestowed on them;

Given that he reestablished the sons of Cotys, Rhoimetalkes, Polemon, and Cotys, his companions who had been brought up with him, in the kingdoms that were due them as heirs of their father and their ancestors, and given that they, enjoying the abundant fruits of immortal grace, are greater than the kings of the past, for the latter held the succession from their fathers, whereas the former became kings owing to the grace of Gaius Caesar in view of the common governance of very powerful gods; and the favors of the gods differ from human legacies as the sun differs from night and eternity from mortal nature. Having become greater than the greatest, and more famous than the most illustrious, Rhoimetalkes and Polemon came to our city-state to participate in the cult and celebrate the festival jointly with their mother, who presides over the contests of the goddess New Aphrodite Drusilla, not as in a friendly city-state but as in their own homeland, because the daughter of kings and the mother of kings, their mother Tryphaina, viewing this as her city-state, established her hearth and home and the good for-

tune of her existence here, and found happiness in the kingdoms of her children spared from divine jealousy. The people,
particularly enchanted by their visit, with unanimous zeal, ordered the magistrates to have a decree adopted and brought to
them in which, before thanking the kings, they would thank
their mother Tryphaina for the benefits that she had graciously
granted to the city-state, a decree by means of which they would
also make manifest the attitude of the people toward them;

It has pleased the people to praise the kings Rhoimetalkes,
Polemon, and Cotys, and their mother Tryphaina; upon their
entry, may the priests and priestesses, after opening the sanctuaries and decorating the statues of the cult *(xoana)* of the gods,
pray for the eternal maintenance of Gaius Caesar and the health
of these kings.

> Inscription, in *Inscriptiones Graecae ad res romanas pertinentes*
> (Paris: Leroux, 1906–1927), vol. 4, 145

K YZIKOS, ON THE southern shore of the Sea of Marmara, the ancient Propontis, around 39–40 C.E. A fairly large city, Kyzikos
had the rank of district capital in the province of Asia, which
means that the proconsul, the provincial governor, regularly held his court
sessions there. This was a sought-after honor; it gave the city-state high
standing. Emperor Caligula, the New Helios Gaius Caesar Augustus Germanicus, came to power after Tiberius was assassinated in 34; Caligula
was assassinated in turn in 41. But the other persons mentioned are the
ones who hold our attention: Tryphaina and her three sons, Rhoimetalkes,
Polemon, and Cotys. Kings, certainly, but of a quite particular sort, and
one that sheds light on the way in which Rome administered large regions
of the Greek part of the empire during this period.

Tryphaina was Antonia Tryphaina, widow of King of Thrace Cotys VIII.
Why was she called Antonia? Because through her mother, queen Pythodoris of Pontus, she descended from the great Mark Antony (and Octavia,
Augustus's daughter), through his daughter Antonia Minor, which means
she was indirectly related to the Julio-Claudian family: Nero, Caligula's
nephew, was the grandson of Antony's other daughter, Antonia Maior,
who married L. Domitius Ahenobarbus. Tryphaina and Cotys VIII had
three sons. Rhoimetalkes, the eldest, inherited the kingdom of Thrace from

his father. In 38, Polemon received the kingdom of Pontus from Caligula; Tiberius had confiscated Pontus in 33, when Polemon I's widow Pythodoris died. The youngest son, Cotys IX, had just received sovereignty over Armenia Minor and probably also over the neighboring region of Sophene. Two of the three young kings, those of Thrace and Pontus, came together to Kyzikos, where their mother usually resided, to celebrate a festival, accompanied by contests, in honor of Caligula's sister (and mistress) Drusilla, who was identified for the occasion with Aphrodite.

But before getting into the heart of the matter, we need to take a look at the way the decree in honor of the three kings and their mother was written. The emphatic character of the vocabulary, the amplitude of the phrases, and their careful balancing are striking. It would be too easy to see in this only a way of attracting the good graces of those honored by the decree through an exaggerated eloquence. To be sure, in the choice of images (and we shall look at these more closely in a moment), hyperbole proliferates, even as it establishes a precise gradation between what applies to the emperor and what is suitable for kings. But we must not see this as gratuitous rhetoric, an attitude of crude flattery, when in fact the intent was first and foremost to honor the kings by using the most beautiful language available, language that delighted the intelligence of cultivated people. The context encourages this rich language and bold imagery; rhetoric was placed in the service of a cause—praising royalty—and it was important to avoid committing any linguistic blunders.

The content of our text is no less rich a source of teaching. In sum, the text tells us that it was henceforth more glorious to hold a kingdom granted by the emperor than one inherited as an ancestral legacy. This is paradoxical discourse, but it suits the occasion, for the three kings had been created by the Roman emperor. The eldest, Rhoimetalkes, had of course inherited his kingdom from his father, but he could not have done so without the emperor's explicit consent. There are excellent parallel examples in other client kingdoms. Upon Herod's death, for instance, his three surviving sons rushed to Rome to get Augustus to recognize their rights of succession; Herod had left a will, but it was Augustus's decision alone that counted. Aretas IV of Nabatene, because he had neglected to seek such authorization, may have been deprived of his kingdom for a few years before being reestablished. In any case, Cotys VIII held his kingdom from Augustus, just as his father Rhoimetalkes I had received it from the same source in 31 B.C.E.: the Thracian dynasty was a Roman creation, on the same basis as the Herodian dynasty in Jerusalem. Even when a royal line could claim legitimacy antedating the Roman presence, Rome managed to transform it into a client dynasty: thus in 30 B.C.E., on various pretexts, Rome deposed the sovereigns of Emesa and of the Amanos kingdom in Cilicia, only to reestablish them about ten years later. Once they had been restored to their thrones, these sovereigns had the same status as the kings created by Rome.

The client kings' close-knit subjection to Roman sovereignty was doubted by no one. Thus it took real audacity to claim that their power was only made more glorious by this means. The author of the Kyzikos decree, a very skillful rhetor, bases his argument on the recent development of the imperial cult. Augustus had proved reticent, and Tiberius even more so, to this proposition on the Greeks' part. However, inasmuch as the cult of sovereigns had a long history in the world of Greek city-states, they had gone along with it. Caligula saw things differently, and, seizing on the Greek tradition of the cult of sovereigns (Chapter 19), supported all the manifestations of the cult directed at himself, going so far as to require such manifestations of those who did not show enough zeal. Did he not want to install his own statue in the Temple of Jerusalem? All the maneuvering skill of the governor of Syria was required to defuse the Jews' anger by dragging things out until the tyrant's disappearance in 41. The Kyzikenes had none of the Jews' reticence, and thus they honored Caligula as the New Helios (Sun) while his sister became the New Aphrodite.

Because the emperor was henceforth a god, his gifts far surpassed those of humans, even if these were kings. Hence the line of argument that appeared audacious at first glance but that is only logical: it is better to hold one's power from a god (the emperor) than from a man (one's father). From this starting point, the author was able to develop a lovely cosmographic image in which the client kings appear like stars around the imperial Sun; their rays mingle with his and shine only thanks to him.

Beyond this cleverly flattering image, the reality was something else again. From the time of its earliest contacts, Rome had often hesitated to administer the Greek world directly: this was the case in Asia Minor in 188, in Macedonia in 168, and in Greece after 146 (when Greece, defeated, was not made a province). Not until 133, under the terms of Attala III's will, was a province finally created. Others followed: Cyrenica in

96, Cilicia at roughly the same time, Bithynia in 74, Syria in 64, Cyprus in 59, and Egypt, finally, in 30. But while the regime of direct administration was being extended little by little, Rome left in its clients' hands vast spaces that had come under its control by right of conquest. This policy found its clearest expression in the period when Mark Antony was administering the eastern Mediterranean, between 42 and 31, although Pompey set the example when Syria was annexed in 64. Pompey had actually deposed the last surviving Seleucid king, but he had left in place a crowd of dynasts who had succeeded in carving out principalities, to the detriment of the old kingdom. Thus there subsisted outside the province not only the Hasmonean state in Judaea, but also the Arab principality of Emesa and Arethusa in central Syria, a principality in the interior of Lebanon, and a host of small tetrarchies (seventeen, according to Pliny) in the mountains in the Syrian interior. Antony in turn made systematic use of government by way of client princes, even giving up certain existing provinces, such as Pontus, which Pompey had created. In Thrace, in interior Anatolia, in Syria, in Judaea, he multiplied client kings. In most cases, he put a local man at the head of the principality, someone very familiar with the region he was to administer. But this cultural correspondence between the prince and his people was challenged on several occasions over time. Augustus was careful not to counter Antony's example on this point, at most making a few replacements. Tiberius followed the same course, although he did proceed to make a few annexations. Caligula pushed the policy to an extreme, restoring kingdoms that had been confiscated by his two predecessors to titleholders or their descendants, but from that point on it seems to have been the case that any prince could reign more or less anywhere. The three kings mentioned in the Kyzikos decree attest to this: born of the union between a Thracian prince and a queen whose ancestors included a Greek rhetor from Tralles, a Roman general, and a king of Pontus, one of the three actually reigned over Thrace, the second over Pontus, and the third over Armenia Minor and Sophene. Similarly, we see that Herod the Great and his successors were authorized to rule over territories populated for the most part by Arabs and Arameans, an Arab from Emesa over a principality of Sophene, and the Jew Aristobulos over Armenia Minor. The client princes became the equivalent of provincial governors who could be changed as the need arose!

The parallel may be a little excessive, but it is not without foundation;

for the most part, these princes were simultaneously kings in their own kingdoms and Roman citizens, for, as members of the elite from Greek city-states, they had often received citizenship, starting in Augustus's reign. In Rome, King Herod was also C. Iulius Herodes. When he came to ask Augustus's pardon after Actium, where he had naturally supported Antony, Herod turned up in a toga, like a simple Roman citizen. Polemon I of Pontus, descendant of the rhetor Zeno of Laodicea, called himself Marcus Antonius Polemo. We could find many more examples among the princes of Galatia, Emesa, Cappadocia, and elsewhere. This dual status created supplementary bonds.

Why not proceed to annexation pure and simple? The reasons doubtless varied from state to state, but generally speaking we may suppose that the regions Rome left in the hands of client princes were the remote and often relatively unpopulated ones—in short, all those that turned out to be neither very Hellenized nor very urbanized. Examples from more or less everywhere prove the rule. Other causes could be added, such as Jewish particularism in Judaea, but the underlying reason always lay in the absence, or the small number, of Greek city-states, those essential cogs in the wheels of the Roman administration.

Apart from the customary tasks of administration—defense of the territory, tax collection—the client princes were very often founders of city-states. We owe them, for example, all the Caesareas—Caesarea by the Sea (Herod), Caesarea of Cappadocia (Archelaos), Caesarea-Arca of Lebanon (Sohaemos), Caesarea of Panias (Herod Philip), but also many other civic foundations, especially in Cilicia. These men, chosen because they were at once natives of the country and Greeks—that is, Greek by culture—proved at least for a time to be valuable auxiliaries of Roman power.

But only for a time, for administration via client intermediaries was not always easy. First, because it deprived Rome of the revenues that went to feed the royal treasury. Every annexation resulted in possession of the royal treasury, which was no small matter. Thus when he decided to annex the client kingdom of Cappadocia, Tiberius could forgive half of the 1 percent tax that was imposed, in Rome, on certain transactions. But most crucially, the client princes were not all up to their tasks. For every Herod, an energetic and highly talented king, there were countless weak ones, incapable of maintaining order. From Augustus's reign on, then, the policy of annexing client states was implemented with increasing frequency.

There is no way to establish a complete and accurate chronology today, but the major phases are well known: Galatia as of 25 B.C.E., Judaea of Archelaos in 6 C.E., Cappadocia in 17, Pontus in 33 (though, as we have seen, it was given back to Polemon II in 38–39), Thrace in 46, Commagene several times between Tiberius and Claudius, then definitively in 68, Emesa in 70–72. The most complex situation concerned the Herodian states that were repeatedly modified, annexed, and restored to dynastic control before their definitive annexation under Agrippa II, although even this took place in stages, between 92 (or 88) and 100. With the annexation of the Nabatean kingdom in 106, upon the death of King Rabbel II, Rome put an end, west of the Euphrates, to a system that had allowed flexible management for more than a century and a half, thanks to the members of the elites whose task had been to prepare for the direct administration of a world that was increasingly Hellenized from then on.

CHAPTER THIRTY-FIVE

Pagan Martyrs in Alexandria, or Greeks and Jews in Alexandria in the First Century C.E.

The city has five quarters named after the first letters of the alphabet, two of these are called Jewish because most of the Jews inhabit them, though in the rest there are not a few Jews scattered about. So then what did they do? From the four letters they ejected the Jews and drove them to herd in a very small part of one. The Jews were so numerous that they poured out over beaches, dunghills and tombs, robbed of all their belongings. Their enemies overran the houses now left empty and turned to pillaging them, distributing the contents like spoil of war, and as no one prevented them they broke open the workshops of the Jews . . .

Multitudes of others also were laid low and destroyed with manifold forms of maltreatment, put in practice to serve their bitter cruelty by those whom savagery had maddened and transformed into the nature of wild beasts; for any Jews who showed themselves anywhere, they stoned or knocked about with clubs, aiming their blows at first against the less vital parts for fear that a speedier death might give a speedier release from the consciousness of their anguish.

> Philo, *Against Flaccus,* trans. F. H. Colson (Loeb Classical
> Library, 1985), vol. 9, pp. 333–335, 339 (VIII, 55–56, 66)

ALEXANDRIA, 37 C.E. Emperor Tiberius had just died. His successor, Gaius, popularly known as Caligula, was a young man, both the great-grandson of Augustus through his mother Agrippa the Elder (daughter of Julia) and the great-grandson of Mark Antony through his father Germanicus, son of Antonia the Younger (Antonia Minor). Here was someone who might not displease Alexandria, given his association with the memory of Antony and the latter's tumultuous love affair with Cleopatra, an affair that also symbolized an earlier attempt to restore Egypt's grandeur. However, one man was afraid: Aulus Avillius Flaccus, the prefect of Egypt (that was the Roman governor's official title) appointed by Tiberius in 32. In the muted struggle that opposed Caligula to Tiberius's grandson, Gemellus, before Tiberius's death, Flaccus had chosen to side with Gemellus: what is more, his friend Macron, prefect of the Praetorium, who had been promised that he would replace Flaccus as prefect of Egypt, committed suicide even before taking up his position—the sign of certain disgrace. Flaccus lived in anguish at the prospect of being recalled to Rome and executed. Panic-stricken, he reached out to people who had been his worst enemies since the beginning of his administration.

Whereas Alexandria's Jewish community had never ceased to benefit from the benevolence of the emperors (and upon Caligula's advent it had not failed to vote a decree of congratulations, which Flaccus had "forgotten" to transmit!), the Greeks, in contrast, had offered silent resistance to the Roman presence. Three of the city-state's leading figures, Dionysius, Lampon, and Isidoros—his former adversaries—came to offer Flaccus their support with respect to Caligula. The offer was vague: on the pretext that the emperors had often showered Alexandria with gifts, the three accomplices promised to intervene with Caligula in favor of the prefect. But their undertaking had a price: in exchange for their good offices at Caesar's court, Flaccus would close his eyes to the elimination of the Alexandrian Jews, which they were planning, and would even contribute his support. The deal was concluded hastily, for time was short.

And the provocations and ill treatments began almost at once. The unexpected visit to Alexandria by King Agrippa I, a friend of Caligula's who had just turned over to him the kingdom of his grandfather, Herod the Great, gave rise to heinous scenes that Flaccus took care not to suppress. Tempers flared, and Greeks demanded that statues of the emperor be placed in the synagogues. Soon, given Flaccus's inaction, people began to attack the Jews' property, and then the Jews themselves, physically. This was the beginning of what in modern terms would have to be called a pogrom.

At least this is the way Philo of Alexandria, called upon to play an important role in the resolution of the crisis, reported events in two works devoted to the matter, *Against Flaccus (In Flaccum)* and *The Embassy to Gaius (Legatio ad Caium)*. Given the events that ensued, the impression remains that Philo's overall analysis was correct: on the one hand, there was a frightened prefect of Egypt to whom the fate of Alexandria's Jews was of little moment; on the other, there were prominent Alexandrians harboring ferocious hatred toward Jews who were prepared to stop at nothing to get rid of them. But why were these Alexandrian Greeks so intensely hostile to the city's Jews?

When it was founded by Alexander, the city was intended to take in Greek and Macedonian colonists, and perhaps to become a future capital of the new empire. But non-Greek populations began to settle there very early: Egyptians, of course, but also Syrians, Phoenicians, and Jews. Josephus even claims that Jews were among the city-state's first inhabitants during the reign of Ptolemy I. This has sometimes been seen as mere propaganda in support of Jewish claims, but Josephus may not be mistaken. Indeed, the entire tradition affirms that the Alexandrian Jewish community essentially constituted a *politeuma*: the term has several meanings, but it has been recently shown to designate, in the Hellenistic period, indigenous and ethnically homogeneous military units recruited by Hellenistic sovereigns (Chapter 27). It is thus probable that some of the Alexandrian Jews were indeed descendants of soldiers recruited, if not by Alexander, then at least by Ptolemy I at the end of the fourth century or the very beginning of the third. The long-standing presence of Jews in Alexandria, with the Lagids' consent, is thus beyond doubt. This community expanded as the city grew, and given that Alexandria became one of the principal Mediterranean ports starting in the third century, it would be astonishing if new immigrants had not come to settle there. Not that the Jews were particularly oriented toward trade and exchange at the time; on the contrary, they were mostly rural types, or soldiers (another politeuma of Jewish soldiers is attested at Heracleopolis around 144–132), but inasmuch as Judaea was under Lagid domination until around 200–198, some Jews must have had dealings with the central government and must have frequented Alexandria. The Tobiads (Chapter 23) maintained a warehouse in Alexandria and kept some of their property there. In addition, rapid population growth in Judaea led more and more Jews to become expatriates and seek land or work elsewhere. Some went no farther than Galilee or southern Syria, but others reached the great Greek cities, Antioch or Alexandria.

The Jewish community of Alexandria—which was only one segment of the Jewish community in Egypt, for there were many Jews on the Egyptian flatlands—maintained fairly good relations with the Lagids. Josephus features a single tragic episode in *Against Apion*: Ptolemy VIII, nicknamed Physcon (the Bloated), is said to have exposed the Alexandrian Jews, naked and in chains, to drunken elephants in the city stadium so they would be trampled.[1] In fact, according to Josephus, this was actually in revenge for the support the Jews had given his sister and rival Cleopatra II, one of whose chief counselors, Onias, was a Jew. But despite the fact that the episode is marred by legendary elements (the elephants turned against Ptolemy's friends), we can retain its exceptional character, and we ought to note that there were high-ranking Jews in the Lagid regime. Some reached that position at the price of abandoning their religion, as was the case, for example, with Dositheos, a Jew who became chief archivist under Ptolemy III and, in 223, the high priest of Alexander and the Lagid dynasty. But others no doubt maintained their fidelity to Judaism, like the Onias mentioned above. Similarly, in 103–102, queen mother Cleopatra III was dissuaded by her Jewish counselor Ananias from launching an attack on Judaea.

But most of the Jews in Egypt, apart from the farmers, were artisans or shopkeepers. There was also a Jewish intellectual milieu, perfectly integrated with Greek culture. Thus when Ptolemy I decided to have Jewish law translated into Greek so as to have a copy that would be useful for the Jews' proper governance, he must have found the necessary translators in Alexandria without difficulty. The lovely story of the seventy or seventy-two Jewish sages, as knowledgeable in Greek as in Hebrew, sent by Ptolemy II to the high priest of Jerusalem has all the elements of a novel; what it underlines for us is that there was nothing implausible about finding a large number of Jewish scholars who knew Greek perfectly. In any case, after the books of the Pentateuch were translated (these were the only ones of interest to the royal authorities because they constituted the Jews' national law), the enterprise continued and led to the complete translation of the Bible into Greek, the Septuagint. But alongside those who produced the Septuagint, other Jewish authors who were Greek by language and culture worked in Alexandria, among them the dramatist Ezechiel the tragedian (*Exagogue* or *The Exodus*), the historians Aristobulos (author of an *Exegesis of the Law of Moses,* around 150–125) and Artapanos (*Response to Manethon,* around 100), or, around 150, the author of the book improperly called *Letter from Aristeas to Philocrates,* a fictionalized account of the translation of the Septuagint. Thus, despite the confirmed anti-Judaism of one Egyptian author, Manethon (who wrote a history of Egypt intended for the Greeks in which he charged the Jews with responsibility for all evils), in Lagid Egypt and especially in Alexandria the Jews experienced three centuries of tranquility.

After Rome conquered Egypt, in 30 b.c.e., the Jews' situation worsened in some respects. The Romans had established differing legal statuses for the inhabitants of Egypt, depending on their origin. Roman citizens constituted a separate category, but during the period that interests us, there were hardly any who had been born in Egypt—Greeks or natives—with the probable exception of some relatives of Philo of Alexandria: his nephew, Tiberius Iulius Alexander, a renegade Jew, became part of the Roman government and even served as procurator of Judaea before becoming prefect of Egypt. The Greeks—that is, the inhabitants of the Greek city-states in Egypt (Alexandria, Naucratis, and Ptolemais)—were at a lower level. They were exempt from certain taxes and paid a reduced head tax *(capitatio).* All others were lumped together with the natives and subjected to the maximum head tax. For the Jews of Alexandria, most of whom were not citizens, being identified with the Egyptians entailed a considerable lowering of status. They tried to take advantage of the confusion that prevailed during the early period of the Roman occupation to make unprecedented requests, essentially by playing with words. They sought support initially from the tradition passed down by Josephus according to which they had been present in Alexandria since its very foundation; this could have implied that they were among the colonists, thus among the founders. In addition, because many of them belonged to the politeuma, they could lay claim to the title *polites,* "citizen": although the military function of the city's Jewish politeuma had disappeared after Alexandria's annexation by Rome, or perhaps even earlier, the term *politeuma* sometimes also designated the civic body of a new city-state (Chapter 26). Finally, as inhabitants of Alexandria, the Jews could also lay claim to the *ethnikos* Alexandreus, or "Alexandrian." By combining these diverse data, they probably tried to convince the new authorities that they had always been citizens of Alexandria, and that they had only recently been deprived of the title. They thus demanded that their ancestral rights be recognized, leaving the nature of these rights somewhat vague.

The Greeks of Alexandria obviously did not see things the same way, and they watched uneasily as the Roman authorities attended to the Jews' claims. If the Jews obtained Alexandrian citizenship from the Romans (which some had indeed obtained over time, but in very small numbers), the number of citizens would turn out to be greatly increased, and this would aggravate the problems pertaining to the food supply, by diminishing the size of individual shares during distributions of free wheat or oil, for example. In view of the risk that the Jewish demands might be met, the leaders of the *polis* made the first move, and once Avillius Flaccus had been neutralized, they threw themselves into the macabre enterprise described by Philo.

The violence went on for weeks and months. To be sure, Philo's account is not that of a neutral observer, but a letter from Emperor Claudius, who put an end to the conflict, confirms the scope of the destructions. The synagogues were burned, looted, and desecrated; personal possessions and sacred books were plundered; individuals were murdered; nothing was spared. The Jews, who had lived dispersed throughout the city—even if they were more numerous in the Delta quarter—were forced to regroup in the Delta quarter alone. It became a sort of ghetto, and sometimes a veritable death camp: "After driving all these many myriads of men, women, and children like herds of cattle out of the whole city into a very small portion as into a pen, they expected in a few days to find heaps of dead massed together, perished either by famine through lack of necessaries . . . or else through overcrowding and stifling heat."[2] As for those who escaped,

> They experienced manifold misfortunes, being stoned or wounded by tiles or branches of ilex or oak in the most vital parts of the body and particularly in the head, the fracture of which proved fatal . . . Most pitiable was the fate of those who were burnt to death in the middle of the city. For sometimes through lack of proper wood they collected brushwood and after setting it on fire threw it upon the unhappy victims, who perished half burnt more through the smoke than by the fire. For brushwood produces a feeble and smoky flame which is at once extinguished since its slightness prevents it from burning steadily like coal. Many too, while still alive, they tied with thongs and nooses and, binding fast their ankles, dragged them through the middle of the market, leaping on them

and not even sparing their dead bodies. For, more brutal and savage than fierce wild beasts, they severed them limb from limb and piece from piece and trampling on them destroyed every lineament, so that not even the least remnant was left which could have received burial.[3]

The Jews could hardly count on the solicitude of Caligula, who was at the same moment attempting to impose a statue of himself at the very heart of the Temple in Jerusalem. As Philo writes, "they were emboldened by having no fear of the vengeance of Gaius. They knew well that he had an indescribable hatred of the Jews, and so they surmised that nothing anyone could do would gratify him more than the infliction on the nation of every kind of ill-treatment."[4] Moreover, in certain synagogues, the aggressors attacked evidence of the Jews' loyalty to the emperor by destroying steles and inscriptions in his honor. In one synagogue they went so far as to use a dilapidated quadriga (a two-wheeled chariot drawn by four horses) as part of a dedication to Gaius:

They fetched a very old one out of the gymnasium, a mass of rust with the ears, tails, feet and many other parts mutilated, and, as some say, dedicated to the honour of a woman, the original Cleopatra, great-grandmother of the last queen of that name. What a serious charge this in itself entailed upon the dedicators is obvious to everyone. What does it matter if it was the new chariot of a woman? What if it was an old chariot of a man? As long as the general fact remains that it was dedicated to someone else? Might not the authors of an offering of this kind in honour of the emperor reasonably feel alarm lest some information should be laid before one who always particularly insisted on his personal gratification? No doubt they had extravagant hopes of getting praise and reaping greater and more splendid benefits for turning our meeting-houses into new and additional precincts consecrated to him, though their motive was not to honour him but to take their fill in every way of the miseries of our nation.[5]

All these troubles did not serve Flaccus's cause well. It may have come to Caligula's attention that Flaccus had failed to transmit the decree of congratulations and joyous advent sent by the Jews. In any case, Caligula's hatred for the man who had supported Gemellus had not diminished, and in 38 he had Flaccus arrested, condemned, and exiled to Andros, where he was assassinated soon afterward by order of the emperor; he was pierced through and through by so many blade-strokes that his body was tossed to the ground in pieces. And Philo concluded that this was "an indubitable proof that the help which God can give was not withdrawn from the nation of the Jews."[6]

A new prefect of Egypt, C. Vitrasius Pollio, had been appointed and had restored order. Nevertheless, two embassies left for Rome: one, consisting of Greeks, was sent to justify the violence and represent the Jews as responsible for the troubles; the other, made up of Jews and led by Philo himself, was sent to request recognition of the Jews' ancestral rights.

The Jewish ambassadors, who left in the winter of 39–40, had to wait a long time to no avail, as Caligula was off on a campaign in Germany. When he returned, he did agree to receive them, but—probably owing to machinations by the Greek ambassadors—he did not take the defense presented by the Jews very seriously, and he dismissed them without giving a clear answer to the questions from either side. After his assassination, on January 24, 41, he was replaced by Claudius, who put off his response, consulted the archives and his advisors, and finally sent a letter indicating, between the lines, what the demands of the two parties were. We have two copies of this crucial text: the version transmitted by Josephus, and the authentic text of the letter, translated into Greek on a papyrus preserved in London, a copy probably intended for some functionary. While these copies are of unequal value, both are of great interest.

The comparison between Josephus's version—which retained only what concerned the Jews—and the original is extremely instructive. Citing Claudius's letter, Josephus asserts that the Jews of Alexandria, residents in the city alongside the Greeks from the very origins of the city-state, enjoyed privileges equal to those of the Greeks through the favor of the Lagid kings; he affirms in addition that these privileges had been confirmed by Augustus and by the successive prefects who had been sent to govern Egypt; consequently, Claudius ordered that the Jews were to regain the rights and privileges they had had before Caligula's reign, and that they should continue to enjoy the right to respect their own customs. Now, the official text of Claudius's letter does not say this, and gives only limited space to Jewish affairs. In fact, Claudius's letter reads like a response to the embassy from the city-state alone, that is, to the embassy of the Alexandrian Greeks. It begins by thanking them for the divine honors granted the new emperor, but Claudius, unlike Caligula, does not want too much to be done in this area, and he refuses the installation of a high priest and a temple that would be dedicated to him. He confirms the advantages already acquired by the Greeks, but leaves for further study the possibility of creating a boule in Alexandria, an old demand of Alexandrians who were trying to make a convincing claim that there had been one in the Lagids' era.

Finally turning his attention to the recent troubles, the emperor shows himself to be extremely severe toward those responsible (which confirms Josephus's version), and warns them to put an end to the violence: "I merely say that, unless you stop this destructive and obstinate mutual enmity, I shall be forced to show what a benevolent emperor can be when he is turned to righteous indignation."[7] And he goes on, along the lines Josephus indicated: "I conjure the Alexandrians to behave gently and kindly towards the Jews who have inhabited the same city for many years, and not to dishonour any of their customs in their worship of their god, but to allow them to keep their own ways, as they did in the time of the god Augustus and as I too, having heard both sides, have confirmed."[8] This may have confirmed the Jews' privilege to respect their Law, but it by no means amounted to granting their claims; quite the contrary. In a paragraph addressed to the Alexandrian Jews, Claudius hammers out his orders:

> The Jews, on the other hand, I order not to aim at more than they have previously had and not in future to send two embassies as if they lived in two cities, a thing which has never been done before, and not to intrude themselves into the games presided over by the *gymnasiarchoi* and the *kosmetai,* since they enjoy what is their own, and in a city which is not their own they possess an abundance of all good things.[9] Nor are they to bring in or invite Jews coming from Syria or Egypt, or I shall be forced to conceive graver suspicions. If they disobey, I shall proceed against them in every way as fomenting a common plague for the whole world.[10]

Thus, for Claudius, the case is closed: the Jews already enjoy sufficient rights in Alexandria, including the right to organize their own affairs; they have no business asking for other rights, in "a city that is not their own." This is markedly different from what Josephus asserts, for without explicitly contradicting Claudius, Josephus plays on words and implies that the Alexandrian Jews enjoy the same rights as the Greeks, that is, the rights of citizenship.

For Claudius and the Roman administration, the crisis was resolved.

The guilty parties remained to be punished, and this helped feed an anti-Roman propaganda in which the administration seemed to have sold out to the Jews while the most eminent personalities of Alexandria were taken off to be tortured. In fact, texts known under the title *Acts of the Pagan Martyrs* preserve the memory of trials of Jewish leaders conducted before the emperor. One of these dramatizes the suit brought by Isidoros, the gymnasiarch of Alexandria and an accomplice of Flaccus against King Agrippa, before Claudius, in an unmistakable echo of the farces of 37. And Isidoros seems not to have escaped torture.

But the history of the Egyptian Jews does not end here; it was to undergo further ups and downs. First, Alexandria, like many other city-states of the eastern Mediterranean and like Rome itself, took in a certain number of survivors of the great revolt in Judaea after the destruction of the Temple in 70. The Alexandrian Jewish community did not budge during the war, which is not surprising: the causes of the revolt were specific to Judaea and in certain respects must have appeared strange to the Alexandrian Jews, who were Hellenized and accustomed to living among pagans. In contrast, in 116–117, a Jewish revolt broke out in Alexandria for reasons that remain unclear; it spread to Egypt, Cyrene, and Cyprus, and was repressed with unprecedented savagery by the Roman army. The effects were disastrous for the Jews from the flatlands. Thanks to the preservation of receipts for payment of the didrachma tax, a tax intended for the upkeep of the temple of Jupiter Capitolinus and paid by Jews alone in the wake of the destruction of the Jerusalem Temple, we observe that whole communities disappeared, either because they had been entirely massacred or because they had fled the villages and blended into urban populations, especially in Alexandria. Thus at Karanis (Fayyum), whereas about a thousand Jews paid the didrachma tax before the revolt, after 115 only one remained! At Apollinopolis Magna (Edfu) in Upper Egypt, not a single receipt for the didrachma tax from after 115 has been found. From that point on, only Alexandria harbored a Jewish community, reduced in size from what it had been, and the city no longer stood as the metropolis of Jews from the Diaspora, that second Jerusalem where the Hellenistic Judeo-Grecian culture had been forged.

CHAPTER THIRTY-SIX

"Let Them Be Free," or Nero
and Greek Freedom

Emperor Caesar proclaimed: "Whereas I wish to reward very noble Greece for her devotion and piety toward myself, I order that as many people as possible from this province gather in Corinth on the fourth day before the calends of December [November 28]."

When crowds had gathered, he made the following speech:

"Greeks, I grant you an unexpected gift (even though one can expect everything of my generosity), a gift such that you would be incapable of asking for it. You all, Greeks, who live in Achaea and what was until now the Peloponnesus, receive freedom and exemption from taxes, something you have never had even in your periods of greatest prosperity, for you were slaves either of foreigners or of one another. I would have liked to make this gift at the time when Greece was at its apogee so that more people could have profited from my beneficence. For this reason, I maintain that time is to blame for reducing the scope of my beneficence. But, such as it is, I grant my benevolence to you not by the effect of my pity but by that of my will, and I reward your gods from whose constant care on land and sea I have benefited, for they have made it possible for me to grant you such benefits. For other princes have granted liberty to city-states, but only Nero has done so for an entire province."

The high priest of the Augusti, for life, and of Nero Claudius Caesar Augustus, Epaminondas son of Epaminondas, proclaims (having first submitted it to the Council and to the people for their opinion):

"Whereas the master of the whole world, Nero, great pontiff, invested with the power of the tribunes for the thirteenth time, Father of the Fatherland, New Helios who shines on the Greeks, has decided to grant his benevolence to Greece and has rewarded and manifested his piety toward our gods, who have been maintained everywhere thanks to his zeal and the security he procures; whereas he, Nero Zeus Liberator, the unique and only great emperor of our time, friend of the Greeks, has granted the eternal native ancestral liberty that had earlier been taken from the Greeks, given that he has manifested that favor (with which he is gratifying us), that he has restored the autonomy and freedom of yesteryear, and that to this immense and unexpected gift he has added the exemption from taxes, wholly and completely, something that none of the previous Augusti had done;

"For all these reasons, it has pleased the magistrates, the councilors, and the people to establish a cult dedicated to him on the existing altar of Zeus Savior and to inscribe there: "To Zeus Liberator Nero forever," and to erect statues of Nero Zeus Liberator and of the goddess Augusta Messalina in the sanctuary of Apollo Ptoios, which he will share with our ancestral gods, so that, after this has been accomplished, it shall be manifest that our city-state has poured every honor and every manifestation of piety onto the house of our master Augustus Nero. It has also been decided to inscribe the decree on a column erected alongside Zeus Savior on the agora and in the temple of Apollo Ptoios."

Inscription, in Maurice Holleaux, Études d'épigraphie et d'histoire grecques, vol. 1 (Paris: E. de Boccard, 1938), pp. 165–185

ACRAEPHIA, BOEOTIA, LATE 67 B.C.E. We are already familiar with this small city-state on the banks of Lake Copais, where a generous benefactor, Epaminondas, son of Epaminondas, sponsored the restoration of the city-state and of the Boeotian federal sanctuary of Apollo Ptoios (Chapter 33). The very same man reappears here, later on, in a precisely dated inscription: the speech was given on November 28, 67 (the era of Nero's thirteenth year of tribunical power), and the decree of thanks adopted on Epaminondas's initiative must have followed shortly afterward, probably less than a month later. But the matter at issue has nothing to do with Acraephia in particular, or rather it concerns the entire province of Achaea. Similar texts may have existed elsewhere, but it is no accident that only the one from Acraephia has survived: we saw earlier how hard Epaminondas worked to develop the imperial cult in his city-state, creating new athletic contests dedicated to the emperor, and associating them with the musical contest that was celebrated at Ptoion. Now, the object of our text is precisely to create a new cult in the city-state, that of Nero Zeus Liberator.

We shall not look closely at this aspect of the text, which is relatively banal even though the cultic epithets attributed to the new god are not. We recall how the Greeks of Asia were the first to divinize Alexander, and how all the Greeks later did the same for the sovereigns who succeeded him. The Roman emperors were simply the beneficiaries of a Greek tradition that the earliest emperors accepted only with reticence. Augustus had even forbidden Roman citizens to participate in his cult in Pergamon, and he had had a cult of the divine Julius (Caesar), his adoptive father, established for their use in Ephesus. Claudius, too, showed a good deal of hesitation in this regard. In contrast, Caligula and Nero seized the opportunity offered them to be ranked among the gods. To be sure, they restrained themselves somewhat in Rome proper, but they allowed the Greeks to multiply gestures of deference and divinization: Caligula did not hesitate to demand honors of the divine type even from the Jews, who could not grant them. The excerpt from Nero's speech cited at the beginning of the Acraephia decree shows to what extent the emperor adapted his language to his divine nature. He, the god, is thanking the other gods for having allowed him to live long enough to be able to shower his benefactions on Greece. To be sure, unlike the Olympian gods, this one is inscribed within time: he is sorry to have come too late to a world undergoing decline and depopulation. This limits the extent of his benevolence, as fewer Greeks will profit from it. But Nero's divinity is not subject to doubt by anyone.

The decree adopted at Epaminondas's initiative inscribes the specific cult of Nero in the religious life of his small city-state. The initial formula of the decree itself is quite unusual, in that it takes the form of a proclamation by the high priest of the imperial cult, a proclamation whose text had first been submitted to the council and the people for their opinion. Epaminondas was determined to personalize a measure that had certainly been adopted at his initiative and that he had surely financed. His designation as high priest stresses once again the ascendancy he exercised over his fellow citizens. Earlier (Chapter 30), we examined the case of benefactors whose power grew to such an extent that they were accused of tyranny.

Epaminondas is perhaps not far from this point; at the very least, he is omnipresent.

After the motives—to which we shall return—have been stated, the measures taken are listed; they turn out to be fairly ordinary, and relatively modest. It is not a matter of giving Nero's name to a civic tribe or to a month of the calendar, or of erecting a temple to him or creating contests in his honor, all possibilities that are well attested for others (Tiberius in Gytheium in Laconia, Claudius in Alexandria). It is enough to devote a cult to him, probably through offerings, on the altar of Zeus Savior, and to inscribe there the name of the new god, Zeus Liberator Nero. This name must have had particular resonance to Boeotian ears, because Zeus Liberator was honored in Plataea to commemorate the victory over the Persians in 479 B.C.E. The next step was to have a statue of the new god erected, along with one of Messalina, goddess Augusta Messalina, thus associating the imperial couple in the same cult, alongside the ancestral gods, within the sanctuary of Apollo Ptoios, where the text of the decree would be displayed.

Much more interesting are the "whereas" clauses of the decree, which plunge us into the heart of a rather fantastic episode in Nero's brief career. We know of Nero's fascination with Greek culture and his ambition to appear as an artist himself. After postponing the journey several times, he ended up traveling to Greece in the fall of 66, and he stayed there over a year. He was the first reigning emperor to visit Greece since Augustus, and, like any imperial voyage, his was at once an honor and a burden for the provincials. It might be an opportunity for them to extract some privileges and advantages, if Nero were satisfied with his welcome. But it was also a burden, for the emperor and his large escort lived at the expense of the locals, requiring board and lodging. The Greeks had many reasons for concern, in reality, for Nero had already had statues and treasures seized from prestigious sanctuaries in Greece, in particular after the great fire in Rome in 64: Athens, Delphi, Olympia, Pergamon, and Thespiae had all had to suffer such looting. Might the emperor's visit provide the occasion to get the stolen goods back?

Nero's trip exceeded all imaginable extravagance. Considering himself to be the greatest of artists, he planned to perform in all the major contests of the *periodos* (Chapter 32). Alas, the calendar had been established long since, and these contests did not take place at the same time, not even in the same year. No matter! Nero had the calendar modified and compelled the Greeks to organize all the competitions within a period of just a few months—including those of the Isthmus, which had been celebrated the previous year and which were to begin again. In Olympia, where there had been only athletic contests, he had a musical component introduced, so he could participate. And, competing as a cithara singer, he won the prize every time! But he had many other talents: he also competed as chariot driver (and even when he fell out of his chariot and had to give up the race, he was still declared the winner); because he announced the results himself, he also won the heraldry contest everywhere. Moreover, the city-states where he was to appear sometimes sent an embassy to give him his prize even before the contest took place. That did not prevent him from manifesting his anxiety, his stage fright, his fear of not being good enough. The public—enthusiastic, needless to say—was obliged to remain in place for hours on end, for it was forbidden to leave the theater, even for urgent causes (women were seen giving birth on the spot). Truly, *qualis artifex!*[1]

Greece came out humiliated by this visit—violated, in a way, despite the gifts and offerings left in the sanctuaries. However, even an ill wind may blow some good. During the Isthmia contests, celebrated in the sanctuary of the Isthmus of Corinth in November, Nero summoned the representatives of all the city-states to meet on the 28th. Before the assembled Greeks, he made an astonishing speech whose inscription in Acraephia unquestionably preserves an authentic citation: he liberated the Greeks of the province of Achaea from Roman control. They became free and exempt from paying tribute. This measure, confirmed by two ancient authors (Suetonius, *Nero*, 24; Plutarch, *Life of Flamininus*, 12–13), has sometimes been viewed as a decision with no real impact. I believe this view is mistaken: the beneficiaries understood the scope of the benefit at once, and this was indeed what justified the institution of a cult of Nero and Messalina in Acraephia.

In the same way that Rome annexed territories, it had the right to liberate them from its own control. After all, in 38, when Caligula returned the Pontus region, annexed in 33, to Polemon II, he cut off part of the empire. We can say the same thing about Judaea, entrusted to Herod and then to Archelaos, then annexed, then returned to Agrippa I, then annexed once again. It might be objected that these were client states, not city-states. But the problem is virtually the same. Moreover, Nero recalled in his speech in

Corinth that before him many Romans had granted liberty and immunity to city-states. In fact, throughout the republican era, Rome granted liberty to city-states in Asia Minor. To take just one example, already mentioned above (Chapter 31), the city-states that refused to carry out Mithridates' orders to kill all Romans received important privileges—liberty and immunity—from Sulla.

Liberty, for a city-state, meant that it was no longer part of the province, that it no longer figured on the *formula provinciae,* the list of communities that made up a given province. In an exchange of letters with Emperor Hadrian, the city-state of Aphrodisias in Caria recalls this self-evident fact: a free city-state since Augustus's reign, it was not subject to any of the levies that could be required by the province, and the governor had no right to intervene in its internal affairs. Pliny the Younger, the proconsul in Bithynia during Trajan's reign, around 110–113, made the same observation on the subject of the free city-states that were geographically located in his province: whatever financial difficulties they might have, he could intervene only if they requested him explicitly to do so.

Nero was thus right to stress the scope of the benefit he was according. Proclaiming the liberty of the Greeks of Achaea and the Peloponnesus amounted purely and simply to eliminating the province of Achaea. This was a reality, for we know of no proconsul of Achaea between 67 and the beginning of Vespasian's reign. That fact could be a matter of chance, for the lists of provincial governors are not complete. But we have a fairly good list of the proconsuls of Achaea, and in the absence of proof to the contrary, this gap corroborates the implementation of Nero's decision.

Nero's liberality did not touch all Greeks, only those of the province of Achaea—that is, those of the old lands of central Greece and the Peloponnesus, to the exclusion of Thessaly, which had been reattached to the province of Macedonia, and some islands belonging once again to Asia. All in all, the number of people involved was not large, but the most prestigious city-states were included: Athens, Sparta, Corinth, Thebes, the Panhellenic sanctuaries of Olympia and Delphi, the crucial sites of Greek history, the Thermopylae, Marathon, Salamis, and Plataea. Nero's gesture could be understood as the homage of the victor to the past grandeur of the vanquished.

In this, Nero's attitude was fairly representative of that of many Romans with respect to the Greeks. He sincerely admired their history, their culture, and their arts. As early as the second century B.C.E., Hellenism had found its way to Rome and had penetrated the governing Roman circles, despite the anger of some conservatives who were attached to the ancestral ways *(mos maiorum)*. Rhetors and artists succeeded one another in Rome, and in the first century no young Roman aristocrat could consider his education complete unless he had studied with a Greek master in Athens, Rhodes, or Ephesus. All the Roman *imperatores* of the late republic counted one or several Greek intellectuals in their entourage.

Nevertheless, scorn for the Greeks was expressed forcefully at the same time, if only in the expression that was often used to designate them: *Graeculi,* "little Greeks." Cicero painted more than one not very flattering portrait of them, although he took care to provide nuances and arguments. Thus in a letter to his brother Quintus he wrote: "Much caution is called for with respect to friendships which may arise with certain among the Greeks themselves . . . Nowadays a great many of these people are false, unreliable, and schooled in overcomplaisance by long servitude . . . one must be careful not to have special friends; I except a very small elite, if there are some who are worthy of ancient Greece. But, in fact, there are among them a host of shallow, treacherous men whom long servitude has fashioned for the excesses of flattery."[2] Which did not prevent him from recognizing what Rome owed Greece:

> We are governing a civilized race, in fact, the race from which civilization is believed to have passed to others, and assuredly we ought to give its benefits above all to those from whom we have received it . . . everything that I have attained I owe to those pursuits and disciplines which have been handed down to us in the literature and teachings of Greece. Therefore, we may well be thought to owe a special duty to this people, over and above our common obligation to mankind; schooled by their precepts, we must wish to exhibit what we have learned before the eyes of our instructors.[3]

This message to his brother, who had been named proconsul of Asia, no doubt better reflects the sentiments of the cultivated Roman elite than the violent anti-Greek diatribes the same Cicero developed in his court speeches, where he sought to undermine the credibility of the witness for the opposition (*Pro Flacco* offers a veritable anthology of such texts).

The feeling that Greece had declined was thus not a novelty in Nero's day, and his allusion to the time when Greece was at its apogee was only a commonplace. The idea had been perfectly internalized by the Greeks themselves, as we see in Plutarch's work, which is entirely turned toward the past. As for the immediate circumstances, we may wonder whether Nero's observation corresponded to any reality beyond the political circumstances. The numerous investigations conducted by historians and archaeologists into the occupation of the territory do not confirm the discourse of decline, which was connected with depopulation and the abandonment of rural areas. Many systematic land surveys have been carried out pretty much everywhere in Greece, and they all seem to indicate a fairly dense reoccupation of the territory in the imperial era. To be sure, the extensive surveys are tricky to use, because they give indications for broad chronological periods but do not allow us to follow the evolution a quarter century or even a half century at a time. Nevertheless, although some inhabited centers do seem to have been abandoned during the Hellenistic period, there was at least some stabilization after the return of the Pax Romana. Moreover, we cannot be content to list the number of occupied sites, for a new way of occupying the land may lead to regroupings without any decrease in population. For the time being, we have to acknowledge that the debate is not over, and many more studies on the ground will have to be carried out if we are to have a clearer image of the real situation.

But for Nero, as for his contemporaries, there was no doubt that Greece's apogee belonged to the past. A few decades later, in a well-known narrative, Dio of Prusa (Dio Chrysostom) described the large island of Euboea as abandoned, returned to the wild state. The story's hero survives by hunting and gathering and by acting as a shipwrecker. Herds graze on the agora of the neighboring city. Is this a moral tale, or a realistic tableau? It is hard to be sure, and Dio's description is not without contradictions. But it seems to me particularly revealing, for our purposes, to note the extent to which Romans and Greeks had accepted the idea that Balkan Greece had undergone an irreversible decline.

By the same token, Nero's gesture associated a symbolic measure with a modest loss for the imperial treasury, and the symbolic impact was reinforced by the fact that Nero had chosen to make his speech in the sanctuary of the Isthmus in memory of the one that Flamininus had made there in 196 B.C.E. After his victory over Macedonia in the battle of Cynoscephales (197), which brought all of Greece under his control, the Roman general in effect proclaimed the freedom of the Greeks while the latter were expecting to be reduced to the status of a province. Nero offered a new version of Flamininus's gesture, all the more dazzling in that, while Flamininus had simply chosen not to take control of the Greeks, Nero had control and chose to give it up. At little cost, for the tribute from Achaea must not have amounted to much. If we take into account the fact that some important cities were Roman colonies and exempt from tribute on that basis (Corinth, Patras), and that other city-states already enjoyed liberty owing to privileges granted earlier (Athens, Epidauros, Troezen, Nicopolis, Delphi, Sparta, Thespiae, and so on), in practice Nero's generosity came as a relief most particularly to obscure small city-states such as Acraephia.

If this proclamation by Nero has often been considered marginal, it is because its effects did not last very long. Nero was assassinated in June 68. The liberation of the Greeks may not have been called into question right away, for Nero's three immediate successors, Galba, Otho, and Vitellius, first had to secure control by force of arms. When Vespasian finally triumphed (proclaimed emperor in Syria in July 69, he entered Rome in late September 79), he hastened to annul the liberation of the Greeks. A new proconsul for Achaea had to be named, a clear sign that the province was being reconstituted. But the dream of liberty restored remained nonetheless as a beautiful memory. And one that lasted: Nero's memory continued to dazzle the Greeks to such an extent that false Neros were seen on several occasions, seeking to stir up the masses against Roman domination.

CHAPTER THIRTY-SEVEN

Eating Roots in Aspendos, or Grain Crises and Speculation in Asia Minor in the First Century

[Apollonius] once came to Aspendus in Pamphylia, a city situated on the river Eurymedon, and the third in importance of the province. Vetch was on sale, and people lived off anything that gave sustenance, as the upper classes were keeping the grain stored up to create a shortage in the territory. People of every age were infuriated with the chief magistrate, and had begun to light torches to burn him alive, even though he clung to the statues of the emperor. At that time these were more feared and sacrosanct than the Zeus at Olympia, since they represented Tiberius. (In his reign, they say, a man was convicted for treason simply for beating his own slave when the slave was carrying a silver drachma with Tiberius's image.) So Apollonius went to the magistrate and by means of a gesture asked him the matter. The man said he had done no wrong, but was being wronged together with the people, and if he could not get a hearing, he and they would perish together.

Turning to the bystanders, Apollonius nodded to them to listen, and out of reverence for him they not only fell silent, but also put their torches on the nearby altars. Recovering his courage, the magistrate said, "so-and-so and so-and-so" (naming several people) "are responsible for the present famine. They are holding back the grain and storing it in different parts of the territory." The Aspendians began to urge each other to go to these estates, but Apollonius shook his head to show that they should not do this, but instead summon the accused and recover the grain from them voluntarily. On their arrival, he could scarcely help breaking into speech against them, being rather moved by the tears of the people, for women and children had gathered, and the aged were groaning as if about to die of starvation on the spot. Yet he obeyed his vow of silence, writing his reproach on a writing tablet and giving it to the magistrate to read. This was his reproach: "Apollonius to the corn merchants of Aspendus. The earth in her justice is the mother of all, but you in your injustice have made her mother to yourselves alone. If you do not stop I will not even let you stand on the earth's face." Frightened by his words, they flooded the market with grain, and the city revived.

Philostratus, The Life of Apollonius of Tyana, in Philostratus,
ed. and trans. Christopher P. Jones (Loeb Classical Library,
2005), vol. 1, pp. 65–67 (I, 15)

ASPENDOS, PAMPHYLIA, on the southern coast of Anatolia, first century C.E., at the earliest during Tiberius's reign, but almost certainly somewhat later. The hero: Apollonios of Tyana. A strange personage who is attested in history but whose biography reads like a novel. He was born in Tyana, southern Cappadocia, in the first third of the first century C.E. After studying with the philosophers and rhetors in Tarsus and Aigai in Cilicia, he led a wandering life that brought him to Egypt, Babylon, and even India, where he met Brahmans. An ascetic Pythagorean philosopher, he enjoyed a visible moral ascendancy. Crisscrossing the Greek world, he endlessly denounced aspects of his compatriots' behavior that he found scandalous. He was annoyed to read Roman names among the lists of ephebes; he fled from a city where spectacles of "human massacre" (contests in the circus and the amphitheater) were held; in short, he accused the Greeks of lowering themselves before their Roman masters. The work Philostratus devoted to him at the beginning of the century is required reading for anyone interested in knowing more about this exceptional individual.

We pick up his story during his visit to Aspendos. This was an old Pamphylian city-state that had resisted Alexander but that had quickly taken on the appearance and institutions of a Greek city-state. Long under Lagid domination in the third century, it later became part of the Attalid kingdom thanks to Rome, before succumbing to the fate of that kingdom upon the death of Attalos III. When Apollonios of Tyana arrived in Aspendos, the city-state belonged to the province of Galatia, which had been created in 25 B.C.E. from the territory of the kingdom of Amyntas of Galatia and a few peripheral territories, including Pamphylia. Located at some distance from the sea, on the banks of the Eurymedon, a river made famous by the striking victory won near its mouth by the Athenian fleet over the Persians in 469 B.C.E., Aspendos shared a rich plain with three other substantial city-states, the ports of Side and Attaleia, and, further into the interior, Perge. Other small city-states were spread out along the coast in the direction of Cilicia. The ruins that remain in Aspendos give only a suggestion of what the city was like, for the monuments remain largely unexcavated. Only the theater attracts attention, its back to a hill: after the theater of Bostra in Syria, this one is the best preserved in the entire Roman world. The aqueducts that ran through the plain north of the city attest to the magistrates' efforts to ensure a water supply for the city, and, as in every sizable city, there must have been several public fountains and thermal baths. In short, though Aspendos was not a huge, sumptuous city like Ephesus, Pergamon, or Antioch, it was hardly an obscure little town. It was a prosperous, well-regarded, heavily populated city that had a vast and rich territory at its command.

And yet, when Apollonios arrived, the inhabitants had been reduced to eating vetch—a leguminous field plant normally reserved for livestock—and even more miserable fare! At least those who had the means to buy in the markets could eat something; many others were literally starving to death. A revolt was brewing, and the people, brandishing torches, were about to set fire to the magistrate charged with procuring supplies; he was presumably an *agoranomos* responsible for the market, or else a *sitones*, a magistrate specifically charged with making sure the grain supply was adequate, either by bringing affordable grain in from elsewhere or by preventing internal speculation. The situation was not unique to Aspendos. In a speech given at Prusa, where he was born, Dio Chrysostom referred to a popular uprising triggered by the lack of grain, an uprising during which the people had tried to burn down his house with his wife and children inside. In Aspendos, had the crowd succeeded it would have committed a great sacrilege (as well as a murder painful to the victim), for the magistrate in question had taken refuge as a suppliant among the divine statues, and this should have protected him from all harm. It was at this point that Apollonios came along, in time to prevent an irreparable act. He said nothing—for he had taken a vow of absolute silence—but he asked questions with his eyes and through signs (similarly, he made his response later on in writing).

The magistrate explained the situation: grain was lacking in the market because some major landowners or merchants were stockpiling it in order to sell it to outsiders at a better price. It was thus not a matter of natural scarcity, owing to a bad harvest or to a structural imbalance between supply and demand; the problem was rather the result of speculation on the part of well-known people: the magistrate was able to name them and indicate where they were keeping their grain. This shows that the crowd was not entirely wrong to judge him an accomplice of those who were starving the city-state: he knew them well and does not seem to have done much up to that point to make them put their grain on the market.

The Greek city-states suffered periodically from crises of this sort in the food supply. We know of similar cases not only in Prusa, mentioned above, but also in Ephesus, Samos (third century B.C.E.), Antioch of Pisidia (around 93 C.E.), Athens (second century C.E.), Tiberias, and elsewhere. And of course many crises left no literary or epigraphic traces. But the preoccupation with the grain supply was never-ending, for grain was the staple food, used in bread, fried cakes, or boiled dishes. We know that, during the classical period, Athens actively sought to make agreements with regions that had excess supplies, in Crimea, Sicily, or elsewhere. A famous speech by Lysias in the early fourth century B.C.E. vigorously denounced the grain merchants who were driving prices up. The city-state had taken steps to ensure a regular supply: every ship carrying grain that stopped in Athens, even if its cargo was intended for a different city-state, was required to sell a certain quantity in the local market; as for the Athenians, they were forbidden to sell grain to other city-states or even to lend money in order to engage in a grain trade that did not have Athens as its recipient. A lengthy decree issued in 347–346 B.C.E. in honor of the Greek princes of the Cimmerian Bosporus (Crimea) thanked the princes explicitly "because they promise[d] the people of Athens to take care of exporting grain as their father had." This father, Leukon, is mentioned by Demosthenes in a speech *(Against Leptines)* as someone who had greatly favored the Athenian grain merchants. A century earlier, the Athenian fleet had taken great care to keep open the route between the Black Sea through the Hellespont (Dardanelles) and the Bosporus, because this was the grain route (among others). When, in a time of difficulties (around 330–324), a merchant from Salamina of Cyprus, Heraclides, got grain for Athens at a low price, he received the considerable honor of a crown of gold and the right to acquire land and a house in Athens—privileges normally reserved for citizens.

As we see, a city-state as powerful as Athens mobilized all its resources, especially at the diplomatic level, to keep itself supplied. It is true that Athens also suffered from special difficulties, because its territory was relatively poor and it had allowed large-scale cultivation of olive trees to be developed to the detriment of grain (olives brought in more profit). The situation in the city-states of Asia Minor mentioned above may have been somewhat different.

The causes of the grain crises in fact seem to have varied from one city-state to another. Thus in Samos, in the third century B.C.E., the city-state suffered from the fact that the part of its territory that was located on the continent had been occupied by Seleucid troops, and King Antiochus had carved out large properties for his intimates. The city-state had thus lost a portion of its resources, for the mountainous terrain on the island itself was mainly given over to vineyards and olive groves. An embassy sent to Antioch returned with assurances that its continental territory would be restored to Samos.

Disastrous climatic conditions come up less often in the surviving texts as causal factors. However, we are told that a very harsh winter ruined the harvests in Antioch of Pisidia. The mountainous Pisidia region did suffer from very hard winters, although in this particular instance late frosts were probably responsible for killing the young shoots. And Antioch was presumably not the only city-state affected; its nearest neighbors must surely have been touched as well. Indeed, an allusion in John's Apocalypse to a general famine in Asia Minor has been related to the inscription from Antioch of Pisidia. Thus it was presumably not just Pisidia that suffered famine but the entire province, either directly through destruction of the harvests or indirectly owing to the impossibility of obtaining supplies from the usual sources. Nevertheless, the cause most often invoked in the texts remains speculation on the part of major producers and merchants. We see this in Athens as early as the fourth century; the same accusations were made in Aspendos in the first half of the first century and again in Prusa at the end of the century. This phenomenon thus warrants special attention.

Speculation is fed by scarcity. We must therefore look for the underlying causes that made scarcity possible at any time, even in periods of abundance. It seems to me that several factors may have come into play, although we cannot assess the weight of each one in the overall picture.

In the first place, grain was difficult to transport, not because it was perishable, but because it was a very heavy cargo in relation to its relatively weak mercantile value (even after speculation). This was especially true for land transportation, which was risky, slow, and limited to modest quantities, whether carts or pack animals were used. In hard times, then, one could not count on bringing in grain supplies from any distance by land. Only shipment by sea offered the advantage of relative rapidity and low cost. This meant that the city-states of Asia Minor had to get their supplies from Syria, Egypt, Sicily, or Africa, all well-known grain-growing regions. Now, ever since Roman rule had been instituted in those regions, the excess grain they produced was reserved for supplying Rome, through the system of the *annona*. It was only through an exceptional privilege granted by the emperor that Ephesus obtained the right to import grain from Egypt. There was thus, properly speaking, no Mediterranean market for grain, no possibility of completely free exchanges.

The result was an extreme fragmentation of the markets, and this was a supplementary encouragement to speculation: how could landowners or merchants resist the desire to stockpile grain and sell it outside the country when they knew that prices could double from one city-state to another? In his address to his fellow citizens in Prusa, Dio Chrysostom points out that they were revolting because in their city-state grain had reached a price that was the normal price elsewhere in periods of abundance. It is probable that even in "normal" periods, if the word "normal" has a meaning, the price of grain varied according to the time of year, that is, according to the time that had passed since harvest. Many city-states must have had trouble making ends meet. The splintering of the markets and the mediocre capacity for transport made it impossible to bring compensatory effects into play.

All of Asia Minor thus seems, even in the period of its greatest prosperity, to have been under the threat of locally insufficient harvests. This may be explained in part by flagrant over-urbanization. Although many city-dwellers were also landowners, and some were farmers, the percentage of people for whom food had to be provided was presumably quite large. It is very difficult to assess the proportion of rural dwellers in relation to city folk, but the strong development of the artisanate suggests that the number of people to be fed often exceeded local resources, at least for certain city-states endowed with small territories.

To this must be added the fact that landowners chose crops that were more profitable than grain. Dio, defending himself, exclaimed before the Prusans: "Have I produced the most grain of all and then put it under lock and key, raising the price? Why, you yourselves know the productive capacity of my farms—that I rarely, if ever, have sold grain, even when the harvest is unusually productive, and that in all these years I have not had even enough for my own needs, but that the income from my land is derived exclusively from wine and cattle."[1] Animal breeding and vineyards were thus more profitable in Bithynia than grain. In other regions, especially along the coasts, olive orchards covered considerable expanses of land.

On the subject of the embassy undertaken on behalf of the inhabitants of Asia by the rhetor Scopelianos of Clazomenae, Philostratus tells the following story:

> The Emperor resolved that there should be no vines in Asia, because it appeared that the people when under the influence of wine plotted revolution; those that had been already planted were to be pulled up, and they were to plant no more in future. There was clearly need of an embassy to represent the whole community, and of a man who in their defence, like another Orpheus or Thamyris, would charm his hearer. Accordingly they unanimously selected Scopelian, and on this mission he succeeded so far beyond their hopes that he returned bringing not only the permission to plant, but actually the threat of penalties for those who should neglect to do so.[2]

As is, the anecdote is incomprehensible, even ridiculous. Fortunately, a passage from Suetonius, in *Life of Domitian*, provides an explanation while indicating both the epoch and the underlying reasons for the measure: "Once upon the occasion of a plentiful wine crop, attended with a scarcity of grain, thinking that the fields were neglected through too much attention to the vineyards, he made an edict forbidding anyone to plant more vines in Italy and ordering that the vineyards in the provinces be cut down, or but half of them at most be left standing."[3] Pulling up the vines was thus not part of a policy directed against the ill effects of alcoholism that might lead to sedition, but it was intended to slow down the decrease in surface areas where grain was grown. Asia must have been particularly concerned, because it sent an embassy in the name of the entire province (the *koinon* was the assembly of the elite) in order to try to get the measure rescinded. Suetonius asserts that Domitian was not concerned with having his edict applied. This is possible, but we may doubt that he made grape-growing obligatory, as Philostratus claims.

The orientation toward speculative crops seems to have been inevitable after Alexander's conquest, for products indispensable to the Greeks, such as wine and olive oil, could not be produced (or could be produced only at a level of quality deemed inadequate) in many of the regions where Greek colonists or Hellenized natives were found. This was the case for Egypt, Mesopotamia, part of inland Anatolia, and the neighboring regions of the Caucasus, for example—and we are not even taking into account the fact that in all the provinces the existence of a wealthy class of Romans and Greeks increased the demand for products of good quality, or reputed to be good. This was true to such an extent that certain products became unavailable in the localities where they were produced. Thus Emperor Hadrian had to issue an edict to require oil producers in Athens to sell a third of their production locally; by exporting everything they no doubt realized large profits, but the city-state ended up lacking oil, and that was going too far!

All this probably helped facilitate speculation on grain, for production must have been just barely sufficient in normal times. Speculators had only to withdraw part of the stock from the market and wait for prices to rise, locally or in a neighboring city-state, to bring in big profits. The producers were not the only ones involved, moreover; certain merchants, and even private individuals, could do the same thing. Dio recalls that although he occasionally lent money, he refused to do so for the purchase of grain, unlike certain other lenders whose names were known to all: "Though I lend money, I am unwilling to supply it for the purchase of grain. There is no need for me to say anything on that score either, for you know both those who lend money in our city and those who borrow."[4]

So what was the solution? When the crisis was circumstantial, as in Antioch of Pisidia, the authorities tried to bring out all the reserves, and they fixed a top selling price that was attractive enough to get merchants to empty their granaries: the provincial governor himself decided that, because the price before the crisis had been eight or nine *as* a bushel, the maximum price would be set at one denier, or sixteen *as*. This doubling in price must have brought the reserves out of hiding. This is probably what happened most often, and speculation ended either because the selling price reached the level desired by the speculators or because a shipment of merchandise brought the price down and merchants had to sell quickly, before the prices collapsed altogether.

Apollonios used a different method: he gave the hoarders a moral lesson and frightened them by announcing immediate punishment by the gods. But this was Apollonios of Tyana, a wise man, not a provincial governor! And Philostratus wrote a biography that he sought to imbue with the piquancy of a novel.

CHAPTER THIRTY-EIGHT

"We, the Greeks of Danaba," or Banditry and Pacification in Syria in the Time of the Herodians

The Greeks living in Danaba, to Menophilos, because of his devotion.

Inscription, in *Inscriptions grecques et latines de la Syrie* (Paris: P. Geuthner, 1929–), vol. 15, ed. Annie Sartre-Fauriat and Maurice Sartre, forthcoming, no. 228

DHUNAIBE, PREFECTURE of Deraa, southern Syria. A small ancient village, built on a hillock overlooking the plain. An ordinary stone lies in the street, near a ruined house: a rough-hewn chunk of local basalt, a rather badly cut block. But on one face there is a Greek inscription, brief and immediately comprehensible: a group of Greeks is honoring one of its own, without giving a reason other than the devotion he has manifested toward them. This could entail practically any sort of generosity, and we need not dwell on the term "devotion," which appears with great frequency in honorific inscriptions.

This particular inscription would hardly warrant our interest, if it were not presented in an almost unprecedented form, and if it did not come from a rather unexpected place and time. For the phrase "the Greeks" is virtually never found. While the Greeks were in the habit of identifying themselves by their *ethnikos* (as Athenians, Ephesians, Alexandrians, Tyrians, and so on), the idea of designating themselves as "the Greeks" was totally foreign. Not that they were unaware of such concepts: they knew perfectly well how to contrast Greeks and barbarians! But it was highly unusual for a small group to designate itself this way. I am aware of only one other group that did so, the residents of Vologesias, in the Parthian empire. But they lived in a milieu in which Greeks were a very small minority, if not absent altogether. Even in Egypt, when the Greeks of the flatlands wanted to distinguish themselves from the indigenous Egyptians, they tended to use circumlocutions such as "the 6,075 of the Arsinoite," or "the people of the gymnasium," and not "the Greeks." So why does this uncommon usage turn up here? And what were Greeks doing in this lost corner of Syria?

The place, first of all. We are in what is called the Hauran today, an area Flavius Josephus knew by the same name, Auranitis. But the modern name covers more territory. Today's Hauran in fact includes the ancient Auranitis, Trachonitis, and Batanea. Properly speaking, the village of Dhunaibe, the one mentioned in the inscription as Danaba, was located in Batanea, but in immediate proximity to the Trachonitis region, the Trachon ("stony") plateau, today called Leja ("refuge"). Readers who know their Bible well may have made the connection between Batanea and the land of Bashan, the kingdom of Og. It is the same country, a rich well-watered plain located between the Mount Hermon massif and the Golan Heights to the west and the Trachon plateau to the east. The road from Damascus passes through here on the way to Jerusalem and points south, toward the Arabian Peninsula and its riches. The Trachon looks very different. Hardly higher than the surrounding plain, a few meters at most, it is the vestige of a recent lava flow that arose from two cones that are still standing at its southeast corner, above the little city of Shahba, the former Philippopolis, homeland of the emperor Philip the Arab. This flow, triangular in shape, with the tip pointing north and the base lying to the south, has remained largely intact. Throughout, the basalt forms either immense, almost smooth slabs or a chaotic muddle of crude blocks, making passage quite difficult. In some places, especially toward the south, rainwater has helped dissolve the lava, producing a rich soil. But these are like confetti spots on the vast plateau, and agriculture is possible only if there is water.

Danaba was near the southwest corner of the Trachon, in a position that was easy to defend, as it constituted an ideal observatory for surveying both the nearby plateau and traffic on the neighboring plain. Thanks to Strabo and Josephus, we are fairly well informed about what happened in this region toward the end of the first century B.C.E. and in the first century C.E. As their two accounts overlap, it will suffice to give just a few brief excerpts. Even though they do not mention the name Danaba, it will be clear that we are not straying from the text that has served as our point of departure.

What does Strabo say during the Augustan era? "[Above Damascus] are situated two Trachones, as they are called. And then, towards the parts inhabited promiscuously by Arabians and Ituraeans, are mountains hard to pass, in which there are deep-mouthed caves, one of which can admit as many as four thousand people in times of incursions, such as are made against the Damasceni from many places. For the most part, indeed, the barbarians have been robbing the merchants from Arabia Felix."[1] The Trachon—which Strabo imagined, inaccurately, as a double chain of hills—was thus only a brigands' hideout. Josephus says essentially the same thing, giving more details: "A certain Zenodorus . . . not being satisfied with [his] revenues . . . increased his income by using robber bands in Trachonitis. For the inhabitants of that region led desperate lives and pillaged the property of the Damascenes, and Zenodorus did not stop them but himself shared in their gains."[2] In fact, Zenodorus had been put at the head of the country by Augustus as a client prince (Chapter 34), to combat the bandits. But Josephus acknowledges that the task was a difficult one:

> For it was really not easy to restrain people who had made brigandage a habit and had no other means of making a living, since they had neither city nor field of their own but only underground shelters and caves, where they lived together with their cattle. They had also managed to collect supplies of water and of food beforehand, and so they were able to hold out for a very long time in their hidden retreat. Moreover, the entrances (to their caves) were narrow, and only one person at a time could enter, while the interiors were incredibly large and constructed to provide plenty of room, and the ground above their dwellings was not high but almost level with the (surrounding) surface. The whole place consisted of rocks that were rugged and difficult of access unless one used a path with a guide leading the way, for not even these paths were straight, but had many turns and windings.[3]

Despite the concordance of the two texts, a modern reader might be tempted to see the description of the Trachon and its immense caverns as fanciful. But that would be a mistake, for anyone who has walked around in the region can attest to the description's accuracy. Thus in Ariqah, in the southern part of the plateau, near an abundant spring, there is a cavern formed by a rise in the basalt crust, a bubble, as it were. One enters through a minuscule passage, crouching down, but once inside the door installed by a restaurant owner with a good business sense, one discovers a gigantic room, more than fifty meters wide and several hundred meters long. I was not able to follow it to the end, but village residents claim that it goes on for more than a kilometer. Strabo's mention of a cavern capable of sheltering more than four thousand men corresponds perfectly to the Ariqah grotto: the presence of the spring at the entrance made it possible to supply men and livestock with water in case of danger.

Many other elements in the descriptions by Strabo and Josephus are confirmed through observation of the landscape. For example, it is very hard to get around, for slabs of basalt rising in all directions cover almost the entire surface of the ground, while deep depressions shelter a few enclaves of tillable soil. Under these conditions, circulation on horseback is quite difficult, and no ordinary troops could have rushed out in pursuit of bandits once they had retreated into their shelters.

Such a situation was highly detrimental to the caravans that came up from Arabia toward Damascus and the Phoenician ports. The inhabitants complained to Varro, the governor of Syria, who informed Augustus. The latter thus dispossessed Zenodorus of what he had been given, and transferred the benefits to a man who had proven himself: Herod. This was around 20 B.C.E., probably a little earlier. Herod's mission was simple: contain the bandits on the Trachon, and wipe them out if he could.

Herod threw himself into the enterprise with zeal. Learning by chance that a troop of Babylonian Jews found itself with nothing to do in the suburbs of Antioch, he hired them and gave them tax-exempt lands in Batanea. The point was clearly to hold the bandits in check. Other soldiers, also Jews, had been recruited in Idumea—that is, in what we know as the Negev desert today—and had settled in the same region, three thousand strong. According to Josephus, the center of that military colonization was found in the village of Bathyra, probably the contemporary village of Basir, located in Batanea but near the Trachon border.

Herod's work was continued by his successors, and several inscriptions found in the region confirm the presence of Herodian troops at various points around the edges of the Trachon. In Sur al Laja, at a point where the Batanea plain shows a deep indentation running toward the heart of the Trachon, a garrison of foot soldiers and "colonist cavalry men" was placed, in the time of Agrippa II, under the command of an Arab officer, Herod son of Aumos (the name of Herod was given in homage to Herod the Great, but the patronymic unmistakably identifies an Arab from the region). Scholars have long wondered why the cavalry men were identified as "colonists," and several commentators have deduced that these men had been recruited from among the Roman colonists who had been sent to settle along the Phoenician coast by Augustus (Beirut) or Claudius (Ptolemais-Akko). This is an absurd hypothesis, for it is hard to see Roman citizens hired as mercenaries in the army of a client prince and placed under the command of an Arab officer! A still-unpublished inscription recently discovered in Sha'arah, a village on the edge of the Trachon, supplies the key to the puzzle. This inscription, the epitaph of a native soldier, dates from year 23 "of the colony"; we do not know the starting point of that particular era, but the unit to which the deceased had belonged was totally unknown in the Roman army and bore a typically local name. There is a good chance, then, that we are in the presence of a soldier in Herod's army. The mention of a "colony" is thus all the more interesting: the military outposts established by Herod and his successors to suppress the bandits must have been called colonies, at least some of them (those in which the colonist-soldiers were exempt from taxation?). It would not be the first time that client princes borrowed from Roman institutions as they had done earlier from the Hellenistic kingdoms. Our colonist-cavalry men from Sur were simply natives of a Herodian colony in the region, and this designation was a way of stressing their privileged status in relation to others.

Have we lost sight of the Greeks of Danaba? They seem to me suddenly to take their place in the landscape. The inscription is not dated, which prevents us from reaching an absolutely definitive conclusion. Still, the writing, which is rather crude and squared-off, is characteristic of the first century C.E. Above all, as I indicated at the beginning of this chapter, the mention of "the Greeks" is meaningful only if the group had to distinguish itself from other groups that were not Greek. Alongside the Babylonian Jews and the Idumeans, and perhaps others of whom we have not yet found any traces, these Greeks formed a homogeneous community, installed on a surveillance post by Herod or one of his successors. We know that Herod recruited Goths, Germans, and Thracians as mercenaries, and used them to maintain order in Judaea itself. He may well also have called upon Greeks—whether from Greece proper, Asia Minor, or Syria—and given them lands in Batanea; at least there is no evidence to the contrary. In this indigenous kingdom, surrounded by Aramean peasants (the Greeks would have called them "Syrians"), cohabiting with garrisons made up of Babylonian Jews, Idumeans, and Arabs, the Greeks had no way to distinguish themselves except by highlighting their only true originality: the fact that they were Greek. And their modest trace suddenly brings back a whole facet of the history of the region.

CHAPTER THIRTY-NINE

The Child in the Cauldron, or Indigenous Gods, Greek Gods in the Near East

For the health of Emperor, Trajan Augustus Germanicus Dacicus, son of Nerva Augustus, Menneas son of Beeliabos son of Beeliabos, father of Neteiros who received apotheosis in the *lebes* [cauldron], thanks to which the festivals are celebrated, [Menneas] supervisor of all the works accomplished here, as a testimony of piety, has offered a dedication to the goddess Leucothea of Segeira.

Inscription, in Julien Aliquot, "Leucothea de Segeira," *Syria 79* (2002): 233 (from French trans. by Julien Aliquot)

ON THE SLOPES OF Mount Hermon (Syria), on the eastern side, at an altitude of about twelve hundred meters. A native village called 'Ayn al-Burj, "the source of the tower," on the border between the territories of Damascus and Sidon. A Greek inscription, copied there in 1885 (but the first copyist was not sure that it came from this village, and did not describe the context of his discovery), transported to Damascus, where it was purchased in 1907 by the great Belgian historian of religion Franz Cumont, then given to the Royal Museums of Art and History in Brussels, where it can still be seen. A curious feature: the inscription is on a piece of marble, not local stone. The apparently simple content turns out to be more ambiguous than it seems, and specialists disagree about how to interpret it. It will nevertheless provide a point of departure, even if we have to acknowledge that we shall not be able to reach a definitive conclusion about the meaning of a difficult passage.

The inscription is presented in the form of a dedication for the health of the emperor Trajan, according to a very common model found throughout the empire, and the titles attributed to the emperor allow us to date it between 103 and 116 C.E. The dedication was erected while construction work was under way in a sanctuary on the site, and it was consecrated to a goddess named Leucothea of Segeira. The mention of Segeira is easy to explain: this was a local place name that Julien Aliquot, who explored the sector, identified with great probability as a forerunner of the current town of Kafr Hawwar, where he found a temple of white marble. The goddess honored was unquestionably the one to whom this sanctuary was dedicated. In contrast, her name invites attention, for Leucothea, the "white goddess," is a well-known Greek divinity, but a sea goddess, the divinity of foam. Her presence in a mountainous region, on a slope facing away from the sea, is somewhat surprising.

The person making the dedication was a native, as his name and genealogy attest: Beeliabos means "Bel has given," and this name was very characteristic of the Mount Hermon region. Similarly, Neteiros (well attested in this same region), who may have been the son of the first Beeliabos or the second (we cannot tell, as the Greek is ambiguous), also bears a wholly Semitic name. This Neteiros is thus Menneas's brother or uncle. The coexistence of all these Semitic names with that of a Greek goddess to which a native topical epithet is attached forms a surprising mix for someone who had never left the Aegean world, but unremarkable for someone who had traversed the Near East. We shall come back to this point.

First, a word must be said about the problematic phrase referring to apotheosis by means of a *lebes,* followed by the mention of a festival. A lebes is a cauldron, generally ceramic but possibly metal, with a large opening; it can be placed on a fire in order to boil a large quantity of water or to cook a large amount of food. The indication that someone "received apotheosis" in a lebes thus appears enigmatic. Many hypotheses have been proposed, some of them extravagant. Some commentators have chosen to see the memory of a human sacrifice. But this appears totally implausible in the middle of the imperial era: even if such a sacrifice had been carried out, it is certain that no one would have boasted of it in an inscription visible to all. Others have privileged the explanation of an initiatory rite, including a dip in purifying water. However, this "apotheosis by cauldron" has most often been related to the myth of Leucothea. According to mythology, this Greek goddess is the mother of Melicertes, who died and was divinized following a fall into a cauldron of boiling water. The myth seems then to support the idea of a funerary rite, rather than an initiatory one in which Melicertes's cauldron had some magical function in view of divinizing the deceased. I myself have defended a somewhat different idea, namely, that Neteiros died accidentally by falling into a cauldron and that this involuntary repetition of the Melicertes myth in a village placed under the protection of the goddess Leucothea would have conferred a privileged status on the deceased; that is why Menneas makes a point of his kinship with the Neteiros in question, who, being only his brother or his uncle, has no a priori reason to be mentioned in the genealogy of the author of the dedication.

Too many unknown factors prevent us from reaching a definitive conclusion. First, because the Greek term "receive apotheosis" may mean that that Neteiros had been divinized, that he had received funerary honors, or even simply that he had died or been buried. Next, because lebes sometimes designates a funerary urn; we could imagine, then, that Neteiros had simply been cremated and that his urn, through an exceptional favor, had been deposited in or near Leucothea's sancturary; let us note, though, that the practice of cremation has never been attested in Syria. Finally, there is some doubt about the link between the lebes and the mention of the festival that follows; most commentators have understood the relative pronoun to refer to lebes, "the *lebes* thanks to which the festival is celebrated," but Julien Aliquot is right to stress that it would be more logical to relate the pronoun to an individual ("the *lebes*, thanks to whom . . ."), Neteiros or, more plausibly, Menneas. By the same token, this would eliminate the relation established between the cauldron and the festival, between Neteiros's cauldron and Melicertes's. I do not believe that a definitive solution to this enigma can be offered, but it is clear that, in death, for a reason that eludes us, Neteiros enjoyed a privileged status in the village, a status that his parents were intent on marking at a time when construction was being undertaken in the sanctuary of Leucothea. It is hard to avoid postulating a privileged relation between the deceased and that goddess.

But let us leave the enigma behind and consider Leucothea. A rapid investigation shows that she was rarely honored in Syria, and that she is mainly found, except for one mention in Tyre, on the Mount Hermon massif, in southern Syria, or in Galilee (but on a stone that I believe must have come from the Golan or the Hauran); on two occasions her son Melicertes is also mentioned. Now, as we have seen, the marine goddess Leucothea symbolized the foam of the sea. First known as Ino, she was the daughter of Cadmos and Harmonia and sister of Semele. Ino served as wet nurse to the infant Dionysus, born of the union between Semele and Zeus. According to one version of the myth, moreover, this was why Hera, jealous, drove her mad. Ino threw herself into the sea with her son Melicertes, but Poseidon, implored by Aphrodite, transformed her into a sea goddess under the name Leucothea, while her son was saved by a dolphin who took him to the Isthmus of Corinth, where he was henceforth venerated under the name Palemon. We would thus expect to see her honored in Phoenician port towns rather than in the mountains or the interior countryside.

This odd detail has led commentators (including myself) to identify the Greek Leucothea in this region with a native goddess, the Syrian goddess par excellence, Atargatis, even though the two goddesses actually have very little in common. But Atargatis's quasi-universal character seemed to make such an identification possible. This was a mistake, as we shall soon see.

Assimilations like this between a native god and a Greek god are well attested in many regions of the Greek world during the Hellenistic and imperial periods. The Greeks recognized equivalents to their own gods in indigenous divinities more or less everywhere, even if some were only approximate. Thus the masters of the pantheon, the gods of the heavens and the elements, were identified with Zeus, with appropriate differentiations through the use of functional or topical epithets. But in the Greek world gods such as Zeus, Apollo, or Athena were already distinguished from one another by their epithets: Zeus Olympios, Zeus Karios, Zeus Epicarpios, and so on; the list is endless. It was thus not hard to extend it further with Zeus Carmel, Zeus Damaskenos, and many others. In certain cases, it was not a matter of discovery, for Greeks had been making these interpretations for a long time. Thus the great god of Tyre, Melqart, had been identified with Heracles, even if it was known that the Tyrian Heracles was different from the Greek version. Even in Egypt, despite the zoomorphic aspects of the indigenous gods, the Greeks had been able to establish correspondences with their own divinities, between Neith of Sais and Athena, between Hathor and Aphrodite, between Thot and Hermes, and so on, on the basis of functional resemblances.

The phenomenon is so ancient and so widespread that historians no longer pay much attention to it, and, by a sort of reflex, behind every mention of a Greek god outside of the "original" Greek world, they seek the hidden indigenous god. Such a figure does exist, often, but caution is called for, because Greek or Macedonian colonists must surely have brought some of their own gods with them, and these latter thus do not mask indigenous gods. Similarly, the dynastic gods popularized by the new kings clearly have no local connections: Apollo and Zeus among the Seleucids and Dionysus among the Attalids are the traditional Greek gods. But it may be possible to go further still, even though we lack elements that would support a definitive answer: is it not conceivable that Hellenized natives adopted Greek gods precisely the better to mark their belonging to the privileged group of "the Greeks"? Not enough texts from the Hellenistic era have survived to support a firm conclusion, but the hypothesis has to remain open, and I do not believe that searching systematically for the indigenous god behind the Greek one is a sound approach unless one has first studied the milieu of the dedicator(s), the place, even the form of the offering or dedication, and perhaps also the era.

Returning to the matter of assimilating native gods to Greek ones (called *interpretatio graeca* by specialists), we need to move ahead with caution, for upon analysis the phenomenon proves to be much more complex than it first appeared, both in the processes that lead to the establishment of an equivalence and—especially—in the consequences that ensue.

Let us note first of all that a number of indigenous gods were never subjected to this sort of assimilation, this Greek "interpretation," and others submitted to it only partially. Thus the great gods of Palmyra continued to be called Bel, Aglibol, Malakbel, and Iarhibol, that of Petra Dushara (Dusares), and similar continuities have been found in Cilicia, Lycia, and Phrygia. What is more, some non-Greek divinities prospered outside of their original region under their indigenous names: Atargatis, Cybele, Men, Isis, and Osiris spread broadly in the Greek and Roman world without being assimilated to Greek or Roman gods, except perhaps in scholarly discourse. Thus the anonymous author of a work devoted to the Syrian goddess Atargatis (attributed to the novelist and polygraph Lucian of Samosata, but there is debate over the author's true identity) speculates about the goddess's real nature—she seems to him to be also Hera or Rhea—and about her *paredros* Hadad, who has been associated with Attis, Adonis, or even Osiris. In the long prayers known as "aretalogies" devoted to Isis, the latter seems susceptible to being identified with all the great goddesses, Greek or not, thus justifying the appellation "Isis of the thousand names."

Establishing equivalence—a term that seems preferable to "assimilation"—is thus not a one-way process, even if references to Greek gods are more frequent than others. But the examples of Isis and Atargatis show that, for the Greeks, the equivalence worked in both directions, and there was no implication of Greek superiority.

How should we understand this phenomenon? Does it mean that the indigenous gods were Hellenized just as individuals were? Or is it a question, on the contrary, of a superficial glaze, a naming artifice intended to "sound Greek," whereas the god remains essentially unchanged? I do not think there is a single answer, and here again we probably have to take into account both the context and the era. Moreover, it is very unusual to be able to analyze a cult as a whole, including its rites, its myths, and its iconography. For a cult's name, all things considered, is only its most superficial aspect. Without seeking to be exhaustive, let us look at a few examples that will shed some light on the complexity of the phenomenon.

The Arabs honored a great goddess named Allat or Lat, whose name signified "the goddess." A goddess of war, she was naturally identified by the Greeks with Athena. The equivalence was established long ago thanks to a dedication at Cordoba in which Allath-Athena is mentioned. But apart from the functional equivalence of the two deities, it is hard to tell, a priori, what this implied for the faithful. We can be certain that the camel herder who watched over his animals in the steppe east of the Hauran and invoked Lat by imploring her protection was unaware of Athena's very existence. But what about in the villages of the Hauran or in Palmyra? In Hauran villages we find several dedications in Greek honoring Athena—without ever calling her Allat—that were erected by faithful followers almost all of whom had indigenous names. Did the decision to call the goddess by her Greek name and not Allat simply reflect the choice of language? Possibly, but how can we be sure? I think the practice went further than this. Traditionally, the Arab divinities were not represented; yet in the Hauran we see the emergence of a type of feminine statue dressed in a long tunic, wearing a helmet and carrying a spear, evoking a goddess of war in a rather primitive style. The association of Allat with Athena is thus translated, at least for a portion of her followers, by abandonment of the traditional aniconism, or prohibition on representation, and this is not a trivial change in the way people conceived of the gods. But they sometimes went further still. During the dig at the temple of Allat in Palmyra, a statue of the Attic Athena was unearthed, one that would have been at home in a sanctuary in Athens or in any other old city-state in the Greek world. The goddess is represented in a very classical manner, with all the attributes of the Attic Athena; her costume can be explained only by reference to the myth of this Greek goddess. While the statues in the Hauran could correspond, a priori, to any goddess of war at all, the one in Palmyra unquestionably represents Athena and no other. And this in a sanctuary dedicated to Allat! Does it mean that, for the faithful, there was complete assimilation, transference not only of the name but also of the iconography, the myths, even the rites of Athena onto Allat? I believe it is impossible to say, and every faithful follower may have had a different conception. The descendant of Greek or Macedonian colonists may have recognized the well-known Greek goddess, but I doubt that the Palmyrene faithful were unaware of the indigenous origin of this Athena. Still, the choice of name and especially of an iconography so characteristic of the Athena of Athens attests to a cultural choice that we may interpret as the will to appear as "Greek" as possible, or as modern as the rest of the Syrian elite. For the choice was indeed made by the elite, not by the faithful masses. And here is where we encounter the limits of interpretation. What lay behind this appearance of Hellenization? Were the rites modified? And what did believers who were more or less Hellenized think of all this?

As for the rites themselves, it is unlikely that they underwent significant transformation. The study of the sanctuaries of Greco-Roman Syria shows considerable long-term stability in their internal organization. We see this as much in the Lebanese mountains as in the Hauran or in Nabatene. Even when the temple decoration helps produce the external appearance of an ordinary Greek or Roman temple, with a colonnade and a podium, the internal organization reveals an arrangement that is completely foreign to Greek customs. Thus in the Nabatene sanctuaries at the center of the temple we observe a platform intended to receive the *betyls* of the god or gods, that is, stones that were not images of gods but symbols of their presence. In the Lebanese mountains and in the Hauran, stairways integral to the stone walls of sanctuaries allowed access to the roof for the celebration of traditional ceremonies. Similarly, the temple was often preceded by a monumental altar quite different from the Greek sacrificial altar. In short, the way the temple was arranged, even when it was dressed up in Greek or Greco-Roman décor, reveals the maintenance of the ancestral rites. Moreover, in Syria, alongside "Greek-style" temples, some open-air sanctuaries have survived, "high places" where there is no sign of the slightest "Hellenization" and that were still in operation in the third century. Thus the faithful, however familiar they may have been with Greek culture, could find both new aspects and traditional elements in the sanctuaries, according to their own tastes or needs.

Nevertheless, the interpenetration must not be underestimated. We have evidence of genuine transferences, which can also turn out to be enrichments. When Melqart was officially named Heracles in Tyre, the authorities there were making a cultural choice. By introducing Heracleia, Greek-style contests, in the Hellenistic period, they were reinforcing the association of the young and dynamic god who was Tyre's protector, Melqart, with the Greek hero who was the protector of the gymnasium. Whatever resistances a portion of the faithful may have had (something we do not know and may well never know), in the long run a fusion of gods took place, at least for part of the population.

But are we seeing the same phenomenon on the slopes of Mount Hermon? Must we admit that the peasants of Mount Hermon called Atargatis Leucothea for reasons that escape us? Julien Aliquot raised the question and even proved decisively that this was not the case. As we saw at the beginning, the cult of Leucothea and her son Melicertes was attested only in this single region of Syria. We are far from the sea, to be sure, but the civic territories of Tyre and Sidon extended as far as the borders of the Damascene territory; in other words, they broadly encompass the slopes of Mount Hermon. Now, two details should have attracted scholarly attention. One, known for a long time, is that Leucothea was the daughter of Cadmos, that is, of the Phoenician hero, the mythic founder of Thebes of Boeotia. And if we look closely at the ancient texts, we observe that Tyre and Sidon each claimed to have been the seat of the house of the "noble Agenorids" (Agenor was Cadmos's father), to use the expression we encountered earlier (Chapter 25). Is it not natural to find on the territories of two rival city-states the cult of the goddess that both claimed as its own? There is no need to go looking for some sort of assimilation to an indigenous goddess: it was customary and proper that two Phoenician city-states that had become *poleis* should include in their pantheon a Greek goddess that had precise and recognized bonds with each of them. The second detail that ought to have put us on the right track—and that did indeed strike Julien Aliquot—is the mention of Melicertes. The latter had no place in a Greek interpretation of Atargatis; yet, after the discovery of a first consecration to Leucothea and to Melicertes, which I had made some fifteen years earlier, a second mention of the same god was found in the Anti-Lebanon Mountains thanks to Julien Aliquot. This is not a matter of chance, and it confirms that Leucothea was indeed the Greek goddess, honored as such with her son. To be sure, Melicertes was never the object of a cult under that name in Greece (he was honored under the name Palemon), but it proves that the Tyrian or Sidonian scholars who had been charged with developing the local civic legends were well acquainted with the god's various avatars and had chosen the name he bore before he was thrown into the waters by his mother. There is no doubt that the diffusion of the cult of Leucothea and Melicertes in this region with one foot in Libya and one in Syria, at the outer limits of the territories of Tyre and Sidon, proceeded from the incorporation into the pantheon of these two city-states, with the goal of embellishing their own identities and increasing their prestige, of an authentically Greek cult, with no local roots other than the Greek tradition itself. Should we be astonished at this? Why should people who claim to be Greek not adopt the Greek cults that did the most to include them in the most ancient aspect of the Greek past, that of myth?

CHAPTER FORTY

Farmers in Flight (163 C.E.), or Agriculture and Rural Life in Greco-Roman Egypt

To Harpocration, strateg[o]s of the divisions of Themistes and Polemon in the Arsinoite nome, from Isidoros, village secretary of Lagis and Tricomia. List of farmers named in place of those who have fled or are disabled for the sowing of the current 3rd year of Antoninus and Verus our Lords.

In place of Protion, son of Amomnius, leasing 2¾ ar. I name Aphrodisius, son of Sarapion son of Aphrodisius.

In place of Papontos, son of Paceies, leasing 22 ar. I name Pisais, son of Collouthus, and Sarapammon, son of Heron, for 2½ ar.; Tithoes, son of Pontus, for 8½ ar.; Chaeremon, son of Onnophris, for 4⁵⁄₁₆ ar.; Anoubas, son of Dius, for 3 ar.; Onesimus, son of Straton, for 2 ar.; Papontos and Panouphis, sons of Amais, for 1¹³⁄₁₆ ar.

In place of Didas, son of Sotas, leasing 8 ar. I name Pasion, son of Charmus son of Areius.

In place of Protion, son of Longinus, leasing 5½ ar. I name Harpoch ( ), son of Bassus, for 2¾ ar. and Peteeus, son of Petesouchus, for 2¾ ar.

From the leasehold of Heron, son of Diodorus, I name Polis, son of Theomnas, to take over 5 ar. and Hermes, son of Dionysius, to take over 1 ar.

In place of Melanas, son of Horion, leasing 4¼ ar. I name Petermouthis, son of Papontos, and Demetrius, son of Longinus.

In place of Heron, son of Heraclides, leasing 7²⁷⁄₃₂ ar. I name Panouphis, son of Petermouthis.

In place of Heron, son of Sabinus, leasing 5 ar. I name Ischyras, son of Ischyras.

In place of Apollonius, son of Heron, leasing 5⅓ ar. I name Petermouthis whose father is unknown and whose mother is—.

In place of Esouris, son of Sansneus, leasing 5⅛ ar. I name Nilus, son of Didas.

In place of Ptollas whose father is unknown leasing 6½ ar. I name Theon and Trallis, sons of Athenion.

From the leasehold of Didymus, son of Heraclides, I name Horion, son of Papontos, to take over 1 ar.; Sarapion whose father is unknown and whose mother is — to take over ¾ ar.; and Didas, son of Sotas, to take over ¾ ar.

In place of Bolus, son of Ision, lessees of 5²³⁄₃₂ ar., I name Diodorus, son of Diodorus, for 2⅛ ar.; Capiton, son of Romanus, for 1 ar.; and Phouonsis, son of Horus, and Longinus, son of Melas, for 2¹⁹⁄₃₂ ar.

In place of Hatres, son of Heron, leasing 3⅝ ar., I name Apollonius, son of Sarapion.

In place of Heron, son of Horus, leasing 1⅜ ar., I name Sansneus, son of Pastoous.

In place of Pelois, son of Anoubion, leasing 3½ ar. I name Miosis, son of the lame Mysthas; Anoubas, son of Onnophris; and Polis, son of Aphrodisius and Esonis.

In place of Paseis, son of Aces, leasing 1 ar. I name Poulemis, son of Poulemis also called —.

Allan Chester Johnson, *Roman Egypt to the Reign of Diocletian*, in *An Economic Survey of Ancient Rome*, ed. Tenney, Frank, vol. 2 (Baltimore: Johns Hopkins Press, 1936), pp. 114–115, no. 43

E GYPT, 163 C.E. A village in the Fayyum region, one of the most fertile areas in Egypt. It is not the Nile Valley, but a sort of subsidiary oasis, a vast depression irrigated by a tributary of the Nile that allows the land to profit from the annual flooding. A huge body of water, Lake Moeris, fills in part of the depression year-round, thus providing reserves of water. The largest villages are spread around the periphery, but in fact the whole region is heavily populated. Moreover, the Fayyum is the only nome (Arsinoite Nome) that is subdivided into three districts, each governed by a strategos, whereas elsewhere the strategos has authority over the entire nome. Here, a single strategos governs two districts or divisions *(merides)*, Themistes and Polemon, at once, perhaps because no one has yet volunteered to take over that role in one of the two districts. We shall come back to this point. Let us note that the name of the strategos is Greek in form but with a strong Egyptian coloration: Harpocrates was the child-god of Isis and Osiris, always represented with a finger over his mouth.

The strategos received from a village secretary, Isidoros—again a Greek name based on a divine Egyptian name, "gift of Isis"—a list containing the names of farmers who had fled (indicating the areas they had cultivated previously) and the names of the farmers the secretary was appointing to cultivate those parcels in their stead. Most of the names—leaving aside the patronymics—are Egyptian, but we also spot some Greek names (Protion, Apollonios, Diodoros, Didymos) and some Latin ones (Capito, Longinus). We must not conclude that there is an ethnic mix here, for sometimes the father of a man with a Greek name has an Egyptian name himself; it is more a question of fashions in naming than of cultural indices—although we cannot rule out the possibility of actual cohabitation between Egyptians and descendants of Greek colonists, or even Romans.

The problem of the moment, in sum, is the flight of the farmers. At least seventeen had left, but the document is incomplete at the bottom, and the list might have been longer. They abandoned the lands for which they held leasing contracts, to go either to another village or, more plausibly, to a city where they would have been able to blend in with the population and find work of some sort. It is the phenomenon of anachoresis, flight from the village. This does not mean that they all fled into the desert: How would they have lived there? Unable to face their fiscal obligations, these farmers had given up their lands for fear of being thrown into prison.

This was not a good thing for the administration, and still less for the village secretary, who was personally responsible for ensuring the collection of farm rents and taxes. He therefore distributed the abandoned parcels—which represented a little over fifty-nine acres—to other farmers. Most of those who fled had only tiny holdings, often less than two and a half acres (one *arura* equaled about two-thirds of an acre), with one exception, Papontos, who by himself had held about a quarter of the whole, twenty-two *arurae* (about fifteen acres). This may be another explanation for their flight: most of them had too little land for their own sustenance. Isidoros thus attributed the vacant lands to others, often dividing them up so the burdens would not be too great. For all the farmers named had to cultivate these lands in addition to the ones they already worked. It was best not to place crushing burdens on the taxpayers who remained; otherwise they might be driven to flee in turn. The vicious cycle thus launched would have ended up emptying out the villages and abandoning the land to the desert.

The crisis that had struck Egypt was not new, and rather than speak of crisis—which evokes a situation that is harsh but temporary—it is better to speak of structural difficulties, more or less aggravated by circumstances. Egypt's wealth ultimately depended on the annual flooding of the Nile, and the degree to which the water rose varied significantly from year to year. But it also depended on the capacity of the administration to ensure the maintenance of the systems of dikes and canals, and to distribute the arable lands among the farmers. Thus, thanks to a systematic cleaning of the canals under Augustus, a rise of twelve cubits was enough to ensure a good harvest, as opposed to the fourteen cubits needed earlier. The Lagid exploitation of Egypt had reached its maximum efficiency in the third century, but overcultivation and administrative ineptitude had led to a clear decline in the second century. To try to bring in more tax money, the Lagids invented a new practice: they held government employees personally responsible for the revenues they were charged with collecting. We can imagine what constraints and brutalities this must have entailed on the part of royal agents who had to make up for shortfalls from their own (meager) holdings. It was also an invitation to require more from those who were better able to pay, in order to constitute reserves. Heightened pressure to collect taxes in fact led to the farmers' flight, and the king was often left with no solution but to issue edicts of amnesty that canceled the debts, in part or in full.

Rome did not innovate much in this area; at most, it systematized the recourse to *leitourgoi* for all administrative functions. The word *leitourgeia* henceforth designated the obligation imposed on an individual to fulfill an administrative function—collecting taxes or policing—at his own expense for a given period of time. The lists of "candidates" were drawn up by village secretaries and transmitted to the strategos of the nome, who made the assignments. We can imagine the innumerable negotiations that must have taken place as people tried to escape from the list! A superb text, notes from a meeting of the council of local dignitaries, relates in detail the process of designating a magistrate for the metropolis of Hemoupolis Magna Nome in 192 C.E. After some discussion, the choice fell on a certain Achilleus, son of Cornelius; we know that he was a man of good family, because his father had also held the same magistracy. But the man refused, for the burden was painful, and he offered to accept a different magistracy while limiting his expenses to two talents and refusing to fulfill some obligations that he deemed dangerous. In fact, there must have been another possible "candidate," who claimed that Achilleus had struck him and insulted him before the meeting, presumably trying to get him to accept the role. In the end, another notable stood surety for Achilleus, who would have to fulfill the function for which he had first been called. We can guess what energy must have been expended if every nomination proved to be as complicated as this one. Moreover, it became obligatory to designate future magistrates well ahead of time: according to an edict by Antoninus Pius, certain magistrates of Egyptian metropolises were designated three years in advance. The difficulty in finding volunteers explains why those who came forward to offer their services were congratulated and honored as benefactors, *euergetai*.

To return to the land, the Roman administration tried to combat the farmers' flight, with variable results. In reality, the problem arose first from the fact that the administration had not managed to adapt its requirements to the realities of production, but based its tax rates on administrative estimates of revenues. Now, depending on the amount of annual flooding, production could vary greatly. If the same requirements applied after a bad season, farmers found themselves indebted for several years, as rates for borrowing money were extremely high. In 150, Antoninus Pius nevertheless took a major step: henceforth taxpayers would make declarations themselves, subject to a posteriori verification by the administration. This was unquestionably a relief, at least as far as taxation was concerned.

But it addressed only one aspect of the problem. On the one hand, the state retained ownership of much of the land, despite the considerable development of private property in Roman Egypt. For these public lands, the administration sought farmers; many rural residents had no recourse except to lease these lands on terms imposed by the state. Yet rents were high, and they did not vary according to the quality or quantity of the harvests. We observe a continuing decline in the average farm rent throughout the first and second centuries, reflecting the difficulty of finding farmers. These temporary tenant farmers were the first to flee when they found themselves unable to pay both their rents and their taxes. The village secretary had no choice but to attribute the abandoned lands, by force, to

351

those farmers who remained. He thus created de facto village solidarity in the face of the royal treasury, because those who stayed behind worked and paid for those who left: in effect, this meant that the state was making taxpayers compensate for the deficiencies of the central administration.

The result was often disastrous. After several years of inadequate flooding, starting in 45, whole villages emptied out. In Karanis (Fayyum), between 150 and 200, the population decreased by 40 percent. This was never irreversible, for the farmers were ready to return as soon as the administration canceled their debts: in the Delta, a number of villages that had been abandoned during the 160s were repopulated and prosperous at the beginning of the third century.

Egypt found itself a victim, in the eyes of its Greek and then Roman masters, of its reputation for limitless wealth. The flooding of the Nile, which so intrigued the ancients, produced a marvelous thing: the flowering of the desert in a land where it almost never rained. As Herodotus had said, Egypt was indeed a gift of the river, but by this he meant primarily that all the country's arable land had been brought by the Nile with its burden of alluvium. From antiquity on, this was understood as a metaphor, and from this gift of the gods, Greeks and Romans alike intended to profit—no matter what it cost Egyptian farmers.

CHAPTER FORTY-ONE

Urinating in Front of Aphrodite, or Jews and Greeks Six Centuries Later

Proclos, son of a philosopher, put a question to R. Gamaliel in Acco when the latter was bathing in the bath of Aphrodite. He said to him, "It is written in your Torah, and there shall cleave nought of the devoted thing to thine hand [Deut. 13:18]. Why are you bathing in the bath of Aphrodite?" He replied to him, "We may not answer [questions relating to Torah] in a bath." When he came out, he said to him, "I did not come into her domain, she has come into mine. Nobody says, The bath was made as an adornment for Aphrodite; but he says, Aphrodite was made as an adornment for the bath. Another reason is, if you were given a large sum of money, you would not enter the presence of a statue reverenced by you while you were nude or had experienced seminal emission, nor would you urinate before it. But this [statue of Aphrodite] stands by a sewer and all people urinate before it. [In the Torah] it is only stated, their gods—i.e., what is treated as a deity is prohibited, what is not treated as a deity is permitted."

Abodah Zarah, trans. A. Cohen, in *The Babylonian Talmud*, ed. Isodore Epstein (London: Soncino Press, 1935–1952), pt. 4, vol. 7, pp. 220–221 (III, 44b)

Akko, or Ptolemais as the Greeks called it, Phoenicia, in the late first or early second century C.E.[1] A highly celebrated Pharisee master, Gamaliel II, his renown emphasized by his title *rabbi*, "master," was president of the Sanhedrin, which had taken refuge in Iamnia after the destruction of the Temple in Jerusalem. But perhaps the text refers only to Gamaliel III, around 220–250; as we shall see, this would make no difference in the matter. His interlocutor is an unknown pagan, probably fictitious, with a fanciful name that nevertheless characterizes the individual: he too is a master in his way, a philosopher, a man who thinks. And who is astonished. Whether the episode was historical or entirely invented is irrelevant here, because the authors of the Mischna, that is, exegetes of the Law, retained it for its exemplary value.

Proclos is quite familiar with the Torah, Jewish Law. He can cite Deuteronomy, one of the five books of the Pentateuch, a highly rule-oriented text that forbids all Jews to be in contact with any pagan sacred object. This is the way we must understand his opening remark: the Torah forbids Jews to touch any object that is *herem,* equivalent to the Latin *sacer,* "consecrated to the gods." Now our pious Jew, a prestigious Torah commentator who knows the text inside out, is there in the city's thermal baths, which are placed under the name of Aphrodite, bathing like any pagan! We can bet that a pious Jew from Jason's day (Chapter 28) would have gasped in horror. Gamaliel explains himself, and without seeming to do so introduces into Jewish thought some absolutely new notions—for which the Greeks are not without a certain responsibility.

Let us look first at a symptomatic detail. According to the Greek tradition, Proclos profits from the relaxed environment in the baths to bring up an intellectual question with his interlocutor. We know that after the Romans conquered the entire eastern Mediterranean region these baths were significantly expanded, while the gymnasium itself came to look like a mere annex. But the institution had been enriched by additional rooms, libraries, and lecture halls, so the bath-gymnasium complex, although it gave priority to caring for the body, did not neglect intellectual preoccupations. Because men all passed several hours a day in the baths, this was the opportunity to meet one's friends and discuss all the issues of the moment and other things besides. The Greek tradition of philosophical conversation under a portico or in the baths had a long history, and its continuance made perfect sense. Gamaliel, in contrast, sets limits to this activity. He probably behaves like everyone else when he speaks of everyday matters; but he refuses to answer one of Proclos's questions: the Torah is not to be discussed in the baths! The study of the Law is undertaken in rabbinical academies; it requires purity of body and spirit, for it is a religious act. Gamaliel thus waits at least until they have left the baths to reply.

His answer may appear convoluted, even tendentious. According the best Socratic tradition of maieutics, he responds to his interlocutor with another question: Would you go naked and impure into the temple of the goddess? Would you urinate before her statue in her temple? Proclos does not need to speak, so obvious is the answer. From this Gamaliel draws the decisive argument in his demonstration: there are situations in which the statue of the goddess is a sacred object, when it is in its temple and venerated as such; there are other situations in which the statue is a decorative object without any particular religious character, on the same basis as molding, a row of ovoid shapes, pearl drops and curlicues, or any other sculpted decoration. Only in the first case is it *herem*, "avowedly forbidden" according to the language in Deuteronomy. And because Proclos questioned him by citing Deuteronomy, Gamaliel bases his reply on another passage from the same book, where he reads: "set fire to the carved images of their gods."[2] Although his answer has the aspect of a citation, Gamaliel does not actually quote from the text itself; instead, he cites a commentary that invites us not to confuse idols with statues. According to standard rabbinical practice, he integrates the commentary on the Law with the Law itself.

Without being a specialist in Talmudic thought, I think I can affirm that Rabbi Gamaliel's reply would not have been at all to the taste of the Hasidim of the second century B.C.E., nor would it have been appreciated by some of his own contemporary colleagues. It attests above all to a spectacular disconnection between the religious life, on the one hand, and daily life, on the other. Jews were now a minority in Judaea, surrounded by pagans, often living at the heart of pagan cities; they had no choice but to adapt their way of life to this new context. Certain scholars assert that rabbis had become marginal and had very little authority over most of the Jewish population, which was becoming integrated with the dominant civilization, that of the Greeks, on a broad scale. I note that it was by issuing rules such as these that they had some chance of retaining authority over Jews at large: in a way, Rabbi Gamaliel is only finding a legal justification, based in Scripture, for a behavior that the vast majority of Jews had already adopted in any case. For if as famous a Pharisee master as Gamaliel frequented the public baths, we may suppose that all the other Jews did the same, without worrying about either the ambient nudity or the presence of statues.

This anecdote seems to me to show that, in a multicultural society, every group, without giving up its own identity, attempts to free itself from rules that isolate it uselessly, the better to preserve what is essential. To keep the Jews from succumbing to the adoration of idols, it was necessary to declare that these were nothing but an insignificant feature of the décor; this was an attempt to find a middle ground between the absolute rejection of images that was required by a rigorous exegetic tradition intent on seeing paganism behind every image, and the invasion by images of the world in which the Jews of that time actually lived. Rabbi Gamaliel in fact understood that, whatever the circumstances, most Jews frequented the baths, where they saw statues of Aphrodite and perhaps other pagan divinities. Could such a rigorous prohibition be respected? Rabbi Nahum bar Simai was admired by the writers of the Talmud because throughout his entire life he never looked at an image, not even on a coin. But such a posture would have to lead to a refusal to use money, because the portrait of the emperor was found on coins. Who could lead a normal life under those conditions? A great rabbi who did not have to worry about doing his own shopping and paying his taxes! For everyone else, it was better to set rules that made life possible without having to renounce one's Judaism. In a way, if I may be permitted the anachronism, coexistence obliged the Jews to undergo a certain "secularization," a separation between what stemmed from religious practice and what was foreign to it. Even the strictest rabbis did not opt to retreat to the desert; they continued to live in towns and villages, for this was the only way to keep any influence over the faithful masses. Between maintaining rules that made life impossible for Jews—which risked driving them into full integration—and fleeing into the desert, retreating from the world as the ascetics of Qumram had done on the shores of the Dead Sea, the rabbis found a middle way by establishing distinctions between what was religious and what was not, and even, at the heart of the religious, between what pertained to the cult and what did not, making what was not cult-related accessible even to Jews as pious as Rabbi Gamaliel. Decoration became a neutral category on the same basis as other fields of human activity, constituting not only a possible ground on which Jews and non-Jews could meet, but a common good, an element of a common culture.

We can see how much such an evolution owes to Hellenism. For it was the coexistence between Hellenism and Judaism that obliged the Jews to question their own practices in the first place. Even as open revolt was breaking out against those who were trying to impose new customs (Chapter 28), borrowings from Hellenism were appearing in works that were most hostile to the Greek presence. As early as the third century B.C.E., a book such as Ecclesiastes (also called Qohelet, "he who brings together") appears to have been largely inspired in its form by the Stoic maxims that were currently in fashion in the Greek world. The beginning is familiar: "Vanity of vanities," says Qohelet, "vanity of vanities, all is vanity" (Eccl. 1:2, NRSV), and, further on, "What has been is what will be, and what has been done is what will be done; there is nothing new under the sun" (Eccl. 1:9, NRSV). Some have wanted to see this succession of disillusioned maxims as a legacy from a Mesopotamian tradition, which did in fact exist. But why privilege Mesopotamian models more than a thousand years old, when we have no evidence that the author of the book had access to them, and when, at the time he was writing, a Greek philosophy with which he could easily have been acquainted was developing the same themes? It seems to me that the warning addressed by another Jewish author, Jesus ben Sira, to his compatriots around 190 B.C.E. invites us to look to Hellenism for Qohelet's models. In fact, in Ecclesiasticus or *Book of the Wisdom of Jesus ben Sira,* without ever explicitly citing the Greeks, the author denounces those of his compatriots who were looking elsewhere for models of life or reasoning when, he says, the Torah provides all the answers to the questions that a Jew might raise. This denunciation of the temptation of new philosophies is meaningful only in the context of a confrontation—still a peaceful one—between Judaism and Hellenism.

The open struggle carried out through the Maccabees' revolt and the success of the adversaries of Jason and Menelas must not lead us to believe that Hellenism had been definitively rejected. Quite to the contrary, I believe that the creation of the Hasmonean state led to a rampant Hellenization of Jewish society, despite a widespread conviction that the state's new independence protected Jews against the temptations of Hellenism. To be sure, it is not hard to find manifest proofs of respect for the Torah in Jewish society: the gradual disappearance of the handles of Rhodian amphorae (and thus of imported wine and other nonkosher products) in step with the Hasmonean conquest of Palestine, respect for the Sabbath (see the Gospels), rules of purity, and the prohibition of images. Generally speaking, we witness a hardening of the rules governing daily life, as if the rabbis were erecting the Torah around the community as an ultimate rampart against the temptations of the Greek lifestyle—although there was some softening, too, as when, following certain passages of the Talmud, Gamaliel is said to have authorized members of his family to use a mirror while cutting their hair, and to learn Greek!

But this is only the most visible, and perhaps the least pertinent, aspect of the new situation imposed by the coexistence between Greeks and Jews. I intentionally emphasized earlier the way Gamaliel borrowed modes of reasoning and teaching that were Greek in origin, Socratic maieutics in particular. We could go further back in time and make the demonstration even stronger. Right after the war of the Maccabees, texts such as the book of Judith bore the unmistakable mark of Hellenism. The book of Judith is an authentic nationalist tract, using a fictitious episode of the Jews' war against the Assyrians to mask the rejection of political control by the Greeks. Yet its form is modeled on the most classical of Greek novels, with the three traditional elements that make a good story: blood, suspense, and sex. Let the reader be the judge: the small Jewish village of Bethulia resists the immense Assyrian army, led by Holophernes. Almost all of the Near East has been conquered, and the fate of Jerusalem depends on Bethulia, which controls the access route. The situation is desperate, and the Elders are ready to capitulate if God does not come to their aid within five days. Judith then comes onstage. She is a lovely young widow who requests a free hand in order to act (suspense). The Elders are worried, but, after all, she is a widow, there is no need to fear for her virginity. Judith leaves the city, approaches Holophernes on the pretext that she can show him a secret passage; she seduces him, promises to yield (sex), but when the general, half drunk, finally joins her in his tent, she cuts off his head (blood) and returns to the city. In the morning, the discovery of Holophernes' body demoralizes the Assyrian army, which lifts the siege: Bethulia is saved. As far as we can see, there is not the slightest historical element in this novel, whose form is entirely Greek, and Judith has to be counted among the works of Greek literature. Is there a more ancient Hebrew or Aramaic original? Possibly, but in its current form it is an adaptation to the Greek taste of the times, and the model, whatever it may be, is nowhere in sight.

The adoption of Greek modes of expression by Jewish authors defending Jewish value systems was not limited to the book of Judith or the book of Esther, another example of an ancient story transformed into a Hellenistic novel. There is a whole Greek literary tradition within Judaism, with Philo unquestionably as its most brilliant representative, but we have seen other examples above (Chapter 35). Thus it is interesting to note that this contamination of modes of thought and reasoning extends into the realm where it would be least expected, that of scriptural exegesis. For the anecdote that served as a point of departure is drawn from the Mischna, that is, from commentary on the Torah.

To come back to the anecdote itself, we see how the multicultural, multireligious, and multiethnic framework in which the Palestinian Jews were living from then on obliged them to reflect on their own identity and on what constituted its essence. And they did this with the tools that Greek rhetoric provided them, as well as with the resources of Jewish exegetics and scriptural commentary. By inventing the neutral category of decoration, the rabbis departed from the traditional vision in which everything was religious. A passage from the treatise of the Talmud on the Sabbath evokes the case of a Jew who, believing he was entering a synagogue, went into a pagan temple.[3] It has been suggested that this confusion had been made possible by the presence of the same decorative elements, which would show, if evidence is needed, that the Jews were no more insensitive to the charms of modernism than the other peoples of the region. Proof that it was urgent to remove from the category of the prohibited what could be removed, distinguishing between the incidental and the essential.

Still, we must not imagine a society of universal tolerance and harmony. We would have no trouble finding evidence to the contrary. Even leaving aside the crises that the confrontation with Hellenism provoked within Judaism—for it was indeed chiefly in terms of cultural identity and integration into the modern world that the problem arose—it is clear that strong resistances to certain aspects of Hellenism persisted, even in the milieus that were most open to the culture of the times. But some Jews no longer feared to emphasize that they belonged to the Greek world. Salome Komaise, a young Jewish woman whose archives have been found on the banks of the Dead Sea, included in her marriage contract "the commitment in good faith of the said Yeshu'a [her spouse] to provide food and clothing for her and her children to come according to *Greek custom* and *manners* at the peril of all his goods." Even if for her it was obviously a matter of stressing a certain quality of life—I am tempted to say a certain "standing"—and if the Hellenism to which she lays claim appears on the surface as a criterion of social differentiation, one can imagine what a long path had been traveled since the author of 2 Maccabees had denounced the creation of a gymnasium in Jerusalem. Under the pressure of Hellenism and with the help of its intellectual tools, Judaism indeed carried out a genuine revolution.

CHAPTER FORTY-TWO

Of the Proper Use of Hellenic Letters, or How to Be Christian and Cultivated

Just as dyers first prepare by certain treatments whatever material is to receive the dye, and then apply the colour, whether it be purple or some other hue, so we also in the same manner must first, if the glory of the good is to abide with us indelible for all time, be instructed by these outside means, and then shall understand the sacred and mystical teachings; and like those who have become accustomed to seeing the reflection of the sun in water, so we shall then direct our eyes to the light itself.

> Basil of Caesarea, "Address to Young Men, on How They
> Might Derive Benefit from Greek Literature," in *Saint Basil: The
> Letters*, trans. Roy J. Deferrari (Loeb Classical Library, 1926),
> vol. 4, p. 385 (II, 39–46)

CAESAREA OF CAPPADOCIA, in the 370s. The author, Basil, had been a bishop since 370, in the city where he was born around 329–331. He did not serve long, for he died when he was still young, in the summer of 378. Born into a Christian family from the Pontus region, Basil was part of a trio known as the Cappadocian Fathers, along with his friend Gregory, bishop of Nazianzus, and his brother Gregory, bishop of Nyssa. Basil wrote rules for monks, compiled an anthology of the works of Origen, and was the author of numerous letters, but he interests us here for a particular work that was addressed to young men—his nephews, in principle—but whose complexity and above all whose countless references to works of classical literature show that he was aiming at a much broader public. Still, let us keep Basil's intention in mind and examine his treatise as if it were indeed addressed first of all to young men, those who had reached the age when it was time to choose masters and schools.

Our excerpt sums up both his message and his method. Facing detractors of classical culture who argued that a Christian ought to avoid reading pagan authors, Basil maintains the contrary position. Basing his demonstration on a comparison that Socrates would not have disavowed, he defends the idea that classical pagan culture—here called "the external sciences," an expression also found in other Christian writers, while the "internal sciences" are the Holy Scriptures—must be an instrument at the service of faith. And, continuing with an image borrowed from Plato's *Republic* (516b), which allows him to put his own advice into practice, he asserts that learning classical culture is the best way for the believer to be prepared to understand the Christian mysteries. All the rest of the bishop's little book develops this idea, with the help of examples.

In addressing young men, Basil makes use of a quite remarkable erudition that attests to the extent of his own culture. Whether they are explicitly cited, alluded to indirectly, or used as sources of borrowed formulae, Homer, Hesiod, Solon (via Plutarch), Aeschylus, Euripides (but not Sophocles), Herodotus, Plato, Plutarch, and a number of other philosophers whom we know today only through fragments, provide marvelous illustrations of the prelate's immense learning. It is true that he had had a good start, for his father and first teacher, Basil the Elder, was himself a rhetor at Neocaesarea (Pontus). Later, Basil pursued his studies in Caesarea (Cappadocia), in Constantinople, and especially in Athens, where he spent four or five years with his friend Gregory of Nazianzus. It was thus a man well versed in rhetorical exercises, a scholar with extensive knowledge of Greek literature from Homer to his own day, who was addressing young people troubled by the contradictory discourses of Christians and by the powerful attacks of certain pagans. And he did so with both discernment and vigor.

Discernment first of all, for Basil was by no means intent on defending the entire legacy that had been developed within the context of the ancient polytheism—a legacy that Christianity, now triumphant and officially installed in the empire, was trying to combat, if not yet to eradicate. Basil distinguished between useful works and the others, between texts that advocated virtue and those that spread moral corruption. While he was not unaware of how much the Attic orators had to teach in the realm of reasoning and fine words, he distrusted them, for their art approached that of lying: as he saw it, their concern with convincing judges at any price had priority over the requirement of truth. To be sure, the ancient orators could praise virtue when the occasion warranted, but Basil believed that they should be used with care. He looked more favorably upon other authors, and he spelled out the principles that must guide Christians in their choice of readings. Using a metaphor that nicely sums up his own attitude toward the ancient authors as a group, he compared a young Christian to a bee that leaves the perfume and color of flowers for all creatures to enjoy, content to draw from the useful flowers alone the substances it needed to make its honey. Generally speaking, philosophers were the ones who found favor with Basil, Plato first and foremost; we find many echoes of Plato in the treatise, especially the Plato of *The Republic,* a text that is mentioned or imitated in some thirty passages at least. This preference reflects the fashion for Platonism and especially for Neoplatonism in late antiquity; the high moral tenor appealed to well-read Christians and pagans alike. But on several occasions Basil also mentioned Cynic or Stoic philosophers, among whom he did not hesitate to acknowledge prefigurations of Christian behaviors, such as scorning wealth or aspiring to virtue. And Basil joined them on still another point: their critique of the depraved morals of the Olympian gods. In a sense, Basil was proposing that his nephews undertake a Christian reading of the ancient texts.

And he made his case forcefully, for assaults against the reading of pagan authors by Christians were proliferating, coming from various horizons. Hostility to Greek literature in fact emerged fairly early in Christianity. It may have a remote origin in some Biblical passages from the Hellenistic period, like the *Book of Wisdom of Jesus ben Sira* (later known as Ecclesiasticus), which reminds readers that the fear of God is the beginning of all wisdom and that the Torah suffices in all circumstances; there is no need for the pious Jew to look elsewhere—that is, in currently fashionable philosophies—for lessons in how to behave. However, explicit texts by Christian authors attacking Greek literature directly are uncommon; instead, we find a diffuse popular sentiment, a mistrust developed among certain groups of monks. By definition, those who rejected classical culture did not write much, so we know of their existence only through their adversaries. Thus in his *Funeral Oration for Basil* (§11), Gregory of Nazianzus asserted that most Christians were strongly hostile toward pagan literature, or at least decidedly suspicious of it.

Among Christian intellectuals, many of whom had something to say on the subject, there was an entirely different discourse. To be sure, all recognized the dangers that awaited a young man eager to learn. As Tertullian said in the early third century in *De anima* (§39), young Christians grew up surrounded by idolatry from the start. And the schools they could attend based their teaching on pagan myths, many of which Christians found scandalous. In the third century, Origen too denounced the risks of attending pagan schools when one had faith (*Epistula ad Gregorium Thaumaturgum,* 2). While Minucius Felix relied on Plato to denounce the falsity and danger of the ancient poets, in a curious way he combined rejection of part of the classical tradition with the use of philosophy (*Octavius,* especially chapter 23). Gregory of Nazianzus, who frequented the schools of Athens along with Basil, regretted that that city was still overrun by idols and their panegyrists (*Funerary Oration for Basil,* PG XXXVI, 524C). And in two fictional speeches titled *Against Julian,* written immediately after the emperor's death, Gregory multiplied his attacks against the pagan authors, seeking repeatedly to make them look ridiculous. But Gregory was in fact indirectly attempting to denigrate Julian himself, and the violently polemical tone of his discourse masks his real attachment to a culture of which Julian had sought to deprive Christians. Moreover, a careful reading of Gregory's text shows that none of his writings attests more eloquently to his complete familiarity with the Greek myths.

For none of these Christian authors rejected Hellenic literature wholesale. Nor did those of Latin culture reject Latin literature; in the late fourth century Jerome wrote to one of his correspondents, Eustachion, that during a self-imposed fast he did not resist the pleasure of reading Cicero or Plautus (Letter XXII, 30), whereas the careless style of the prophets put him off, Horace seemed far superior to the Psalms, and Virgil outshone the Evangelists. Tertullian had said pretty much the same thing two centuries earlier (*De praescriptione,* VII, 9). In the third century, Clement of Alexandria, who had denounced the Greek contests with exceptional violence (*Protrepticus,* 34) and had denounced myths and all pagan practices as well, attacked just as vigorously those who were "frightened at Hellenic philosophy, as children are at masks."[1] He points out that there are truths in Greek philosophy that could only have been inspired by God or borrowed from the Holy Books (see especially *Stromateis,* VI, 67, 1; see also *Protrepticus,* 6–7). Nor does he hesitate to call Plato to the rescue to discover God, a Plato whom he judges to have touched on truth by looting the Holy Scriptures, like all the Greek philosophers (*Stromateis*, VI, 1–5). During the same period, in Anatolia, a former student of Origen known as Gregory Thaumaturgus congratulated himself for having studied the Greek philosophers and poets (*Panegyrics*, 11 and 13). Gregory of Nazianzus considered that one must study the pagan sciences before reading the Holy Books (PG XXXVII, 1577). In the fifth century, the Church historian Socrates Scholasticus also noted that the Holy Scriptures did not give instruction in oratory and thus did not teach people how to defend the truths of the Gospel with conviction. Moreover, it is possible that some clerics took such an attitude a little too far: Jerome occasionally lashed out against bishops and priests who attempted to compete with the pagan rhetors in their sermons and made a display of their classical learning.

As we can see, the question of the relationship between Christian faith and Greek culture arose sharply as early as the third century. And the debate was not confined to Christian circles. During the fourth century, the term "Hellenism" gradually came to designate what we call paganism but what can better be identified as the traditional polytheism of the societies encompassed by the Roman Empire. Emperor Julian the Apostate took a further, decisive step that obliged Christian "intellectuals" to react. Proclaimed emperor by his troops in Paris in early 360, he officially succeeded Constantine II upon the latter's death in 361, and he wasted no time before putting into practice a policy of restoring paganism. He began by lifting all the prohibitions that had been imposed on the cults and sanctuaries. In the spring of 362, during a sojourn in Antioch of Syria, where he was preparing an expedition against the Persians, this man trained in rhetoric and Neoplatonist philosophy took a series of measures that have been compared to veritable encyclicals (Glen Bowersock introduced this term in his biography of Julian the Apostate): he ordered that all bullying directed against pagans be stopped, and then turned the prohibitions back against the Christians. Among the measures he took on June 17, 362, one imperial edict that looked anodyne on the surface stirred up a commotion, because an explanatory letter by Julian spelled out its meaning. Julian proclaimed in his edict that schoolmasters and professors must set themselves apart first of all by their *mores*, that is, by their good morality, and secondly by their eloquence. He thus decided that no one could teach without authorization by a decree from the *curiales*, the members of the municipal council, of whom "the best" (for Julian, these were undoubtedly the pagans) were supposed to be unanimous; and to avoid errors Julian submitted their decrees to his own approval (so that, as he put it, "such teachers may enter upon their pursuits in the municipalities with a certain higher honor because of Our judgment").[2] The desire to entrust the education of children to the best masters appeared praiseworthy, but it masked a very different concern. The accompanying letter revealed the actual goal of the edict: to remove Christians from teaching. The argument went as follows. The first quality of a teacher is loyalty: "Whoever thinks one thing and teaches another to his pupils appears to me as far from true education as he is from honesty." Without naming the Christians, Julian attacked them directly by adding a little further on:

> Did not Homer, Hesiod, Demosthenes, Herodotus, Thucydides, Isocrates, and Lysias recognize the gods as guides for all education? . . . I find it absurd that someone who comments on their works scorns the gods whom they honored . . . I do not require of educators of youth that they change their opinions, but I leave them the choice: that they cease to teach what they do not take seriously, or else, if they wish to continue their lessons, that they preach by example above all else and that they persuade their pupils that neither Homer nor Hesiod nor any of those whom they are explicating [was as stupid as they want to make them out to be] after accusing them of impiety, madness, and error on the subject of the gods.[3]

Christian masters had only to submit or resign, because Julian was establishing as an incontestable truth that classical culture bore in itself the values of paganism and could not be dissociated from them. Julian had understood quite well what was at stake in teaching, and he may have hoped to wipe out the Christianity of the cultivated elites, those who attended the schools and learned grammar, rhetoric, and philosophy. This amounted to preventing the "Galileans"—as he called the Christians, the better to distinguish them from the "Hellenes" and thus from the pagans—from running schools and teaching classical culture, as if they lacked legitimacy in that realm. He did not forbid them to attend schools—he even hoped to cure them of their folly—but excluding Christians from teaching was a way of letting them know that classical culture did not belong to them.

For Basil, as for all educated Christians, this was intolerable. His address to the young people made it clear, after Julian's death and the abolition of his edict, to what extent Greek culture remained a common good belonging to Christians and pagans alike. To be sure, Basil proved selective in the use of ancient authors: "just as in plucking the blooms from a rose-bed we avoid the thorns, so also in garnering from such writings whatever is useful, let us guard ourselves against what is harmful."[4] But this attitude was not the exclusive property of Christians. Plato had already deemed that certain stories reported by Homer or Hesiod, obvious lies, could only have a bad influence on young minds, that many stories told by those authors actually painted unfavorable pictures of the gods and heroes, and that there was a risk that young children would fail to understand the difference between allegory and reality (see especially *The Republic*, 378).

But times had changed, for Plato, in his day, had not had to defend classical culture against anyone. Eight centuries later, pagan rhetors could be astonished at the Christians' ambiguous attitude. In a fictional speech that he addressed to his fellow citizens, Christians for the most part, the pagan rhetor Libanius of Antioch, who had tried to defend that city-state in texts addressed to Julian, went back to some of Julian's own arguments. He urged his Christian compatriots to avoid the emperor's anger by restoring the city-state to Zeus and the other gods, adding: "Homer and Hesiod instructed you about them in earliest childhood, long before the emperor did. You expect to be admired for your educational system, and you call epic poetry part of it, and yet on matters of prime importance you employ other teachers; you turn your backs upon instruction when the road lies open to it, though when it was barred you should have been loud in your laments," a direct allusion to Julian's edict.[5] For Christians complained of being prevented from teaching rhetoric or philosophy, but if by chance they were caught citing Plato or Pythagoras, they would invoke the bad influence of their mothers, their wives, their stewards, or their cooks! And Libanius took sly pleasure, a few paragraphs later, in illustrating his demonstration by drawing examples from the stories of Ajax, Pericles, and Oedipus. Without necessarily approving Julian's extreme measures, Libanius more or less ordered the Christians to clarify their position: for or against the Hellenic cultural legacy.

Basil's approach, while not original, was inscribed in an intellectual process that was fundamental for the survival of Hellenism, the process by which Christians claimed "ownership" of the best of the classical tradition. The responsibility for the loss of whole segments of classical culture has too often been imputed to ignorant monks. This is both untrue and unfair. To be sure, there was a monastic tradition that was hostile to literature, Greek or not, and that privileged extreme forms of asceticism to the detriment of any study, especially in Syrian monachism. But this was the tendency of a minority, and one that surely did not represent the opinion of many bishops or educated clerics. In reality, the loss of a number of classical works occurred well before the triumph of Christianity, owing to accidents in the history of the texts and perhaps also to choices made in Alexandria during the Hellenistic era. By producing anthologies and other compilations, the scholars of the Hellenistic period were condemning the integral original work to oblivion. But more than anything else, fires and other accidents of daily life may have caused works that had been preserved in a single copy to disappear forever. Who can know how many works definitively disappeared in the successive fires in the Library of Alexandria, not the pseudofire of 47 B.C.E.—which affected only cases of books intended for export—but also the disastrous fire of 270 during the Palmyrene invasion and the one in the Serapeion annex in 391? To blame the Christians alone thus seems exaggerated at the very least. And unfair, for it means forgetting that the classical tradition was essentially passed along to us by the copyists of the early Middle Ages, the large majority of whom were monks and clerics. And they did not hesitate to transmit works that had little or no relation to Christian faith and morality, and that sometimes seriously contradicted Christian tenets.

Basil, through his fictitious address, staked out a clear position: classical culture belongs to all, including Christians. This was a post mortem response to Julian and to the overzealous pagans, but it also served to bring an internal debate to a close. By the weight of his unquestionable moral and intellectual authority, Basil reassured educated clerics and Christians, definitively gave them access to pagan writings, and at the same time ensured the survival of those works by bringing them into the field of a broadened Christian culture.

CHAPTER FORTY-THREE

The Death of Hypatia, or Remaining Pagan in a Christian World

Wherefore she had great spite and envy owed unto her; and because she conferred oft, and had great familiarity with *Orestes,* the people charged her that she was the cause why the Bishop and Orestes were not become friends. To be short, certain heady and rash cock-brains whose guide and captain was *Peter* a Reader of that Church, watched this woman coming home from some place or other; they pull her out of her Chariot; they hale her into the Church called *Kaisareion;* they stripped her stark naked; they raze the skin, and rend the flesh of her body with sharp shels, until the breath departed out of her body; they quarter her body; they bring her quarters unto a place called *Kinaron,* and burn them to ashes.

> Socrates Scholasticus, in Eusebius Pamphilus, Socrates Scholasticus, and Evagrius Scholasticus, *The Ancient Ecclesiastical Histories of the First Six Hundred Years after Christ,* trans. from the Greek by Meredith Hanmer, 6th ed. (London: Abraham Miller, 1663), p. 382 (VII, 15)

ALEXANDRIA OF EGYPT, May 415 C.E. A woman was viciously assassinated, in a church, no less, the one that stood on the site of the former imperial sanctuary known as Kaisareion. We do not know who the assassins were, except that their leader was a certain Peter, a cleric who served as lector in the Alexandrian Church. Indignant at the savagery of the act, the ancient authors (including Christians) were not generous with details about the exact context; this leaves room for the imagination and—at least in modern historiography—allows Hypatia to stand as the emblematic victim of Christian intolerance or even obscurantism.

Hypatia, whose memory remains vivid in Byzantine literature as the model of a wise and learned woman, drew renewed interest in the West after a book devoted to her was published in London in 1720 by the Englishman John Toland, under the title *Hypatia, or the History of a Most Beautiful, Most Virtuous, Most Learned and in Every Way Accomplished Lady; Who was Torn to Pieces by the Clergy of Alexandria, to Gratify the Pride, Emulation and Cruelty of the Archbishop, Commonly but Undeservedly Titled St. Cyril.* Toland represented the cultivated young heroine as a victim of the Christian intolerance embodied by Cyril, patriarch of Alexandria, who had just been elected to the post in 412 after the death of his uncle Theophilus. Toland's book inaugurated a trend that, from Voltaire to our day, not without idealizing Hypatia, has made her death the symbol of a certain end of antiquity, the end of culture and freedom of thought, the end of the philosophical tradition and the taste for beauty. Leconte de Lisle, Gérard de Nerval, and Maurice Barrès, to cite only a few French literary celebrities, made use of the figure.[1] Because the tradition assures us that Hypatia remained a virgin all her life, she is imagined as young and attractive, and her assassination becomes all the more atrocious. The arguments that anticlericals and freethinkers, opponents of Catholic dogma and admirers of ancient Greece, managed to develop around Hypatia's death are hardly surprising. Indeed, as early as 1721, Toland's book received a scathing response from Thomas Lewis, *The History of Hypatia, a Most Impudent School-Mistress: In Defense of Saint Cyril and the Alexandrian Clergy from the Aspersions of Mr Toland* (London, 1721), which was presented, starting with the title, as a defense of Cyril and his fellow clergy. In other words, Hypatia's story was removed from the historians' purview before it even came into focus, and the ideological stakes that have been attached to her name for nearly three centuries have somewhat obscured the realities. Yet despite the uncertainties of the sources, both the figure of Hypatia and the conditions of her death can be pinned down more accurately without diminishing the individual and her tragic end—even if we must clearly give them a different meaning from the one imagined by her earliest admirers.

Hypatia was the daughter of a famous scholar, Theon of Alexandria, a member of the Museum continuing the work of a brilliant scientific school whose reputation endured intact until the fourth century C.E. She was probably born around 355, and not in the 370s as previously believed, for

Synesios of Cyrene, who studied with her, speaks of her respectfully as an older woman. At the time of her death, she was thus around sixty; this in no way detracts from the atrocity of the crime, but it dispels the fantasies related to the image of a virgin stripped naked.

Her first teacher was her father, and he remained her most important master. The texts we have offer few details about her training, but by sifting what information there is we can come up with a fairly precise idea of her personality and her teaching. Hypatia began by following in her father's footsteps as a mathematician and an astronomer; her father had written valuable commentaries on Euclid's *Elements* for use by students, and on Ptolemy's *Almagest*. Although for a long time scholars believed that none of Hypatia's own works had survived, specialists today think that the text we have of the *Almagest* and its *Easy Tables* is none other than the edition revised by Hypatia. At all events, the young woman soon surpassed her father and tackled more difficult mathematicians, such as Apollonios of Perge (third century B.C.E.)—she wrote a commentary on his *Conic Sections*—and above all Diophantus (mid-third century B.C.E.), whose work is considered the most complex in all antiquity. Portions of his *Arithmetica* in thirteen books have survived: six books in Greek and four others in Arabic, with many notes and interpolations that may go back in part to commentaries by Hypatia.

Hypatia also turned toward philosophy. A Neoplatonist like most of the great philosophers of late antiquity, she was nevertheless familiar with the other schools and had read their major works. In the surviving letters that Synesios of Cyrene wrote her, specific allusions to her teaching allow us to appreciate the extent of her reading and the importance of her commentaries on Pythagoras, Plato, and Aristotle.

Hypatia also managed to surround herself with a small circle of faithful followers and pupils. Even dressed in the poor philosophers' mantle (the *tribon*), she remained one of the most prominent teachers in the city-state. In reality, while she may have given some public classes and lectures, she influenced mainly a narrow circle of faithful friends, of whom a handful—four, to be precise—seem to have benefited over many years from her teaching, delivered in her home. First among these was Synesios of Cyrene, her fellow student from their younger days; he left an abundant correspondence, including at least seven letters addressed to Hypatia. He spent time in Alexandria on several occasions and frequented Hypatia's house.

A Christian, he became bishop of Ptolemais of Cyreniaca in 411 (shortly before his death, in 413). Another of Hypatia's close disciples, Kyros of Panopolis, became bishop of Cotyaeum in Phrygia. We must also note Herculianus, Kyros's brother, and the Syrian Olympios, a major landowner in the region of Seleucia Pieria. But many other prominent men from Alexandria or elsewhere were frequent visitors in Hypatia's home; we find their names scattered throughout Synesios's 156 letters. They all belonged to the upper classes of society, and many later held high positions in the imperial administration or in the Church. And many, if not most, were clearly Christians.

Hypatia was by no means a pagan fanatic entirely oriented toward a Hellenic past peopled with gods and heroes. In this respect she differed from several of the Alexandrian masters of her day, who were very attached to the gods and often served in their sanctuaries: the philosopher Olympios was associated with the sanctuary of Serapis, the grammarian Ammonios was a priest in the service of Toth-Hermes, and his colleague Helladios had the same relation to Zeus Ammon. While many pagans continued to engage in religious practices that had been outlawed by Theodosius's edicts in 391 and 392, Hypatia in contrast appeared relatively indifferent toward the pagan gods. This may well be why her name was never mentioned in the bloody events that shook Alexandria in 391–392. In the wake of the imperial edicts that forbade pagans to engage in any public worship, Theophilus, patriarch of Alexandria, incited Christian mobs to destroy pagan places of worship, including the most famous one in the city, the Serapeion. The events mobilized a number of pagan intellectuals, led by the Neoplatonist philosopher Olympios, for the Serapeion contained not only the statue of the god by the sculptor Bryaxis (fourth century B.C.E.), but also an important library consisting in copies of the works in the celebrated Library of Alexandria, which had probably been partially destroyed during the siege of the city by the Palmyrenes in 270. Hypatia must have been between 35 and 40 years old at that point, and her reputation must already have been considerable. Yet no ancient text associates her name with the Serapeion episode, as if she had kept her distance from it. The most probable explanation is that she did not view the destruction of a pagan sanctuary, no matter how prestigious, as an event of major importance. Her philosophy, as well as her scientific skills, must have led her to see concrete manifestations of cults, whatever they were, as rather futile.

Nor did Hypatia ever appear hostile to Christians. We have seen that two of her pupils and closest friends became bishops. She frequented Alexandria's sophisticated circles, which were almost all Christian. For she belonged to a certain cultivated social elite that gave her access to the highest spheres of local society. Her personal prestige attracted everyone who counted in the city. Cyril's jealousy has been thought to stem from the fact that he saw prominent figures throng to Hypatia, seeking instruction or advice. True or false, the supposition reveals the respectability she had acquired and the moral authority she enjoyed owing to her own virtues: uprightness, constancy in her quest for truth, devotion to her city-state, uncommon intelligence, but even more, her *sophrosyne,* a notion difficult to translate that encompasses at once wisdom, reserve, modesty, chastity, and dignity in all circumstances. This explains her frequent contacts with Orestes, the augustal prefect of Egypt—relations that seem to have been behind her assassination.

The account by Socrates Scholasticus that served as point of departure for our investigation and that has nourished most of the later commentaries, despite certain variations, indicates clearly that Hypatia's paganism played no role in her death, at least not officially. Ever since the election of a new patriarch in October 412, an event that coincided more or less with the arrival of augustal prefect Orestes the same year, tension between the patriarch and the civil authorities had been rising; it reached a peak in 414–415. On the one hand, there was Cyril, nephew of the previous patriarch Theophilus. He had been elected with difficulty over his opponent, his uncle Timothy; he seems to have been eager to impose the Church's influence in every sphere and to extend its control to the civil authorities. Obsessed by the struggle against heretics—he had the Novatians of Alexandria expelled and their churches closed—and Jews much more than pagans, he clearly intended to exercise a sort of moral authority to which all state authorities would have to conform. On the other hand, there was the prefect, Orestes, who sought—probably with the support of the city's leaders—to keep the patriarch confined to his own sphere. Orestes did not hesitate to arrest and subject to torture a certain Hierax, an informer in Cyril's pay whose seditious machinations had been pointed out to him by the city's Jews. Violent incidents involving Jews and Christians ensued. Christians led by Cyril in person were seen to ransack synagogues and the entire Jewish quarter. Orestes, appalled by these disturbances, had no choice but to inform the emperor, whom Cyril for his part was petitioning to act against Orestes. Emperor Theodosius did no more than urge them to reconcile.

The crisis only got worse, and Orestes, supported by the city's leaders, refused reconciliation with the patriarch. Cyril called five hundred monks from Nitria (the desert region south of Alexandria) to the rescue, and they attacked the prefect; one of them, Ammonios, even threw a stone that hit the prefect in the head and caused profuse bleeding. The prefect had him arrested and tortured to death, while Cyril made him a martyr.

Hypatia, like all the civic leaders, undoubtedly supported the augustal prefect, whom she encountered frequently. This was the meaning of Socrates' allusion to the role Hypatia was said to have played in preventing reconciliation between Orestes and Cyril. This interpretation probably credits her with more influence than she actually had, but it is true that Cyril and his clan might have feared that Hypatia's many friends and students, well placed in the emperor's entourage and in high administrative positions, would bring Theodosius around to the augustal prefect's side. Whatever the truth of the matter, we know that, in a situation like this, what the crowd believes counts for more than the actual facts. For Cyril's partisans, Hypatia embodied the obstacle to any reconciliation, and they turned on her the anger they felt toward Orestes.

Who were Hypatia's assassins? This is not a secondary question, for Cyril's own responsibility is at stake. A single ancient source, the Byzantine encyclopedia known as the *Suda,* probably relying on a passage from Damascius's *Life of Isidorus,* accuses Cyril of providing the assassins with weapons. A single individual is named, Peter, a lector, that is, a cleric who had taken minor orders. The assassins were not an amorphous crowd but a specific group. No one mentions the monks, who had been severely beaten during the attack on Orestes and had retreated to their convent in the desert. Cyril's name is not mentioned either, and he cannot be held directly responsible. But various indications show that the organized group that had stirred up the attack—for there is evidence of premeditation— was quite likely to have been the *parabalanai,* the group of eight hundred "ambulance men" responsible for gathering up the poor and the sick in the streets and helping them; the men of this group also served as the patriarch's personal guards. Under these conditions, it is hard to see how Cyril could be completely exonerated from any ties to Hypatia's murder. Even if he did not give the order, his exasperation could have fed the hatred of his entourage, and his bodyguards could have thought they were responding to an unacknowledged wish on the patriarch's part by ridding him of this cumbersome woman. Not to mention that for these fervent Christians, who obviously knew nothing at all about Hypatia's largely esoteric teaching, the murder of this pagan, who was viewed more or less as a magician, could almost be seen as an act of devotion.

However this may be, Hypatia's murder seems to have been at bottom the consequence of a conflict among Christians, between temporal power and spiritual power. Hypatia paid the price of her fame, her influence, her moral authority, and also her commitment to a limitation on Church powers. It was only marginally, perhaps for some of her uneducated assailants, that her paganism could have justified the murder. We are clearly a long way from the image conveyed by John Toland and Voltaire of Reason and Liberty assassinated by "Cyril's tonsured mastiffs, followed by a band of fanatics" who "went to seize her on the rostrum where she was dictating her lessons, dragged her by the hair, stoned and burned her, without the slightest reprimand from Saint Cyril."[2]

Voltaire was not exempt from a certain bad faith, moreover, for when he returned to the subject in an article in the *Dictionnaire philosophique* ("Hypatie"), he established an audacious comparison underlining the opposition between civil power and ecclesiastic power:

> I will suppose that madame Dacier had been the finest woman in Paris; and that in the quarrel on the comparative merits of the ancients and moderns, the carmelites pretended that the poem of the Magdalen, written by a carmelite, was infinitely superior to Homer, and that it was an atrocious impiety to prefer the Iliad to the verses of a monk. I will take the additional liberty of supposing that the archbishop of Paris took the part of the carmelites against the governor of the city, a partisan of the beautiful madame Dacier, and that he excited the carmelites to massacre this fine woman in the church of Notre Dame, and to drag her naked and bloody to the Place Maubert—would not everybody say that the archbishop of Paris had done a very wicked action, for which he ought to do penance? This is precisely the history of Hypatia. She taught

Homer and Plato in Alexandria, in the time of Theodosius II. St. Cyril incensed the christian population against her.[3]

Without exonerating Cyril and his circle of this abomination, we cannot view Hypatia's murder as the symbol of Christian obscurantism. With Hypatia, an exceptional woman disappeared, but it was not the end of ancient Greek culture or of paganism.

In Alexandria itself, after Hypatia's death, the philosopher Hierocles developed an eclectic Neoplatonism, and this tradition lasted until the Arab invasion in 648. Aristotle was held in growing esteem. Similarly, Alexandria remained an active site for research in mathematics and astronomy, and the city had a sort of intellectual apogee around the turn of the fifth and sixth centuries, with men such as Ammonios, Damascius, Simplicius, Asclepios, Olympiodoros, and John Philiponus. In a parallel movement, philosophico-religious circles were attempting to revive the ancient paganism by revalorizing Egyptian wisdom and the Greek and Egyptian rites, around the philosopher Horapollon the Elder (under Theosodius II) and his school.

But Egypt was not the only ultimate repository of this ancient pagan culture. Damascius, whose name has come up several times before, was a Neoplatonist originally from Damascus but trained both in Athens and in Alexandria; his *Life of Isidorus* offered a wealth of information about these last pagans who continued to keep the ancient culture alive throughout the fifth century and the beginning of the sixth. The travels of a small band of Platonist philosophers to southern Syria around 480 in search of the sources of the Styx, a voyage recounted by Damascius, illustrates both the vibrant character that pagan culture had maintained in this intellectual milieu and the pagans' growing isolation in an increasingly alien world. But the study of Plato and Aristotle did not die out, during the sixth century, until shortly before it was taken up by the Arabs, who found ample material for reflection and commentary in the rich libraries of Syria and Egypt.

If Hypatia's death does not symbolize either the end of the ancient culture or even the triumph of intolerance and obscurantism (although neither phenomenon is absent), it does tell us something about the situation of Greek societies at the moment when state Christianity finally had a majority both in the general population and in the governing circles. Hypatia

was located at the crossroads of an immense relational network that recalls to some extent the one centered around her elder, Libanius (314–393),
in Antioch. Pagans and Christians mingled in this network without com-
plications; they were all from the same milieu, and they shared a common
culture—they were all readers of Homer, Hesiod, Plato, and Aristotle.
What bound the group together, even beyond culture, was the sort of life
they led: the comfortable life of landowners and people who held power in
the city-state or in the imperial administration. But this society of prominent individuals represented only a tiny minority at the summit of the social hierarchy, and the bulk of the population—still largely pagan in rural
areas, more often Christian in the cities—was excluded. Relying on this
urban throng that could be quickly stirred up and on monks who were
largely unfamiliar with classical culture (although here again there were
exceptions), the bishops could be tempted, when they themselves came
from the lower classes of society, to impose their spiritual authority in the
face of political power, to subordinate civic authority to their injunctions.
This was indeed what frightened the municipal and imperial aristocracies,
who saw only too well that such subordination would inevitably be translated by a reduction of their own freedom to act and a rise in intolerance.
The refined culture that unified them was totally foreign to the monks and
the Christian populace alike; it was seen only as the residue of paganism,
sorcery, and magic. Hypatia was a victim of this mix of envy and fear, ignorance and fanaticism. Yet no one in her powerful circle seems to have
done anything at all to avenge her: Orestes asked to be recalled to Constantinople, while her students remained dispersed and did no more than
piously preserve her memory. Cyril was not disturbed, and while in 416
the emperor reorganized the body of the parabalanai and reduced its number from eight hundred to five hundred, there is no evidence that Hypatia's
murder had anything at all to do with this change. Hypatia's story, very
quickly forgotten by most, became available as summed up in its final episode to feed the imagination of poets, philosophers, and polemicists enam-
ored of the freedom to think and to believe.

Afterword

WHY STOP, when there is still so much to say? I address to myself the same reproaches that others may well formulate, but these gaps reveal my ignorance rather than my lack of interest. In the preface, I acknowledged my taste for the margins of the Greek world; I should have specified the eastern or southern margins, for the west remains largely foreign to me, not very well known. Of course I have traveled through Sicily and Campania, visited Syracuse, Agrigentum, Paestum, and even Ampurias in Catalonia, but shall I confess that I have never been to Marseille? Perhaps it is this lack of firsthand knowledge of the sites that keeps me from writing.

But more than on these lacunae, my regret as I complete this book has a different focus. Might I not have contributed to an image against which I have constantly fought in my teaching (and in other books, I think), an image of a Greek world in which there are only Greeks or indigenous peoples who became Greek? I hope not, for this would be quite contrary to what I believe, and to countless testimonies. But let us not be naive: nothing would be more absurd, in the name of some politically correct conception, than to place all cultures, all ancient civilizations, on the same level. There is no question of making a value judgment—in the name of what, and according to what criteria, would a historian do such a thing? But it has to be acknowledged that the attractions exercised from one direction and the other are not the same. To be sure, the Greeks of Egypt were seduced by the gods of the country and by its culture; they became "Egyptianized" to the point that it is sometimes hard to identify them. Similarly, the Acts of the Apostles do not fail to emphasize the attraction that Judaism exercised in the Greek milieus of Asia Minor and Greece, through the beauty of its festivals and its moral exigency. Men like Manethon the Egyptian, Berossus of Babylon, Philo of Alexandria, and Flavius Josephus the Jew unquestionably helped enrich Greek literature and thought, and helped introduce new ferments that led to new conceptions. But the fact remains that each of them situated himself in relation to Hellenism. No Greek author felt it necessary to learn Aramaic, Egyptian, or some other language spoken in the world that emerged from the Alexandrian conquest in order to have direct contact with the culture that it transmitted. And is not too much sometimes attributed to the authors who originated in the Near East? Must we believe that the Greek philosophers born in Phoenicia, so numerous both in the Hellenistic period and under the Roman Empire, introduced something "Semitic" into Greek thought? Most of them were only born in Tyre, Sidon, or Byblos; they were trained in Rhodes, Ephesus, or Athens, and they taught in these same cities or in Rome, Herculanum, or elsewhere. What ties did they retain with their countries of origin? We do not know, and we do not even know whether they knew Phoenician or Aramaic. Regarding Porphyry of Tyre, who spent nearly all his life in Herculanum and in Rome, Fergus Millar used to point out that, in the very rare passages in his work where Syria was mentioned, Porphyry relied on the testimony of Greek authors! How better to express the strength of a culture that seemed to dominate the others?

But more generally, the Greek way of life had a power of attraction that extended far beyond cultivated and Hellenized circles. Gymnasia, theaters, colonnades, and houses with peristyles spread everywhere; it was indeed the Greek lifestyle that appeared attractive and was adopted by the locals, not the reverse. We have to observe that for nearly a thousand years, throughout the Mediterranean region and sometimes far beyond, Greek culture was deemed the culture of reference, the one that had to be acquired by anyone who wanted to appear modern. Paul Veyne has recently shown, dazzlingly and not without provocation, as he knows so well how to do in order to get us to abandon our conventional schemas, that the Roman Empire was Greek in its culture.[1] I can only agree, for the most part. And how could such a culture not have fascinated others, through the wealth and depth of its thought, the variety and multiplicity of its accomplishments, in all areas and for such a long time? From Homer to Damascius, what a long road was traversed, but also what continuity in systems of value and thought! Is this not, finally, what continues to attract us today?

NOTES

GLOSSARY

INDEX

Notes

1. Theseus Unites Attica's Inhabitants

1. Plutarch, *Theseus,* in *Plutarch's Lives,* trans. Bernadotte Perrin (Loeb Classical Library, 1914), vol. 1, p. 55 (XXV, 2).

2. Ibid.

3. Thucydides, *History of the Peloponnesian War,* trans. Charles Forster Smith (Loeb Classical Library, 1919), vol. 1, p. 19 (I, 10).

2. The Theraeans Embark for Cyrene

In the original epigraph to Chapter 2 and elsewhere in this book, the English translation is based on the French translation provided by the author in the original French edition, in cases where no published English version is readily available.

1. Plutarch, *Solon,* in *Plutarch's Lives,* trans. Bernadotte Perrin (Loeb Classical Library, 1914), vol. 1, p. 445 (XV, 5).

3. Lydian Coins, or the Origins of Money

1. Cited in Hélène Nicolet-Pierre, *Numismatique grecque* (Paris: Armand Colin, 2002), pp. 85–87. The inscription concludes: "How prosperous was his reign!"

4. Graffiti on Ramses II's Leg

1. Martin Bernal, *Black Athena: The Afroasiatic Roots of Classical Civilization* (New Brunswick, N.J.: Rutgers University Press, 1987).

2. *Herodotus,* trans. A. D. Godley (Loeb Classical Library, 1920), vol. 1, p. 473 (II, 160).

3. Ibid., p. 281 (II, 5).
4. Ibid., p. 317 (II, 35–36).
5. Ibid., p. 337 (II, 50).

5. Phalaris's Bull

1. Aristotle, *The Athenian Constitution,* trans. H. Rackham, in *Aristotle* (Loeb Classical Library, 1952), vol. 20, p. 51 (XVI, 7).
2. *Herodotus,* trans. A. D. Godley (Loeb Classical Library, 1920), vol. 3, p. 77 (V, 68).

6. "You Will Destroy a Great Empire!"

1. The Lydians had been sent to the oracular sanctuaries of Delphi and Oropos of Boeotia.
2. *Herodotus,* trans. A. D. Godley (Loeb Classical Library, 1920), vol. 1, p. 55 (I, 47).
3. Lucian's *Alexander the False Prophet* is devoted to him.

7. The Bases of Athenian Democracy

1. The fundamental work on this topic remains that of Pierre Lévêque and Pierre Vidal-Naquet, *Cleisthenes the Athenian: An Essay on the Representation of Space and Time in Greek Political Thought from the End of the Sixth Century to the Death of Plato,* ed. and trans. David Ames Curtis (Atlantic Highlands, N.J.: Humanities Press, 1996 [1964]).
2. *Herodotus,* trans. A. D. Godley (Loeb Classical Library, 1920), vol. 3, p. 79 (V, 71).

9. An Ostracizing Potsherd

1. Plutarch, *Aristides,* in *Plutarch's Lives,* trans. Bernadotte Perrin (Loeb Classical Library, 1914), vol. 2, pp. 231–233 (VII, 2).

10. Complaints of a Bastard

1. Philippe Gauthier, "'Générosité' romaine et 'avarice' grecque: Sur l'octroi du droit de cité," in *Mélanges William Seston* (Paris: E. de Boccard, 1974), pp. 207–215.
2. *Pericles,* in *Plutarch's Lives,* trans. Bernadotte Perrin (Loeb Classical Library, 1967), vol. 3, p. 109 (XXXVII, 3–4).
3. We know that historians of antiquity complain about not having the

quantified data that exist for other epochs, but as soon as they do have a figure, they proceed to show that it is unreliable, or impossible. I shall stay out of this debate and take Plutarch's figure for what it is worth.

11. Hippolytus's Prayer to Zeus

1. Aristophanes, *Women at the Thesmophoria*, in *Aristophanes*, ed. and trans. Jeffrey Henderson (Loeb Classical Library, 2000), vol. 3, p. 503 (340–350).
2. Plutarch, *Lycurgus*, in *Plutarch's Lives*, trans. Bernadotte Perrin (Loeb Classical Library, 1914), vol. 1, pp. 245–247 (XIV, 3–4, 7).

12. The Story of a Broken Sigma

1. Aristophanes, *Birds*, in *Aristophanes*, ed. and trans. Jeffrey Henderson (Loeb Classical Library, 2000), vol. 3, pp. 161–163 (1040–1042).

13. Two Thousand Helots Gone!

1. Critias, in Libanius, *Oratio* 25, §63.
2. Jean Ducat, "Le mépris des hilotes," *Annales ESC* (1974): 1451–62.
3. Myron of Priene, in Felix Jacoby, *Die Fragmente der Griechischen Historiker*, vol. 2 (Berlin: Weidman, 1993), 106 F 2.

14. Naked and Unarmed in the Dark

1. Strabo, *The Geography of Strabo*, trans. Horace Leonard Jones (Loeb Classical Library, 1928), vol. 5, p. 157 (X, iv, 21).
2. Ibid.
3. Plutarch, *Lycurgus*, in *Plutarch's Lives*, trans. Bernadotte Perrin (Loeb Classical Library, 1914), vol. 1, p. 283 (XXV, 3).
4. Strabo, *Geography*, vol. 5, p. 159 (X, iv, 21).
5. Lafitau was the author of *Moeurs des sauvages amériquains comparés aux moeurs des premiers temps* (Paris: Saugrain l'aîné, 1724).

15. Nicocles of Salamis in Cyprus

1. Isocrates, *Discours*, vol. 2, ed. and trans. Georges Mathieu (Paris: Les Belles Lettres, 1938), p. 143.
2. Philippe Gauthier, *Symbola: Les étrangers et la justice dans les cités grecques* (Nancy: Université de Nancy II, 1972), p. 202.

16. Pasion Bequeaths His Wife

1. Aristophanes, *Acharnians*, in *Aristophanes*, ed. and trans. Jeffrey Henderson (Loeb Classical Library, 1998), vol. 1, pp. 119–121 (502–508).

2. Euripides, Erechtheus, frag. 360 (Nauck).

18. The Susa Weddings

1. Ulrich Wilcken, *Alexander the Great* (New York: Dial Press, 1932), p. 208.

19. A Hymn for Demetrios Poliorcetes

1. F. Bilabel, "Fragmente aus Heidelberger Papyrussammlung," *Philologus* 180 (1925): 149 (inventory of the Heidelberg Papyrus Collection, no. 1716).

20. In Io's Footsteps

1. I am leaving aside here the indigenous city-states that were promoted without name changes, such as the Phoenician city-states, which I discuss in Chapter 26.

2. Victor D. Hanson, *The Wars of the Ancient Greeks and Their Invention of Western Military Culture* (London: Cassell, 1999).

3. *The Chronicle of John Malalas*, trans. Elizabeth Jeffreys, Michael Jeffreys, and Roger Scott (Melbourne: Australian Association for Byzantine Studies, 1986), pp. 105–106 (VIII, 12 [199–200]).

4. Ibid., p. 106 (VIII, 12 [201, 201–202]).

21. Long Live Poverty!

1. Plutarch, *Agis*, in *Plutarch's Lives*, trans. Bernadotte Perrin (Loeb Classical Library, 1914), vol. 10, p. 9 (III, 1).

2. Ibid., p. 15 (V, 4).

3. Ibid., p. 11 (IV).

4. Ibid., p. 15 (VI, 3).

5. Ibid., p. 21 (VIII, 2).

6. Plutarch, *Life of Cleomenes*, in *Plutarch's Lives*, trans. Bernadotte Perrin (Loeb Classical Library) (XI, 1).

7. Polybius, *The Histories*, trans. W. R. Paton (Loeb Classical Library, 1922), vol. 4, pp. 419–421 (XIII, 6).

8. Ibid., pp. 421–423 (XIII, 7).

22. A Capital on the Banks of the Amu Darya

1. Paul Bernard, Georges-Jean Pinault, and Georges Rougement, "Deux nouvelles inscriptions grecques de l'Asie centrale," *Journal des Savants* (2004): 227–356.

2. Athenaeus, *The Deipnosophists*, trans. Charles Burton Gulick (Loeb Classical Library, 1927), vol. 6, p. 527 (XIV, 652–653).

23. Education and Citizenship in the Hellenistic World

1. Jeanne Robert and Louis Robert, *Bulletin épigraphique* (1978): 434–435, n. 274.

2. Inscription, in Wilhelm Dittenberger, *Sylloge Inscriptionum Graecarum*, 3rd ed. (Leipzig: S. Hirzelium, 1915–1924), no. 578.

24. A Wild Ass for the King

1. Many commentators believe that these figures correspond to Hyrcanos's deposit alone, but the text is not clear enough, for Onias responds to Heliodoros that the total deposit consisted of property entrusted by widows and orphans in addition to Hyrcanos's property.

2. Josephus, *Jewish Antiquities*, trans. Ralph Marcus (Loeb Classical Library, 1958), vol. 7, pp. 117–119 (XII, 230–233).

25. An Epigram from Sidon

1. Isocrates, *Panegyricus*, in *Isocrates*, trans. George Norlin (Loeb Classical Library, 1928), vol. 1, p. 149 (50–51).

2. Benjamin Isaac, *The Invention of Racism in Classical Antiquity* (Princeton: Princeton University Press, 2004).

3. C. P. Jones, *Kinship Diplomacy in the Ancient World* (Cambridge, Mass.: Harvard University Press, 1999).

27. Steles of Mercenaries from Sidon

1. Flavius Josephus, *Jewish Antiquities*, trans. Ralph Marcus (Loeb Classical Library, 1976), vol. 7, p. 79 (XII, 150–152).

28. Jason the Impious

1. The signal was a gong announcing the beginning of the distribution of oil.

2. H. Cotton and M. Wörrie, "Seleukos IV to Heliodoros: A New Dossier of Royal Correspondence from Israel," *Zeitschrift für Papyrologie und Epigraphik* 159 (2007): 191–205.

30. Let Us Pray for Archippe's Recovery!

1. Inscription, in Helmut Engelmann, *Inschriften von Kyme* (Bonn: Habelt, 1979), no. 13.

2. Because the Greeks had no system for designating eras, a given year is designated by the name of the eponymous magistrate for that year.

31. "Kill Them All"

1. Appian, *The Mithridatic Wars*, in *Appian's Roman History*, trans. Horace White (Loeb Classical Library, 1912), vol. 2, p. 281 (IV, 23).
2. Inscription, in *Sylloge inscriptionum Graecarum*, ed. Wilhelm Dittenberger, 3rd ed. (Leipzig: S. Hirzelium, 1915–1924), 742, preamble.

32. Prizes for an Athlete from Miletus

1. Euripides, *Autolycus*, frag. 282 (Nauck).
2. Clement of Alexandria, *Protreptics* 34, 2.

33. Epaminondas Offers a Banquet

1. An association of Boeotian city-states whose delegates were sent to meetings of the koinon of the Achaeans and Panhellenes, along with delegates from the other leagues and city-states of the Roman province of Achaea.
2. The Great Ptoia contests were held in connection with a festival celebrated in honor of Apollo Ptoios.
3. A triclinion is a group of three beds around a dining table.
4. *The Geography of Strabo,* trans. Horace Leonard Jones (Loeb Classical Library, 1917), vol. 6, p. 295 (XIV, i, 24).
5. Ibid., pp. 295–297.

34. "The Sun and the Stars"

1. The hipparch was the chief magistrate in Cyzikos; he gave his name to the year.

35. Pagan Martyrs in Alexandria

1. Josephus, *Against Apion*, in *Josephus,* trans. H. St. J. Thackeray (Loeb Classical Library), vol. 1, p. 315 (II, 53–55).
2. Philo, *The Embassy to Gaius*, in *Philo,* trans. F. H. Colson (Loeb Classical Library, 1962), vol. 10, p. 63 (124).
3. Ibid., pp. 63–67 (127–131).
4. Ibid., p. 67 (133).
5. Ibid., pp. 69–71 (135–137).
6. Philo, *Against Flaccus*, in *Philo,* trans. F. H. Colson (Loeb Classical Library, 1985), vol. 9, p. 403 (191).
7. "The Letter of Claudius to the Alexandrians," in Victor A. Tcherikover

and Alexander Fuks, *Corpus Papyrorum Judaicarum* (Cambridge, Mass.: Harvard University Press, 1957), vol. 2, no. 153, p. 43.

8. Ibid.

9. *Kosmetai* were magistrates responsible in particular for the public festivals and contests in the capitals of nomes in Egypt and Alexandria. The post was very costly.

10. "Letter of Claudius to the Alexandrians."

36. "Let Them Be Free"

1. Suetonius claims that as he was dying Nero exclaimed: "Qualis artifex pereo!"—"What an artist the world is losing!" Suetonius, *Nero*, in *Lives of the Caesars* and *Lives of Illustrious Men*, trans. J. C. Rolfe, rev. Donna W. Hurley (Loeb Classical Library, 1997), vol. 2, p. 171 (49, 1c). For Nero's speech, see C. P. Jones, "Nero Speaking," *Harvard Studies in Classical Philology* 100 (2000, published 2001): 453–462.

2. *Cicero's Letters to His Brother Quintus*, in *Cicero*, trans. D. R. Shackleton Bailey (Loeb Classical Library, 2002), vol. 28, p. 19 (1.1, 16).

3. Ibid., p. 31 (1.1, 27–28).

37. Eating Roots in Aspendos

1. Dio Chrysostom, "The Forty-Sixth Discourse: Delivered in His Native City prior to His Philosophical Career," in *Dio Chrysostom*, trans. H. Lamar Crosby (Loeb Classical Library, 1946), vol. 5, p. 285 (§9).

2. Philostratus, *The Lives of the Sophists*, trans. Wilmer Cave Wright, in *Philostratus* (Loeb Classical Library, 1922), vol. 4, pp. 85–87 (I, 21). Thamyris was a highly skilled Thracian musician who was challenged by the Muses because of his boasting. If he won, he would sleep with all nine; if he lost, they would deprive him of his sight and his gifts. He became blind. He was also said to have been the first man to fall in love with another man (Hyakinthos), but that is not why Philostratus mentions him here.

3. Suetonius, "Domitian," in *Lives of the Caesars* and *Lives of Illustrious Men*, trans. J. C. Rolfe, rev. Donna W. Hurley (Loeb Classical Library, 1997), vol. 2, p. 333 (§VII).

4. Dio Chrysostom, "Forty-Sixth Discourse," p. 285 (§9).

38. "We, the Greeks of Danaba"

1. *The Geography of Strabo*, trans. Horace Leonard Jones (Loeb Classical Library, 1917), vol. 7, p. 265 (XVI, ii, 20).

2. Josephus, *Jewish Antiquities*, trans. Ralph Marcus (Loeb Classical Library, 1963), vol. 8, p. 167 (XV, 344–345).

3. Ibid., pp. 167–169 (XV, 346–347).

41. Urinating in Front of Aphrodite

1. Later, Acre or Saint-Jean-d'Acre. On this whole issue, see Seth Schwartz, "The Rabbi in Aphrodite's Bath: Palestinian Society and Jewish Identity in the High Roman Empire," in *Being Greek under Rome: Cultural Identity, the Second Sophistic, and the Development of Empire,* ed. Simon Goldhill (Cambridge: Cambridge University Press, 2001), pp. 335–361.

2. Deuteronomy 12:3, in *The Jerusalem Bible,* ed. Alexander Jones (Garden City, N.Y.: Doubleday, 1966).

3. *Shabbath,* trans. H. Freedman, in *The Babylonian Talmud,* ed. Isodore Epstein (London: Soncino Press, 1935–1952), vol. 1, p. 346 (72b).

42. Of the Proper Use of Hellenic Letters

1. *The Writings of Clement of Alexandria,* vol. 12, trans. William Wilson, in *Ante-Nicene Christian Library* (Edinburgh: T. & T. Clark, 1869), p. 350 (*Stromateis,* VI, 80, 5).

2. Julian, in *The Theodosian Code and Novels and the Sirmondian Constitutions,* trans. Clyde Pharr (Princeton: Princeton University Press, 1952), p. 388 (13.3.5).

3. Letter 61, in Julian, *Lettres et fragments,* trans. J. Bidez (Paris: Les Belles Lettres, 1960). There is a gap in the text, for which I have adopted the passage suggested by Bidez.

4. Basil of Caesarea, "Address to Young Men, on How They Might Derive Benefit from Greek Literature," in *Saint Basil: The Letters,* trans. Roy J. Deferrari (Loeb Classical Library, 1926), vol. 4, pp. 391–393 (IV, 47–51).

5. Libanius, Oration 16, "To the Antiochenes: On the Emperor's Anger," in *Libanius: Selected Works,* trans. A. F. Norman (Loeb Classical Library, 1969), vol. 1, p. 241 (46–47).

43. The Death of Hypatia

This chapter is a slightly modified version of an article published in *L'Histoire,* no. 306 (February 2006); I thank Valérie Hannin, editor, for generously authorizing me to reproduce it here. On Hypatia, see the full treatment in Maria Dzielska, *Hypatia of Alexandria,* trans. F. Lyra (Cambridge, Mass.: Harvard University Press, 1995).

1. Leconte de Lisle published two quite different versions of Hypatia's story. His poem *Hypatie* was written in 1847 and published in 1852 in *Poèmes antiques* (Paris: M. Ducloux); a minidrama, *Hypatie et Cyrille,* appeared in the second, revised and expanded edition of *Poèmes antiques* (Paris: A. Lemerre, 1874). Only the second version took up the anti-Christian argument concerning Hypatia's death. Nerval alluded to Hypatia in his *Nouvelles,* I: *Les filles du feu, Angélique* (Paris: Calmann Lévy, 1854), and Hypatia was the subject of Barrès's "La vierge assassinée," in *Sous l'oeil des barbares* (Paris: A. Lemerre, 1888).

2. Voltaire, *Examen important de Milord Bolingbroke ou le tombeau du fanatisme écrit vers la fin de 1736* (Paris, 1768), p. 185.

3. Voltaire, "Hypatia," in *A Philosophical Dictionary,* translated from the French (Boston: J. P. Mendum, 1852), vol. 2, p. 23.

Afterword

1. Paul Veyne, *L'Empire greco-romain* (Paris: Le Seuil, 2005).

Glossary

Agonothetes: A magistrate in a city-state responsible for organizing a competition.

Annona: The Roman system for requisitioning various food products, especially wheat, to supply Rome or the Roman army.

Archon (pl. archontes): The principal magistrate of Athens; the term means "the one who commands." The eponymous archon gave his name to the year of his archontate, or period of service.

Atimia: Total or partial deprivation of civic and civil rights, according to the seriousness of the offense.

Bouleutes (pl. bouleutai): A member of the Council (boule).

Census classes: The Athenians were divided into four census classes, according to their income: *pentakosiomedimnoi* (those who harvested more than 500 measures of produce from their own property), *hippeis* (horsemen) (between 300 and 500 measures), *zeugitai* (between 200 and 300), and *thetes* (below 200). This was an ancient classification revised by Solon at the beginning of the sixth century. The *medimnos*, which served as a unit of measure, was the equivalent of about 52 liters in Athens in Solon's day.

Cleruchy: A colony of citizen-soldier-farmers (cleruchs) sent by the Athenians to settle on the territory of allied city-states that had revolted and been conquered (Imbros, Skyros, Chalcis of Euboea in particular). In the Hellenistic period, this was a way of allocating plots of land to soldiers.

Cubit: A unit of length equivalent, in Athens, to about 0.44 meters.

Cypris: An epithet for Aphrodite, goddess of love.

Deme: An Athenian district corresponding to a single village, or to several villages and hamlets, or to a quarter of the city of Athens.

Diadochs: "Successors." Used alone, the term designates Alexander's successors; the latters' successors are known as "Epigones."

Dionysia (Great Dionysia): The principal Athenian festivals in honor of Dionysus, which included, most notably, a theatrical competition.

Dual monarchy, or diarchy: A political system operating in Sparta, in which two families, the Agids and the Eurypontids, traditionally supplied kings who ruled jointly. Within each family, kings succeeded one another, in principle, in the order of male primogeniture.

Electrum: A natural blend of gold and silver.

Ephebeion: A public building in which part of the training of *epheboi* (young men) took place.

Ephebia: A system of military training for young men.

Ephor: One of the principal magistrates in Sparta. Ephors were five in number, elected annually; they held virtually all political power.

Ethnikos: An indication of the city-state of origin that followed the name and patronymic, at least when they were mentioned outside their city-state of origin.

Favissa: The term for a trench or pit intended to receive worn-out sacred objects that could not be destroyed without sacrilege.

Greco-Persian Wars: Two wars opposing certain Greeks to the Persians. The first took place in 490 (when Athens, helped by some Plataeans, won a decisive battle at Marathon); during the second, which went on from 481 to 479, some thirty Greek city-states came together under Sparta's leadership and defeated the Persians at Salamis, off the coast of Athens (480), and then at Plataea in Boeotia (479) and at Cape Mycale in Asia Minor (479).

Heliaia (tribunal of the): A people's tribunal, made up of citizens drawn by lot every day, generally sitting in sections of 501 members.

Hetaireia (pl. hetaireiai): A group of young aristocrats brought together by familial, political, military, or religious ties.

Hoplite: A heavily armed footsoldier recruited from among the well-to-do citizens of the city-states.

Intercalary month: In many Greek city-states, the year was made up of twelve months of thirty days each. To make up for the gap with respect to the lunar-solar cycle, either intercalary days were added at the end of the year or a supplementary month was added at regular intervals.

Irenarch: The magistrate responsible for public safety, especially in Asia Minor; the word literally means "chief of the peace."

Leitourgeia: A system for distributing public responsibilities among well-to-do citizens, who were designated either to finance a spectacle (choregy), to equip a warship (trierarchy), or to support the operation of a gymnasium (gymnasiarchy).

Magistracy: The name given by historians to the responsibilities incumbent upon the individuals elected or chosen by lot who had to implement the decisions of the popular assembly, command the army, or manage the finances of a city-state.

Metic: A foreigner in a city-state who enjoyed the status of resident protected by laws, once he signed a registry and paid a small tax. Metics were subject to the same military obligations as citizens of similar economic means, but they were not allowed to join the cavalry in Athens.

Nome: An administrative subdivision of Egypt. Nomes varied in number between forty and fifty, depending on the period.

Oliganthropy: A lack of men, or, more precisely, of citizens.

Paidonomos: A master responsible for training boys in the gymnasium.

Paredros: A divinity that in principle "assisted," "seconded" a principal god; often actually the secondary divinity in a divine pair.

Phratry: In Athens, a group of citizens who claimed a common ancestor; belonging to a phratry proved the legitimacy of one's birth and marriage, and made it possible to verify the identity of individuals and their right to citizenship.

Pnyx: A space set up at the foot of the acropolis, to the southwest, where the people's assembly met.

Pre-Dorian populations: The Greeks distinguished, among themselves, the Ionians and the Dorians. In their wake, historians believed for a long time that the renewal of Greek civilization in the tenth and ninth centuries was due to the arrival of new Greek populations, the Dorians. Although that theory was abandoned long ago, the term *pre-Dorian* is sometimes used to characterize the peoples who settled in the Aegean world before that period, whether they were Greek or not.

Proscynesis: Prostration before the sovereign as a sign of submission. Contrary to what the Greeks thought, it was not a gesture of adoration.

Proxenos: A citizen of city-state *A* charged by city-state *B* to defend the interests of the citizens of *B* in *A*; he was neither a consul nor an ambassador but rather an official host who served as intermediary and protector for any citizens of *B* who had to deal with courts of law in *A*.

Prytaneum (pl. prytanea): A building in which the prytaneis stayed during their term of office, and where the city-state provided free food to the citizens or foreigners it wanted to honor.

Prytaneia: The Athenian political year was divided into ten prytaneiai of thirty-five or thirty-six days, the period during which one of the ten tribes took responsibility for the Council (boule).

Prytaneis: Members of the boule who were on duty during a *prytaneia*.

Publican: An agent who purchased the (temporary) right to collect taxes on behalf of the Roman state.

Pythia: A young girl from Delphi charged with transmitting the response of the god Apollo to the pilgrims who came to consult him.

Sanhedrin: The supreme council of the Jews, assisting the high priest. The word comes from the Greek *synedrion,* meaning "sitting together."

Sophists: Masters of rhetoric and eloquence, who taught in the fifth century that everything can be learned and that everything can be subject to discussion. Despite the pejorative character the term *sophist* took on even in antiquity, the sophists were the true founders of modern teaching.

Stephanephoros (pl. stephanephoroi): The eponymous magistrate in many cities of Asia Minor, comparable to the archon in Athens. The term means "the one who wears the crown."

Synoikismos: A meeting of several communities or city-states in a single city-state.

Tetrarchy: A small principality whose leader, appointed or recognized by Rome, did not have the royal title. Tetrarchies were especially numerous in Syria.

Thirty Tyrants: The name given to a group of thirty citizens who governed Athens after the defeat of 404 and produced a reign of terror that lasted several months.

Tribe: A civic structure to which all citizens belonged and that served in particular to distribute military responsibilities (in Athens, each tribe supplied one thousand hoplites and one hundred horsemen); the number of tribes varied according to the city-state (there were usually three, four, six, ten, or twelve tribes).

Index